Japanese Diasporas

Today three million people of Japanese descent, known as Nikkei, are citizens of other nations. Hundreds of thousands of Japanese reside outside of Japan permanently or temporarily but, unlike some other migrations such as the Chinese or Irish diasporas, the Japanese have received little attention from anthropologists, sociologists, and historians. Adachi redresses the balance by examining the relationship of overseas Japanese and their descendants with their home and host nations, focusing specifically on the political, social, and economic struggles of the Nikkei. Frequently abandoned by their homeland, and often suffering alienation in their host nations, the people of the Japanese diaspora have attempted to carve out lives between two different worlds. *Japanese Diasporas* provides new perspectives in the study of the diaspora within a transnational context, looking at the historical factors that first led nineteenth-century Japan to mass emigration and the impact of contemporary issues such as racism, human rights, and racial and ethnic identity.

The essays provide descriptive and analytical case studies of Japanese migration to all geographic locations where a significant overseas Japanese population can be found. These important studies contribute to a better understanding of the cultural practice of transnational migration as the subjects of assimilation, acculturation, and resistance are discussed. With contributions from leading scholars in Asian American studies, *Japanese Diasporas* will be essential reading for those studying contemporary globalization, Asian American history, and ethnic studies.

Nobuko Adachi is Assistant Professor of Anthropology at Illinois State University, USA. She is co-editor of *Pan-Japan: The International Journal of the Japanese Diaspora*.

Asia's transformations
Edited by Mark Selden
Binghamton and Cornell Universities, USA

The books in this series explore the political, social, economic, and cultural consequences of Asia's transformations in the twentieth and twenty-first centuries. The series emphasizes the tumultuous interplay of local, national, regional, and global forces as Asia bids to become the hub of the world economy. While focusing on the contemporary, it also looks back to analyze the antecedents of Asia's contested rise. This series comprises several strands:

Asia's Transformations aims to address the needs of students and teachers, and the titles will be published in hardback and paperback. Titles include:

Debating Human Rights
Critical essays from the United States and Asia
Edited by Peter Van Ness

Hong Kong's History
State and society under colonial rule
Edited by Tak-Wing Ngo

Japan's Comfort Women
Sexual slavery and prostitution during World War II and the US occupation
Yuki Tanaka

Opium, Empire and the Global Political Economy
Carl A. Trocki

Chinese Society
Change, conflict and resistance
Edited by Elizabeth J. Perry and Mark Selden

Mao's Children in the New China
Voices from the Red Guard generation
Yarong Jiang and David Ashley

Remaking the Chinese State
Strategies, society and security
Edited by Chien-min Chao and Bruce J. Dickson

Korean Society
Civil society, democracy and the state
Edited by Charles K. Armstrong

The Making of Modern Korea
Adrian Buzo

The Resurgence of East Asia
500, 150 and 50 year perspectives
Edited by Giovanni Arrighi, Takeshi Hamashita and Mark Selden

Chinese Society, 2nd edition
Change, conflict and resistance
Edited by Elizabeth J. Perry and Mark Selden

Ethnicity in Asia
Edited by Colin Mackerras

The Battle for Asia
From decolonization to globalization
Mark T. Berger

State and Society in 21st Century China
Edited by Peter Hays Gries and Stanley Rosen

Japan's Quiet Transformation
Social change and civil society in the 21st century
Jeff Kingston

Confronting the Bush Doctrine
Critical views from the Asia-Pacific
Edited by Mel Gurtov and Peter Van Ness

China in War and Revolution, 1895–1949
Peter Zarrow

The Future of US–Korean Relations
The imbalance of power
Edited by John Feffer

Asia's Great Cities
Each volume aims to capture the heartbeat of the contemporary city from multiple perspectives emblematic of the authors' own deep familiarity with the distinctive faces of the city, its history, society, culture, politics, and economics, and its evolving position in national, regional, and global frameworks. While most volumes emphasize urban developments since World War II, some pay close attention to the legacy of the longue durée in shaping the contemporary. Thematic and comparative volumes address such themes as urbanization, economic and financial linkages, architecture and space, wealth and power, gendered relationships, planning and anarchy, and ethnographies in national and regional perspective. Titles include:

Bangkok
Place, practice and representation
Marc Askew

Beijing in the Modern World
David Strand and Madeline Yue Dong

Shanghai
Global city
Jeff Wasserstrom

Hong Kong
Global city
Stephen Chiu and Tai-Lok Lui

Representing Calcutta
Modernity, nationalism and the colonial uncanny
Swati Chattopadhyay

Singapore
Wealth, power and the culture of control
Carl A. Trocki

Asia.com is a series which focuses on the ways in which new information and communication technologies are influencing politics, society, and culture in Asia. Titles include:

Japanese Cybercultures
*Edited by Mark McLelland and
Nanette Gottlieb*

Asia.com
Asia encounters the Internet
*Edited by K. C. Ho, Randolph Kluver
and Kenneth C. C. Yang*

**The Internet in Indonesia's New
Democracy**
David T. Hill and Krishna Sen

Chinese Cyberspaces
Technological changes and
political effects
*Edited by Jens Damm and
Simona Thomas*

Literature and Society is a series that seeks to demonstrate the ways in which Asian Literature is influenced by the politics, society, and culture in which it is produced. Titles include:

**The Body in Postwar Japanese
Fiction**
Edited by Douglas N. Slaymaker

**Chinese Women Writers and the
Feminist Imagination, 1905–1948**
Haiping Yan

Routledge Studies in Asia's Transformations is a forum for innovative new research intended for a high-level specialist readership, and the titles will be available in hardback only. Titles include:

1 **The American Occupation of
   Japan and Okinawa***
   Literature and memory
   Michael Molasky

2 **Koreans in Japan***
   Critical voices from the margin
   Edited by Sonia Ryang

3 **Internationalizing the Pacific**
   The United States, Japan and
   the Institute of Pacific
   Relations in War and Peace,
   1919–1945
   Tomoko Akami

4 **Imperialism in South East Asia**
   'A fleeting, passing phase'
   Nicholas Tarling

5 **Chinese Media, Global
   Contexts**
   Edited by Chin-Chuan Lee

6 **Remaking Citizenship in Hong
   Kong**
   Community, nation and the
   global city
   *Edited by Agnes S. Ku and
   Ngai Pun*

7 **Japanese Industrial Governance**
Protectionism and the licensing state
Yul Sohn

8 **Developmental Dilemmas**
Land reform and institutional change in China
Edited by Peter Ho

9 **Genders, Transgenders and Sexualities in Japan**
Edited by Mark McLelland and Romit Dasgupta

10 **Fertility, Family Planning and Population Policy in China**
Edited by Dudley L. Poston, Che-Fu Lee, Chiung-Fang Chang, Sherry L. McKibben and Carol S. Walther

11 **Japanese Diasporas**
Unsung pasts, conflicting presents, and uncertain futures
Edited by Nobuko Adachi

*Now available in paperback

Critical Asian Scholarship is a series intended to showcase the most important individual contributions to scholarship in Asian Studies. Each of the volumes presents a leading Asian scholar addressing themes that are central to his or her most significant and lasting contribution to Asian studies. The series is committed to the rich variety of research and writing on Asia, and is not restricted to any particular discipline, theoretical approach, or geographical expertise.

Southeast Asia
A testament
George McT. Kahin

Women and the Family in Chinese History
Patricia Buckley Ebrey

China Unbound
Evolving perspectives on the Chinese past
Paul A. Cohen

China's Past, China's Future
Energy, food, environment
Vaclav Smil

The Chinese State in Ming Society
Timothy Brook

Japanese Diasporas
Unsung pasts, conflicting presents, and uncertain futures

Edited by Nobuko Adachi

LONDON AND NEW YORK

First published 2006
by Routledge
2 Park Square, Milton Park, Abingdon, Oxon OX14 5RN

Simultaneously published in the USA and Canada
by Routledge
270 Madison Ave, New York, NY 10016

Routledge is an imprint of the Taylor & Francis Group, an informa business

Transferred to Digital Printing 2009

© 2006 selection and editorial matter, Nobuko Adachi; individual chapters, the contributors

Typeset in Baskerville by Wearset Ltd, Boldon, Tyne and Wear

All rights reserved. No part of this book may be reprinted or reproduced or utilized in any form or by any electronic, mechanical, or other means, now known or hereafter invented, including photocopying and recording, or in any information storage or retrieval system, without permission in writing from the publishers.

British Library Cataloguing in Publication Data
A catalogue record for this book is available from the British Library

Library of Congress Cataloging in Publication Data
A catalog record for this book has been requested

ISBN10: 0-415-77035-1 (hbk)
ISBN10: 0-415-49745-0 (pbk)

ISBN13: 978-0-415-77035-4 (hbk)
ISBN13: 978-0-415-49745-9 (pbk)

Contents

List of illustrations	xii
Notes on contributors	xiii
Acknowledgments	xvii
Introduction: theorizing Japanese diaspora	1
NOBUKO ADACHI	

PART I
Origins of the Japanese diaspora — 23

1 The Japanese diaspora in the New World: its Asian predecessors and origins — 25
   ROGER DANIELS

2 Japanese emigration and immigration: from the Meiji to the modern — 35
   JAMES STANLAW

3 Instructions to emigrant laborers, 1885–94: "Return in triumph" or "Wander on the verge of starvation" — 52
   JONATHAN DRESNER

PART II
Cultural identity: from the incipient diaspora to classic diaspora — 69

4 Paradise lost: Japan's agricultural colonists in Manchukuo — 71
   GREG P. GUELCHER

5 The intermarried issei and *mestizo* nisei in the Philippines: reflections on the origin of Philippine Nikkeijin problems 85
SHUN OHNO

6 Constructing Japanese Brazilian identity: from agrarian migrants to urban white-collar workers 102
NOBUKO ADACHI

7 A stone voice: the diary of a Japanese transnational migrant in Canada 121
KEIBO OIWA

8 The Japanese of Peru: the first-century experience and beyond 142
DANIEL M. MASTERSON

9 Japanese Latin Americans during World War II: a reconsideration 159
LANE RYO HIRABAYASHI AND AKEMI KIKUMURA-YANO

PART III
Constructing identities in the Okinawan, Nikkei, and permanent resident diasporas 173

10 Four governments and a new land: emigration to Bolivia 175
KOZY AMEMIYA

11 Acting Japanese 191
GARY Y. OKIHIRO

12 Crossing ethnic boundaries: the challenge of Brazilian Nikkeijin return migrants in Japan 202
TAKEYUKI TSUDA

13 Overseas Japanese and the challenges of repatriation in post-colonial East Asia 217
MARIKO ASANO TAMANOI

14 **Negotiating work and self: experiences of Japanese
    working women in Singapore**   236
    LENG LENG THANG, MIHO GODA, AND
    ELIZABETH MACLACHLAN

    References   254
    Index   274

Illustrations

Figure

I.1	Construction of a diasporic community	7

Maps

2.1	Sources of highest early Japanese emigration, by prefecture	44
6.1	Japanese settlements in São Paulo State	108

Tables

I.1	Japanese overseas long-term and permanent residents, 1999 and 2003	18
2.1	Agricultural conditions in Japan at the time of emigration	37
2.2	Number and destination of pre- and post-World War II Japanese emigrants	48
2.3	Japanese nationals living overseas, by country	49
2.4	Japanese permanent residents living abroad in 1996 and 2002, by country	49
2.5	Nikkei (overseas Japanese) populations in the mid-1990s	50
2.6	International marriages by selected countries, 1970, 1996, and 2000	51

Contributors

Nobuko Adachi received her PhD in anthropology from the University of Toronto in 1997. She is the editor of *Pan-Japan: The International Journal of the Japanese Diaspora*, and is Assistant Professor of Anthropology at Illinois State University where she teaches classes on the Japanese diaspora, Asian American studies, feminist anthropology, and linguistics. Her research interests are Japanese immigration in South America, ethnohistory, ethnic identity, transnationalism, cultural and human globalization, and sociolinguistics. She has co-edited *Exploring the Myth of Japanese Women's Language*, and translated and annotated Masako Itoh's *"Oh, No! I'm Married to the Company!": Japanese Society as Viewed by its Women*. Both books are currently under review. Her publications include "Japonês: A Marker of Social Class or a Key Term in the Discourse of Race?" in *Latin American Perspectives*.

Kozy Amemiya received her PhD in sociology from the University of California, San Diego. She is a research associate at the Japan Policy Research Institute and has been investigating Okinawan immigration to Bolivia since 1996. She has contributed to *Okinawa: Cold War Island* (Japan Policy Research Institute 1999), *Encounters: People of Asian Descent in the Americas* (Rowman & Littlefield 1999), and *New Worlds, New Lives: Globalization and People of Japanese Descent in the Americas and from Latin America in Japan* (Stanford University Press 2002).

Roger Daniels, Charles Phelps Taft Professor Emeritus of History at the University of Cincinnati, is a leading historian of Asian American immigration. His numerous books include *The Politics of Prejudice: The Anti-Japanese Movement in California and the Struggle for Japanese Exclusion* (University of California Press 1967), *Asian America: Chinese and Japanese in the United States* (University of Washington Press 1988), and *Coming to America: A History of Immigration and Ethnicity in American Life* (Harper 1990).

Jonathan Dresner received his PhD from Harvard University and is Assistant Professor of East Asian History at the University of Hawaii, Hilo.

His dissertation research was on Japanese emigration from Yamaguchi Prefecture to Hawaii, focusing on the social and economic effects of labor migration and return migration on sending communities.

Miho Goda received her PhD in sociology from Konan Women's University and teaches at the Chinese University of Hong Kong. She researches in the area of Chinese communities in Southeast Asia, and her current project is a comparative study of clan associations in Singapore and Hong Kong.

Greg P. Guelcher is Associate Professor of History at Morningside College in Sioux City, Iowa. He received his PhD from the University of Illinois at Urbana-Champaign in 1999. In 2003, Guelcher was an inaugural recipient of the Sharon Walker Faculty Excellence Award at Morningside College.

Lane Ryo Hirabayashi received his PhD in anthropology from the University of California at Berkeley in 1981. He is currently a Professor in the Department of Ethnic Studies at the University of California, Riverside. He is the senior editor of *New Worlds, New Lives: Globalization and People of Japanese Descent in the Americas* (Stanford University Press 2002).

Akemi Kikumura-Yano is Director of Research and International Relations at the Japanese American National Museum, Los Angeles. She is the editor of *Encyclopedia of Japanese Descendants in the Americas* (AltaMira Press 2002) and a co-editor of *New Worlds, New Lives: Globalization and People of Japanese Descent in the Americas* (Stanford University Press 2002).

Elizabeth Naoko MacLachlan is Assistant Professor in the Department of Japanese Studies at the National University of Singapore. She is the author of numerous articles on Japanese mass media production and popular culture flows, and is the writer and co-producer of the documentary film *The Second Wave: Japanese Women Working in Singapore* (2002).

Daniel M. Masterson is Professor of Latin American History at the United States Naval Academy, Annapolis, Maryland, where he has taught since 1979. He has authored or edited five books and numerous articles on the issues of Latin American race relations, civil–military conflict, and immigration. His most recent books are: *Fuerza armada y sociedad en el Perú moderno* (Lima: IEPE 2000), and *The Japanese in Latin America* (University of Illinois Press 2004) with Sayaka Funada-Classen.

Shun Ohno is a visiting professorate lecturer at the Center for International Studies at the University of the Philippines in Manila, a visiting professor at Mindanao International College in Davao, and a research fellow at the Institute for International Mutual Understanding at Tezukayama Gakuin University in Osaka. He has been a staff writer, foreign correspondent, and assistant editor for Japan's *Mainichi Shimbun* newspaper for twenty-two years. He received his PhD from the Australian National University in 2005. His publications include *Hapon: Firipin Nikkeijin no Nagai Sengo* [The Long Agony of the Philippine Nikkeijin after the War] (Daisan Shokan 1991), and "Hito no Gurôbaru-ka ga Susumu Ajia Taiheiyô no Nakano Nippon" [Japan in the Human, Globalized, Asia-Pacific], in *Nippon Keizai Saisei no Jôken*, ed. Shigeo Nakao (Chikuma Shobô 2003).

Keibo Oiwa is a cultural anthropologist and teaches International Studies at Meijigakuin University in Yokohama, Japan. He is the author of *Rowing the Eternal Sea. The Story of a Minamata Fisherman* (Rowman & Littlefield 2003), co-author of *The Other Japan: Voices Beyond the Mainstream* (Fulcrum Publishers 1999), and *The Japan We Never Knew: A Journey of Discovery* (Stoddart Books 1996) both with David Suzuki. He also edited *Stone Voices* (Véhicule Press 1991).

Gary Okihiro is Professor of International and Public Affairs and Director of the Center for the Study of Ethnicity and Race at Columbia University. He is author of, most recently, *Common Ground: Reimagining American History* (Princeton University Press 2001), and *The Columbia Guide To Asian American History* (Columbia University Press 2001). He received the Lifetime Achievement Award from the American Studies Association, and is a past president of the Association for Asian American Studies.

James Stanlaw is Professor of Anthropology at Illinois State University. He is a contributing editor to *Anthropology News* and is co-editor of *Pan-Japan: The International Journal of the Japanese Diaspora*. His most recent work is *Japanese English: Language and Culture Contact* (Hong Kong University Press 2004).

Mariko Asano Tamanoi received her doctorate in anthropology from Northwestern University. She is Associate Professor of Anthropology at the University of California, Los Angeles. She is the author of *Under the Shadow of Nationalism: Politics and Poetics of Rural Japanese Women* (University of Hawaii Press 1998). Her articles have appeared in the *Journal of Asian Studies, Annual Review of Anthropology, American Ethnologist, Positions: East Asia Cultures Critique*, and *Comparative Studies in Society and History*.

Leng Leng Thang is Associate Professor in the Department of Japanese Studies at National University of Singapore. Her research interests include the anthropology of aging, intergenerational relationships, gender, and Japan–Singapore sociocultural relations. She is the author of *Generations in Touch: Linking the Old and Young in a Tokyo Neighborhood* (Cornell University Press 2001), co-editor of *Old Challenges, New*

Strategies? Women, Work and Family in Contemporary Asia (Brill Academic Publishers 2004) and producer of the documentary film *The Second Wave: Japanese Women Working in Singapore* (2002).

Takeyuki Tsuda is Associate Director of the Center for Comparative Immigration Studies at the University of California at San Diego. He is the author of *Strangers in the Ethnic Homeland: Japanese Brazilian Return Migration in Transnational Perspective* (Columbia University Press 2003). He has published articles in the *Journal of Asian Studies*, *Journal of Japanese Studies*, and *Ethos*.

Acknowledgments

Early versions of most of the chapters in this book were presented at several sessions at the panel "Unsung Pasts, Unimaginable Futures, and the Ongoing Negotiations of Human Rights: Japanese Transnational Migrants and Their Descendants in a Globalized World" at the 101st Annual Meeting of the American Anthropological Association in 2002. We are very grateful to the following organizations for sponsoring these sessions: the Society for Urban, National, and Transnational/Global Anthropology, the Society for East Asian Anthropology, and the Society for the Anthropology of North America.

Many people worked hard to make this book possible, especially the contributors, to whom I owe a great debt for all their support and encouragement. However, I want to thank especially Mark Selden, Harumi Befu, and Rosemary Carstens who all went "beyond the call of duty" – or obligations of friendship or colleagueship – in helping me make this project a reality.

Introduction
Theorizing Japanese diaspora

Nobuko Adachi

Today, three million Nikkei[1] – people of Japanese descent who were born and raised overseas – are found throughout the world. In addition, hundreds of thousands of Japanese reside outside of Japan permanently or temporarily. This volume examines these dispersed Japanese populations: their histories, the diverse contemporary communities they have formed, and the political, economic, social, and cultural pressures they have faced. In contrast with other groups of migrants – notably African, Jewish, Chinese, and Irish – Japanese and Nikkei have received little attention from anthropologists, sociologists, and historians. Nor does much of the existing literature consider them as members of a "diaspora." For example, the term *diaspora* hardly appears in the most influential works on Japanese Americans such as those of Ronald Takaki (1983, 1998) or Yuji Ichioka (1988), nor do we find it in the growing literature on Japanese in Latin America such as that of Harvey Gardiner (1981) or Joshua Roth (2002). When it does appear in these monographs, authors are often "cautious about using" the word as it is such a "slippery term" and not clearly defined (Azuma 2005: 219).

Although the experiences of the internment camps in North America during World War II are well known, other issues concerning overseas Japanese and Nikkei, such as their racial, cultural, and economic positions in a Latin American or North American racial, cultural, and economic context; issues of assimilating or maintaining cultural integrity; and issues of Nikkei "returnee" labor migrants in Japan, have been little investigated. In addition, problems of human rights, racism, and racial and ethnic identity have yet to be examined in a Japanese transnational context. This book addresses these issues while considering the appropriateness of the diaspora concept for encompassing the varied experiences of different groups of Japanese overseas and their relationship to Japanese society.

Theorizing a diaspora

Diaspora is one of the most frequently, yet most ambiguously, used terms in migration and globalization studies. The term *diaspora*, meaning dispersal or scattering, originated in Deuteronomy and came into general use in the late nineteenth century to describe the dispersion of the Jews from their homeland in Judea (Palestine), and eventually to many parts of the world. For more than a century, diaspora has been commonly used to refer to Jewish expatriate communities and the identities that developed via their historical experience that continue to link them in cultural, and sometimes political, terms to their homeland.

In recent decades, the term has been applied to numerous migrant groups including Africans, Armenians, Chinese, Indians, Palestinians, and Afghans, to mention only a few. During the Civil Rights Movement in the United States in the 1960s the word *diaspora* was enlisted to describe attempts to form a Pan-African community, linking populations of New World Blacks who were forced to disperse from their homelands to the non-African world where they were economically and politically marginalized (see Winkler 1999: A11). Focusing on cultural identities formed through experiences of dispersal and alienation, since the 1980s Asian and Asian American specialists have applied the concept of diaspora to communities of overseas Chinese and other Asian migrants.

All of the authors in this volume use the term *diaspora* when discussing various Japanese communities overseas. Among us, there is general agreement that we are examining the societies, cultures, economics, politics, and histories of communities of people who have left their ancestral homeland, yet who continue to maintain cultural and emotional group identities that link them to it. For some, the movement was forced by such factors as poverty or war. For others, it was a matter of seizing an opportunity. Some have been marginalized or oppressed in their adopted nations; others have been tremendously successful. Each author focuses on the evolution of personal and ethnic identities that have emerged as a result of these varied experiences. However, it is worthwhile at this point to examine the notion of diaspora when used as an analytical tool for the description or analysis of data, or as an aid in the formation of research hypotheses, and how it applies in the Japanese case.

Competing terms

The notion of a diaspora overlaps with terms such as "travel," "refugee," "transnationalism," and "immigration" – all of which also describe the global movements and experiences of people. But in what ways does diaspora differ, or go beyond such terms?

Unlike travel, diaspora involves the creation and maintenance of migrant communities (Clifford 1994: 308). Although both diasporee and refugee confront migration and incorporation into a different society and culture, the latter term focuses on *leaving* a home and nation (Schiller *et al.* 1995: 48; Takaki 1998), while the former focuses on a collective home away from home, together with others of the same group. People in a diasporic community, then, articulate roots and routes to establish these collective homes, by which they construct identity as a means to both strengthen their own solidarity and to gain cultural citizenship in their adopted nations (Clifford 1994: 307–8).

Transnationalism, a term originally widely used to describe corporate structures with established organizational bases in more than one state, has also been applied to movements and linkages of people, ideas, goods, beliefs, values, and capital across national borders (Schiller *et al.* 1995; Levitt 1998; Baía 1999; Braziel and Mannur 2003). Transnationalism, then, "emphasizes the dynamic process of nation-making as anchored across nations (and states), privileging neither place of origin nor adopted land, and collapsing time and space into a single social field" (Hoffman 2004: H-Net Reviews). When diaspora researchers look at the movement of transnational migrants, they focus on how cultural ideologies and identities are formed at the ethnic boundaries in host nations. They look particularly at how transnational migrants – and their descendants – relate to local people socially, culturally, economically, or politically.

The connections of diasporees with their homeland also differ from those of immigrants. The latter emphasizes departure from the country of origin, but the immigrant is never fully assimilated into the new nation, and in certain ways inhabits a space that is politically detached from both worlds (Hoffman 2004). On the other hand, diasporees may focus more on maintaining ethnic identity through language, culture, or religion associated with the homeland, and their desire to continue to maintain relations with likeminded others, fostering an "ethno-communal" consciousness in the nations in which they currently reside (Safran 1991: 84).

Previous approaches to the study of diaspora

Cohen (1997) proposed several classifications of diaspora based on ethnic group and migratory features. He classified the Jewish migration, consisting of many expatriate minority communities overseas, as a *prototypical* diaspora; the African or Armenian transnational migrations as *victim* diasporas; the Chinese and Lebanese who sought business or economic opportunities abroad as *trade* diasporas; and Indians who left for jobs abroad as a *labor* diaspora.

In fact, however, diverse factors shaped both the migrations and the community formations and other patterns of dispersal of each of these and others. For example, Jews were not only part of a *victim* diaspora; many became prosperous merchants, thus forming part of a *trade* diaspora. Among Chinese migrants, coolies were certainly members of a *labor* diaspora. But others, including merchants, students, and intellectuals, went abroad for quite different reasons and led dissimilar lives. In other words, ethnic diasporas are typically composed of varying components and subtypes, whose differences may range from the rationale for dispersal to factors including occupation, class, assimilation to a new culture, and ties to the original homeland, to mention a few salient factors.

Instead of classifications of diasporas by ethnicity, William Safran (1991: 83–4) posits six historical and sociological features which define a diaspora: (1) dispersal from a central place to two or more foreign or peripheral regions; (2) retention of a shared (expressed) collective memory/mythology about their homeland; (3) alienation in the host society; (4) desire to eventually return to their ancestral homeland; (5) commitment to maintain, restore, or assure the safety and welfare of their original homeland; and (6) definition of ethnic identity through the homeland, and desire to continue to maintain relations with likeminded others, fostering an "ethno-communal" consciousness.

However, while no one denies the diasporees' desire to maintain strong ties to the original homeland, including the desire to return to live there, we must remember that these communities are often very diverse. James Clifford (1994), while acknowledging Safran's comparative approach to diasporas as "certainly the best way to theorize a complex discursive and historical field" (p. 305), observes that no diasporic community, not even the prototypical Jewish diaspora, fits this ideal type. Clifford particularly criticizes the emphasis on strong attachment to the homeland and the desire for actual physical return, a point that might be applied to many other diasporic communities. The point is not to deny the possibility that some not only maintain strong ties to the original homeland, including the desire to return to live there, but to stress the diversity of communities on this and many other points.

This applies to attachments to Africa expressed by American Pan Africanists. As Sheffer (1986: 11) observes, most Black Americans do not experience themselves as part of a diaspora in the sense that their imagined home is where they and their parents were born and live, not in Africa. This is underlined by the fact that most have at best scant awareness of the region, tribal group, or language from which they originated. Black American political leaders have rarely looked toward physical return, concentrating instead on strengthening their collective group identity as a basis for negotiating with the majority in their transplanted nation's societies (see also Clifford 1994: 308).

In order to understand diasporas in modern society, we need to look at their range of experiences abroad, including not only political, economic, and social marginalization, but also the nature of cultural identity and perceptions of an imagined homeland.

Cultural identities and diasporas

Stuart Hall (1990) distinguishes two types of cultural identity found in diaspora communities. The first, which shares some of the features enumerated by Safran, refers to the collective memory of the shared historical experiences and common ancestry of a people. Hall argues that this kind of cultural identity tends to be stable and unchanging. Beneath the shifting divisions and vicissitudes of history, it offers a stable frame of reference and meaning (1990: 223). This first type of cultural identity might be called "historical memory."

The second type of cultural identity – which is ever in flux – could be called "cultural construction." Cultural construction is a *process*, transcending place, time, and history. Far from being eternally fixed in some essentialized past – which members of the group share – this kind of cultural identity focuses on the continuous *play* of history, culture, and power. Unlike historical memory, which can secure our sense of "who we are" long after it is formed, cultural construction is constantly (re)shaping people's identity in relation to contemporary social situations and needs (1990: 225).

However, we must realize that these two types of cultural identity are not clearly separated, nor can they be defined in absolute terms. Historical or collective memory is not invariably frozen. To take one example, the historical memory of World War II for many Japanese has shifted in the post-war era. Some, embracing pacifism or critical reflection on the past, have one narrative, while others, hewing to a nationalist stance, have quite different recollections. The result has been continuing contention over the war within Japanese society, as well as between Japanese and people in nations that Japan fought.

Historical memory, which inculcates values in a diaspora community, may *tend* to be as stable and unchanging as Hall defines it, but it is influenced by cultural construction (and vice versa). The two types of cultural identity are not mutually exclusive. Dynamic cultural constructions are overtly or tacitly being created under the influence of historical memory. For example, the experiences of Japanese–North American internees during World War II (see Oiwa, Chapter 7) are today often discussed – and thought about – in terms rather different from those of the 1940s. This has led to some divisiveness in the Japanese American community. For instance, Japanese American filmmaker Emiko Omori's recent *Rabbit in the Moon* generated controversy by portraying internment camp rebels and draft resisters in a more positive light than many earlier interpreters. This contrasted with the image of resisters as troublemakers who only made life harder for everyone, a view favored by more accommodating and "patriotic" organizations such as the Japanese American Citizens League.

Japanese diasporas

The use of the concept of diaspora has proven to be extremely productive in the study of people of Japanese ancestry overseas. Today, millions of people of Japanese descent are citizens of other nations, hundreds of thousands more live and work outside of Japan, and hundreds of thousands of "returnee" *dekasegi* migrants from Latin America now work in Japan as manual laborers.

In most of the countries where Japanese have emigrated, they have achieved a degree of economic success, often after suffering economic hardship and social isolation. Some have come to be classified as members of a "model" or "positive" minority – exemplary success stories in several nations of how minorities might become economically and socially assimilated. Others still suffer from problems of human rights, racism, and racial and ethnic conflict. In some places Nikkei occupy an ostensibly neutral place in various racial dichotomies – being neither "white" nor "black," they are often thought to occupy a middle ground in some of the most explosive social conflicts.

What do all these people share in common? Is there a Pan-Nikkei community? When there are differences among these groups, why do they exist, and how are they manifested? What forms of hybrid cultures have emerged through the processes of migration, integration, and intermarriage? When they "return" to Japan, are Nikkei treated as lost relatives – or as strangers, even foreigners? It is precisely these kinds of questions that can be best answered by using diaspora as a theoretical construct and analytic tool, the lens through which to more sharply view and understand these phenomena.

Many diasporees see their community through the lens of a shared diasporic experience, which is constituted from at least three factors: historical, external, and internal. Historical factors are the physical realities of the political economy, such as depressions, famines, wars, and internments. But they are constructed both internally and externally, as these historical factors are usually interpreted differently by outsiders and insiders. Insiders, for example, see the world internally through the lens of earlier immigrant generations. Such internal factors reflect individual psychological states as well as group consciousness. But communities are also constructed with reference to external factors, the psychological attitudes and states of those outside the group. Outsiders, usually being in the mainstream or the majority, have the power to impose a particular privileged view or narrative on historical events. For example, until recently governments and societies in both North and South America felt that the internment of Japanese populations in their countries in the 1940s was justified due to wartime expediency. Thus, the diasporic experience results from the interplay between these three overlapping perspectives (as seen in the intersection in Figure I.1).

But such shared diasporic experiences are not at all static; their very dynamism is inherent in their structure. Thus, the shaded area in the intersection is constantly in a state of flux, expanding and contracting depending on context and participants, even possibly in the same community at different times.

Introduction 7

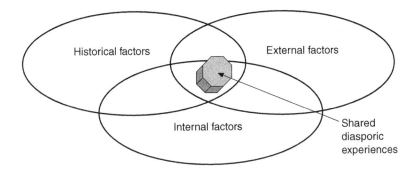

Figure I.1 Construction of a diasporic community.

Three features important in all diasporic communities are highlighted in this volume's discussion. First, while numerous factors – such as political disenfranchisement, economic and cultural insecurity, and social discrimination, but also pride in community and in the successes of its members – shape the formation of a diaspora, diasporic communities seek to draw on a common cultural identity in order to gain political rights and strengthen economic and social bonds.

Second, diasporic communities everywhere experience constant change over time, both in terms of the nature and composition of the community and in its relationship to the original homeland, the recipient community, and nation. Third, diasporic communities invariably include diverse subtypes – based on the particulars of the political, social, ethnic, cultural, and economic situation of its members and their relations to each other. Diasporas constantly change their social, political, economic, and cultural complexion, and these integral processes define who gains wealth, power, and prestige, and who is impoverished and marginalized. Six subtypes of the Japanese diaspora are discussed in this volume: *incipient, displaced, model or positive minority, Okinawan, Nikkei,* and *long-term and permanent-resident* diaspora. Each possesses unique characteristics.

The incipient diaspora

The majority of pre-World War II Japanese emigrants went abroad initially as temporary workers to earn income in foreign lands and then return to Japan (see Daniels, Chapter 1). Myron Weiner (1986: 47) points out that such foreign workers should not be considered immigrants since they were not allowed to remain in their host country and they could be forced by the government to leave at any time. Furthermore, they were entitled neither to citizenship nor to social and political benefits and rights. Most importantly, in contrast to European immigrants, they could not look forward to achieving citizenship rights. They lived in a state of legal and political subordination, economic insecurity, and social marginalization. Their children were in an even more ambiguous position. They, too, were expected to *return home* with their parents despite feeling more *at home* in the host country in which they grew up than in the land of their parents.

Weiner terms such groups an *incipient* diaspora. Weiner's characterization is useful, as it adds a processual dynamic that is rarely considered. Instead of focusing exclusively on how diasporees were marginalized from mainstream society, and how they formed their own identities at the margins, Weiner's concept reminds us that all diasporas have a unique history. Often in the initial stages, new immigrants are socially marginalized and face political and economic restrictions as foreigners. In spite of such difficulties, some migrants find ways to thrive in their new environment. By learning from the historical particulars of the formation of incipient diasporic communities, we are able to discover why these immigrants constructed and adopted the identities that they did.

By Weiner's definition, the majority of pre-war Japanese migrants were part of an incipient diaspora. Many Japanese workers and their overseas-born children (who often were not entitled to automatic citizenship in the host nation) wished to remain in their adopted nations. However, being classified as foreigners of a specific type, they could not do so. Japanese migrant workers experienced legal, political, and economic marginality and discrimination, sometimes specifically targeting only Japanese. For example, the Philippines' Public Land Act of 1903 prohibited non-citizens from owning land. This had a great impact on Japanese emigrant life and social structure, for example, causing many Japanese to choose Filipino wives (see Ohno, Chapter 5). In the United States, California strictly enforced the Alien Land Laws of 1913 and of 1920 that denied citizenship and the right to own real property to Japanese immigrants. Although Japanese migrant farmers tried to get around these laws through various technicalities such as leasing land in the name of American citizens, these restrictions profoundly affected the lives of Japanese immigrant farmers (Ichioka 1988: 227; Niiya 2001: 111).

The Canadian government restricted fishing licenses for Japanese in 1919. At that time, the majority of Japanese migrant workers lived in British Columbia and engaged in fishing. They had established a thriving and successful community, and were becoming an economic influence in the Province. Japanese fishermen held 1,958 commercial finishing licenses out of a total 4,722 issued (Adachi 1991: 57). The restriction of fishing licenses cut most of them off from their livelihood, forcing the majority of Japanese in Canada to become cannery factory workers (see Oiwa, Chapter 7).

In Peru, the Eighty Percent Law of 1932 required that 80 percent of employees in every business be Peruvian citizens – including small Japanese-owned shops in Japantown that served Japanese monolingual patrons. They could not hire Peruvian-born Japanese to circumvent this restriction as the Immigration Law of 1936 prevented citizenship for children of aliens, including those who were born in Peru (see Masterson, Chapter 8). In Brazil, the Estado Novo (New State) Law of 1937 banned foreign-language teaching and closed down Japanese schools. However, in the Japanese communities in the rural areas most people were monolingual Japanese speakers, and their children maintained verbal fluency, though their reading and writing ability in Japanese declined rapidly (see Adachi 2004; Chapter 6, this volume).

Prior to World War II, Japanese remained closely linked to their homeland. For example, Japanese overseas communities regularly received Japanese newcomers. These people were usually recruited through *imingaisha* (emigration companies; see Dresner, Chapter 3; Adachi, Chapter 6), many of them were invited via the *yobiyose* system whereby relatives and families sponsored immigrants, and some came as picture brides. In welcoming new members from Japan, overseas Japanese societies revitalized and reified their Japaneseness.

Tens of thousands of Japanese migrant workers' children who were born in the adopted nations were sent back to Japan for a Japanese education.[2] In Japan, many of these *nisei* children were raised by grandparents or other relatives. After attending school for a few years, or sometimes completing their entire education, they were reunited with their parents abroad.

Japanese performers as individuals or in troupes regularly toured Japanese overseas settlements. Money and gifts also flowed back and forth between the host nations and Japan. For example, Japanese immigrants, like many other immigrant groups, regularly sent money to support their families back in Japan and, when natural disasters occurred in Japan, they pooled money and sent care packages.

Following the incipient diaspora period, most Japanese and their children wanted to remain in their host nations. Since World War II, many, indeed, were granted citizenship either by birth or by naturalization. However, in spite of their new legal status and their many contributions to their new countries, they often could not overcome being seen as "foreigners." Some of these attitudes still prevail. However, before we examine contemporary Japanese diasporas, we need to look at the *displaced* diaspora – a time in which people of Japanese ancestry living in countries throughout the Americas and Asia were once again forced to move, this time by events of World War II.

The displaced diaspora

World War II everywhere had a shattering effect on Japanese communities abroad, especially those in Asia and the Americas, inviting comparison with exile-based diasporas similar in certain ways to exiled Jewish or African communities abroad, yet unique in their own right. The socioeconomic and political relationships, between home nation and host nations and between migrants and the states and societies to which they had gone, changed dramatically. Throughout the Americas, many host nations placed Japanese and Nikkei in prison camps and confiscated their farms, businesses, and homes (as discussed in many of this volume's chapters).

Japanese settlers and their children were branded as enemy aliens, especially in Canada, Cuba, Mexico, and the United States. Japanese and Nikkei were forced to relocate, with many being sent to internment camps (in effect, concentration camps). These governments imprisoned over 135,000 Japanese nationals and Nikkei who were born as citizens of these nations[3] (see Hirabayashi and Kikumura-Yano, Chapter 9).

In most cases, the property of the detainees was auctioned off by the host governments or stolen or destroyed by the local populace. Thus, many Japanese had nothing to return to even after being freed from the camps. After the war, the governments of some host nations prohibited Japanese and Nikkei from living in their pre-war locales. Indeed, Canada offered this choice to released detainees: return to Japan or relocate east of the Rocky Mountains. This order remained in effect until 1949. Japanese immigrants and their children who returned to Japan also suffered discrimination. Having been residents or citizens of former enemy nations, some saw them as traitors. Some, therefore, later returned to their host nations (Oiwa, Chapter 7). Thus, many overseas Japanese and Nikkei found themselves, in effect, homeless; that is, alienated from both their host and home nations.

Japanese adults and children in several Latin American nations, such as Peru (Masterson, Chapter 8), Bolivia (Amemiya, Chapter 10), and Chile, were sent to camps in the United States with the Japanese Americans. Hirabayashi and Kikumura-Yano (Chapter 9) point out that the number of internees from Latin America was a relatively small percentage of the local Japanese population when compared to North America, where almost the entire Japanese and Nikkei population was interned. However, the impact of the demolition of these Latin American Japanese communities could be as far-reaching as it was for those in the North. Many were sent to the United States at gunpoint and without passports (Higashide 1993). My interviews with Japanese Peruvians in the 1990s revealed that the families who were left behind in Latin America were devastated, never knowing when it would be their turn to be deported or whether their families and communities would ever be restored. The social, cultural, and psychological impact of relocation during World War II is one of the most important factors in the formation of social identity among later generations.

Even in Brazil, although Japanese were not relocated to concentration camps as in North America and other Latin American nations, lives were inexorably changed. When Brazil and Japan severed diplomatic relations, taking opposite sides in the war, Japanese in Brazil lost all support from the Japanese government for their communities (see Adachi, Chapter 6), and many urban Japanese, forced to leave the cities, fled to the interior to live with their rural compatriots.

In Asia, the situation for Japanese abroad was sometimes even more devastating. In Manchuria, Japanese diasporees were even persecuted and displaced by their own army. The military had its own occupying agenda – trying to pacify an increasing hostile population – and had few qualms about using local Japanese civilians for their own ends, or forcing them to do much of their dirty work (e.g., spying instead of farming) (see Guelcher, Chapter 4; Tamanoi, Chapter 13). Moreover, in the wake of Japan's military defeat in 1945, many were killed and many children lost. In the Philippines, the wartime and post-war situation for Japanese and Nikkei was also catastrophic (see Ohno, Chapter 5). During World War II, the Japanese military forced Japanese settlers to help arrest anti-Japanese Filipinos. Since the majority of Japanese settlers' wives were Filipinas they often had to arrest relatives, even their parents-in-law. This created such severe tensions that after the war all Japanese nationals were expelled from the country, and some were murdered by vengeful Filipinos. Rather than follow their husbands and fathers to Japan, most Filipino wives and their children chose to stay behind. Nevertheless, they were discriminated against because of lingering wartime hatreds, and most lived their lives hiding their Japanese connections.

The model or positive minority diaspora

After the war, overseas Japanese and Nikkei rebuilt their lives and their families. Education provided social mobility for many. The number of Nikkei who have obtained higher education or become professionals in North America has increased steadily since World War II. Historically, Japanese have valued education highly. By the middle of the Edo period (1600–1867), even many children of the lower classes, such as merchants and farmers, went to temple schools where they learned reading and writing from Buddhist monks. The number of students in Japan in the eighteenth century was among the highest in the world. By the end of the Tokugawa period (1600–1867), about 40 percent of boys and 10 percent of girls were receiving some kind of formal instruction, ranking Japan among the top three countries worldwide in terms of rates of literacy and access to education (Jansen 2000: 190). Furthermore, in the late nineteenth and early twentieth centuries when Japanese emigration began in earnest, Japan was in the middle of a time of energetic Westernization and industrialization. In this rising meritocracy, education was thought to be the path for both personal social mobility and national growth and development. Japanese migrants carried this respect for education with them. As soon as they established a Japanese community, a Japanese school was founded, and many even sent their children back to Japan for schooling, if they were financially able.

After World War II – when Japan lost power and prestige, so that studying there became less attractive – new generations of Nikkei concentrated on education in their adopted nations, and many attended universities and colleges. They put their education to good use, and many Nikkei in the Americas especially distinguished themselves professionally and economically. Nikkei leaders were usually well educated, earning the respect of both Japanese and mainstream communities. Their apparent economic success and social and cultural assimilation of the community led many in the host nations to view the Nikkei as a "model" minority (in North America) or "positive" minority (in South America).

In many venues, the Japanese have gone from being marginal farmers or migrants to mainstream neighbors, professionals, and co-workers. They are often held up as prime examples in their countries of what minorities can achieve. While at least some of this may be exaggerated or wishful thinking, it reminds us once again that diasporic communities and their perceived place in the larger society are always in flux.

Many Nikkei members of the model or positive minority diaspora have indeed successfully adopted the manners and customs of their adopted nations. However, some community leaders nevertheless continue to stress consciousness-raising, and strive to preserve a Japanese ethnic identity as a means to maintain communal solidarity and to secure political gains for the community.

Nikkei activists also seek to unify the community and demonstrate leadership by highlighting and protesting the racial and ethnic discrimination they, their parents, and grandparents experienced during and after the war. The bitterness of the wartime experience was thus turned into a basis for solidarity for winning civil rights, a strategy that may be linked with their new image as a model/positive minority diaspora. In 1988 Japanese Americans won an official public apology from President Reagan. Each surviving wartime detainee from World War II was paid $20,000, and Japanese Canadians CD$21,000, in redress awards from their governments. This accomplished something that no other North American minority, and few elsewhere, had ever achieved.

The case of interned Latin Americans is still under negotiation. Up to several thousand Latin Americans were deported to internment camps in the United States during World War II. However, not being U.S. citizens, they received no redress at the time of the North American settlement in 1988. Finally, in 1998, President Clinton gave an apology and offered US$5,000 to every Latin American surviving ex-internee. However, since this amount was less than a quarter of that for North Americans, it was rejected by Nikkei Latin American community leaders. Even within Japanese diasporic communities all are not equal; there are those who are more marginalized than others. And as for redress from their homelands in Latin America, there has been almost nothing. Part of the reason for this is that a great many Latin American Japanese internees were never able to return home. Because they were sent to the United States without passports, visas, or proper documents, they fell through various legal cracks.

Many of the model or positive minority diasporees have successfully established their social position in the society of their adopted nations through education, economic advancement, and political achievement. This has given them a degree of confidence and security unknown by previous generations. They can voice their grievances over current or past inequities or mistreatment. They have the power to insure their political rights. In other words, unlike incipient and displaced diasporees, the model/positive minority diasporees have many advantages as citizens of their adopted nations. Besides the obvious benefits for day-to-day living, this has also given them a more important power: the ability to control their own historical images and to construct their own historical narratives.

The Nikkei diaspora

One of the characteristics of the Japanese diaspora is that scores of thousands of Nikkei have "returned" to their ancestral homeland. While every dispersed ethnic group has seen some members return to their place of origin, the unique aspect in the Japanese case is the institutionalization of this process in what I will refer to as the *Nikkei* diaspora.

Nikkei diasporees in contemporary Japan fall into two main categories: (1) *dekasegi* migrant workers – mostly from Latin America – who were encouraged by the Japanese government to "return" to help overcome a labor shortage in the country; and (2) overseas *orphans* of Japanese, who were born and raised by people in host nations and recently who were invited to migrate to Japan by the Japanese government.

Due to later marriages and an increasing number of women who are postponing or avoiding marriage and motherhood, Japan's birth rate is currently 1.29 children per woman, one of the lowest in the world (Clark 2005), dropping from 1.36 as late as 2000 (Asahi Shimbun 2002: 35). This is substantially less than the 2.1 needed to maintain a population at its current level. In addition, the Japanese population is aging at the highest rate in the world (Keizai Koho Center 2004: 14). Of the 127.4 million people in Japan in 2002, 23,626,000 were over sixty-five years old, almost 20 percent of the population. In contrast, there were only 25,296,000 people under twenty years old[4] (Keizai Koho Center 2004: 16), about an equal percentage. The aggregate size of the workforce is declining. In 2001, for example, the potential "labor force population" – the total number of persons aged fifteen or older who worked or sought work – dropped by 140,000, and has been declining ever since (Asahi Shimbum 2002: 78). These demographic facts highlight the severe labor shortage Japan has been facing for the past decade and a half and the prospect that the situation will worsen substantially in the coming years.

In one attempt to combat the shrinking workforce, the Japanese government issued special working visas to people of Japanese descent, thinking that Nikkei would adjust better to Japan than other migrants. The recent influx of hundreds of thousands of labor migrants, mostly descendants of Japanese Latin Americans, has created a type of reverse diaspora. Increasing numbers of Nikkei have returned to work as dekasegi workers in Japan. Many of them work as unskilled laborers, including some who were white-collar workers in their host nation, attracted by Japan's high wages. For example, unskilled Japanese Brazilian dekasegi factory workers make about $20,000 per year in Japan, or five to ten times what they could earn in Brazil (Tsuda 1999b: 693). Even after Japan's economic bubble burst in the 1990s, the number of Nikkei dekasegi workers continued to increase (Komai 1998: 104). The Brazilian case is especially striking: 56,000 Brazilians of Japanese descent were living in Japan in 1990, 233,000 in 1997, and 266,000 in 2001, the vast majority being dekasegi workers (Asahi Shimbum 1992: 39; 1998: 63; 2002: 37).

Most Nikkei returnees anticipated that they would settle down in their parents' or grandparents' homeland with little difficulty. However, this has not been the case. As foreign workers, not only do they not share in the same social benefits or political rights as Japanese citizens, but most have only two-year work permits. Moreover, many are not eligible for permanent residence. Indeed, their legal status resembles that of Japanese labor migrants to the Americas a century ago. They are, then, in a sense, incipient diasporees in Japan, living in a state of legal and political ambiguity, as did earlier generations of Japanese in foreign countries. Moreover, upon their arrival in Japan, Japanese locals treat them not as returning compatriots but as foreign migrant workers.

Although the majority of the young generation of Nikkei – especially those who grew up in Latin American cities – have limited command of the Japanese language (see Tsuda, Chapter 12), many understand some Japanese and some speak it fluently. However, their language is generally a mixture of turn-of-the-twentieth-century Japanese farm dialects and the languages of the host nations, mostly Portuguese or Spanish. These Nikkei dialects generally lack the polite grammatical forms found in today's standard Japanese. This reinforces a view among Japanese that the Nikkei are uneducated or rude (Adachi 1998, 1999, 2001). Language is the threshold in the creation of a social boundary between Japanese locals and Nikkei workers. Consequently, most Nikkei are relegated to menial labor in Japan, even highly trained professionals. Tsuda (Chapter 12) argues that as long as Nikkei workers did not attempt to penetrate Japanese society, remaining in the category of *gaijin* (foreigner), they did not experience undue ethnic conflict. Often seen as exotic, they received sympathetic attention from Japanese locals. While generally not held in as high esteem as "white" gaijin, they are more highly regarded than other foreigners from Third World countries, who are generally viewed negatively by local

Japanese. However, once these Nikkei try to "become Japanese" they encounter cold shoulders from neighbors, landlords, and co-workers, causing many to feel alienated and discriminated against. Being viewed as foreign laborers rather than long-lost relatives, Nikkei discover their non-Japaneseness – their differences rather than their similarities – in Japan. This recognition – or the resistance encountered by those who try to become Japanese – compels them to reconstruct a new cultural identity while in Japan: identifying themselves as Brazilians or Latin Americans – or perhaps Latin American Nikkei – rather than Japanese.

For example, in 1996, six samba dance teams – consisting of 360 Nikkei Brazilians – performed in a carnival in Ôizumi in Gumma Prefecture (Jomo Shinbun 1997: 109). Started in 1991, the carnival has grown to become one of the most famous Nikkei ethnic cultural events, attracting both Nikkei and local Japanese (see Tsuda, Chapter 12).

Such cultural symbols of Nikkei Latin Americans have been invented in Japan. Although carnivals and samba dances are national events in Brazil, these are expressions of Afro-Brazilian culture, and Nikkei rarely participate in them there. Traditions and ethnic symbols may be invented and constructed within a short period by making connections to the past (Hobsbawm 1983); in the case of diaspora communities, the past is reconstructed through an image of their "homeland," as Brazil and Latin America are now homelands for people of the dekasegi diaspora. These Nikkei re-create their image by calling attention to their Latin American heritage, thereby fostering an ethnic solidarity and communal consciousness in Japan.

A component of the Nikkei diaspora consists of children who were left behind overseas when their parents returned to Japan, or orphans who were adopted by local people. The key feature of this group is that they have been raised by people of an adopted nation rather than by their Japanese families. The majority of these Nikkei have no direct knowledge or memory of their parents' homeland. They construct their imagined homeland differently from children of immigrants who grew up with Japanese-born parents in overseas Japanese communities. After "returning," these orphans often find themselves treated as aliens, even by their own biological parents and grandparents. Not only do they lack Japanese citizenship, they often do not share Japanese language or cultural values. They are in fact nationals of other countries, albeit of Japanese ancestry.

Almost 1.5 million Japanese had settled in Manchuria in the years 1931 to 1945 (see Tamanoi, Chapter 13). In the chaos of the war's end – when Japanese colonists in China fled in the attempt to return to Japan following the Soviet invasion – as many as ten thousand Japanese children were left behind. Most were adopted by Chinese parents, grew up Chinese, married Chinese citizens, made their own families in China, and forgot much of the Japanese they had learned as children.

In the early 1980s the Japanese government officially recognized their existence and started allowing those identified by their Japanese parents to come to Japan (Tamanoi, Chapter 13). More than three thousand have done so, yet their situation is far from settled. Invited by the Japanese government, they find on arrival little support from either national or local governments to restart their lives. Because they are called *zanryû koji* (left-behind orphans), many Japanese think of them as children, yet most are already in their sixties. Growing up with Chinese parents in China and having only Chinese communicative competence, these people are seen by Japanese in Japan as adult Chinese instead of descendants of Japanese. Japanese locals tend to treat them no differently than foreign migrants from other poor nations. As children of Japanese parents who were at war with their Chinese foster-parents during the Manchurian occupation, they have experienced deep conflicts of identity, finding themselves outsiders in both Japanese and Chinese society.

The Okinawan diaspora

The Japanese diaspora was never homogeneous. Important divisions hinged on class, education, urban or rural residence, and native place. For example, even during the incipient diaspora from the Japanese mainland, Okinawans were in a class of their own due to the historical relationship between Japan and Okinawa.

In 1879, Japanese forces occupied the Ryûkyû kingdom, making it Japan's first overseas conquest, after informally exercising control over the preceding two centuries. The Ryûkyû Islands subsequently became a prefecture of Japan (called Okinawa, based on the name of its largest island). Before World War II, Okinawans lived in what was then and still is the nation's poorest prefecture. Okinawa also had the lowest levels of education and Okinawans were generally regarded by mainlanders as second-class Japanese citizens. Prior to leaving their homeland, Okinawans experienced many of the social, economic, political, cultural, and linguistic problems of colonized peoples, but upon arriving in an overseas host nation, Okinawans were simply considered Japanese. Okinawans confronted not only the discrimination and alienation faced by all Japanese nationals in their host countries, they also faced discrimination from mainland Japanese immigrants (Amemiya, Chapter 10; Okihiro, Chapter 11).

Japanese officials branded Okinawans as inferior to other Japanese, and they were marked as troublemakers who might jeopardize the positive emigrant image that the Japanese government was trying to create (Mori 2003: 49–54). They also blamed Okinawans for demonstrations against plantation owners or calls for improved working conditions. Japanese migrants, re-enacting the kinds of prejudice directed toward Okinawan migrants to Japan's main islands, also complained about Okinawans, especially their meat-eating diet and their tattooed wives (see Okihiro, Chapter

11). The Japanese government, therefore, often restricted emigration from Okinawa. Okinawans could not emigrate until 1899, and again were prevented from leaving between 1913 and 1916. After 1919, Okinawans were completely prohibited from leaving (Mori 2003: 50).[5] Nonetheless, by the start of World War II, 75,424 Okinawans had left their homeland for overseas. This was almost 10 percent of all Japanese emigration before the war (*Ryukyu Shimpo* 1995). Only Hiroshima prefecture, which provided about 100,000 persons, saw more emigration (see Ishikawa 1975: 63).

In 1945, Okinawa, devastated by the U.S. invasion that resulted in the loss of more than a quarter of the islands' population, became a United States military colony. It was not returned to Japanese jurisdiction until 1972, and then on terms that perpetuated U.S. domination of the islands through the maintenance of the military base structure. Thus, the status of the Okinawan diaspora became more complicated after Japan's defeat in World War II. For example, regarding the Japanese diaspora in Bolivia after World War II, Amemiya (Chapter 10) argues that four governments of varying degrees of power and status – Japan, Okinawa, Bolivia, and the United States – organized, sponsored, or encouraged immigration programs for both mainland Japanese and Okinawans. The eastern lowlands of Bolivia were isolated and undeveloped, but fertile, and awaited immigrants to populate and cultivate them. Okinawa and Japan encouraged emigration in the hope that it could solve serious domestic problems of overpopulation and political instability. Okinawans, facing poverty and limited economic opportunities at home, actively sought a better life through migration both to the main Japanese islands and, in large numbers, abroad.

Okinawans have contributed substantially to the Japanese diaspora and constitute a disproportionate number of diasporees. According to the *Ryukyu Shimpo* (1995), in 1995 there were some two million Nikkei, of whom 300,000 were of Okinawan descent. In the early twenty-first century, there may be as many as half a million Okinawans among the three million Nikkei residing around the world.

The long-term and permanent-resident diaspora

According to the Japanese Ministry of Foreign Affairs,[6] in 1986 there were 497,981 Japanese nationals living abroad; this number had almost doubled by 2003. Since the 1970s and 1980s, then, a new type of Japanese diaspora – the *long-term and permanent-resident* diaspora – has emerged as the number of Japanese overseas of this status has increased year by year.

Table I.1 clearly shows these changes in Japanese-overseas demographics. For example, the number of Japanese residents living overseas was almost 800,000 in 1999, increasing to over 900,000 in 2003, one-third of whom were permanent residents of other nations (about 280,000 in 1999 and 290,000 in 2003). North America had the largest number of

Table I.1 Japanese overseas long-term and permanent residents, 1999 and 2003

	1999		2003	
	Number	Percent	Number	Percent
WORLD TOTAL	795,852	100	911,062	100
perm. res.	280,557	35.3	291,793	32.0
long-term	515,295	64.7	619,269	68.9
Asia total	159,114	(20)	206,521	(22.7)
perm. res. (% of world perm. res.)	6,602	(2.4)	7,399	(2.5)
long-term (% of world long-term)	152,512	(29.6)	199,122	(32.2)
Oceania total	45,137	(5.7)	63,018	(6.9)
perm. res.(% of world perm. res.)	20,776	(7.4)	27,866	(9.5)
long-term (% of world long-term)	24,361	(4.7)	35,152	(5.7)
North American total	324,295	(40.7)	369,639	(40.6)
perm. res.(% of world perm. res.)	125,596	(44.8)	129,606	(44.4)
long-term (% of world long-term)	198,699	(38.6)	240,033	(38.8)
Central American total	6,950	(0.9)	7,584	(0.8)
perm. res.(% of world perm. res.)	2,490	(0.9)	2,528	(0.9)
long-term (% of world long-term)	4,460	(0.9)	5,056	(0.8)
South American total	103,796	(13.0)	94,310	(10.4)
perm. res.(% of world perm. res.)	97,114	(34.6)	88,819	(30.4)
long-term (% of world long-term)	6,682	(1.3)	5,491	(0.9)
Western Europe total	139,667	(17.5)	152,833	(16.8)
perm. res.(% of world perm. res.)	26,249	(9.4)	33,540	(11.5)
long-term (% of world long-term)	113,418	(22.0)	119,293	(19.3)
Eastern/Central Europe total	4,413	(0.6)	5,715	(0.6)
perm. res.(% of world perm. res.)	331	(0.1)	455	(0.2)
long-term (% of world long-term)	4,082	(0.8)	5,260	(0.8)
Middle East total	6,054	(0.8)	5,857	(0.6)
perm. res.(% of world perm. res.)	972	(0.4)	1,108	(0.4)
long-term (% of world long-term)	5,082	(1.0)	4,749	(0.8)
Africa total	6,386	(0.8)	5,541	(0.6)
perm. res.(% of world perm. res.)	427	(0.2)	472	(0.2)
long-term (% of world long-term)	5,959	(1.2)	5,069	(0.8)

Source: Japan the Ministry of Foreign Affairs: mofa.go.jp/mofaj/took/tokei/hojin/04/pdfs/3-2-2.pdf.

Note
For regions, percent refers to the total of *all* Japanese long-term or permanent residents respectively (e.g., 6.602, or 2.4% of all permanent residents in 1999 lived in Asia, as shown in row 2 in the left-hand column).

permanent residents, followed by South America.[7] The rest were "long-term" residents (*chôki-taizai-sha*) – those who stay on long-term visas (over three months), but are not on permanent resident visas, of the host nation.

There are several different categories of recent Japanese transnational migrants who have become part of the long-term and permanent resident diaspora. One such group is career-oriented Japanese females in their twenties and thirties who leave Japan because of dissatisfaction with the workplace (Befu 2000: 34–5). Their numbers are gradually growing. For example, in 1999, 402,575 Japanese long-term and permanent-resident Japanese women were living abroad and this number grew by more than 10 percent in 2003 (Japanese Ministry of Foreign Affairs[8]). Many choose to go due to some degree of dissatisfaction with career opportunities in Japan, while others leave with positive motivations to study, to experience another culture, meet different people, and perhaps find interesting jobs with international businesses or NGOs. Whatever the motivation, however, these people are generally not among those sent overseas by a corporation.

Many Japanese women quit their jobs and become full-time housewives soon after they have children. This is largely due to a lack of daycare facilities in Japan, as well as some disapproval of childcare outside the home among Japanese in general (Liddle and Nakajima 2000: 11). These women often return to the workforce later in life, but they can usually only do so only as part-timers. This is because employers often do not want to hire women as full-time employees to save on benefits. In addition, some women do not wish to have full-time jobs because of a tax system which discourages a dual-income family (Liddle and Nakajima 2000: 11). As a result, although about 41 percent of all Japanese women were working in 2002, more than two-thirds were part-timers (Keizai Koho Center 2004: 109). Yet almost 50 percent of Japanese females receive higher education, a proportion that is almost the same as men (ibid.: 120).[9] Thus, increasing numbers of Japanese women feel shackled by such obvious economic inequities. In addition, many are torn between the expectations society has of Japanese women – to be caregivers for their children, provide domestic support for their husbands, and take care of aging relatives and in-laws – and their own desires for personal fulfillment (Rosenberger 2001: 2).

There remain institutional and social constraints on Japanese women seeking professional careers or aspiring to positions of leadership. Increasing numbers of Japanese women have concluded that living and working overseas will provide greater opportunities for professional advancement and personal growth. Once overseas, they find many of their beliefs about the inequalities of Japanese society confirmed. For example, Yuko Ogasawara (1998: 1) gives the following account in her book *Office Ladies and Salaried Men*:

> Most Americans I talked to in university circles had heard of the male-biased career structure in Japan ... [and] asked, "Is it really *still* like that?" When I replied with an emphatic yes, my American friends responded with sympathy for Japanese women and wondered how these women can stand it.

Obviously, foreign countries are not necessarily paradises for women, and some Japanese women are surprised to find an ongoing struggle for women's rights abroad. Ogasawara goes on to ask herself "Are Japanese women oppressed, or not? Are they powerless, or powerful?" (ibid.: 2). But significant numbers of young Japanese women relocate in other nations to seek freedom from real or perceived cultural expectations and restrictions in their own country.

Because Japan is a rich country and the currency is strong even after fifteen years of economic doldrums, many young women are able to travel overseas to satisfy their curiosity about foreign lifestyles. Even women who have been in the workforce for only a few years can save up enough funds to travel abroad and stay long enough to become established (Befu 2000: 35). These women may even accept jobs overseas that pay less than those in Japan. Unlike earlier emigrants who left Japan due to economic hardship, these Japanese leave for personal reasons. Economic success makes possible Japanese women's place in the long-term and permanent-resident diaspora (see Befu 2000: 33–6). Some women become permanent residents through marriage to local men.

There are also long-term and permanent-resident professionals who went overseas as students and stayed on after graduation or graduate school. While not members of a diaspora in the usual sense, their large numbers contribute to the establishment and maintenance of overseas Japanese communities. Many find jobs at university and research institutes, in government or in international companies, including some with ties or partnerships with Japan. The largest numbers of such people are found in North America (e.g., 82,382, or 34.3 percent of all Japanese living abroad, in 2003) and Western Europe (40,188, or 33.7 percent). There are also significant numbers of workers for Japanese corporations who are sent abroad as managers and mid-level executives. According to Japan's Ministry of Foreign Affairs,[10] there were 135,798 (68.2 percent) such employees in Asia in 2003, 132,005 (55 percent) in North America, 52,983 (44.4 percent) in Europe, and 2,706 (49.3 percent) in Latin America. Most of these are men, and many are accompanied by their wives and children. These long-term and permanent residents have also been driven by Japan's economic success.

Reconsiderations of diaspora through overseas Japanese and Nikkei experiences

This volume examines the concept of diaspora with a focus on the evolution of cultural ideologies and identities through analysis of various Japanese migrant and Nikkei experiences. It highlights five primary aspects: (1) the initial state of diaspora (the incipient diaspora); (2) the racial discrimination and marginalization of diasporees in their host nations (the displaced and Nikkei diasporas); (3) the political movements and formation of ethnic identity to overcome diasporees' marginal social conditions in their adopted society (the model/positive minority); (4) the subcultures and subgroups that have developed, reflecting the fact that a diaspora is not experienced monolithically by all diasporees (the Okinawan diaspora); and (5) the potential for global economic success of diasporees abroad (the long-term and permanent-resident diaspora). The contributors not only provide a more textured understanding of each parameter of the diaspora experience; they have also extended the definition of diaspora to include its dynamic and situational characteristics.

Our examination of diaspora makes three contributions to general diaspora studies and theory. First, the Japanese case reveals that notions of home, homeland, and host countries are not static – but very dynamic concepts – for diasporees in a modern global society. For example, in looking at Japanese Brazilian Nikkei returnees in Japan, the notion of home country and host country are quite situational. When they were in Brazil, many viewed Japan positively. While Japan was not believed to be a homeland per se, they never thought they were going to work in a "host" country. However, when they began working in Japan as dekasegi migrant workers, Nikkei Brazilians came to see Japan as a host nation, and their Brazilianness is discovered and reified.

Second, we find that the primary elements of diasporic communities are not defined by a national unit but through historical or collective memory. For example, when arriving in host nations, Okinawans were considered to be Japanese nationals. However, when faced with Japanese from the homeland, they confronted a social barrier and found that they were regarded as members of an Okinawan, rather than a Japanese, diaspora. Finally, we reveal that the formation of diasporic communities is not always defined by the political, economic, social, or cultural confrontations that exist between diasporees and local people. Diasporees come in many "flavors," and may unite for a broad range of reasons, including legal or political expediency or even simply convenience, or just because of a shared nostalgia for home.

This book offers an international perspective on the study of Japanese transnational migrants and Nikkei. Besides Hawaii and the United States, it discusses Nikkei communities and Japanese migration to Manchuria and China, Canada, the Philippines, Singapore, and many countries in Latin America. The Nikkei experience is compared with that of Japanese transnational migrants living abroad. This work connects theoretical issues of ethnic identity in the Japanese diaspora to the realities of modern diasporas. Each contributor attempts to uncover the hidden dynamics of the social construction of race, ethnicity, and homeland, and to locate, in a broad sense, how diasporees today are being transformed by, and are themselves transforming, a globalizing society in which permanent and temporary migration and the interplay of cultures and peoples are commonplace. The chapters reveal diaspora as a vital concept perennially in flux. Members of a diasporic community often seek to demonstrate cultural identity in order to gain political, economic, and social capital, and the community itself is influenced and reshaped over time by both external and internal factors. It may consist of several subtypes – based on the particulars of the political, social, and economic situation of each subculture in an ethnic group and their relations to each other. This volume reveals diaspora as something vigorous, kinetic, and divergent.

Notes

1 Among the various ethnic groups having displaced populations, the Japanese idea of Nikkei is distinctive. Nikkei-jin – people of Japanese descent who for whatever reason are residing overseas – are thought by many Japanese in Japan to share certain racial and cultural affinities. For many Japanese in Japan, then, Japanese ancestry trumps citizenship. This is often true even when the people residing overseas see themselves merely as people of Japanese ethnicity rather than occupying a special Nikkei category.
2 Nisei who receive a Japanese education in Japan and return to their host nations are referred to by special terms, using the *ki-* (returning) prefix and the Japanese abbreviation of the host nation's name, such as *kibei* (lit. returning to the United States), *kika* (returning to Canada), or *kihaku* (returning to Brazil).
3 Some 110,000 Japanese and their children were interned in the United States. We can add to this number another 10,000 who were born in the camps or were sent there by Latin American nations. About 12,000 Japanese and their children were interned in Canada, as were 2,800 Japanese in Mexico, and 300 in Cuba.
4 In 2002, almost 50 percent of all eighteen-year-old Japanese were engaged in higher education (Keizi Koho Center 2004: 120), and were not in the workforce.
5 It is unclear how strictly this was enforced or when the restriction was repealed.
6 Japanese Ministry of Foreign Affairs statistics given at http://web-Japan. org/stat/stats/21MIG31.html (accessed March 6, 2005) and Japanese Ministry of Foreign Affairs: mofa.go.jp/mofaj/took/tokei/hojin/04/pdfs/3-2-2.pdf (accessed April 8, 2005).
7 However, the number of permanent residents in Latin America has remained the same or declined. For example, in 1996 there were 85,896 permanent residents in Brazil and 10,858 in Argentina, but these numbers dropped in 2002 to 69,978 and 10,798, respectively. This is because many Nikkei Latin Americans are migrating to Japan as dekasegi workers.
8 mofa.go.jp/mofaj/took/tokei/hojin/04/pdfs/3-2-2.pdf (accessed April 8, 2005).
9 In 2001, almost 33 percent of Japanese women went on to colleges and universities upon graduation from high school compared to almost 47 percent of men. Traditionally, more Japanese women go on to junior colleges than do men (almost 18 percent vs. around 2 percent in 2001). Now, however, the percentage of female students who go to colleges and universities rather than junior colleges is increasing, resulting in a decline in junior college enrollment (Asahi Shimbun 2002: 228).
10 mofa.go.jp/mofaj/took/tokei/hojin/04/pdfs/3-2-2.pdf (accessed April 8, 2005).

Part I
Origins of the Japanese diaspora

1 The Japanese diaspora in the New World

Its Asian predecessors and origins

Roger Daniels

The purpose of this chapter is to outline the beginnings of the Japanese diaspora and to summarize the development of Asian immigration to the Caribbean, Hawaii, the United States, and Canada.[1] To understand the Japanese diaspora in the New World it is useful first to consider the prior migration of other Asians, chiefly from China, to various parts of the plantation world beginning early in the nineteenth century. The British civil servant and scholar Hugh Tinker (1974) has called this migration "a new system of slavery," in which Asians, mostly indentured, were used as surrogates for enslaved Africans at a time when first the Atlantic slave-trade and then slavery were being outlawed. There had been a fragmentary migration of East Asians to the New World as early as the seventeenth century. Spanish and Nahuatl texts describe both Chinese and Japanese in early seventeenth-century Mexico, who came as supercargoes on the fabled Manila galleons. Chinese seamen were present in American east coast ports in the years immediately after the American Revolution, followed by the occasional merchant (Nuttall 1906; Brunhouse 1940; Schurz 1959; Leon-Portilla 1981; Calvo 1983). These and other migrations from Asia involved very few individuals, probably fewer than a hundred before 1800.

The Chinese diaspora in the New World to the 1920s

Early in the nineteenth century the nature and size of Asian migration changed radically. Even before the end of the slave-trade some British writers, seeing the handwriting on the wall, suggested using indentured Chinese to replace enslaved Africans. As one naval officer put it, Chinese came from the best cultivated country on Earth, were inured to a hot climate, and very industrious. He might have added that the peoples of South China had long migrated into *Nanyang* (Southeast Asia). What became known as the "Chinese coolie trade" began in 1806 with a shipment of 200 Chinese indentured laborers to Trinidad.[2] Eight of them – 4 percent – died in transit, a rate that remained fairly constant in the trade from China to the British Caribbean, although in one bad year, 1853, 189 of 1,824 who left Chinese ports for the West Indies died at sea, more than 10 percent (Higman 1972; Lai 1993: 292, table 23).

As was the case in most nineteenth- and early twentieth-century international migration, these and later indentured laborers were chiefly adult males; a recent careful estimate of Chinese brought to Jamaica between 1860 and 1884 judges that about 15 percent were female. Nearly 200,000 Chinese were brought to the Caribbean, some 150,000 of them to Cuba; perhaps 18,000 went to the British Caribbean islands, chiefly Jamaica; about 2,500 to the Dutch colonies, and a smaller number to Central America. Chinese workers were never a very significant factor in the contract labor force within the British Empire in the Americas (Mintz 1985),[3] but they were of great importance in four different parts of the New World. Indentured Chinese immigrants played major economic roles in Cuba, Peru, and Hawaii; Chinese workers also played a major role in the Canadian and American West where indentured labor existed only among Native Americans in thrall to Spanish Mexican missions. Except in North America, the sugar plantations absorbed most of their labor.

The treatment of Chinese in Cuba was quite harsh and their indenture existed alongside African and Afro-Caribbean slavery until 1886. The importation of Chinese began in 1847, broke off for six years, and recommenced in 1853. From then until 1874, laborers – more than 90 percent of them male – left China for Havana every year: a total of 150,000 Chinese. An investigatory commission set up by the Chinese government concluded in 1870 to 1871 that "of the Chinese laborers who have proceeded to Cuba, 8 or 9 of every 10 have been conveyed there against their will." It estimated a voyage mortality rate of some 11 percent; more than 16,000 Chinese died *en route* to Cuba (Helly 1993: 38, 42). The conditions under which the Chinese worked in Cuba can only be described as barbaric: Robert L. Irick's (1982: 300) judgment that "nothing in the slave trade literature reads worse than the accounts of maltreatment in Cuba" is surely an overstatement, but not by much. The mortality rate within Cuba was quite high from accidents and illness. In addition, the Cuba Commission reported in 1876 that some 500 Chinese were committing suicide every year (cf. Pastrana 1983).

Conditions in Peru were probably worse. Most of the 80,000 to 100,000 Chinese who were brought there between 1849 and 1875 worked on sugar and cotton plantations, but a particularly wretched minority, perhaps one-fifth and all male, were put to tasks on Peru's guano islands where apparently most were simply worked to death. The shipboard mortality rate – as high as 41 percent in some terrible years – seems to have averaged about the same 11 percent that prevailed on the longer trip to Cuba. Chinese mortality in continental Peru also ran high, although there are no good data. A Lima newspaper reported in 1871 that: "The greatest part of those being newly contracted by the plantations are coming to replace, not those who are completing their contracts, but rather those who died fulfilling them" (Stewart 1951: 105; see also Gonzales 1985).

There are many common factors in the Chinese presence in the Caribbean and Peru. They had no provision for return transportation in their indentures as did contract laborers from India and, unlike the case in Hawaii or North America, no sizable number is believed to have returned to China, although a few economically successful returnees are reported as early as the 1860s (Lai 1993: 203). Chinese in Trinidad moved quickly away from the plantations and into small-scale market gardening and eventually into commerce. In British Guiana, where Portuguese occupied most of the petty producer niches, the move from the plantation was less rapid, but it occurred. As Clementi pointed out, there were some spectacular economic success stories among the British Guiana Chinese, but the overall picture is one of steady population decline, caused by the absence of Chinese women, emigration to other parts of the Caribbean, and entry, often illegal after 1882, into the United States (Clementi 1915).

By the early twentieth century there was at least a small Chinese presence everywhere in the hemisphere. Large numbers of Chinese were merchants, shopkeepers, and entrepreneurs. (Many of these came direct from China.) And, as is so often the case with what some style "middlemen minorities," Chinese were often the targets of nativists. This was nowhere more true than in Mexico, where, by 1910, there were some 13,000 Chinese. To note merely the bloodiest incident, some 300 Chinese in a community of about 400 in the northern Mexican city of Torreón were massacred in one bloody night in 1911 by revolutionary troops under Francisco Villa (Jacques 1974: 233–46).[4]

In addition to their mobility, which was one element in the acculturation of Chinese in the Caribbean area, many Chinese entered into family arrangements, formal and informal, with women of other ethnicities. Walton Look Lai, speaking of Trinidad, estimates that at most 20 percent entered into such unions, which were much more often with the more numerous creole women, black and mulatto, than with the daughters of Indian immigrants. Most Chinese men who came to the New World in the nineteenth and early twentieth centuries either died without issue or participated in what one scholar (Li 1977) has called "mutilated marriages": the husband was abroad and the wife remained in China.

Although China suppressed the "coolie trade" in 1875, that did not stop the flow of Chinese labor to the New World. Both contract and free immigration of Chinese to Hawaii and their free immigration to the North America mainland continued until inhibited by statute, as did sporadic immigration to Latin America. The initial movement of Chinese laborers to Hawaii was part of the coolie trade, but the contract system that evolved there was unaffected by its end (Takaki 1983). The first cargo of 180 coolies was imported into Hawaii in 1852 by the newly founded Royal Hawaiian Agricultural Society, one of whose purposes was introducing "coolie labor from China to supply the places of the rapidly declining native population" (Coman 1978: 11–12).

In that year, the governor of Hong Kong, Sir John Bowring, described the procedures at the barracoons where the laborers were kept under guard until their ships came:

> I have myself seen the arrangements for the shipment of coolies at Amoy; hundreds of them gathered together in barracoons, stripped naked, and stamped or painted with the letter C (Cuba), P (Peru), or S (Sandwich Islands) on their breasts.[5]

Those brought to Hawaii were bound by contract to serve for five years at US$3 per month plus food, clothing, and shelter. While servitude in Hawaii seems not to have been quite as brutal as in the Caribbean or Peru, it was servitude in an oligarchy dominated by white, largely American, plantation owners (Coman 1978: 11–12). A few Chinese peddlers and merchants had preceded the laborers to the islands, the first being reported in Honolulu in 1823. The census of 1853 reported 123 Chinese men (and no Chinese women) living in Honolulu in addition to the contract laborers noted above (Fuchs 1961: 86–7). All told, some 46,000 Chinese contract laborers came to Hawaii before American annexation in 1898 brought the islands under the jurisdiction of United States law which outlawed contract labor and prohibited further Chinese labor immigration (Lind 1968: 195).[6] By 1860, laborers who had completed their indentures were leaving the plantations and going into business for themselves in Honolulu and other urban centers in the islands. Since in the 1880s and 1890s they comprised more than one-fifth of the urban population, these free Chinese constituted what Hilary Conroy has called "troublesome elements in a class society" in which most Asians were bound to the plantations (Conroy 1953: 58).

Chinese in large numbers began coming to the United States just before the California Gold Rush of 1849. By 1882 some 250,000 Chinese had arrived, more than 90 percent of them male. Almost all came from the Pearl River delta of Guangdong province of South China, a traditional area of emigration. Many immigrants financed their passage by using a "credit ticket" system. Evidence from the 1850s speaks of a $70 advance ($50 for the ticket and $20 for expenses) resulting in a $200 obligation (Zo 1978). As early as 1852 American diplomatic officials in south China reported to Washington about the return of immigrants who had been "fortunate at the gold mountain [California]" (Davids 1973: 149).[7] This goal – to be successful abroad and return home with a nest-egg of, say, $400 – seems to have been the motivation of most of those who set out to sojourn on the Gold Mountain (and, after the 1854 discovery of gold in Australia, on the "New Gold Mountain" as well). Both migrations were primarily of laborers, but some students, merchants, and political exiles also went to each place.

While some immigrants were able to return to China as "rich men," most remained poor and became settlers rather than sojourners, as did large numbers of nineteenth-century male immigrants from Europe who came with the same intention. Chinese built railroads, engaged in mining, cleared land, and were pioneers in agriculture in the underdeveloped American West (Chan 1986). After 1880 many Chinese migrated to large cities and engaged in urban pursuits, the majority of them in Chinese-owned labor-intensive businesses requiring little capital, such as laundries and restaurants.

Although Chinese were thought necessary by entrepreneurs such as the railroad builder Charles Crocker, laboring men, their organizations, and the politicians who sought their votes disagreed; they insisted that "The Chinese Must GO!"[8] More than a decade of agitation eventually resulted in the passage of a federal Chinese Exclusion Act by an overwhelming majority in 1882. The stated reasons may be boiled down to a single phrase: the Chinese, it was claimed, worked cheap and smelled bad. One disapproving senator, Oliver P. Morton (R-IN), put it well: "If the Chinese in California were white people, being in all other respects what they are, I do not believe that the complaints and warfare made against them would have existed to any considerable extent."[9]

There were some 125,000 Chinese in the United States in 1882 when the first Chinese Exclusion Act was passed. The Exclusion Act did not end all legal Chinese immigration – merchants, their families, students, and elite travelers could all enter the country, and certain former residents could return – but Chinese laborers were barred. Between the enactment of exclusion and its 1943 repeal, immigration records show nearly 95,000 legal Chinese entries, an annual average of about 1,500. About 90 percent of these entries were males, so that well into the 1940s Chinese America maintained a gender ratio characteristic of the early stages of migration, while its total population shrank from about 125,000 in 1882 to nearly 62,000 in 1920 (Daniels 1988: 1, 69, table 3).

The 1882 exclusion of Chinese laborers was a nodal point in the development of American immigration law, the hinge on which the "golden door" began to swing toward a closed position. In addition, Chinese and other Asians in the United States faced serious legal disabilities: none could become naturalized citizens, as federal law limited naturalization to "free white persons" before 1870 and to "white persons and persons of African descent" from then until the bars were removed between 1943 and 1952. Asians born on American soil or in Hawaii after 1898 were citizens with all the presumed rights of other citizens, although *de jure* equality did not free them from many of the same kinds of discrimination – segregation and the like – that African Americans faced after they became free in 1865 (Daniels 2004).

The factors that drew Chinese to the United States – a relatively high standard of living and a relative shortage of labor – also attracted Chinese to the Canadian west, where their incidence was much larger. At the beginning of the twentieth century, for example, the nearly 15,000 Chinese in British Columbia constituted more than 8 percent of the province's population while California's 45,000 was just 3 percent of the state's. Sex ratios were even more skewed in the north: While in the late nineteenth century females were perhaps 5 percent of the Chinese American population, the most detailed Canadian count (by a Chinese government official) found just 154 women in a Chinese Canadian population of some 10,000, or about 1.5 percent. In both Canada and the United States, Chinese took jobs no one else wanted, acted as a depressant on wages (and, on occasion, as strike breakers), and were crucial in the construction of the first transcontinental railroads. Testimony given to Royal Commissions in 1885 and 1902 shows Canadian racism to be indistinguishable from American (cf. Canada 1885, 1902). The Canadian government was somewhat less responsive to its subjects' demands, reflecting a lower level of democracy there and the continuing existence of a deference society. This galled British Columbians who knew that within the British Empire, Australia, New Zealand, and later, Natal, had all halted Chinese immigration (Huttenback 1976). Canada imposed a head tax on Chinese entrants that was $500 after 1904, but it did not end legal Chinese immigration until 1923.

Origins of the Japanese diaspora

Unlike China, which lost control of its most important ports to Westerners in the early nineteenth century, or India, which had been colonized, conquered, and ruled by Europeans during what the noted early twentieth-century Indian historian K. M. Panikkar (1959) calls the Vasco da Gama Epoch of Asian History (1498–1945), Japan retained its sovereignty throughout the age of colonization. Until an American naval officer, Matthew Calbraith Perry, and his "black ships" forcibly opened Japan up to foreign trade in 1854, it was effectively closed to almost all foreigners and its subjects forbidden to travel abroad.

The major reason that Japan's leaders, however reluctantly, bowed to American demands was that they were all too aware of what was happening in China, which had been defeated, humiliated, and forced to cede aspects of its sovereignty to Britain and then other Western powers beginning in the first Opium War of 1840 to 1842. Similarly, these men knew something of the horrors of the coolie trade. They and their successors well into the twentieth century were determined not to allow such treatment to emigrant Japanese. They assumed, correctly I think, that if overseas Japanese became coolies it would be detrimental to Japan's aspirations to an equal place with the Western powers.

Despite this resolve, both outside pressures and internal problems resulted in nineteenth-century contract labor agreements first with Hawaii and then with Peru, and in the twentieth-century large-scale emigration to every part of the New World. The most important population centers were Hawaii, the United States, Peru, Canada, and Brazil. This latter locale became (sometime in the second half of the twentieth century) the most populous center of the Japanese diaspora.

We can date the beginning of the Japanese diaspora with the so-called *Gannen-mono* (Meiji first-year people), a shipment of 141 Japanese men, six women, and a child to Hawaii under three-year contracts in 1868, the first year of the Meiji era. Although theoretically sojourners, the majority chose not to return to Japan and became the founders of the Japanese community in the islands; see Van Sant (2000: 97–116) for further details.

Japan refused to allow further contract labor emigration for sixteen years. During the years that contract labor emigration continued (1885–95) more than 30,000 Japanese came to Hawaiian plantations, so that by the end of the nineteenth century some 76,000 East Asian contract workers were brought there. The planters saw the Japanese as both an additional source of labor and a counterweight to the Chinese on whom they had been dependent. But most Japanese workers also failed to renew their contracts and many created the same kinds of problems for the planter society as had the Chinese. Although the last Japanese contract laborers came in 1895, Japanese free immigrants continued to come to Hawaii for more than a decade, as their coming was not stopped by American law. Many also used Hawaii as a stepping stone to the United States mainland even before the 1898 annexation. Near the end of the Japanese contract labor period – 1894, when accurate statistics cease – 771 laborers who had fulfilled their contracts were listed as having departed for America.

The annexation of Hawaii facilitated this movement to the American West Coast. Until the Gentlemen's Agreement cut off the entry of Japanese laborers into both Hawaii and the American mainland in early 1908, some 40,000 Japanese made the secondary migration from Hawaii to the American mainland. All told, some 180,000 Japanese had migrated to Hawaii by 1924. The census of 1900 showed that they had become the largest single ethnic group in the islands and by 1910 there were nearly 80,000 Japanese there. Between 1908 and 1924 significant numbers of Japanese women were able to come to Hawaii, which nearly balanced the gender ratio. In 1910 females made up just 31.2 percent of the Hawaiian Japanese population; by 1930 they were 46.3 percent of a total of some 140,000.

Apart from a few castaways,[10] diplomats,[11] and elite travelers, the first true Japanese immigrants to North America were a small group of political exiles who tried to found an agricultural colony at Gold Hill, California, near Sacramento in 1868 (Daniels 1962: 2–3; Van Sant 2000: 117–30). As late as 1880 the census recorded only 148 Japanese, eighty-six of them in California. There were nearly 25,000 in 1900 and perhaps five times that number when the 1924 immigration act ended their immigration for almost three decades. Anti-Japanese movements within the United States would surely have resulted in restrictive legislation in the early twentieth century had not Japan been a rising power. American presidents as diverse as Theodore Roosevelt, William Howard Taft, Woodrow Wilson, and Calvin Coolidge each sought to prevent popular anti-Japanese legislation for reasons of state. Local discrimination produced crises involving school segregation in San Francisco in 1905 to 1906 and Alien Land Acts in California and other western states in 1913 and 1920 to 1922. Politicians in Tokyo were willing to accommodate the Americans because they were convinced that a "Japanese Exclusion Act" would mitigate against their aspirations to great power status. Japanese were spared the humiliation of total exclusion for two decades in the United States and even longer in Canada.

The *modus vivendi* for postponing exclusion by the United States was the so-called Gentlemen's Agreement of 1907 to 1908, an executive agreement effected by a series of notes. Japan agreed not to issue passports to "laborers" for either Hawaii or the United States, and the United States arranged to block persons with Japanese passports moving from Hawaii to the mainland. The United States did agree to permit the return of laborers formerly domiciled in the United States, to allow those presently domiciled in the United States to leave and return, and, most importantly, to allow family reunification. Under these provisions, not only were existing families reunited, but tens of thousands of Japanese bachelors were able to bring wives from Japan, many of them the so-called picture brides, married by proxy to men in North America whom in many cases they had not seen prior to marriage. Females, who had comprised only 12.6 percent of the mainland Japanese population of 72,157 in 1910, were 41.1 percent of the 1930 population of 138,834. By 1940, 62.7 percent of all 126,000 Japanese Americans were native born (Daniels 1988: table 4.2, p. 127; table 5.1, p. 156).

The bulk of the Japanese immigrants settled on the West Coast and although significant numbers worked as right-of-way maintenance crews for railroads, in lumbering, and in scattered urban pursuits, most engaged in agriculture. Usually they began as migrant laborers, as so many Chinese had done, but large numbers of them soon became leaseholders or proprietors. By 1919 about 10 percent of the market value of California agriculture – some $67 million – was produced by Japanese farms. Despite – or because of – their economic success, the Japanese in California and elsewhere in the American West encountered persistent prejudice and discrimination in both law and custom. Much of the legal discrimination was facilitated by the fact that the immigrants were barred from becoming naturalized. But their citizen-children also faced widespread discrimination, especially in employment and housing, even though they had, in theory, equality before the law. Japan's growing power deferred the ultimate discrimination – exclusion from immigration – until 1924. All the evidence –

including a number of referenda in western states – demonstrates widespread popular racist support for the anti-Japanese measures and practices that were adopted, and a willingness to support more draconian actions.

A similar situation prevailed in Canada where a smaller number of Japanese Canadians (about 25,000 in 1940) were even more highly concentrated in British Columbia (95 percent in 1941) than West Coast Japanese Americans (88 percent in 1940). The chief Japanese economic niche in Canada was fishing, particularly salmon fishing, although sizable numbers were in agriculture, lumbering, mining, and urban pursuits (Roy 1989). Anti-Asian sentiment in the Canadian west reached boiling point in the Vancouver Riot of September 1907, when a mob of at least a thousand people invaded the small ethnic enclaves in which the city's Chinese and Japanese lived. After an unopposed sack of Chinatown, it met resistance in the Japanese quarter and beat a hasty retreat. There was property damage and injuries, but happily no fatalities; the Canadian government eventually paid $35,000 in compensation. A royal commissioner, future prime minister William Lyon Mackenzie King, was appointed to investigate both the riot and "the methods by which Oriental laborers have been induced to come to Canada" (Sugimoto 1978). Negotiations between Canada and Japan quickly ensued, resulting in a December 1907 Canadian "Gentlemen's Agreement": Japan agreed to limit the number of new passports issued for Canada to 400 per annum and Canada agreed not to exclude Japanese. In May 1928, four years after the United States had put a halt to all Japanese immigration, Canada persuaded Japan to issue only 150 passports annually and to bar picture brides.

While prejudice against Japanese and other Asians was all but identical on each side of the Canadian–American border, legal discrimination varied due to constitutional differences. In Canada, Japanese and other Asians could become naturalized citizens since naturalization was controlled by the national government. Citizenship was crucial to Japanese Canadian fishermen, who as aliens could not get licenses. But suffrage was controlled by the provinces and, in British Columbia and Alberta where almost all of Canada's Japanese lived, persons of Asian ancestry were barred from voting even if they were citizens, either naturalized or native-born. In addition to denying them suffrage, British Columbia forbade Canadian-born Asians from serving as school trustees, on juries, or from obtaining licenses for hand logging. They could not be hired by public works contractors. They could practice medicine, dentistry, and nursing, but not law or pharmacy. And, as in the United States, de facto employment discrimination prevailed where statute law did not apply.

In reading the above, some may get the impression that the Asian migrants who began what is now a diaspora amounting to many millions of people were simply in the grip of blind, impersonal forces. That such forces existed and had their influence cannot be doubted, but even those dedicated determinists, Marx and Engels, admitted on a number of occasions that men – we would now say "persons" – make history. Many if not most of those who participated in the formative years of these and other diasporas were making a conscious effort to change their personal history by embarking on a journey whose outcome they could hardly imagine.

In an interview conducted in 1935, Sentaro Ishii – apparently the last survivor of the *Gannen-mono* – reported that he had signed up because conditions in his part of Japan were awful and working for four dollars a month seemed a "splendid offer." He recalled that he did not know what sugar cane was or where Hawaii was located (Van Sant 2000: 113). But he dared, and survived. The thriving world of Japanese Hawaii was, at least in part, the result of what he and other seemingly insignificant individuals had begun sixty-seven years before.

Notes

1 For an earlier look at this topic see Daniels (2000) which includes comments on the southern regions.
2 The trade still awaits its historian. Campbell (1923) is geographically limited and out of date. Irick (1982) focuses on government actions; for Latin America see Meagher (1978).
3 For Chinese in South Africa see Richardson (1982).
4 Five Japanese were also killed "by mistake." See also Schwartz (1998).
5 Letter, August 3, 1852, as cited by Irick (1982: 27).
6 Hawaii had passed its own Chinese Exclusion Act in 1886, but exceptions covering 15,000 new laborers were freely granted before annexation (Fuchs 1961: 87).
7 Peter Parker to Daniel Webster, Dispatch 24, January 27, 1852.
8 For more on the anti-Chinese movement see Miller (1969), Saxton (1971), Sandmeyer (1973), and Aarim-Heriot (2003).
9 For a massive assemblage of contemporary views see United States Congress, Senate. *Report of the Joint Special Committee to Investigate Chinese Immigration.* 44th Cong., 2nd sess., Report No. 670. Washington, DC: GPO, 1977. Crocker's testimony is at 666–8. Morton is quoted in United States Congress, Senate. *Misc. Document 20.* 45th Cong., 2nd sess., 1879: 4.
10 The most famous castaway, known as Joseph Heco, published two autobiographies, *Hyoryuki* (Edo, 1863), translated as *Floating on the Pacific Ocean* (1955) and *The Narrative of a Japanese: What He has Seen and the People He Has Met in the Course of the Last Forty Years* (1895). See also Van Sant (2000: 21–48).
11 Miyoshi (1979) describes the first diplomatic mission in 1860.

2 Japanese emigration and immigration
From the Meiji to the modern

James Stanlaw

This chapter presents a cultural–historic overview of what has come to be called the Japanese diaspora – that mass movement of people of Japanese ancestry to all parts of the world including "returnee" immigrants. At least 800,000 people (JICA 1994), and perhaps as many as a million, left Japan before World War II, and another 300,000 have relocated since then. Probably at least three million people of Japanese descent live as citizens of fifty-five countries, and three-quarters of a million Japanese nationals live abroad as temporary or permanent residents (Japanese American National Museum 1999: 14). While the greatest migration has occurred over the last 150 years, Japanese have migrated abroad from at least the fifteenth century.

A history of migration from Japan

Population shifts in Japan have long been tied to historical developments. While there had always been migration back and forth between Japan and the Asian mainland (especially Korea and China), Europeans began arriving in the fourteenth century during the Western "Age of Exploration." The Tokugawa shoguns, however, finally unifying Japan after centuries of intermittent civil war, had successfully closed the country by the mid-1600s ostensibly to eradicate Christianity from the nation's shores. European traders and missionaries had brought their political and religious conflicts with them as they traveled throughout Asia, and the Japanese government lost patience trying to make sense of these differences. In addition, the shoguns worried about how much influence the Europeans had over the local warlords, and feared renewed uprisings if they became too powerful. In any case, the nation sealed its borders, preventing Japanese from leaving, and foreigners from entering, for the next two and a half centuries. It was not until a notorious American commodore, Matthew Perry, "opened" the islands in the mid-nineteenth century that Japan again had legal involvement with the rest of the world.

Soon after the period of national isolation ended, Japanese emigration started. As we will see in other chapters of this volume, the instant contact with the West caused great social and economic upheavals in Japan around the turn of the twentieth century. Rural areas were especially hard-hit, forcing many Japanese farmers to seek work overseas, particularly in Guam, Hawaii, mainland North America, and Latin America. The Japanese government even encouraged such migrations as a means to ameliorate population pressures, and established organizations to facilitate it (see Amemiya, Chapter 10; Dresner, Chapter 3; Adachi 1999).

Motivations for emigration

I will now look at nine specific reasons why Japanese emigration took the forms that it did. These, of course, are rather arbitrary divisions, and not always distinct.

1 Taxation and economics

On January 3, 1868, revolutionary forces from the western prefectures of Chôshû and Satsuma (along with those of Tosa, Echizen, and others) overthrew the reigning fifteenth Tokugawa shogun, Yoshinobu. The Tokugawa family had ruled Japan for over 250 years as regents for the Emperor (who, in actuality, had no real political power). These young revolutionaries – the oldest of them being no more than 43 – immediately transformed Japanese society. At their behest, the newly rehabilitated Emperor Meiji issued his *Go-ka-jô no Go-seimon* (Oath of Five Articles) in 1868, which declared that:

> The common people, no less than the civil and military officials, shall each be allowed to pursue his own calling so that there may be no discontent.... Evil customs of the past shall be broken off and everything shall be based on the just laws of Nature.... Knowledge shall be sought throughout the world so as to strengthen the foundations of imperial rule.
>
> (quoted in Hane 1986: 86)

In other words – in theory, at least – the old feudal class distinctions were abolished, and Japanese farmers (more than three-quarters of the population)[1] were relieved of their class obligations to the samurai warriors or landowning warlords.

In actuality, however, things were not so simple (see Table 2.1). The new government, in its attempt to modernize overnight to meet the coming Western threat, had a very long and expensive wish list. The army had to be reorganized and modernized, schools needed to be built because of the now-compulsory education requirement, and new industries had to be established. Land tax was the chief source of governmental income (about 80 percent of all tax revenue), but budgeting and plan-

Table 2.1 Agricultural conditions in Japan at the time of emigration

c.1880	
Total Japanese population	38,000,000
Number of farm families	5,500,000
Number of farmers	15,588,000
Percentage of labor force in farming	75
Percentagee of national income due to farming	35
Percentage of net value of farm products	64.2
Total cultivated agricultural land	4,735,000 hectares; 18,300 sq. m.
Cultivated land area per worker	0.3 hectares; 0.75 acre
Average size of farm of one farmer	9 *tan*, 8 *se* (2.5 acres)
Percentage of farmers cultivating 1.1 acres or less	40
Percentage cultivating 1 *chô* (2.45 acres) or less	70
Percentage of land used to grow rice	53
Total rice yield	2.0 metric tons/hectare of plant. rice 0.8 metric tons/acre of planted rice
Average yield of a 1 *tan* (0.245 acre) rice paddy	1.6 *koku* (7.94 bushels)
Total production of brown rice	5,293,000 metric tons
Total agricultural economic output	¥1,332,000; $3,996,000
Average agricultural economic output (land)	¥281/hectare; ¥112/acre $850/hectare; $330/acre
Average agricultural economic output (people)	¥86/person; $250/person
Tax rate	3% (dropped to 2.5% in 1872)
Percentage of crop income taken to taxes	35
Percentage of farm taxes paid to income brought in	11.2
Changes	
Percentage of labor force in farming, c.1880	75
Percentage of labor force in farming, c.1930	45
Percentage of tenant farmers, c.1870	30
Percentage of tenant farmers, c.1900	40
Percentage of tenant farmers, c.1908	45
Percentage of rent paid by tenant farmers, c.1870	50
Percentagee of rent paid by tenant farmers, c.1900	50
Percentage of rent paid by tenant farmers, c.1908	50
Percentage of farm taxes paid to income, 1880	11.2
Percentage of farm taxes paid to income, 1882	15.5
Percentage of farm taxes paid to income, 1883	20.2
Percentage of farm taxes paid to income, 1884	25.0

Source: Data taken from Myers and Yamada (1984: 424); Yoshida (1909: 380); Reischauer and Craig (1978: 141, 204–5); *Kodansha Encyclopedia* (1993: 1219–20); Ericson (1983: 134); Hane (1982: 29, 31); Duus (1976: 139); Lone (2001: 9–10).

Note
Dollar conversions are made at approximately ¥1 = $3.00 at the turn of the nineteenth century.

ning had always been difficult as the taxes were tied to a percentage of a farm's annual yield. A more dependable means was to make taxes dependent on land values. Thus, a fixed tax rate was established, eventually leveling off at 2.5 percent of assessed land values. However, more importantly, these assessments were relatively permanent, and did not vary according to market price. This resulted in an increase in land tenancy, because farmers who could not afford to pay their taxes in years of bad harvests now had to sell off their land. About a quarter of the farmers were tenants before the new tax system began, and this rose to almost half by 1908 (Reischauer and Craig 1978: 140).

Those who opposed the new tax assessments – said to be necessary for the success of the new nation – were often thought to be not only miserly, but unpatriotic. One prefectural governor told his farmers that "Those who oppose the government's land assessment will be deemed traitors and they and their entire families will be stripped naked and exiled to foreign lands" (Hane 1982: 22).

But there were other problems facing the farmers in the late nineteenth century. Due to rapid changes in the economy, in 1880 Japan was experiencing general inflation as well as paper-currency depreciation. In an effort to halt both, Masayoshi Matsukata, the new Meiji (1868–1912) government finance minister, enacted a series of draconian economic reforms. He increased direct and indirect taxes, sold off government holdings, and revamped the commercial banking system. Although these actions guaranteed the eventual long-term stability of the Japanese economy, they entailed high cost and sacrifice from small businessmen and farmers. Between 1883 and 1890 more than 10 percent of all independent farmers lost their lands due to failure to pay taxes. One-seventh of all arable farmland was taken due to foreclosed mortgages in 1884 and 1885 alone (Ericson 1983: 134). To put things another way, in 1885 there were 108,000 farm bankruptcies, meaning that at least 400,000 persons lost their livelihood that year (Hane 1982: 23). In addition, as seen in Table 2.1, the percentage of taxes on farmland to farmland income rose dramatically, from 11.2 percent in 1880 to 25.0 percent in 1884.

Yet, unfortunately, there were even more pressures put on these strapped farmers. Bad weather in 1885 destroyed the crops, not only ruining farmers' incomes, but also sending the whole nation into a famine. The saké excise tax was raised by 250 percent, the tobacco excise tax by 750 percent, and the price of rice collapsed in the late nineteenth century, which hurt them even more. Once again, the government ignored market factors and demanded a pre-established fixed tax per *koku*[2] of rice, regardless of what it was actually selling for (even if the price was *less* than the tax).

These conditions caused many riots and "incidents of intense violence" (*gekka jihen*), large and small. In 1876, farmers from four central provinces demanded the government to reassess the excessively high rice tax rate. When the Meiji government refused, 10,000 farmers in Mie Prefecture (on the east coast of south-central Japan) rioted in the streets and destroyed public buildings. Although the unrest spread, these acts were sporadic and uncoordinated, and the government was able to suppress the revolt. Over 50,000 people were punished or fined, and the leaders of the initial Mie protest were executed or imprisoned for life (Hane 1982: 22).

But it was not only farmers who suffered under the new Meiji government's economic reforms. For example, in Saitama Prefecture, near Tokyo, the price of raw silk dropped 50 percent in one year in 1882. Townsmen, and even professional gamblers, could often not pay back their debts. Members of the *Jiyû Minken Undô* (Freedom and People's Rights Movement) and *Kômintô* (Indigent's Party) led between 6,000 and 8,000 armed peasants on a march on government offices and money lenders' shops. Within two weeks the government cracked down hard on these protesters, and the army or police arrested some 3,000 persons. Seven were sentenced to death. The consequence was that:

> the largest armed peasant uprising to confront the Meiji government ended, and the peasants learned that they could not hope to succeed in having their grievances redressed by force of rebellion.... The suppression of the Chichibu Uprising signaled the end of any attempt on the part of the poor people's parties to rely on force to protect their interests.
>
> (Hane 1982: 27)

2 Compulsory military service

The new Japanese government started universal military conscription in 1873. Conscription actually may have had the most profound impact on everyday Japanese life because now warfare was something all males would be involved with, not just the samurai warrior class. Ideally, the draft was intended to democratize the army and allow for a European-style modern military to develop, but the majority of Japanese saw things differently. Indeed, the peasants called this new obligation *ketsuzei* (lit. a blood tax) and generally viewed it as just one more way the Meiji government was exploiting the masses. Most saw the three years of required service for all men over the age of twenty as another type of the corvée labor so vigorously rejected in Tokugawa times (Hane 1982: 18).

Public outcry was loud and resistance great. In 1881 in Nagasaki alone, not one man responded to the draft. Anti-conscription riots were common, and eventually 20,000 people were arrested. Although the Sino–Japanese War in 1894 stirred patriotic feelings and damped down some of the resistance to the draft, there was little doubt that it was both a special hardship and loss of manpower for farming families. It also contained many injustices and irregularities. For example, until this loophole's repeal in 1889, a man could be exempted if he paid ¥400 (around US$1,200).[3] This was several years' annual salary, which no farmer could afford to pay (ibid.: 21–2).

3 Demographics

Accurate statistics kept by the Tokugawa shoguns suggest that Japan's population held constant at about 30,000,000 people from the middle Edo Period until the last half of the nineteenth century. For example, the population in 1721 was 26,065,425 and only slightly more in 1846 at 26,907,625 (Totman 1993: 251).[4] As Perez points out (2002: 15), scholars are at a loss to explain this. The usual suspects cited by demographers – war, famine, and pestilence – were natural checks on population growth. It is likely, however, that farmers became aware of the inescapable connections between land, standard of living, poverty, and family size, and made conscious attempts to limit births.

After the Meiji Restoration, however, the population increased steadily, an equally perplexing puzzle. In 1872 the population was 33,100,000 (growing 0.57 percent from the year before). The population increased to 41,000,000 in 1892 and to 52,100,000 in 1912, an annual average population growth rate of 0.5 percent per year (Duus 1976: 135). The population doubled, then, from pre-Meiji times to 73,000,000 in 1940. Regardless of the reasons, Japan's population, and its population density, was significantly increasing during the Meiji Period (1868–1912). Population density went from 224 persons per square mile in 1872 to 317 persons per square mile in 1902. Although there are obvious differences from region to region, it is likely that this overall increase in population pressure was a major contributing factor in family decisions to emigrate.

4 Natural tragedies and earthquakes

In 1923, the Great Tokyo Earthquake (*Kantô Dai-shinsai*) registered about 7.9 on the Richter scale. Of all the natural disasters that can plague a nation, Japan is most susceptible to earthquakes (having had twenty-three with a measure of 6 or higher – indicating a highly "destructive" earthquake – in the twentieth century alone). In the Great Tokyo Earthquake, centered between Yokohama and Tokyo, 100,000 people apparently were killed instantly, with the official toll of the dead or missing being more than 142,000. Over 100,000 people were injured (most due to the firestorms and cyclones caused by the rapidly heating air). At least three million people were left homeless, and at least another nine million were directly affected (Kodansha 1993: 1596).

With Tokyo being the capital of the country, this disaster could hardly have been worse. The cost in 1990 U.S. dollars was about $51.7 billion, or 40 percent of the country's GNP at the time (Hadfield 1995: 13). The government was on the verge of collapse, and with Prime Minister Yûzaburô Kato having died on August 24 – and Gonbei Yamamoto being appointed the new Prime Minister only the day after the earthquake on September 1 – the cabinet was at a loss to take the drastic action necessary to help the people, let alone stay in power. Chaos was rampant, martial law was declared, and 35,000 soldiers were sent to the area (Kodansha 1993: 1596). However, right-wing thugs and police used this confusion to attack leftists, anarchists, social activists, union organizers, and Chinese and Korean minorities. Perhaps 3,000 Koreans (Andô 1973: 39) and 1,000 others were killed in such incidents, and no one was ever brought to justice for these crimes (Perez 1998: 138).

While the Great Tokyo Earthquake was just one incident, it had tremendous repercussions for the whole Japanese economy. Much of Japan's capital and industry was destroyed – 9,000 factories alone – sending the country back into the depression from which it had not yet recovered. While not a direct or immediate cause for farmers to emigrate, the social and economic climate created by the earthquake was undoubtedly a contributing factor.

5 Social unrest: labor activity

It was not only the farmers who were suffering on Japan's road to modernization (though they seemed to carry a disproportionate share of the burden). The growing demand for export goods increased the number of factory workers, but little was done to provide safe working conditions and health protection, or to eliminate child labor. Interest in socialism and labor organizing grew, as did the number of strikes. For example, in 1914 there were fifty strikes involving 8,000 workers; this grew to 500 strikes with 60,000 workers in 1919 (Hane 1986: 210).

After the actions of the authorities during the Great Tokyo Earthquake, union membership, and the number of strikes, increased. Conditions on the farms were still not improving very rapidly either, with the average tenant farmer earning about half the daily wage of a factory worker. Intellectuals, workers, and socialists moved their campaigns to the countryside, and by 1922 the *Nihon Nômin Kumiai* (Japan National Farmers Union) was formed, swelling in membership to 150,000 in four years. However, "the landlords had the law on their side, thus creating a situation in which it was almost impossible for the tenant unions to make much headway" (Hane 1986: 212). In other words, this social unrest, combined with a stagnant and bleak economic future, probably led many – especially socialists and communists – to consider emigration as a potential alternative.

6 Social unrest: rice riots

Social unrest, especially the *kome sôdô* (rice riots), also grew from other sources. The most famous of these was in 1918. The Japanese economy was already in a recession at the start of World War I, and reduced foreign trade due to the fighting collapsed the price of rice and other foodstuffs. However, as the war continued and Japan achieved a surplus balance of payments by supplying the Western powers with necessary commodities, inflation took over the economy. The price of rice then actually doubled during 1917 (Hane 1982: 196–7).

Protests turned to populist rebellion as the price of rice continued to climb. In 1918, from July to mid-September, riots "unparalleled in modern Japanese history in their magnitude, diffusion, and violent intensity" (Radin 1984: 310) swept the country. The first disturbances started in out-of-the-way Toyama Prefecture (in northwestern Japan), but soon spread to many other places. These protests escalated from "peaceful petitioning of officials to riots, strikes, looting, incendiarism, and armed clashes" (Kodansha 1993: 1263). Riots occurred in thirty-six cities, 129 townships, and 145 villages, and the army was sent to establish order in sixty locations (Andô 1973: 386). At least two million people, and perhaps as many as thirteen million, participated in the riots. Added to this were some 150 labor strikes involving 35,000 workers. More than a thousand protestors were killed or wounded when the army was finally called out, and 25,000 people were arrested. Seventy-one received sentences of ten years in prison or more. However, the riots forced the collapse of the government, with Prime Minister Masatake Terauchi resigning in September.

These riots directly reflected the "social impact of economic change and market commercialization" that was taking place in the late Meiji and early Taishô (1912–26) periods. While perhaps not an immediate impetus for emigration, the rice riots were certainly a contributing factor. The geographic pattern of the spread of the riots "directly corresponded with the regional pattern of concentration of industrial development and population redistribution" (Radin 1984: 311).

7 Famine

One of the concomitant features of Japanese modernization was frequent famine. During the Meiji Period there were twenty-four years of famine (mostly in the north), and four in the Taishô era (1912–26). The whole country was hit with crop failures in 1885. "People were reduced to eating roots of plants, tree bark, and dead horses.... A government report stated that 70 to 80 percent of the people of Aomori prefecture [in northern Japan] were living like animals" (Hane 1982: 114).

The two most severe famines were in 1905 and 1934. In 1934, several years of bad harvests preceded the ruining of the rice crop due to cold and wet weather. Yields dropped by about one-third, and in some villages by as much as 50 to 100 percent (that is, no yield at all). The national average infant mortality rate climbed to 13 percent, and in Iwate Prefecture in the north, the hardest hit area, it reached 50 percent. But besides imminent starvation, the famine had other consequences as well. As one contemporary journalist explained:

When they have no resource they sell their daughters [to brothels in the cities]. The parents insist that they will never let their daughters go, even if they cannot eat, but the daughters say they cannot bear to see their parents suffer.... Even when they sell their daughters, the parents seldom get as much as 100 yen in advance.

(Hane 1982: 115)

However, the central government was unwilling or unable to do much to alleviate this suffering, and landlords continued to try and collect rents (even if these were as much as the total harvest). As Hane (1982: 117) states, given the government's lack of action, poor farmers could (1) passively accept their fate, (2) become revolutionaries, or (3) become followers of right-wing militants. All of these factors contributed to Japanese emigration.

8 Geography

A cursory glance at Map 2.1 (cf. Yoshida 1909: 380–1; Ishikawa 1975: 61) shows that, geographically, emigration was not distributed evenly throughout mainland Japan.[5] The prefectures in the southwest – around the Inland Sea and Kyûshû – contributed a major portion of early emigrants (in some years, more than half of the total). In particular, the five prefectures of Hiroshima, Okayama, Yamaguchi, Kagawa, and Ehime – the so-called Setouchi region surrounding the Inland Sea – sent many more of their residents overseas prior to World War II than did any other region.

Research by historians and demographers indicates that at least one-third of all emigrants came from these five Setouchi prefectures until the 1930s (e.g., Ishikawa 1975: 63; Yoshida 1909: 380–3). This fact of geography has important repercussions for the structure of overseas Japanese society. As Adachi argues in this volume (Chapter 6), in the early days of Japanese immigration, associations and business relationships were often based on former locale, and people from the same prefecture often settled in the same areas (even long after the original migrants arrived). But the question naturally arises as to why these prefectures contributed proportionally more than their share of immigrants. Ishikawa (1975) claims that there are at least two reasons: the Inland Sea's natural environment, and its historically poor economy.

As for the natural environment, the soil of the Setouchi prefectures is notoriously poor, especially for rice agriculture. It is too hilly to farm easily, but not mountainous enough to allow people to gather wild plants as a dietary supplement. In addition, the farms in these areas were incredibly small, some being less than one-tenth of an acre. Hiroshima plots were the smallest in all of Japan. Thus, the idea of making a living on a larger, more productive, plot of land no doubt appealed to many of those who went overseas from these regions.

44 *James Stanlaw*

Map 2.1 Sources of highest early Japanese emigration, by prefecture.

There was also another important economic reason why Setouchi people went overseas to work: the need for cash. These farmers were very poor; around 1900 the average Japanese per capita income nationally was about ¥506 (approximately US$1,500). However, for Hiroshima, for example, it was only ¥382 (about US$1,100) (Yoshida 1909: 383), but the new modern Meiji state was predicated on participating in a globalized international economy. Hard cash was therefore needed to pay taxes, pay rent or buy land, repair houses, or keep up ancestral shrines and cemeteries. As a result, even many eldest sons who had familial responsibilities at home went abroad to become migratory workers. They intended to send the cash they earned to Japan to buy back their ancestors' lands and pay off their family debts.

9 Social imperialism and the global economy

Schumpeter (1951) introduced the term "social imperialism" to describe how problems of social conflict and the agenda of industrial capital became intermixed at the turn of the twentieth century. That is, as Young (1998: 308–9) describes in the Japanese context:

> The social imperialist thesis looks at empire building as a political strategy of elites to produce social stability and win support of the masses. Faced with the emergence of a politically organized working class demanding social reform, entrenched political elites promoted the social and economic benefits of colonial expansionism as an alternative to social welfare policies.... [This was] one of a range of socially interventionist policies developed to deal with the consequences of uneven capitalist development and social unrest.... Japanese social imperialism ... emerged with the greatest force ... in rural peripheries of political and economic power. It was in the agrarian political economy that the impact of uneven economic growth was felt most keenly and in the world of the village elites that social imperialism became the answer to calls for social justice by an agrarian proletariat of tenant farmers. For the countryside, the advent of industrial capitalism meant the incorporation in and increasing vulnerability to a national and global market, a process that pitted landlord against tenants in the struggle to achieve social security against the vagaries of the market.... In Japan, ... agrarian social imperialism forged new links between agriculture and empire.

Korea and Taiwan, which were literally colonies of Japan, had almost three-quarters of a million Japanese residents by 1930. More than a quarter of a million Japanese had settled in Manchuria. In fact, this institutionalized state-sponsored social imperialism is perhaps best seen in the Japanese policy towards Manchuria (see Guelcher, Chapter 4; Tamanoi, Chapter 13). In 1931 the Japanese army conquered the province during its war with China, and until the end of World War II it remained a Japanese puppet state. The last Chinese emperor Pu-yi (of the Qing Dynasty, and thus technically a Manchu) was installed at the Japanese army's behest as the leader of the "independent" state of Manchukuo.

In 1937 the Ministry of Agriculture and Forestry, with local prefectural support, began to finance in earnest the mass emigration of village farmers to Manchukuo. The ostensive reason for this policy was to solve an overpopulation problem in many rural areas. However, such pressure seems not to have always been a factor in decisions to emigrate. For example, prefectures in Kyûshû with the highest population densities (such as Ohita and Nagasaki) sent very few immigrants to Manchuria, while those that were less crowded (such as Fukushima and Miyagi in the north) sent the most. There were also again regional concentrations. While early emigrants around the turn of the twentieth century came from prefectures in the southwest surrounding the Inland Sea, the emigrants to Manchukuo in the 1930s came from the northeast and central areas, especially from the prefectures of Nagano, Yamagata, Fukushima, Niigata, and Miyagi (see the shaded area in the upper-right corner of Map 2.1). The Setouchi prefectures around the Inland Sea sent 11 percent of the emigrants to Manchuria; almost three times that number came from these central-northeast prefectures. Nagano and Yamagata sent more than 16 percent alone (Young 1998: 328–39).

Young suggests a plausible reason for these differences. She argues (1998: 330) that it was not overcrowding which caused these population shifts. Instead, it was local crop failures, bad weather, and the drop in silk and rice prices that caused the collapse of household finances and village structure. The Tôhoku region was one of the hardest hit areas, and the six prefectures in this region – Yamagata, Fukushima, Miyagi, Akita, Aomori, and Iwate – sent 66,522 people to Manchukuo (or 20.6 percent of the total). Nagano, the largest contributing prefecture, had been Japan's number one silk producer (Young 1998: 330).

And yet, as Young says (1998: 331), a disproportionate share of economic hardship did not necessarily translate into emigration: "Clearly, economic hardship provided a necessary but not sufficient condition for the development of an emigration movement." Rather, what the districts had in common was a tradition of sending emigrants overseas – as Young says, "long histories of involvement with colonization." The Shinano Overseas Emigration Association (*Shinano Kaigai Kyôkai*) of Nagano sponsored a village in Brazil (Alicança, which is discussed by Adachi in Chapter 6). Toyama, Tottori, Yamagata, Miyagi, and Niigata Prefectures had similar activities. Such organizations and government sponsorship established an aura of legitimacy and safety among potential emigrants who may have been harboring doubts. The contribution of these overseas emigration associations to the Japanese diaspora is incalculable, as Dresner demonstrates in Chapter 3.

One last comment should be made about the role of advertisements as inducements to emigration, which was apparently significant. Young (1998: 333), for example, mentions that between 1932 and 1935 the Nagano overseas organization promoting emigration to Manchukuo held 200 lectures, distributed 4,000 books and 15,000 pamphlets, and put up 350,000 posters. Yoshida (1909: 384) also says that at the turn of the twentieth century there were some thirty different pamphlets circulating with titles such as "The New Hawaii" or "Guide Book to Different Occupations in America." He also notes that, generally speaking, "they have exaggerated the abundance of opportunities in the United States and stimulated emigration in over-attractive descriptions." Diaries, letters of emigrants, oral histories – and even a fascinating contemporary cartoon strip (Kiyama 1999) – show that this is no understatement.

In sum, then, social and economic hardship caused many of the million Japanese emigrants to leave their homeland in search of better lives abroad. However, Japanese emigration cannot be explained by these factors alone. Prefectures suffering the most economically did not always send the most people overseas. As we have seen, emigration was often as much personal choice as anything else – depending upon such things as government sponsorship, individual social networks, advertising, and even personal ideologies.

The results of Japanese emigration: rejections and acceptance

Regardless of the reasons, hundreds of thousands of Japanese left for work overseas. Table 2.2 shows the numbers and destinations of Japanese emigrants in the years 1868 to 1941 and 1946 to 1989. Over 180,000 Japanese went to Hawaii from the 1890s to the 1920s, making them the largest ethnic group in the islands. Some of these people went on to the American mainland, especially California. Records show some 275,000 Japanese had directly entered the mainland United States from Japan by 1924,[6] and 15,000 went to Canada. Between 1899 and 1930, more than 20,000 Japanese had emigrated to Peru. Almost 300,000 people went to Manchuria. By 1930 more than 100,000 Japanese went to Brazil, starting a trend that would last until World War II began. In 1933 and 1934, 45,000 more Japanese went to Brazil, and from 1935 to 1941 25,000 more followed. By 1940, then, there were 240,000 people of Japanese ancestry living in Brazil (Daniels 2000: 15–17).

Since the struggle of Japanese North Americans and Japanese Latin Americans is amply discussed in other chapters, I will only briefly mention a few highlights here. As is well documented, American and Western immigration laws, and World Wars I and II, altered Japanese emigration patterns significantly. The "Yellow Peril" threat at the turn of the twentieth century caused many governments to limit the number of Japanese who could migrate to their country. For example, by 1900 more than 61,000 Japanese were living in Hawaii (about 40 percent of the total population of the islands), and 24,000 were living in California. From 1902 to 1907 more than 39,500 Japanese came to California directly from Japan and almost 33,000 from Hawaii (Hane 1986: 200). However, all this effectively stopped under various laws, including the Gentlemen's Agreement of 1908 and the Immigration Exclusion Act of 1924. Australia closed its borders to Japanese in 1898, and Canada and the United States tried to curtail local Japanese population growth by statutory means. For example, American laws effectively barred people of Japanese ancestry from owning farmland in California by the 1920s. As a result, Japanese emigrants turned to Latin America as their new destination, particularly Brazil and Peru.

Japanese emigration and immigration today

The emigration of hundreds of thousands of Japanese in the late nineteenth and early twentieth centuries has left a modern legacy for our

Table 2.2 Number and destination of pre- and post-World War II Japanese emigrants

	1868–1941	1946–89
Korea	712,583	na[a]
Taiwan	397,090	na
Manchuria (Manchuko)[b]	270,007	na
Hawaii	231,206	na
Brazil	188,985	71,385
United States (mainland)	107,253	135,084[c]
Canada	35,777	11,260
Paraguay	na	9,616
Bolivia	na	6,359
Peru	33,070	2,615
Mexico	14,667	na
Argentina	5,398	12,068
Russia/Soviet Union	56,821	na
Philippines and Guam	53,115	na
Singapore and Malaysia	11,809	na
Indonesia	7,095	na
New Caledonia	5,074	na
Hong Kong and Macao	3,815	na
Sarawak/North Borneo	2,829	na
Australia	3,773	1,558
India	1,885	na
New Zealand	1,046	na
Dominican Republic	na	1,390
Other countries	7,980	10,565
Total	1,041,605	261,900

Source: Based on figures taken from *Kodansha Encyclopedia of Japan* (1993, p. 335).

Notes

a Unavailable or not applicable at that time; only countries with more than 1,000 Japanese emigrants are listed; individual figures are available for Europe, Africa, or western Asia.
b Manchuria was a Japanese puppet state established after its annexation in 1931; these figures are based on 1932–45 statistics.
c This includes Hawaii.

twenty-first-century world. Table 2.3 shows the Nikkei population – the descendants of these previous sojourners – in seventeen countries. But Japanese emigration and immigration continues to this day, though in modified forms. Table 2.4 shows that more and more Japanese nationals are living abroad each year, with more than 800,000 being overseas in 2001. A comparison of Table 2.4 with Table 2.5 shows that some 35 percent of these people are permanent residents in their host countries, creating a new kind of "permanent resident diaspora." In addition, about 8,000 Japanese women marry foreigners every year (Asahi Shumbun 2002: 37), the vast majority of them moving abroad with their husbands, as seen in Table 2.6.

Table 2.3 Japanese nationals living overseas, by country

Country	1990[a] Number	%	1996[b] Number	%	2001[c] Number	%
United States	236,401	38.1	273,779	35.8	312,936	37.4
Brazil	105,060	16.9	89,005	11.7	73,492	8.8
China	na	na	na	na	53,357	6.4
United Kingdom	44,351	7.2	55,375	7.2	51,896	6.2
Australia	15,154	2.4	25,355	3.3	41,309	4.9
Canada	21,846	3.5	26,545	3.5	34,446	4.1
Germany	20,913	3.4	24,117	3.2	26,402	3.2
Singapore	12,701	2.0	25,688	3.4	23,174	2.8
Thailand	14,289	2.3	23,292	3.0	22,731	2.7
Hong Kong	13,980	2.3	24,500	3.2	na	na
France	15,026	2.4	20,060	2.6	21,785	2.6
Other countries	120,435	19.4	176,262	23.1	176,216	21.0
Total	620,174	100	763,977	100	837,744	100

Sources:
a Based on figures in *Asahi Shimbun Japan Alamanac* (1993: 39).
b Based on figures in *Asahi Shimbun Japan Alamanac* (1999: 63).
c Based on figures in *Asahi Shimbun Japan Alamanac* (2003: 37).

Table 2.4 Japanese permanent residents living abroad in 1996 and 2002, by country

Country	1996 Number	%	2002 Number	%
United States	98,777	36.3	101,395	35.5
Brazil	85,896	31.6	69,978	24.5
United Kingdom	6,034	2.2	9,457	3.3
Canada	16,403	6.0	22,878	8.0
Australia	12,111	4.4	20,041	7.0
Singapore	813	0.2	1,037	0.4
Hong Kong	1,017	0.3	na	na
Germany	3,221	1.1	4,285	1.5
Thailand	2,655	0.98	583	0.2
France	3,008	1.1	5,331	1.9
China (PRC)	454	0.1	992	0.3
Taiwan	747	0.27	598	0.2
Korea	389	0.1	24	<0.01
Argentina	10,858	4.0	10,798	3.8
Indonesia	443	0.1	1,311	0.4
Malaysia	437	0.1	714	0.2
India	na	na	154	0.05
Other countries	28,672	10.5	36,129	12.6
Total	271,935	100	285,705	100

Source: Based on data in *Japan 1996: An International Comparison* (Keizai Koho Center): 108; *Japan 2004: An International Comparison* (Keizai Koho Center): 130.

50　*James Stanlaw*

Table 2.5 Nikkei (overseas Japanese) populations in the mid-1990s

Country	Total population[a]	Nikkei population[b]	Nikkei population per 100,000	Year of first arrival[c]
Argentina	34,673,000	29,262	83.6	1907
Bolivia	7,165,000	7,986	111.7	1916
Brazil	162,661,000	1,620,370	381.2	1908
Canada	28,821,000	55,111	190.8	1891
Chile	14,333,000	2,292	15.3	1903
Columbia	36,813,000	1,106	0.32	1921
Costa Rica	3,463,000	57	0.17	na
Cuba	11,007,000	842	0.73	1907
Dominican Republic	8,089,000	583	0.74	na
Ecuador	11,446,000	152	0.13	na
Guatemala	11,278,000	113	0.10	na
Mexico	95,772,000	11,926	12.6	1892
Paraguay	5,504,000	6,054	109.0	1930
Peru	24,523,000	55,472	224.3	1899
Uruguay	3,239,000	436	1.23	1930
Venezuela	21,983,000	828	3.6	1931
United States	266,476,000	848,000	318.2	1868

Sources:
a 1996 figures from the *Wall Street Journal Alamanac* (1998: 501–2).
b 1993 figures from "International Nikkei Demographics," The Japanese American National Museum, http://www.inrp.org/pre/english/demogrph.htm; and *Statistical Abstract of the United States* (1996: 31).
c "International Nikkei Demographics," The Japanese American National Museum, http://www.inrp.org/pre/english/demogrph.htm.

Increasing globalization guarantees that immigration to and from Japan will continue to play an important part in all discussions of international migration. The study of the Japanese diaspora – and of immigration into Japan – will help provide insights about the flow of peoples everywhere. If nothing else, such an examination shows how problems of race and accommodation – and acculturation and acceptance – demonstrate how views of foreign "others" reflect and reify ideas of domestic "selves," even in an alleged homogeneous nation like Japan.

Notes

1 For some, this number may seem small. However, as Ohnuki-Tierney says, "Researchers are increasingly aware that Japanese culture and society have never been as homogeneous as once claimed. The representation of the entire nation as 'agrarian Japan' denies the heterogeneity of Japanese society throughout history by portraying the Japanese as a monolithic population consisting entirely of farmers" (1993: 82). Even a standard reference (Kodansha 1993: 16) says that prior to the Meiji Restoration only 80 percent of the population was engaged in farming.

Table 2.6 International marriages by selected countries, 1970, 1996, and 2000

(a) Japanese men marrying foreign women in selected years

Nationality of wife	1970		1996		2000	
	No.	%	No.	%	No.	%
China	280	13.3	6,264	29.6	9,884	34.9
Philippines	na	na	6,645	31.4	7,519	26.5
Korea	1,536	72.9	4,461	21.1	6,214	21.9
Thailand	na	na	na	na	2,137	7.5
Brazil	na	na	na	na	357	1.3
United States	75	3.6	241	1.1	202	0.7
Other countries	217	10.3	565	2.6	2,013	7.1
Total	2,108	100	21,162	100	28,363	100

(b) Japanese women marrying foreign men in selected years

Nationality of husband	1970		1996		2000	
	No.	%	No.	%	No.	%
Korea	1,386	40.3	2,800	38.8	2,509	31.6
China	195	5.7	773	10.7	878	11.1
United States	1,571	45.7	1,357	18.8	1,483	18.7
Brazil	na	na	na	na	279	3.5
United Kingdom	na	na	na	na	245	3.1
Other countries	286	8.3	2,280	31.6	2,539	32.0
Total	3,438	100	7,210	100	7,937	100

Sources: *Asahi Shimbun Japan Almanac* (1999: 63); *Asahi Shimbun Japan Almanac* (2003: 37).

Note
"No." indicates the number of marriages by nationality in a given year; "%" reflects marriage by nationality as a percentage of all foreign marriages with Japanese that year.

2 One Japanese *koku* was approximately 5.12 U.S. dry bushels (or about 180 liters or 41 U.S. gallons).
3 This would be about US$1,200, assuming that ¥1 = US$3.00 at the turn of the century.
4 Totman (1993) reminds us that we must add to these figures some two million samurai and their subordinates, several thousand court nobles, and various others – such as beggars and poor people – who missed being counted.
5 Emigration from Okinawa was subject to many of the same forces discussed here for mainland Japan, but there were some particulars unique to the region (see Masterson, Chapter 8; Hirabayashi and Kikumura-Yano, Chapter 9; Amemiya, Chapter 10, for more details).
6 But Daniels (2000: 14) points out that this number is inflated, as repeated entries are included in these tallies.

3 Instructions to emigrant laborers, 1885–94
"Return in triumph" or "Wander on the verge of starvation"

Jonathan Dresner

The opening up of Japan to foreign trade in 1853 after more than two centuries of closure also made it possible for Japanese to travel overseas. The earliest travelers were diplomats and students, but as Japan became more integrated into the world economy, it became clear that Japanese labor could be a valuable commodity, as had occurred with Chinese and Irish labor. It also became clear that there were dangers associated with overseas migration of laborers, both for the laborers and for the government of Japan. As a result, when the Japanese government re-authorized labor migration in the 1880s, it strove to protect its citizens as well as its own international image by carefully managing the migrants and the migration system. The migration system has been studied in some detail (e.g., Irwin and Conroy 1972; Wakatsuki 1979; Moriyama 1985: 11–32), including analyses of the role of Japanese embassies and consulates in overseas Japanese communities (Iriye 1972; Kimura 1988; Takaki 1989), but there has been no analysis of the Japanese government's attempts to influence the emigrants themselves through information and exhortation.[1]

From the earliest stages of the *kan'yaku imin* (government-sponsored emigration) program,[2] problems prompted official attempts to control the laborers through selection and social pressure. Hazama and Komeiji, for example, cite low morale, gambling, drinking, and absconding among the pioneer 1885 group (1986: 22; also see Kimura 1988: 6–7). Recruitment drives were increasingly limited to more "successful" rural communities and according to more stringent participation limitations. In addition, officials tried to modify the behavior of emigrants through education and moral suasion. Specifically, the government distributed the Rules for Migrant Workers and forced emigrants to sign pledges of good conduct, and also issued gubernatorial proclamations. These documents reveal the Japanese government's perspective regarding the emigration program: potential for economic gain, but also risk of national embarrassment. Officials tried to improve emigrant behavior, and therefore Japan's international position, by appealing to practical benefits, personal pride, family connections, group and legal obligations, and benefits accruing to fellow Japanese.

From the very beginning of the Meiji era (1868–1912), the Japanese government was reluctant to allow Japanese to travel overseas as unskilled labor, and results from emigration in the early years largely supported this position (Dresner 2001: 10–13). Three groups of labor emigrants left Japan in the first years of Meiji: the 150 *Gannen-mono* (Meiji first-year people) who went to the Kingdom of Hawaii, the forty-two who went to German-controlled Guam the same year, and the dozens of Aizu-Wakamatsu samurai and their families who went to northern California after the defeat of the Shogunal loyalist domain. The Aizu-Wakamatsu group and the Guam migration were unmitigated failures, complete with high death rates. The Hawaii *Gannen-mono* had more success: about one-third of the group returned to Japan before a full year, but over half of the group remained in Hawaii after their three-year contract period was over, and were well regarded as laborers. In the 1870s and through the rest of the century there were also Japanese who went to Asia, including a large number of women who worked as prostitutes, mostly in the Western-dominated treaty ports of China and elsewhere.

With the exception of those in the Aizu-Wakamatsu group, who were political refugees, Japanese workers were drawn overseas by the wage gap between Japan and the rest of the world; those workers who endured did well financially and Japanese labor remained in demand. But the Japanese government refused to allow substantial overseas migrations until 1884 for two reasons. First, the government was concerned about the poor treatment its nationals suffered, so Japan needed to gain strength and prestige to better serve its citizens overseas. Second was the image problem, created by farm workers and prostitutes, at a time when Japan was assiduously trying to present a "civilized" face to the world (Moriyama 1985: 32; Ichioka 1988: 4; Takaki 1989: 46). To mitigate both problems, the emigration program was deliberately structured and adapted to improve the success rate of emigrants.

The Hawaiian government lobbied Japan for fifteen years to gain access to Japanese labor, but the Japanese government demurred until the 1880s. By then, rural economic distress caused by the Matsukata Deflation (1881–3) had created enough pressure to overcome reservations about image, and Japan's foreign relations had advanced to a point where there was greater confidence about monitoring and protecting emigrants (Takaki 1989: 43–4). The agreements under which Japanese traveled to Hawaii and Australia were carefully constructed to provide support and protection for the laborers, and even involved the Japanese government in the process of labor recruitment and selection (Conroy 1978 [1953]: 44–53; Suzuki 1992: 57). To promote the program and reduce confusion, the government distributed information about Hawaii and the labor contracts, and used local notables to proselytize (Dresner 2001: 86–8).

Government-managed migration was closely monitored by Japanese officials and results from the first few rounds quickly led to changes in the system (Kodama 1992: 129–34). Kimura argues that the workers were under-prepared for the rigorous work and for the sometimes violent and repressive control imposed on workers by many plantations, which led to alcohol abuse and work stoppages (Kimura 1988: 6–9, 131–5). The Japanese consul in Hawaii was replaced and the status of the post upgraded to Consul General. Tarô Andô, Japanese Consul General in Hawaii from 1886 through 1889, sent an inspection report back to the Foreign Ministry that was extremely complimentary of emigrants from rural areas including Hiroshima, Yamaguchi, Kumamoto, and critical of the urban emigrants who were a small portion of the whole (Doi 1980: 85–8; Hiroshima Prefecture 1991: 38). The Japanese government responded by restricting recruitment to "remote agricultural villages" of the four prefectures whose pioneers presented Japan in the best light (Ichioka 1988: 41–2). These four prefectures, along with Okinawa, eventually accounted for the vast majority of Japan's international emigration. The Japanese government was trying to select emigrants who would both benefit from the program and impress non-Japanese with their character and abilities. Officials tightened restrictions on the emigration of women and of males with industrial or entrepreneurial experience (Kodama 1978: 29–30). They also expanded the pre-departure moral exhortation program of pamphlets and pledges.

For the program to succeed, the government needed the migrants to learn new habits and to adapt to new institutions. To this end, emigrants were given supplementary materials, sometimes very detailed, which the government tried to make as binding as the actual labor contract. These materials were produced at all levels of government and they varied in length, detail, and content. They have been described as paternalistic (Doi 1980: 82; Kimura 1988: 132), which is certainly true. They display great hope for the emigration program, as well as hand wringing about the ability of the emigrants to live up to their potential.

The Yamaguchi program

The four documents discussed in this chapter are from the high-emigration Yamaguchi Prefecture.[3] First is a fine example of the Rules for Migrant Workers (hereafter Rules) genre produced nationally: detailed, edifying, and persuasive.[4] Second is a proclamation from the governor of Yamaguchi Prefecture, full of rhetorical flourishes to drive home the necessity of hard work and perseverance. Third is an early example of a written pledge signed by a group of emigrants from the town of Kuga in Yamaguchi, short but containing all the basic elements. The fourth document is a later example of a group pledge, slightly longer and on a preprinted form.

All of these documents are from the government-sponsored emigration period (1885–94). Document one (Rules) mentions using postal money orders through the consulate, which suggests that it was written between 1889 (when the Japanese Postal Savings Bank opened a branch at the Honolulu consulate) and 1892 (when both remittance transmission and forced withholding duties were turned over to private banks) (Suzuki 1992: 68; Dresner 2001: 108–12). Doi implies that similar rules were distributed from 1885, and other sources support this. Doi also suggests that Governor Hara's Proclamation was a relatively late addition (Doi 1980: 82). It does mention tens of recruitments: There were twenty-six groups of laborers under the program, so a literal reading would place it relatively late. Yasutarô Sôga, in whose memoir the Hara Proclamation appears, came to Hawaii in 1897 at the age of fourteen as a contract laborer. It is interesting that he remembered and included a document produced earlier by a governor who was no longer in office (Sôga 1953: 8–13). Both the Rules and the Hara Proclamation refer to past migrants' experiences, both positive and negative, which suggests that they should be placed after 1888, when the first three-year contracts would have been completed. The two types of good behavior pledges we discuss are dated early in the decade: the handwritten document from January 3, 1886, and the printed version from April 26, 1888.

These written and printed materials raise the question of the literacy rate of Japan's emigrants. It seems futile for the Rules to have insisted that it be reread regularly if the vast majority of the emigrants were illiterate. Rural Yamaguchi was not noted for educational achievement, and many of the emigrants did communicate with family through literate friends and neighbors, particularly village headmen (Masaharu Ano, a local historian known for his work on the imperialist Yôsuke Matsuoka, personal communication). The majority of emigrants, who were relatively young as a group (Moriyama 1985: 17), probably had a few years of schooling (Rubinger 1986: 213). School attendance in Yamaguchi in 1877 was around 40 percent but, due to the expansion of compulsory education, by 1900 the elementary school attendance rate was 87 percent, and it rose as high as 98 percent by 1912 (Yamaguchi Prefecture 1963: 680). Moreover, the written pledges were signed in the presence of village headmen, sometimes with guarantors as well, sometimes in groups, so it is likely that these documents were read aloud at some point in the process. Thus, the content of the materials was certainly heard and understood.

There are a variety of strategies employed by these documents. They all set standards for acceptable and successful behavior, and they mobilize social and psychological pressure at a variety of levels to reinforce the character and will of the emigrants. All four documents use various synonyms of "strictly" (e.g., *kataku, gen ni, kenjiki*), most in reference to the labor contract or to their own moral formulas.[5] The government intended these documents to be – or seem, as discussed below – binding on the emigrant, though there were rarely legal repercussions for violations. Morality and hard work are presented as being in the emigrants' best interests, and it is suggested that immorality and laziness would result in personal financial ruin and the loss of opportunities for other Japanese. Emigration is for the mutual benefit of workers and employers, and both are expected to look out for the interests of the other.

The Rules includes very pragmatic instructions about work and life in Hawaii, to prepare rural migrants for the conditions they will face. The pamphlet seems to have been produced by the national government and distributed nationally. It was distributed in both Yamaguchi and Hiroshima prefectures, and a copy is in the archives of the Japanese Foreign Ministry (Hiroshima Prefecture 1991: 10). It opens with a reminder to adhere strictly to the labor contract, then adds: "they [workers] are also expected to resolve to preserve the following points." The first point is a caution that the work will be hard and hot, but that the earnings will be extraordinary. The next two points are about packing for the trip, then there is the section on "Salary" that opens one of the dominant themes of the piece: sick days. Taking too many, it says, will not only cut into your salary, but will also cost the employer money and give all Japanese workers a bad reputation. It is important to avoid "making mountains out of molehills" or getting sick through self-neglect. Health comes up again and again. There is a paragraph on what we would now call a disability discharge. The paragraphs on "Food" focus on maintaining strength and avoiding diseases such as beriberi and diarrhea. The section, "Work Hard and Honestly," reiterates the earlier warnings about "feigned illnesses" as well as the importance of resting if one is actually ill (Doi 1980: 76–82).

The labor contracts included provisions for medical care by Japanese doctors who were paid by the Hawaiian Board of Immigration. That money came first from the plantation owners and later from worker wage deductions, and was a constant source of tension in the labor migration system (Moriyama 1985: 22, 27; Irwin and Conroy 1972: 47–51). On the plantations, work avoidance and alcoholism collided with real exhaustion and overseers with neither medical training nor sympathy (Hazama and Komeiji 1986: 40). Ameliorating this conflict was clearly a goal of the pamphlet.

Time discipline, a perennial issue for workers moving from pre-modern to modern conditions (Gordon 1988: 27–30; Smith 1988), is also stressed. The first section of the rules warns that work time will be different than in Japan. "Time" has its own heading where the rigidity of work time is explained, as well as the importance of worker flexibility about overtime. The concept of Sunday as a day of rest is also introduced here.[6] This segues into a plea for good worker–employer relations: honesty (sick-days are discussed), obedience, determination, and self-abnegation are the foundations of successful earning. Emigrants are encouraged to be law-abiding and obedient, particularly "In the unlikely event that the employer of the emigrant's services violates the contract or offers bad treatment," which should be handled through self-examination and proper channels. In fact, employee abuse was not at all unlikely at the beginning: plantations maintained their own private police forces, for example, traditionally holding a great deal of authority over plantation workers (Doi 1980: 76–82; Hazama and Komeiji 1986: 19–22, 40; Takaki 1989: 134–6, 140).

Financial matters take up the longest sections of the Rules pamphlet. Hard work and savings will pay off, it says under the heading "Savings" (Doi 1980: 80):

> Those who come to work and do not squander their money but rather put it away, can return to Japan after three years with a great deal of money, and buy land, or pay off their parents' debts and reclaim their pawned treasures or land, and thus return in triumph (*nishiki o kazaru*, lit. "exhibit the brocade") to their hometowns, which requires staunch determination and adherence to moral advice.

This is the essence of the emigration project: financial redemption (Takaki 1989: 45; Dresner 2001: 102–5). Section 10 of the Rules also reiterates provisions of the contract related to salary and forced savings, then strongly encourages the workers to deposit or remit any extra money above expenses, to avoid theft or temptation. Modern banking was still developing and evolving in Japan in the 1880s, so there is some detailed explanation of the savings and remittance process. On the home front, Yamaguchi Prefecture officials pushed the families of emigrants to save remitted monies by having them sign their own semi-contractual agreements, committing, in one example from Kuga, to saving 5 percent of the remittances in a postal savings account for the emigrant to use on his return (Kodama 1992: 171). The pamphlet assumes that its readers comprehend percentages, interest accrual, and currency conversions at a "good market rate."

"Gambling" threatened the success of the individual emigrant and created an atmosphere of vice that soiled the Japanese reputation overseas. Gambling is described as illegal, as isolating the gambler from friends and family, as financially draining and generally having "only disastrous consequences," including the possibility of being forever stranded overseas. Gambling was a powerful attraction for the workers, linguistically and physically isolated from non-plantation society, and it was widely recognized as a principal vice of the overseas Japanese communities. Not only is it mentioned directly in these types of documents, but it is repeatedly cited in Japanese consular reports along with alcohol and prostitution (Hazama and Komeiji 1986: 22, 39–40; Ichioka 1988: 84–8, 177–9).

Several strategies are apparent within the Rules that apply pressure to the emigrant. First, those who are not willing to work hard are told that they "will not endure but half a year." Later, they are warned that "People who will not follow the rules should not go overseas in the first place ... because if you cannot put forth the effort, you will not earn great money." On the other hand, the rewards of success are substantial, shared with family and community. Next, the pamphlet invokes an obligation to the employer, going so far as to say, "You will work hard for your employer without making a distinction between working for them or working for yourself." If Japanese workers fail to be productive, "the Japanese will become known as poor workers, so the Chinese or Portuguese will get the jobs. This will make it impossible for Japanese to make these good salaries" (Doi 1980: 76–82).

These precepts may sound like a nationalistic appeal, but since emigration was highly concentrated in poor regions (Dresner 2001: 93–4) this is primarily a threat to the welfare of the emigrants' home towns.[7] But though it had no legal force, the pamphlet concludes with a legal formulation: "Those who take this document and go to Hawaii are acknowledging their agreement to strictly preserve the above points, and will be treated accordingly. This is, therefore, an important document and should be taken out and read occasionally while in Hawaii." This vaguely threatening invocation of authority is a technique that was repeated in the good behavior pledges. Some pledges also afford the Rules for Migrant Workers roughly equal weight with the labor contract. This use of quasi-legal contractual formulas echoes the vague authority of pre-modern governments, rather than the strictly defined powers of the modern state.

Yamaguchi Prefecture Governor Yasutarô Hara strongly supported the development of the emigration program, and lent his voice to the effort to improve emigrant outcomes (Dresner 2001: 100–8). Hara still holds the record as the longest serving Governor of Yamaguchi Prefecture (February 1881 to March 1895), working from the Matsukata Deflation era through the entire government-sponsored emigration period, finally ending his term after overseeing the intense mobilization of Yamaguchi in support of the Sino–Japanese War (Dresner 2001: 115, 166, 171). Hara also carried out land tax reform and agricultural improvement programs to build up the region's economy, and he is credited with reversing the decline in Yamaguchi's fortunes which began in the 1860s (ibid.: 79–80, 113–15, 119).

Hara's Proclamation to Yamaguchi Prefecture citizens going to labor in Hawaii was apparently given to emigrants when they left the prefecture for Yokohama, where they would take passage (Doi 1980: 82). Sôga describes it as "being extremely kind, naturally having the feeling of a parent's farewell to a child departing for overseas, in which you can clearly discern the thinking of the Japanese government at that time towards the Hawaii emigrants" (Sôga 1953: 15). While it is certainly paternalistic, it has more the structure of a short sermon, framed with the promise of success through effort and "pure heart" and complete with interjections and rhetorical questions. Hara starts with the possibility of earning "not a small amount" of profit, as well as the risk of harming the prospects of other emigrants. He continues with warnings about bringing "ridicule" and "shame on the Japanese people" and about the possibility that failed emigrants might "wander on the verge of starvation." But to fulfill their true goal of enriching their families, Hara offers "these clear warnings." Returning to the theme of group reputation, he encourages obedience to local law and mutual aid, so as not to "shame the Japanese people overseas." He enjoins emigrants against squandering money, which seems an oblique reference to gambling and other vices, and invokes both family and "the pure heart of your beloved homeland." Finally, these platitudes are called a "parting gift" that will allow the emigrants to "return home with health and prosperity." It mentions neither the contract nor the employer.

Should the quasi-legal warnings of the official gravitas of Hara's Proclamation fail to impress, Yamaguchi emigrants were also required to sign contract-like pledges of good behavior[8] (Doi 1980: 83–4, particularly "Early Good Behavior Contract" and "Pre-Printed Good Behavior Contract" sections). These pledges were signed by emigrants on the verge of departure in groups based on village or town of origin (Doi 1980: 83–4). The earliest pledges were handwritten, but from 1887 on these forms were preprinted and filed as official documents with village headmen as countersigners. These documents employed multiple forms of social pressure, including group obligation, respect for authority, and the obligation of the personal oath. The contract pledges were short and straightforward, promoting obedience and hard work and rejecting gambling.[9]

In addition, some pledges[10] required emigrants to "send money for support periodically and without fail" to their families in Japan. Such a pledge was signed in January 1886 by twenty-five emigrants from the town of Kuga on Yashiro, a southeastern island of Yamaguchi Prefecture (more officially known as Ôshima County). There were thirty-seven people from Kuga in that third round of recruitment (twenty-five men and twelve women); this made up 4 percent of the entire group of 927 laborers (and almost 8 percent of all Yamaguchi emigrants) (Doi 1980: 43). Unmarried women were not permitted to emigrate, so all the women had husbands in the group serving as heads of household and signing as guarantors for their wives. There were sometimes, however, marriages of convenience (Kawakami 1993: 12). In some cases unmarried daughters were permitted to emigrate, but probably only very young ones. Kuga sent enough emigrants to Hawaii that in 1928 there were two Kuga expatriate associations in Honolulu, distinct from the Ôshima County association (Doi 1980: 74, 137).

A similar preprinted pledge was signed by a group emigrating from the town of Kuga, this time in 1888 as part of the fifth group of emigrants (Doi 1980: 59). It was more legalistic than familial, choosing instead to emphasize "strict" observance of contract conditions, employee obligations, and the Rules for Migrant Workers strictures. It adds a temperance pledge to the mix. Alcohol was a significant expense for the Japanese in Hawaii, and saké was one of Japan's largest exports to Hawaii, though it was almost entirely consumed by the Hawaiian Japanese (Hazama and Komeiji 1986: 39–40). Alcohol was considered second only to gambling as a source of trouble for the laborers. The pledge closes with resolve and determination.

The renunciation of work stoppages in this particular pledge reflects real concern over labor unrest. In addition to being bad for worker–employer relations, Japanese labor activism could harm Japan's image and relationships with countries hosting its workers. Particularly following the establishment of the Republic of Hawaii in 1893, U.S.-oriented Republic leaders were extremely suspicious of Japan and of the Japanese in Hawaii, partially due to Hawaii's dependence on Japanese labor. An 1894 editorial warned that "Until then [annexation] she [Hawaii] cannot afford to quarrel with a Power 18,000 of whose subjects reside in Hawaii and who constitute the backbone of her labor force" (Conroy 1978 [1953]: 120–1). Ironically, organized labor unrest increased sharply after annexation (Takaki 1989: 142, 148–55). By 1920, the Japanese were the largest single ethnic group in Hawaii and a local newspaper repeatedly charged Japan with means and motive to become a credible "yellow peril" (Okihiro 1991: 78–81). Japanese diplomatic officials tried to smooth over these conflicts, but the increasingly independent overseas communities were not pleased with their compromises (Kimura 1988: 135–41).

Hiroshima Prefecture: a second region of high emigration

Hiroshima Prefecture sent over 11,000 residents to Hawaii through Japan's emigration program – almost 700 more than Yamaguchi Prefecture – and has been closely studied by Japanese scholars.[11] Over four-fifths of Hiroshima's government-sponsored emigrants came from four counties and the city of Hiroshima, all in the western coastal region (Hiroshima Prefecture 1993: 72–3) bordering Yamaguchi's high-emigration southeastern region (Dresner 2001: 93–4). A similar campaign of education and exhortation was directed at Hiroshima emigrants, but with some intriguing differences.

Hiroshima Governor Jôgyô Senda issued a statement on May 5, 1885, directed specifically at its second group recruited for Hawaii (Hiroshima Prefecture 1993: 78–9; Hiroshima Prefecture 1991: 10). One-sixth the length of Hara's sermonette, it touched on many of the same points. Obedience to local law and preservation of one's health were the first points, followed by a reminder to do the job properly and behave morally. Emigrants were warned to avoid incurring national dishonor and urged to save their wages so they could *nishiki o kite* (wear the brocade), i.e., return home in triumph. Senda expressed his wish that every one of them work hard. The *Hiroshima-ken Ijûshi* (History of Hiroshima Prefecture Emigration) suggests, without explanation, that "this sort of leadership and position taken regarding the emigrants" was a contributing factor in the strong reputation of Hiroshima workers (Hiroshima Prefecture 1993: 79).

On October 3, 1893, Hiroshima Governor Miki Nabeshima issued a Proclamation to the emigrants departing in the twenty-second Hawaii-bound group, this one closer in tone and length to Hara's (Hiroshima Prefecture 1991: 29–30).[12] There are even some very similar phrasings: Nabeshima proclaimed that if emigrants were not serious and hard-working, their money would evaporate and they would be "on the verge of starvation." He insisted that emigrants keep this idea "in their heart day and night without forgetting."

Nabeshima's Proclamation is in two parts: the Proclamation itself – including admonitions that emigrants preserve their health and follow orders – followed by a half-dozen specific charges. The first article says that emigrants "should not forget they are subjects of the Japanese Empire and should not leave a shameful impression overseas." The rest of the articles are typical – work according to the contract agreement and behave ethically; avoid gambling and liquor; be careful with your earnings and send them home – except for the third, which says, "emigrants should consider one another as family and help one another," and certainly should never fight. This Confucian language is a sharp departure from the secular and practical wording of other documents.

Hiroshima Prefecture emigrants, starting with the second group of recruits, also signed and sealed short written pledges (Hiroshima Prefecture 1993: 78; Hiroshima Prefecture 1991: 7–8).[13] Both personal guarantors and village officials affixed their seals as countersignatories. There were three articles, each with a helpful, if broad, injunction:

Article One: During the sojourn in Hawaii, do not to fight or do other unethical things.
Article Two: Do not get wrapped up in debt problems.
Article Three: The expectation is that you work hard during the sojourn in Hawaii.

These pledges had teeth: emigrants promised to repay any monies lost or other appropriate penalties as a result of failing to complete the contract, even to the extent of auctioning personal property, and should emigrants be unable to pay their share, the guarantor and family of the emigrant would be liable for the balance. In contrast with the Yamaguchi written pledge, this is a more powerfully binding document with real penalties, but the moral charges to the emigrant are more vague. It is noteworthy, though, that the Hiroshima authorities imposed this regimen on emigrants who were already considered to be among the best Japanese workers.

Emigration documents: purposes, omissions, and failures

One area these documents all address is the difficulty rural Japanese workers had adapting to plantation work, including the year-round nature of Hawaiian agriculture. The labor contracts required constant and consistent labor, ten or twelve hours a day, six days a week, for three years (Moriyama 1985: 173–5). Although there was some ebb and flow in the sugar plantation workload, it was not the cycle of temperate agriculture to which the Japanese were accustomed (Takaki 1989: 133). Absconding and work avoidance were apparently common in the early years of emigration (Hazama and Komeiji 1986: 40). Coming from a rural pre-modern environment – that is, a culture in which work time was seasonal and flexible – the emigrants were not accustomed to the discipline of paid plantation labor, which is why these documents repeatedly make the point that the contract must be "strictly" followed. In the 1890s, some of the sugar plantations adapted their work schedules to be more flexible and attractive, but this mainly applied to independent immigrants and former contract workers who had already completed their three-year terms (Hazama and Komeiji 1986: 41).

There are two direct references to work requirements in the Rules for Migrant Workers set forth in the Yamaguchi emigration program. In the very first section it says, "you must work without rest during different appointed hours than in Japan." And later, under the heading "Time," it clarifies "your duty to your employer, to be done without saying unkind things about your boss, or resisting." The Rules also state (Doi 1980: 81):

> Labor time (*rôdô jikan*) is entirely time for work (*shigoto jikan*), and time for breaks, meals and getting to and from the worksite is separate ... there are times when it will be difficult to stick strictly to the time limits, and it may be necessary to work 30 or 40 minutes over the normal time to get the job done.... If the emigrant is unused to the work it may take a bit longer than the expected time, so you must realize that the times are minimums, and if your employer asks you should be prepared to accept that.

This wording is clearly aimed at preventing employer–worker conflicts by making the workers more flexible, at the same time preparing them for inflexible employers. Both pledge contracts discussed here stressed obedience to the employer and adherence to the contract, and all four of the documents examined proclaim the necessity of hard work. This seems unnecessary for emigrants who came from rural areas with strong farming and fishing backgrounds and traditions of *dekasegi* migrant labor, but plantation life was hard and foreign to the Japanese workers.

There are some interesting omissions in these documents. Most glaring are the sparse references to women. Prostitution is not mentioned, though it was part of the overseas laborers' community life and a significant drain on emigrant resources and energy (Takaki 1989: 51). There are only two references to women as emigrants in the long Rules document used in the Yamaguchi program: women's salaries are specified and if the male emigrant should die in Hawaii, "his wife and/or children may be returned to Japan without charge if they wish" (Doi 1980: 76–82). All other references to women are to wives and mothers left behind. About one-fifth of the government-sponsored emigrants were women traveling with their husbands or fathers (Ishikawa 1967: 87; Moriyama 1985: 16–18; Takaki 1989: 47–51).[14] In addition to being a significant component of plantation labor, these women performed an important role in the overseas Japanese community in their domestic capacity: cooking and cleaning for the unmarried men was a lucrative business for women who were not under contract with the plantations (Hazama and Komeiji 1986: 33, 53; Takaki 1989: 134–5).

In the early years of emigration married couples were more likely to return immediately following their contract term than were single emigrants (Dresner 2001: 129). But many unmarried men who chose to settle in Hawaii wanted to start families, leading to picture brides, and other forms of long-distance marriage arrangements, though those were still rare during the government-sponsored era. It may be simply that emigration documents were directed at males by a patriarchal official class drawing on traditions of male responsibility and female invisibility (Nolte and Hastings 1991), as evidenced by the fact that the Kuga pledge was signed by the male emigrants only.

Appeals to moral or ethical abstractions are also sparse. Religious language is not invoked: there are no references to Shinto purity, to Buddhist karma, or even to Confucian filial piety. Obedience is stressed, but in the most practical terms. Except in Hara's Proclamation, the language is unrelentingly concrete, legalistic, and practical. Nationalistic language is rarely invoked, and most references to "other Japanese" point out the economic benefits that accrue through the program. Hara's Proclamation refers to *aikoku no sekishin* (the pure heart of the beloved homeland) and *Nihon shinmin* (people of Japan), though it also threatens starvation and exile as practical consequences of moral failure. Hiroshima Governor Nabeshima's 1893 proclamation (Hiroshima Prefecture 1991: 29–30) refers to *Nippon teikoku* (the Japanese Empire), which is the most nationalistic language in any of the documents examined from the Yamaguchi and Hiroshima prefectures, and it argues for *oyako-kyôdai* (familial) relations among emigrants, which is a rare reference to Confucian relational values. The Rules of Migrant Workers actually takes the time to explain how the actions of Japanese can affect each other in the eyes of foreigners, which suggests that the authors did not expect their emigrants to have a strong sense of national identity or solidarity.

Japanese diplomats worked to reduce tensions with host countries, frequently at the expense of the overseas Japanese workers' interests (Kimura 1988: 131–41; Dresner 2001: 33–8). Japanese officials even considered ending emigration as early as 1887, when the Kingdom of Hawaii imposed a new anti-Asian constitution (Conroy 1978 [1953]: 96–7; LaFeber 1997: 54–6). They did not do so because they were trying to portray themselves as reasonable and unthreatening, and were concerned that a unilateral decision ending emigration might be seen as high-handed. Later on, for example, in the midst of the San Francisco school segregation uproar (1907–8), the Japanese Foreign Minister subtly "revealed that the Japanese government shared the American prejudice against immigrant laborers as less than equal members of society and had no qualms about unequivocally eliminating their travel," which was, in fact, the result of negotiation (Sawada 1991: 352). The interests of the emigrants do not seem to have been the first priority, except insofar as their treatment reflected Japan's status in the world. With few exceptions the overwhelming message of the documents cited here is that the emigrants are on their own, rather than being strongly backed by their government.

Some emigrants failed, and in the racialist atmosphere of the late nineteenth century these failures cast doubt upon the character of the Japanese as a race and the advancement of Japan as a nation. Japanese consuls in Hawaii and the U.S. mainland labored in vain to bring the wild lifestyle of the Japanese community under control, because disorder contributed to anti-Japanese rhetoric. The increased length and specificity of the two Hiroshima proclamations and of the two Yamaguchi written pledges discussed above strongly suggest that the government's concerns and involvement escalated over time. Even success could be problematic. Japanese migrants had evolved and grown into the largest single ethnic group in the territory, increasingly prosperous and powerful, but the purpose of the program was to provide temporary labor: emigrants who stayed in Hawaii and established families and businesses were seen as an unwelcome Japanese foothold in the islands, further complicating an already tense racial environment and difficult diplomatic situation.[15]

In spite of their successes, the general reputation of Japanese overseas remained low even in Japan. An aspiring Japanese lawyer, musing on emigration in 1925 on his way to Hawaii, wrote:

> It is a pity that Japanese emigrants were not very successful in the past. Rather they have left a history of failure behind. They lacked prudence and foresight.... In the future, I would like to see emigrants of noble character who are sturdily built, strong-willed, and cultured. This may be too big an expectation, but at the least I hope we send spirited, lively people who can raise the Japanese reputation and gain the trust and respect of others.
>
> (Nakamura 1981: 77)

He proposed the establishment of a "training school for emigrants" which would provide up to a week of instruction prior to departure (ibid.: 78). Successful completion of classes in "Moral education," "Attire," and "Manners, etiquette and the proper usage of language" would be required for passports to be issued, and the classes would be taught by "some schoolteachers, ladies' association or benevolent volunteers" (ibid.). Although this proposal clearly echoes the indoctrination program that produced the documents discussed here, by 1925 the 1924 U.S. Immigration Act had closed off even *yobiyose* (family unification migration), limiting Japan to a few hundred migrants per year. Most Japanese emigrants in 1925 were going to Korea, Taiwan, and Brazil. It is emblematic of the low esteem in which Japanese elites still held their emigrants – imprudent, unprincipled, weak-willed, and unpresentable – which may have been an extension of the traditional urbanites' disdain for rural society, or a more modern class stereotype. Either way, the bad behavior of some Japanese overseas greatly overshadowed the success and integrity of the remainder of the community, in the eyes of both their sending and receiving societies.

Conclusion

The Japanese government did try to reduce the emigrant failure rate through selectivity and indoctrination. The recruitment system selected emigrants for good work habits, and the high likelihood of return and pre-departure education programs tried to promote acceptable behavior. Officials encouraged and tried to enable success by promoting savings, contract completion, and pointing out particularly common problems. They displayed concern about the frequency with which emigrants succumbed to pitfalls such as gambling and alcohol, and tried to alleviate the problems by applying every conceivable form of social pressure. They linked individual interests with family, community, nation, and even foreign employers. They used legal forms and group oaths to reinforce the rigid contractual nature of the program. They enlisted local, prefectural, and national political authority to coerce compliance. There is, however, little evidence that this education program had a significant effect separate from pre-recruitment information distribution or from the contract itself. Anyone who has traveled overseas can imagine the blur of excitement that a rural Meiji-era Japanese would experience traveling first to urban Yokohama, then to the strange but beautiful Hawaiian islands. Under those conditions, it is unlikely that the pleas of Japanese officialdom were "taken out and read occasionally" (Doi 1980: 76) or "preserved in [their] hearts day and night without forgetting" (ibid.: 82–3). However, it is worth noting that most of the extant examples of the governors' proclamations come from the collections of Hawaiian immigrants.

The Japanese government would not have undertaken the labor

emigration program if it had not offered real benefits. Public perception of the emigrants was not as positive as the Japanese government had hoped, but the program may be judged to have been more successful than not. Data from Kuga town, for example, show that the first two groups of emigrants had about an 8 percent rate of early return, and a 12 percent death rate (Kuga-gun yakusho 1889: 406). In spite of that, official evaluations of the program based on its returnees was extremely positive, mentioning particularly the high rate of remittances, the rising standard of living for returnees and the community at large, and the complete absence of "Emigrants who troubled their families by failing to communicate" (Dresner 2001: 105–6). Thousands of underemployed workers were able to take advantage of the wage gap between Japan and Hawaii; in addition to their personal enrichment, the underdeveloped rural areas from which they came were lifted from poverty (ibid.: 106–7, 129–32). On the national level, the foreign exchange brought back to Japan in the form of emigrant earnings was a small but noteworthy contribution to Japan's balance of payments (ibid.: 131).

The vast majority of Japanese who participated in this program did carry out the conditions of their contracts. Demand for Japanese labor remained strong. The Caucasian leadership of the Republic of Hawaii (1898) was concerned about the strength of the Japanese community and tried to shift to other sources of labor, mostly from China and Portugal (Conroy 1978 [1953]: 120–30). They also abrogated the labor migration treaty in the expectation that fewer Japanese would move to Hawaii. However, the number of Japanese migrating through emigration companies and independently grew dramatically until the 1908 Gentlemen's Agreement, and the economy of Hawaii absorbed the labor easily (Moriyama 1985: 52). The demand for Japanese labor was based not only on the wage differential, which narrowed after the turn of the century, but also on the effectiveness of Japanese workers. Whether its exhortations had any effect, the government program did send out thousands of earnest, hard-working, reliable, and frugal workers.

Acknowledgment

Some of the research for this chapter was supported by a Japan Foundation dissertation fellowship and by a dissertation fellowship from the Edwin O. Reischauer Institute for Japanese Studies. The University of Hawaii supported research at the Hamilton Library, University of Hawaii at Manoa. Special thanks to Tokiko Bazell and her colleagues at the East Asian and Hawaiian Collections at Hamilton Library, including the Kajiyama Collection. Unless otherwise indicated, all translations from Japanese are the work of the author.

Notes

1 The only English-language reference to this program is in Kimura (1988: 4–7, 131–2): she dismisses it as grossly inadequate to prepare emigrants. There has been more mention, if not analysis, in Japanese-language scholarship. For example, Ishikawa (1967: 31) quotes in its entirety an example of the paperwork that migrants needed to do before leaving, but says nothing about the content of the document itself. The *Hiroshima-ken Ijûshi* (History of Migration in Hiroshima Prefecture) includes a written pledge in its documents (Hiroshima Prefecture 1991: 7) and reprints a page of the original in the narrative volume (Hiroshima Prefecture 1993: 78) but reference to it in the text is very limited (ibid.: 78–9). The Hiroshima Prefecture (1980: 994, fig. 245) reprints the same written pledge with different signatories, though the headman was the same, but the text says only that recruits were carefully screened and applicants were required to submit these.
2 Japanese migration to the United States before World War II is usually divided into three "eras": (1) *kan'yaku imin* (the government-sponsored emigration period from 1885 to 1894; (2) *jiyû imin* (the free emigration period from 1894 to 1908 [also sometimes called the *imin-gaisha*, or emigration companies period]); (3) the *yobiyose imin* (the era of family unification between the Gentleman's Agreement in 1908 and the 1924 Immigration Act). Almost every scholar has some distinctive variation on this chronology, e.g., Doi (1980: 128–9); Moriyama (1985: xvii–xviii); Suzuki (1992: chs 3 and 4); Kawakami (1993: 2–8).
3 I first found the documents in Yatarô Doi's 1980 work. The Yamaguchi Rules for Migrant Laborers was originally translated as Appendix One of Dresner (2001: 157–65). It may also be found in Hiroshima Prefecture (1991: 10–16). Hara's Proclamation was reprinted from Sôga's (1953) memoir, and Doi's comments about the Proclamation are also from Sôga. The earlier Kuga pledge appears to be from Doi's family archives – his grandfather Yashirô Doi was a local notable who sometimes served as a conduit for communication and remittances (112–13), and other Doi family members also appear in his documents. Doi's unsigned document is from archived local government documents; the signed version is from Ishikawa (1967).
4 The term *kokoregaki* is also used for several other kinds of documents in the context of emigration, including guidelines for limiting recruitment and descriptive pamphlets designed to explain the program to emigrants (Kodama 1992: 107–11).
5 Various terms that can be translated as "strict" or "strictly" appear eleven times in the four documents discussed herein, including thrice in the Rules and six times in the preprinted pledge. It also appears in both the introduction and conclusion to the Hiroshima written pledge.
6 The national government began closing offices on Sunday in 1876, so it is likely that most Japanese were at least nominally familiar with the concept by 1885, though it was not widely practiced in rural communities (Ito 1973: 230–1).
7 On local versus national identification, see Gardner's discussion (2003: 81) of inter-prefectural marriages as "mixed."
8 Documents are found in Doi (1980: 83–4) and also a version of a written pledge with a signature is found in Ishikawa (1967: 31).
9 Being short and straightforward texts cloaked in ritual and obligation, I suspect, without evidence, that they probably had more effect on their signers than the longer Proclamation or the Rules of Migrant Workers.
10 The document is found in Doi (1980: 83–4).

68 *Jonathan Dresner*

11 Tomonori Ishikawa and Masa'aki Kodama are the current leading scholars, and Hiroshima Prefecture has published its own detailed history of emigration with documents.
12 Kimura has a slightly more liberal translation (1988: 4–5). Her copy came from a Honolulu-based archive, as did the copy in the Hiroshima Prefecture collection, but it is unclear if they are from the same collection.
13 It is frustratingly common that these histories note the beginning of a practice but make no mention of an end, so it is unclear whether this was a short-term or continuing process. This particular document came from the village of Jigozen in Saeki County, a high-emigration region bordering southeastern Yamaguchi.
14 Curiously, Moriyama (1985) says that the Hawaiian Bureau of Immigration tried to limit female workers (to keep the Japanese from settling) while Takaki (1989) says that they "actively promoted" female migration. Sôga (1953: 13) says that most emigrants came alone as a matter of convenience for themselves, which was also how the employers wanted it.
15 Suzuki (1992: 64) suggests that selection and encouragement of return – i.e., sojourn rather than settlement – failed, with lower rates of return as time passed. Overall, about half of the government-sponsored emigrants had returned to Japan by 1897.

Part II
Cultural identity
From the incipient diaspora to classic diaspora

4 Paradise lost
Japan's agricultural colonists in Manchukuo

Greg P. Guelcher

Although never annexed formally, the puppet state of Manchukuo (*Manshûkoku*) was often spoken of as the "jewel" of Japan's wartime empire. Established in 1932 under the auspices of Japan's Kwantung Army stationed in Manchuria, Manchukuo also attracted the attention of Japan's economic developers and soon became a vital source of the foodstuffs and raw materials needed to sustain the nation's growing war effort. To better secure Japan's hold over the territory, between 1932 and 1945 the Japanese government colonized Manchukuo with large numbers of landed emigrants from the Home Islands. Carefully planned as a national project during wartime, and justified largely on strategic grounds, the eventual settlement of some 270,000 Japanese (of an originally projected five million) still stands as the largest emigration project in modern Japanese history. It should be noted here, too, that the Japanese government also promoted Korean emigration to Manchuria during the interwar years (Korea was annexed by Japan in 1910, and remained a Japanese colony until 1945). Some 700,000 Koreans were living in Manchuria at the time of the so-called Manchurian Incident in 1931, but this number grew to over two million by 1945 (Kodansha 1993: 828, 915).

Most settlers soon discovered, with varying degrees of dismay, that the Japanese government had prepared them poorly for the realities of life in Manchuria. Fed rather hazy images of the wondrous "New Paradise" under construction in pro-emigration propaganda, many colonists departed Japan with little more than a vague expectation of instant gratification: an extensive landholding, suitable housing, generous financial aid, white rice every day, an honored position atop the rural social order. Yet rarely did Manchuria meet the colonists' heightened expectations.

Trials of the initial agricultural colonists

The pioneer group of 492 colonists, which arrived in Manchuria on October 8, 1932, proved no exception. They reached Jiamusi – the urban center nearest their settlement site – the following week and began tilling the soil. While the colonists may have initially come with an idyllic picture of what life in Manchuria would be like, they quickly found that things were hardly a paradise.

Kaneo Tômiya and Kanji Katô, the main architects of the colonization program, had deliberately misled both the Ministry of Colonial Affairs and the candidates themselves with false assurances that anti-Japanese forces in Manchuria had already been suppressed (Ishihara 1944: 216). In fact, the newly "independent" state of Manchukuo was still very much in turmoil. Official estimates conservatively placed the number of so-called bandits (anti-Japanese elements) at 360,000 in 1932 (Yamada 1962: 67), responsible for an average of four raids per day (Young 1938: 160). In such a situation of pervasive internal unrest, the military role of the colonists not surprisingly took immediate precedence over their putative agricultural tasks. That security concerns were paramount seemed confirmed by both the content of the group's pre-departure training, which emphasized spiritual exhortations, and its brevity, lasting a mere nineteen days in September (Kita 1944: 104).

Any illusions the first group of trial colonists may have harbored concerning the true nature of their mission were quickly dispelled. Marshall Nobuyoshi Mutô, Commander-in-Chief of the Kwantung Army and Japan's first ambassador to Manchukuo, himself welcomed them on October 10. He immediately cautioned the apprehensive "settlers":

> It is necessary that you prepare to farm and fight since the security situation in Manchukuo is not yet good. Always strengthen your military spirit, train yourself for battle, be well informed about the bandits surrounding you on all sides, and never let your guard down.
> (Manshû Takushoku Iinkai Jimukyoku 1938: 120–1)

Muto's warning proved well founded, for the city of Jiamusi came under attack the very evening of the group's arrival by ship.

As the officer in charge of "bandit suppression," Tômiya pressed the colonists to reinforce the unreliable Manchukuo puppet troops under his command. It proved a long and trying winter for the colonists. Japanese army units stationed in Jiamusi reportedly fought pitched battles against anti-Japanese forces "every day and every night" that winter, often entrusting the defense of the city to the newly arrived colonists (Kita 1944: 106). Freezing winter temperatures that dropped to minus thirty degrees Celsius, moreover, made the colonists anxious and bitter. Lacking proper housing, they found themselves billeted in a ramshackle storage building requisitioned from a local grain merchant (Tôa Keizai Chôsa-kyoku 1933: 8). Both their food and clothing were of such poor quality and insufficient quantity that the colonists frequently complained of being cold and hungry (ibid.: 10; Kuwajima 1992: 138).

Above all, the colonists resented having been placed under the direct authority of the Manchukuo National Army and pressed into unexpected military service. Expecting to be farmers in the wilds of Manchuria, they instead found themselves confined to a remote Japanese-held bastion until April 1933, performing the same dangerous guard duties as regular conscripts. During a three-and-a-half-month period, while regular army troops were occupied elsewhere, the trial colonists reportedly assumed sole responsibility for defending the strategic city of Jiamusi – a total of seventy-four days (Tôa Keizai Chôsa-kyoku 1933: 10). Having bowed to rising "Manchuria fever" back home, and expecting immediate and ample reward in the form of free land abroad for their "sacrifice," few colonists were prepared for the combination of bitter cold, fear, and boredom that had suddenly become an inescapable part of their lives (ibid.).

Unlike the soldiers alongside whom they fought, moreover, the trial colonists had had little time to forge a sense of loyalty or discipline within the group. Beset by unanticipated hardships, the colonists vented their growing frustrations on the local Chinese populace in petty violence and outright brutality. The first group's legacy would act like a millstone around the necks of later colonists, helping to guarantee that they would nearly always confront a wary and hostile Chinese community.

The Chinese in the Jiamusi area soon learned to hate and fear the colonists from Japan. On their first day, local military authorities had marched the new colonists in rank through the streets of Jiamusi in an effort to intimidate the locals (Tôa Keizai Chôsa-kyoku 1933: 8). This action helped insure that the local Chinese would look upon the first agricultural colonists with the same loathing usually reserved for the Kwantung Army itself. Once settled in the town, the colonists proceeded to fulfill the worst expectations of Jiamusi's Chinese residents. The colonists refused to pay for meals in restaurants. Livestock, even dogs, disappeared into the cooking pots of the Japanese. Colonists guarding the entrance to the city reportedly shook down travelers, beating to death those who resisted. One desperate Chinese family was swindled by a Japanese colonist who passed himself off as a doctor and sold ordinary tooth powder as medicine. Rapes were frequent, and the perpetrators sometimes broke into homes in broad daylight to reach their hapless victims (ibid.: 141, 143–4). Colonists even began to fight among each other, with the result that several were deported.

Life did not improve noticeably for the colonists upon reaching their settlement site at Yongfengchen, southeast of Jiamusi, the following spring. Yongfengchen, like the locations selected for the next several waves of agricultural colonists, was of interest to the Kwantung Army primarily as an area where anti-Japanese activity was exceptionally troublesome. Iyasaka Village, as the settlement became known, was located in "a region destitute of communications, and swarming with Chinese bandit and guerilla forces" (Jones 1949: 87). Equally significant, the Red Spears, which was a sort of private militia system forged along settlement lines and designed to resist outside incursions, maintained a significant presence in the area. Whereas the initial trial group survived that first venture into the Manchurian countryside, they lived in constant fear of attack. As a result, the residents of Iyasaka Village (as well as many later colonists) farmed their fields literally with gun in one hand and hoe in the other (Hinkôshô kôsho 1940: 195; Katô 1943: 38–9).[1]

The colonists' reputation for violence preceded them to their settlement site, where their reluctant Chinese neighbors perceived the Japanese as another irritating bandit group to defend against. As they had done previously when bandits were near, most of Yongfengchen's residents fled their homes ahead of the invading Japanese menace. The colonists, with the encouragement of the Kwantung Army, subsequently took over the "abandoned" farmland and homes. Yet more was needed. In a process of land acquisition that was to become all too typical, Kwantung Army troops extorted Chinese farmers under threat of violence to sell their ancestral homes and lands, and at a price far below fair market values. In the case of Iyasaka Village, for instance, the Chinese so coerced received the unreasonably low sum of five yen per family member (Kuwajima 1992: 160). When necessary, Japanese soldiers reportedly burst into the dwellings of recalcitrant landowners and forcibly seized the desired land titles (ibid.: 205). Such actions were in direct violation of an earlier agreement with local Chinese leaders in which the colonists had promised not to purchase land already under cultivation; yet nearly one-third of the land procured for the first Japanese settlement had been previously cleared and in use (Okabe 1990: 184). Such duplicity on the part of the Japanese did little to endear the colonists to their Chinese neighbors, who in their frustration vilified the government's Bureau of Land Development (*Kaitaku-kyoku*) as the "Bureau of the Unsheathed Sword" (*Kaitô-kyoku*) (Yamamuro 1993: 286). Eventually, in the spring of 1934, Chinese anger boiled over in the so-called Ilan Incident (also sometimes referred to as the Doryûzan Incident). Six to seven thousand (mostly unarmed) Chinese descended suddenly on the two existing Japanese settlements in hopes of reclaiming lost lands.

For the initial agricultural colonists, the Ilan Incident was of great personal consequence. Of the thirty-nine deaths ultimately experienced by these two groups, most were attributable to this popular revolt (Kita 1944: 450). The hostilities forced the second trial group to abandon its original settlement site permanently, and kept the better-established first group under siege for two long months. Large numbers of colonists deserted the program in the revolt's aftermath, leaving behind slightly more than half the original complement to carry on in either settlement (ibid.: 113, 139).

The Japanese government successfully censored news of the Ilan Incident back home, while strenuously denying the truth of reports appearing in foreign newspapers such as the *New York Times*. A pattern of obfuscation concerning conditions in rural Manchuria was set in motion, which over time worked to stifle public criticism of the colonization program by concealing potentially damaging information. Insufficient, slanted information rendered moot any public discussions that might have encouraged reasonable preparations to cope with the special rigors of life in Manchuria.

Conditions of settler life in Manchuria

Personal safety turned out to be only one of many difficulties facing unsuspecting newcomers to Manchuria. How to protect one's health was another. Life in Manchuria, contrary to the images of cheerful young housewives and their rosy-cheeked progeny that flooded the print media back home, could be particularly unkind to Japanese women and children.

A comprehensive 1944 study of Japanese villages in Manchuria disclosed winter temperatures that dipped as low as −32.8 to −47.3 degrees Celsius in some areas (Kita 1944: 442).[2] For the entire year, in fact, the average late-morning temperature for all colonized areas hovered around 3 degrees (ibid.: 442). It turned so cold, recalled Patriotic Youths Corps member Kôsaku Nakase, that guard duty in the settlement had to be conducted in brief, one-hour shifts. Despite that, Nakase explained, "my eyelashes still turned to ice, my nose became frostbitten, and urine ... froze immediately upon reaching the ground, where it collected like an inverted icicle" (personal interview with Kôsaku Nakase, July 12, 1991, Toyama). Water, too, commonly solidified the instant it began flowing from well pumps ("Kaitakuchi no Seikatsu Shidô" 1944: 46). Expecting the "new paradise" of their propaganda-fed dreams, at least a few naïve colonists came woefully unprepared for their initial Manchurian winter. Kenji Takizawa, a Kwantung Army soldier on leave in the northern Manchurian city of Qiqihar in January 1943, speaks of a newly arrived emigrant couple encountered during a blizzard:

> The scrawny man didn't even have a hat on and wore only a summer cloak. The woman, quite noticeably pregnant, was dressed in a thin, fluttering kimono with a summer shawl wrapped around her shoulders.
>
> (Gibney 1995: 109)

Against such bitter cold, veteran agricultural colonists sealed up their homes tightly and struggled to keep their children layered in heavy cotton outer garments copied from the Chinese.

A ruddy glow in children's cheeks sometimes signaled a fever tormenting young bodies weakened by more serious illnesses. According to the journal *Kaitaku* [Frontier], nearly half of all children surveyed at a child-care seminar in Manchukuo suffered from poor health, with rickets, beriberi, digestion problems, and skin diseases being most prevalent.

In one village alone, between 60 and 70 percent of all small children reportedly displayed signs of rickets. Health officials concluded that many Japanese children in Manchuria were simply undernourished. Most disheartening, however, were the consistently high infant-toddler mortality rates recorded by the agricultural settlements. At about double the rate of Japan proper, such dismal results mocked official claims of Manchuria's salutatory effects on child health (Takaguchi 1944: 48–50).

Reality likewise clashed with official propaganda when the same health officials surveyed the much-praised lifestyles of female colonists in Manchuria. Nobuko Yoshiya, in an influential 1944 article in a popular women's magazine, played on the vanity of her female readership when she reassured them that:

> Despite my expectations that Continental Brides would appear all covered in dirt, with their bodies darkly tanned from working morning through night [in the fields], they instead looked quite pretty with their pale skin.
>
> (Yoshiya 1940: 85)

A pale complexion, of course, had long been regarded in Japan as a hallmark of female beauty, one affected primarily by women of leisure. Japanese health experts canvassing Manchuria, in contrast, highlighted the enervating effects of *émigré* life on Japanese women. Health officials warned that many of the young mothers surveyed were plainly too worn out by the hardships of life on the Manchurian frontier to care properly for themselves, much less their children. The necessity of working in the fields from dawn until dusk afforded female colonists little time to fulfill their primary gender role as "good wives and wise mothers." So, while the male colonist refreshed himself on hot summer days with a nap lasting one or two hours "as a rule," his harried wife had to forsake such indulgences in her rush to "clean up after lunch, feed the baby, change its diaper, put the baby down for a nap, do the laundry and the sewing" and so much more. Deprived of the extended family network common to rural life back home, the young "Continental Bride" of Manchuria was denied the assistance that might normally have lessened her domestic burden: "the mother-in-law to guide her, the younger sister to help her, the niece to baby-sit or clean for her." Alone with her husband, health officials concluded only half in jest, "the woman with one, two, or three children literally needs extra bodies" (Takaguchi 1944: 50).

Elsewhere, a confidential report on a settlement named Mizuho Village flagged tuberculosis as a spreading health problem "demanding immediate attention." Health officials had recorded 263 cases of respiratory disease among the 2,703 residents of the village, but estimated the true number of cases to be much higher as many residents avoided the local clinic to save money. The report cited unspecified "housing problems" and "unsanitary conditions" as the root causes of the colonists' health problems (Hinkôshô kôsho 1940: 238–9; personal interview with Jirô Fujimori, April 5, 1995, Tokyo).[3] One can surmise that homes sealed off tightly in winter to keep out the bitter cold would quickly lead to stagnant, fetid air within. That fact, plus vitamin deficiencies brought about by a changed diet (particularly the loss for many of fish as a regular source of vitamin D), and the settlements' limited access to potable water (Takaguchi 1944: 52), likely facilitated the spread of communicative illnesses such as amebic dysentery and typhoid fever throughout the Japanese community (Sugano 1939: 39–42).

Illness and disease spread relatively unhindered in agricultural communities where clinics were under or poorly manned and medical supplies in short supply, and their remoteness made transportation of all but the basics difficult and expensive. Furthermore, the lack of commensurate rewards discouraged top-quality medical personnel from seeking employment there (Nichiman Nôsei Kenkyû-kai 1942: 12). Of those doctors intrepid enough to try their fortunes in Manchuria, the more capable ones retained the option of deserting the agricultural settlements for more lucrative employment in the cities. As a result, dissatisfaction with medical services was rife within the agricultural community. During a tour of settlements, the writer Kensaku Shimaki wrote of being deluged with complaints about elderly village doctors who could barely get around by themselves to visit sick patients. "We would give up if there wasn't any doctor at all," complained one irate Japanese colonist to Shimaki. "But we also shouldn't have to die without the doctor being there to check our pulse, should we?" (Shimaki 1940: 124–5). According to Kiyoshi Komiya's post-war memoir, it appeared to many at the time that only "the losers who couldn't otherwise hope to get a job" could be enticed to rural Manchuria (Komiya 1990: 83). Komiya went on to describe in detail his own village's alcoholic doctor, whose hands shook visibly whenever he treated patients and whose medical treatments soon became the laughingstock of the community (ibid.: 82–3).

Komiya, in retrospect, understood full well the problem of recruiting capable doctors for agricultural settlements that were located "in the middle of nowhere" (ibid.: 38). For the vast majority of agricultural settlements, geographical isolation was *the* most fundamental reality. Isolation accounted for many of the inconveniences of colonial life; ultimately, it also foretold the failure of the colonial enterprise's publicly stated goals.

The trial colonists who settled in Manchuria in 1932 and 1933 had fared comparatively well in this regard. The authorities placed the initial settlements no more than five kilometers from the nearest railroad station or river port. Year by year, as the Kwantung Army's interest in the strategic aspects of the agricultural colonization program grew, the settlements crept further and further into Manchuria's rugged north. As they did so, the distance from settlement to nearest transportation hub increased. By the ninth and tenth waves of Japanese settlement in 1940 and 1941, for instance, villages were being situated forty to fifty kilometers distant *on average*. Several exceeded 100 kilometers, with a nearly untraversable 147 kilometers reportedly separating one village from its closest railroad line (Kita 1944: 448). The train station was a full day's ride by truck, recalled Kurihara Sadako, a former Continental Bride, of her village, and "we had only the one truck" (Kurihara 1995, personal interview). As for communications, it was not unusual for a single telephone line to serve an entire rural community (Hinkôshô kôsho 1940: 197).

Isolation exacerbated pre-existing feelings of betrayal to spawn a powerful strain of homesickness, known by the newly coined term *tonkonbyô* (roughly, frontier mission illness), which sapped the will of scores of Japanese agricultural colonists. When the attentions of Katô and Tômiya later turned to the recruitment of adolescents for a Patriotic Youths Corps program, it was in part because they blamed *tonkonbyô* for the high drop-out rate among the earliest adult colonists. Katô and Tômiya reasoned that it would be easier to instill the proper spirit of sacrifice in younger, presumably more adaptable minds (Kami 1973: 84). Events soon demonstrated the extent of their miscalculation. Patriotic Youths Corps members, many barely out of childhood, proved particularly susceptible to bouts of severe homesickness.

Some youthful victims of virulent homesickness turned inward, lying around listlessly all day, suffering both loss of appetite and sleep. The worst cases among them committed suicide. Other reputedly homesick youths turned aggressive and violent, venting their frustrations on whomever or whatever was within reach. The following list of serious incidents, all recorded by Patriotic Youths Corps training centers in Manchuria within sixteen months of opening, point to the depths of this frustration and anger: twenty-one arson cases, twelve shootings, twelve major brawls, and six suicide attempts; 177 trainees reportedly went AWOL and another 137 were expelled from the program for "bad behavior" (Kami 1973: 99–100). Many "lesser" examples of delinquency, particularly the often brutal hazing of younger members by older ones, commonly went unreported.

Depression, in the final analysis, remains a difficult cost to assess precisely. Yet the positioning of agricultural settlements in the north impaired the colonization program in more readily quantifiable ways, too. Despite the incessant talk of self-sufficient farming communities as the ideal, northern Manchukuo proved particularly ill-suited to successful agriculture. In many areas, the colonists worked soil that was either too sandy or too alkaline to support most crops (Kita 1944: 445). Few Japanese settlements, therefore, could grow the white rice that so often overflowed mealtime bowls in pro-emigration propaganda. "I expected white rice," mused Sadako Kurihara, "but all I ever got was soybeans and potatoes" (personal communication with Sadako Kurihara, February 1995, Tokyo).

Kaoliang (sorghum), the staple of both the Manchurian diet and of Japanese-inspired propaganda, likewise withered in the rain-parched, frostbitten soil of the north. Most rural communities in consequence eked out a living raising oats, barley, and a little wheat (Hinkôshô kôsho 1940: 458; Irie 1941: 14).[4]

The economics of agricultural colonization

Self-sufficiency was largely precluded by the climatic and geographical peculiarities of Manchuria. For even daily necessities, the colonists had to trade outside the village, where once again isolation hindered success. Japanese villages were established at such a frantic pace, and with military necessity usually overriding all other concerns, that the infrastructure to aid their economic growth lagged woefully behind. "There still isn't a proper system to connect rural villages with [urban] markets," lamented one concerned scholar as late as 1944 (Kita 1944: 451). Many settlements balked at the expense of transporting the harvest from the settlement to the nearest train station, whether by truck or horse-drawn cart (ibid.: 449). Nor could the later settlements compete well with the earlier, better-situated ones. "The cost of shipping our soybeans and corn was too high," protested a former member of an eighth-wave settlement, "we couldn't compete with the immigrants settled [earlier] along the railway lines" (personal communication with Akira Niizu,[5] January 1995, Tokyo). Japanese farmers could barter more profitably with nearby Chinese communities or supplement their modest incomes by selling vegetables and saké to nearby Kwantung Army bases (personal communication with Aki Mugishima,[6] February, 1995, Tokyo).

Side businesses seem to have been a common, but worrisome, trend among agricultural colonists trying to compensate for economic shortfalls elsewhere. The researcher Hisao Irie questioned the place of such activities in a program premised on full-time, self-sufficient farming communities. "So long as it remains only a side business it's fine," Irie (1941: 48) wrote, "but we can't allow [the colonists] to turn their side businesses into their main business." The attentions of Japanese colonists should be redirected back to the primary goal of farming, he advised, lest they begin to leave agriculture for more lucrative occupations elsewhere.

Irie's fear that the agricultural colonists were beginning to lose sight of their assigned goal was echoed by those who decried the colonists' extensive reliance on native labor. Critics worried that the settlement program was creating a class of Japanese absentee landlords rather than the hardy, self-sufficient yeomen of wartime propaganda. In truth, the Japanese agricultural community in Manchuria depended heavily on hired native assistance. A government survey of the supposedly "self-farmed" fields of Mizuho Village in 1939, for example, discovered that the settlement's 148 Japanese households employed fully 173 Chinese on annual contract. During peak periods, such as seeding, weeding, and harvesting, many additional part-time contract employees were taken on. Worse yet, in the view of Japanese officialdom, the residents of Mizuho Village had tenanted out even more land to Chinese than they themselves still claimed to farm (1,508 versus 1,356 *chô*, respectively)[7] (Hinkôshô Kôsho 1940: 375). Mizuho Village was by no means unique. A follow-up sampling of villages from the first through sixth waves (which included those villages founded between 1932 and 1937) disclosed a tenancy rate averaging 26 percent (Kita 1944: 478), with cases of individual colonists personally working as little as one-tenth of their allotment not uncommon (Irie 1941: 65).

By 1944, an alarming trend had become apparent: the older or more established the settlement, the larger the amount of village land tenanted out to the natives (Kita 1944: 520). Ironically, in many Japanese villages the tenanted portion ultimately best met the stated goal of self-sufficiency. Provided with land, Chinese farmers drew upon their long experience of tilling the Manchurian soil to grow traditional subsistence crops. In contrast, tradition frequently worked against the Japanese newcomers, particularly with regard to their heavy reliance on labor-intensive agricultural practices. Insufficiently skilled to work their new fields properly, Japan's transplant community also frequently lacked the necessary manpower. The nuclear family units that comprised most Japanese agricultural settlements reportedly provided less than half the hands needed to manage the new, larger fields (ibid.: 478). Inherent economic inefficiencies dragged most Japanese agricultural communities into a self-defeating cycle. Overwhelmed Japanese farming families resorted to hiring native labor that added significantly to their overheads. According to various contemporary estimates, the wages paid to hired laborers accounted for anywhere between 49 and 66 percent of total village expenditures (Irie 1941: 34; Kita 1944: 479). Such unacceptable outflows, in turn, encouraged the leasing of "excess" lands to a growing number of Chinese tenants, with the inevitable result that supposedly self-sufficient Japanese farmers became increasingly alienated from the land and hence divorced from their *raison d'être*.

Tenanting out land could do little more than slow a rising tide of red ink that likely tempered the expectations of quick profits held by many colonists. "In my village," explained Akira Niizu, "we despaired of ever achieving successful self-management. Some who still had houses in Japan dropped out of the program and returned home. Those of us who were poor, though, had no choice but to stay" (personal communication with Akira Niizu, January 1995, Tokyo). Well before the war's end, in fact, cries of alarm over the agricultural settlements' deteriorating economic conditions were being raised. Highlighting the issue of hired native labor in 1941, Hisao Irie surmised that a tripling of wages since 1937 had likely erased the modest profits recorded previously by the earliest Japanese agricultural settlements. Irie further predicted that the colony's overall economic situation would likely worsen in the future as an ever-increasing number of settlements confronted not only wage–price hikes, but also the loss of tax and loan repayment deferrals accorded them during their initial five years (Irie 1941: 35–8). Itsuo Kita, after analyzing the seemingly insurmountable economic difficulties troubling Japan's later settlements, subtly called into question the depth of the government's commitment to the colonists' economic well-being. Noting both the scarcity of studies and the seeming ignorance of colonization officials, Kita worried aloud that the casual observer "might well misunderstand and conclude the authorities were trying to cover up the economic failure of Japanese farmers [in Manchuria]" (Kita 1944: 509). Research official Renjirô Iijima likewise chided the government in mid-1942 for its perceived failure to bring public expectations concerning the colonists into closer alignment with the economic realities of Manchuria. Iijima cautioned that an expanded war effort had burdened the agricultural settlements with dire shortages of nearly all vital necessities: farming tools, livestock, seeds, agricultural and animal specialists, medical doctors, and even basic manpower, especially in critical village leadership positions (Nichiman Nôsei Kenkyû-kai 1942: 8–13). In closed session he intoned: "Unless the government increases the budget or lends more money to the settlements, they won't be able to survive financially and the whole program will face imminent collapse" (ibid.: 47).

Such dire warnings, however, fell on deaf ears. A resource-starved Japanese government could do little so late in the war beyond sending the agricultural settlements an ever-dwindling supply of fresh colonists. The national emergency demanded that the colonists sacrifice their economic viability, even as it frustrated their attempts to achieve minimal self-sufficiency. Food-processing equipment and facilities, in which many settlements had invested heavily, languished as the government asserted its own pre-emptory claims over agricultural production. Even older and more established settlements faced a future of mounting debts so long as 80 percent of the soybean harvest was being diverted to government use (Nichiman Nôson Kenkyû-kai 1942: 6). Official wartime decrees banning the conversion of raw agricultural produce into finished by-products such as *miso* paste, saké soy sauce, and ketchup either forced the colonists to do without, or depleted precious cash reserves to purchase what they had once produced themselves. Similar prohibitions designed to safeguard Manchuria's resources for the war effort kept the colonists from shearing sheep for their wool, slaughtering pigs for their meat, or "diverting" milk supplies for the production of butter or cheese (Kita 1944: 544–5). To many colonists it must have seemed as though a callous government was requisitioning their crops "down to the very last bit of grain" (ibid.: 544).

The question of landownership

Promotion to the coveted status of private landowner may have compensated somewhat for the colonists' economic difficulties in Manchuria. Yet even in issues of land and landownership circumstances were not as they seemed. First, there would be no immediate pay-off for acceding to emigration – the colonists received merely the promise of land at some unspecified point in the future. The exigencies of initial settlement demanded that Japanese colonists begin farming under a system of communal management of lands and property. Agencies facilitating this settlement anticipated that most Japanese villages would likely not make the transition to individualized management for at least three to six years (Irie 1941: 26; Kita 1944: 478).[8] Even then the colonists would not receive fully twenty *chô* of land (approximately forty-nine acres), the amount most often mentioned in pro-emigration propaganda. Rather, the government intended to distribute only half that amount (for a fee) to individual families. An official "Outline of Recruitment" for certain subgroups of colonists such as the Patriotic Youths Corps, moreover, tellingly included no mention of the exact amount of land to be distributed (Amano 1940: 477–93).

Nor did the authorities guarantee colonists the freedom to manage their lands as they saw fit. Due to the strategic thrust of the colonization program, land often came with specific stipulations regarding its use. A Colonial Ministry proposal late in the war, for instance, sought to divide up the colonists' fields as follows: wheat (35 percent), soybeans (30 percent), barley (15 percent), rice (10 percent), Chinese millet (5 percent), and foxtail millet (5 percent) (Irie 1941: 26). Another program apparently required at least some agricultural colonists to devote 10 percent of their fields to the cultivation of hemp for the Japanese military, despite the obvious lack of benefit to the colonists (Nichiman Nôsei Kenkyû-kai 1942: 38).

More importantly, in light of the colonists' pre-departure expectations, they would not be receiving title to the land, but rather a carefully limited right of permanent *tenancy* (*Orient Year Book* 1942: 514). The Manchukuo government retained actual ownership. Whereas the colonists' tenancy rights were to be considered hereditary and indivisible, it was a far cry from the sort of private ownership common in Japan and aspired to by many colonists (Shimaki 1940: 308; Araragi 1994: 127; personal communication with Gensuke Matsuda,[9] 1992, Toyama; personal communication with Hoshiko Misawa,[10] 1995, Tokyo).

Social status and the agricultural colonists

At least one aspect of the emigrant experience did initially fulfill the agricultural colonists' expectations: their elevated position vis-à-vis the natives. Every Japanese expatriate, even the socially outcaste *burakumin*,[11] was entitled to the perks and privileges of membership in Manchuria's new "leading body" by mere virtue of their ethnicity. All could pride themselves on being a part of a larger Japanese colonial enterprise; at least rhetorically, all were also accorded a valued role in its advancement. Kwantung Army soldiers guaranteed Manchuria's security, for example, while Japanese civilians of all classes were lauded for their contributions to Manchuria's economic growth.

The collapse of the colonial enterprise

War's end, however, stripped the agricultural colonists of their privileged status relative not only to the Chinese but also to their fellow countrymen. Few rural colonists found inclusion in the evacuation that followed the Soviet invasion of August 9, 1945. According to all accounts, access to the evacuation trains was prioritized by an unofficial (and unyielding) social ranking: first, the Kwantung Army; second, military dependants; third, government officials and their dependants; fourth, the employees of major companies established under wartime policy and their dependants (often in order of company size and importance); fifth, other urban Japanese (Tamura 1953: 178–9). No provision was made to assist stragglers from the rural settlements, a grievous slight that bitterly confirmed their true standing within Manchuria's expatriate community.

Conclusion

Proponents of colonization, in sum, deliberately sold their countrymen a much-distorted vision of the "New Paradise." Although Manchuria's belated emergence as a wartime battlefield did afford the colonists some unanticipated benefits, such as sparing them the worst ravages of wartime rationing or attack by Allied bombers until quite late in the conflict, the promised rewards remained elusive. Lacking accurate information about Manchuria, the colonists confronted unexpected hardships for which their training, with its misplaced emphasis on spiritual exhortations, provided few answers. Long after knowledgable observers had raised serious reservations about the colonization program privately, the government continued to spin its web of illusions publicly, often sending colonists off with bland reassurances such as the following:

> Emigration to Manchukuo means a continuation of your current lifestyle; therefore, prior to leaving there's no need to prepare more than what you currently have on hand or are using now.
> (Amano 1940: 492)

Furthermore, the colonists learned to expect little if any practical assistance from the authorities.

World War II did intervene finally to bring an end to the agricultural colonization of Manchuria. Considering the difficult economic straits into which official duplicity forced many settlements from the start, it appears that the war merely accelerated the preordained collapse of a terminally ill program.

Notes

1 Kanji Katô Kanji himself admitted as much several years later. Katô, in recalling the troubles the first group of 500 self-defense colonists experienced with so-called bandits, lauded the group's perseverance against overwhelming odds "with sword in the left hand and hoe in the right" (Katô 1943: 38–9). An official report on a later settlement released in 1938 simply reversed the above order to make the same point. The Japanese, the report noted, still went to work "with a hoe in the right hand and a gun in the left" (Hinkôshô kôsho 1940: 15).
2 Summer, in turn, could become unbearably hot. One Japanese village reported a one-time high temperature of 39.7 degrees Celsius (or 103.5 degrees Fahrenheit) (Kita 1944: 442).
3 Fujimori disclosed that like so many of his fellow Patriotic Youths Corps members, he soon contracted tuberculosis while in Manchuria (Fujimori 1995).
4 Irie reported that annual rainfall in Manchuria was only about one-half to one-third as much as in Japan, with half again that amount concentrated in just two months of the year: July and August. "In Japan," Irie cautioned, "how to eliminate excess water from the vegetable fields is a problem; in Manchuria, by contrast, how to retain moisture in the fields is the problem" (Irie 1941: 14).
5 He is a former Patriotic Youths Corps member.
6 She is a former agricultural colonist.
7 A *chô* as a unit of measurement is equivalent to 2.451 acres.
8 A sizable number of Japanese settlements had therefore not yet dispensed with communal management before the war's end.
9 Former Patriotic Youths Corps member.
10 Former agricultural colonist.
11 A minority group that historically suffered discrimination on the basis of occupation and family.

5 The Intermarried issei and *mestizo* nisei in the Philippines
Reflections on the origin of Philippine Nikkeijin problems

Shun Ohno

In Baguio City on Luzon Island, the 100th Anniversary Celebration of the First Japanese Workers in the Construction of Benguet Road was held on February 20, 2003. The distinguished guests for the celebration were the Japanese and Filipino ambassadors, based in Manila and Tokyo respectively, and members of the Japanese Diet and the Philippine Congress.[1] In Davao City on Mindanao Island, the Philippine–Japan Centennial Celebration was held from August 22 to 27 in that same year. Among many events, a centennial parade attracted the biggest attention for local Filipinos. The 400 participants included both young descendants of pre-war Japanese immigrants, who wore Japanese *yukata* (casual cotton kimonos) or indigenous tribal costumes, and Davao-raised old Okinawans. They paraded with fancy *Omikoshi* (Japanese traditional portable shrines) down the main streets of the city shouting in Japanese, "*yoisah, yoisah*" (heave-ho),[2] saddening the Davao citizens lining the road who once again heard loud chants in the language of their former occupiers.

Both celebrations were initiated by local associations of Philippine Nikkeijin,[3] descendants of Japanese migrants who were born, raised, and remained in the Philippines after World War II. The Philippine Nikkeijin emphasized their Japanese ancestors' great economic contribution to the Philippines during centennial speeches and with a photo exhibition of pre-war Japanese migrants. These events taught young Filipinos and Japanese an unknown history of pre-war Japanese migrants to the Philippines and informed them about Philippine Nikkeijin issues.[4]

The Philippine Nikkeijin had to contend with many difficulties after the war. Many of their Japanese fathers had died, and all of those who survived were repatriated back to Japan and often cut off from communications with their Filipino wives and *mestizo*[5] children who had been left behind in the Philippines. It was not unusual for Nikkeijin families to be divided between the Philippines and Japan, and sometimes to be forced to live separately in the two countries after the war. Although many first-generation Japanese migrants and their children were conscripted as *gunzoku* (paramilitary personnel), and many of them died during the war, they or their families were rarely granted military pensions or survivor benefits by the Japanese government. Their cultivated land and other properties – the fruits of the issei's hard labor – were confiscated by the Philippine government or local Filipinos, and were mostly not returned to the original owners after the war.

Moreover, today many of the Nikkeijin have serious self-identity problems. Their Japanese citizenship became uncertain after the war; many lost or abandoned their identification documents amid the confusion. Many changed their Japanese names to Filipino names to conceal their Japanese ancestry, fearing revenge and other hostilities by Filipinos who had suffered Japanese soldiers' cruelties. Many Filipinos continued to hate the Japanese long after the war. Since the 1970s, after Filipinos' sentiments toward the Japanese improved, *mestizo* nisei began to come out as Nikkeijin and demanded that the Japanese government tackle their problems. These problems originated mainly from land disputes regarding property the issei administered before the war, and from their collaboration with invading Japanese forces during the war. To understand the scope of these difficulties, we must also examine the background of issei intermarriage with local Filipino women.

Issei land problems in Davao

A substantial proportion of Japanese immigration to the Philippines commenced after the United States took over the Philippine Islands from Spain in 1898. For American administrators, Manila was too hot to work, especially during the dry season. The United States colonial government decided to establish a summer capital in Baguio, located in the highlands of northern Luzon Island, and to construct the Benguet Road that would be extended to Baguio. Because of the insufficient quantity and alleged poor quality of native laborers, an American official in charge of the construction employed foreign laborers, including Japanese immigrants. Around 2,800 Japanese immigrants were engaged in the construction of the Benguet Road between 1903 and 1905 (Tôa Keizai Chôsa-kyoku 1936: 212). They were called "Benguet migrants" by the Japanese, and became the first group of issei. The completion of the road, however, made more than a thousand issei jobless. While many of them went back to Japan, a substantial number remained in the Philippines.

For jobless issei, the most attractive frontier was Davao, which faces the southeast coast of Mindanao Island. Early American settlers, mostly veterans, started *abaca* (Manila hemp) plantations in the Davao Gulf region, which has fertile soil and a typhoon-free climate.[6] The most serious problem for pioneer *abaca* planters was a severe shortage of good-quality laborers in Davao. Kyôzaburô Ohta, a Japanese merchant based in Manila, initiated the full-scale dispatch of Japanese immigrants to Davao, sending hundreds of issei there beginning in 1904. Many of them were Benguet migrants (Furukawa 1956: 120–2) who became pioneers on the plantations.

Origin of Philippine Nikkeijin problems 87

For Japanese cultivators on Davao, a big problem was the Philippines' Public Land Act of 1903, which prohibited alien individuals from acquiring public lands. However, this law allowed corporations, regardless of their owner's citizenship, to purchase or lease agricultural public lands up to 1,024 hectares (Guerrero 1967: 71). Thus, Ohta was able to found an *abaca* plantation company known as the Ohta Development Company in 1907. Ohta originally created job opportunities for Japanese immigrants through an independent cultivator system. This was a de facto tenant farming system under which Japanese cultivated land owned by agricultural companies. These tenants were required to hand over 5 to 15 percent of the harvest to the company as a "sales handling fee." This system was very suitable for Japanese immigrants with no capital because many local Filipinos and even governmental officials were willing to lease their arable land to Japanese cultivators in the names of their wives, relatives, or friends in order to collect such fees (Goodman 1967: 4). In 1914 another Japanese businessman, Yoshizô Furukawa, set up the Furukawa Plantation Company in Davao. That same year World War I broke out, leading to an *abaca* boom as demand rose for rope for naval use. Many issei with less capital also began to establish smaller *abaca* plantation corporations in Davao. Around the end of World War I, in 1918, the number of Japanese-owned plantation companies based in Davao reached sixty-five (Maeda 1941: 74).

The Philippine government, however, took countermeasures to protect the land from Japanese planters by enacting a revised public land act in 1919. The new law provided that no individual or corporation could purchase or lease land unless 61 percent of the capital stock was owned by Americans or Filipinos. Moreover, the crash of *abaca* prices that same year discouraged Japanese immigration. Japanese settlers in Davao rapidly decreased to 2,693 in 1923 from 5,533 in 1920 (Kamohara 1938: 746).

However, the remaining issei did not give up *abaca* cultivation, and sought to retain possession of arable land. In 1919 Rafael Medina, Division Chief of Forest Lands and Maps, reported to the Director of Forestry about several methods employed by Japanese settlers to keep possession of land. According to this report, Japanese settlers acquired land not only by establishing joint venture corporations in accordance with the law, but also by surreptitious methods such as subleasing lands previously leased by Filipino and American individuals and corporations. They also induced native Filipinos to apply for, or occupy, certain tracts of land with rewards and other incentives, and bought leasing rights from native Filipinos. Moreover, Medina pointed out that Japanese male settlers used intermarriage with non-Christian Filipinas as a means for gaining control of land (Manuel L. Quezon Papers 1919). At that time, the vast majority of land available for *abaca* cultivation was owned by non-Christian indigenous peoples.

Issei intermarriage in Davao and northern Luzon

As Medina points out, the rapid increase in Japanese settlers and the expansion of cultivated farmlands led inevitably to ethnic conflicts over landownership and the right of cultivation between indigenous Filipinos and Japanese settlers. The native ethnic group with whom Japanese settlers in Davao came in contact most regularly was the Bagobo,[7] because a substantial portion of ancestral Bagobo lands overlapped land cultivated by Japanese pioneers. Young Bagobo males did not hesitate to attack or ambush foreign intruders to protect their sacred lands. Their attacks were seen as justified and considered gallant within the Bagobo community. The exact number of Japanese victims is unknown. However, according to Hiroji Kamohara, a Japanese journalist based in pre-war Davao, in all about 600 Japanese settlers had been killed by "local aboriginals," mainly Bagobo (Kamohara 1938: 116, 725–7, 1235).

Some acculturated "Bagobo-ized" issei settlers mediated conflicts between their fellow settlers and local Bagobo. Enzô Yoshida, a Benguet migrant from Fukuoka Prefecture, was the most famous of these in the Davao Japanese community. According to his recollections, after running away from an *abaca* plantation because its Filipino manager overworked and underpaid him, and after threats from native Filipinos caused him to even leave his own plantation in the mountains, he chose to try to assimilate into a Bagobo community. He took on a male Bagobo appearance and worked hard, residing in their community for three years without seeing any Japanese (Furusawa 1936: 89–90; Shibata 1942a: 58–64). After he had mastered the Bagobo language and gained the goodwill of a Bagobo chieftain, he married the daughter of a *datu* (chieftain). Later, he became President of Bayabas Plantation Company, which owned around 2,000 hectares of *abaca* lands and employed around 500 Japanese and 500 Filipinos (Shibata 1942a: 59). Yoshida was able to help many Japanese settlers who had troubles with the Bagobo (Kamohara 1938: 1461–2; Shibata 1942b: 288–90; Yanami 1936: 186–7).

Not only Yoshida, but also other Japanese settlers married local women, mainly Bagoba[8] in Davao, and Igorot in northern Luzon. In Davao, many of the Japanese were Benguet migrants from the early settlement days. It has been estimated that over 200 Japanese settlers intermarried with Bagobo women in the region (Nakahara 1943: 13). In addition to the Bagobo and the Igorot, the issei also married women from other "tribes" such as the Moro, Bilaan, Mansaka, and Mandaya.[9] Some issei intermarriers even became datus in indigenous Filipino communities. Some prestigious issei married local Filipinas, mainly from Christian communities. Osao Mizobe, President of the Tibungco Lumber Company based in Davao, who was once called "king of the lumber industry in Davao," married a Visayan nurse (Kamohara 1938: 1448; Furukawa 1956: 192–4).[10]

A significant number of intermarriages between Japanese male issei and Filipino women also took place in Baguio City and the surrounding areas of Mountain Province in northern Luzon. Some Benguet migrants settled down on the outskirts of Baguio, such as in La Trinidad Valley, following completion of the road. Many of them began vegetable farming after they were leased land by local native Igorot[11] landowners, and planted Japanese vegetables such as cabbage, radishes, leeks, and carrots, which gradually became popular foods for Filipinos. The seeds of these vegetables were originally sent from Japan and planted by Benguet migrants (Kanegae 1968: 369, 690). Baguio's cool climate was comfortable for issei residents and suitable for cultivating Japanese vegetables (Irie 1938: 436–7). The issei who stayed behind in the Baguio area were mainland Japanese.

By 1940, around 500 Japanese adult males and 200 adult females were residing in Baguio City and vicinity (Hayakawa 1940: 24). In Mountain Province, sixty-four Japanese men were confirmed to have intermarried with Filipinas in 1939 (Philippines Commission of the Census 1941: 465). While the majority of issei males living in the downtown area of Baguio married Japanese women, many issei males living in rural areas intermarried with native women, the majority of whom were Igorots (Hamada 1983: 24). This was a reflection of the differences in economic status between the urban issei and the rural issei. If an issei male wished to marry a Japanese female, he was required to have enough financial capability to pay for his bride's transportation along with her belongings from Japan. This arrangement was easily afforded by many urban issei, such as store managers, but was difficult for rural issei.

Gradual Japanese penetration into Davao and northern Luzon was accompanied by intermarriage due to several factors. The first was the very unbalanced sex ratio of the Japanese population in both areas. Although the opening of Davao as an international port in 1926 triggered more female immigration from Japan, many male issei remained single given a severe shortage of Japanese female partners. According to the Japanese consulate in Davao, there were about 4,000 unmarried Japanese men in 1935 whereas there were around 3,000 married Japanese men. A substantial number of fifty- or sixty-year-old male issei were still single even after having worked for more than twenty or thirty years in the Philippines (Furusawa 1936: 77–8). Japanese journalists who visited Davao in 1935 were surprised at their fellow countrymen's severe shortage of companionship, what they described as a "wife famine" (Inobushi 1936: 305).

Many issei turned to local Filipinas as an alternative choice for wives. In Davao, the Bagobo were particularly attractive to Japanese settlers. They wore colorful jackets and skirts made of hemp, and many rings on their ears, necks, and arms. Yoshiroku Shirota, a former teacher at the Davao Japanese Elementary School, wrote that all Bagoba who married Japanese settlers were good-looking (Shirota 1985: 19). His description is supported by Keisuke Matsuo, a *mestizo* nisei of Japanese and Bagobo parentage. His father, Ichimatsu Matsuo, who emigrated from Okayama Prefecture to Davao in 1917, told Keisuke that "It was said among Davao Japanese migrants that they had better marry a Bagoba. Among Bagobo women, there are many beauties."[12]

Intermarriage in these two regions made it possible for an issei to control the arable land held in his wife's or wife's relatives names under Philippine land law that strictly prohibited individual foreigners (except Americans) to own and manage land. As Medina pointed out (Manuel L. Quezon Papers 1919), it was frequently advantageous for issei males to intermarry with Bagobo women from influential families, many of whom possessed vast tracts of land. Some Filipino scholars also believe that Japanese settlers wanted Igorot women as wives for similar reasons – to acquire land through lease or sale through intermarriage. However, it may not be true that issei intermarriages with local women were motivated only by their wish to acquire arable lands. Bagobo women, even after marriage, still continued to own land that could be administered by their landless husbands. In Bagobo communities, inheritance of property was transferred from parents to children, but not from wife to husband (Gloria 1987: 85). There is also evidence showing that some male issei married landless Filipinas. For instance, Yasutarô Takamori from Hiroshima Prefecture, who married a landless Bagoba, made his livelihood by hunting wild animals.[13] There were many cases of intermarriage by non-farming issei such as carpenters, mining workers, and engineers. In the cosmopolitan Baguio area, out-marriage by Filipino women was not at all an unusual practice. Other foreign males such as Americans, Spaniards, and Chinese also intermarried with Igorot women (Bagamaspad and Hamada-Pawid 1985: 227, 235).

Bagobo families and datu chieftains generally welcomed and encouraged their daughters' marriages with Japanese men because this could bring more wealth to the families. The Bagobo could learn more modern methods of crop cultivation from their hard-working Japanese partners, and landless Bagobo could get jobs at Japanese-managed *abaca* plantations as laborers. In Davao, Japanese settlers encouraged their Bagobo relatives or friends to gain ownership of land by applying for homesteads.[14] Many Bagobo who married Japanese were influential people in their community and had the biggest houses in their town (Gloria 1987: 85). Therefore, the Bagobo had a generally favorable attitude toward the Japanese, more so than toward Christian Filipinos.[15]

Finally, cultural similarities between the Japanese and the native Bagobo and Igorot deserve attention. The former teacher of a Japanese elementary school in Davao, Yoshiaki Yoshida (1993: 397–403), points out that the countenance of the Bagobo was similar to that of Japanese farmers living in the mountains of Japan, and the women's stature was also similar to that of Japanese women who were born during the Meiji era.

Marriage customs were also often not so different from those of the

Japanese. As a Bagobo tradition, parents or relatives of the bridegroom selected a bride, and negotiated their match with the parents or the head relative of the bride. Upon agreement, the bridegroom had to stay at the bride's residence and serve the bride's family for a certain period. After both families were convinced that a couple was getting along well, relatives of the couple and a local datu determined the value of a bridegroom's marriage gifts, which were usually at least several *agong* (Bagobo traditional large copper gongs), or sometimes horses or slaves.[16]

Undoubtedly, hundreds of Japanese–Bagobo and Japanese–Igorot intermarriages contributed to improving bilateral relations and ironing out troubles between the ethnic groups. In Davao, for example, these issei intermarriers played a significant role in attracting more Japanese immigrants to the region (Shibata 1942a: 58). By 1934 there were 13,065 Japanese residents in Davao, or 62.8 percent of all Japanese residents in the Philippines (Kamohara 1938: 747; Japan Gaimushô Ryôji Ijû-bu 1971: 166–7).[17] According to the report of then Acting Governor General George Butte, who inspected Davao in February 1932, Japanese interests controlled all timber production, 80 percent of *abaca* production, and 50 percent of copra production in Davao (Goodman 1967: 20–1). By the mid-1930s, Davao was already "one of the most important hemp-producing centers in the world," according to Joseph Hayden, Vice-Governor of the Philippines (1933–5) (1942: 718–19). In Davao, the issei could succeed in various businesses partly because of superior corporate organization and adequate capital support, and also because they used indigenous methods of accumulating land to achieve both economies of scale and a well-organized labor pool (Abinales 2000: 82). I would add that intermarriages with native women played a significant role in alleviating land conflicts between Filipinos and Japanese, and in the development of Davao into one of the most prosperous provinces in the pre-war Philippines.

Many issei in the Philippines, especially intermarriers, achieved the first stage of acculturation, or "cultural or behavioral assimilation" (Gordon 1964: 69). After they decided to become permanent residents and not sojourners, they married local women and mastered native languages. Some agreed to their Filipino bride's family's request to be baptized as Christians. Some tried to become naturalized before the war, although their applications for naturalization were all suspended by the Philippine government in Davao, perhaps because the government did not wish to cause any international problems between the United States and Japan (Furukawa 1956: 77–9). The intermarried issei were the front-runners for assimilation in their host communities, and helped to make possible the gradual Japanese penetration into many areas of the Philippines.

Ethnic attitudes and marital behavior in a plural society

After J. S. Furnivall studied the economic and social development of the Netherlands East Indies (current-day Indonesia), he labeled it "a plural society." By his definition, a plural society comprised two or more elements or social orders which co-exist "side by side, yet without mingling, in one political unit" (Furnivall 1939: 446). If we follow his view, pre-war Davao was also a plural society where indigenous non-Christian Filipinos, Christian Filipinos who migrated in from other parts of the islands, Japanese, and many other ethnic foreigners co-existed, each retaining their cultures and customs (though there was some intermarriage). The area where the Japanese were most concentrated was Davao City. The inhabitants of the city fell into three categories: Christian Filipinos (26,731), non-Christian Filipinos (6,209), and foreign residents (12,639) as of July 1937. The overwhelming majority of foreign residents were Japanese (11,487), accounting for nearly a quarter of Davao City inhabitants (Shibata 1942a: 302–4). The population of Japanese residents in the entire Davao Province (including Davao City) reached 17,888 in 1939. This figure constitutes 61.6 percent of the total Japanese population in the Philippines (Philippines Commission of the Census 1941: 428).

A self-contained Japanese community developed in Davao, containing many Japanese bazaars, schools, hospitals, Buddhist temples, and Shinto shrines. Thus, Davao came to be called "Davaokuo" in the Philippine and American media, a term coined to resemble "Manchukuo" after Manchuria became a puppet government of the Japanese Empire in 1932 (see Guelcher, Chapter 4). However, Japanese settlers in Davaokuo were not ethnically homogeneous, but were composed of two kinds of Japanese: the Okinawans and non-Okinawans (the mainland Japanese). Although about half of the Japanese in Davao were Okinawans from the late 1920s until the end of World War II,[18] the number of Okinawan intermarriages with local women was relatively small. There are several reasons for this. One was the Okinawan women's preference for marrying Okinawan emigrants to Davao, in contrast to women from the main Japanese islands. After 1920, the price of brown sugar, Okinawa's main agricultural product, declined sharply in the international market. Consequently, poorer Okinawans had to eat even the poisonous *sotetsu* (sago palm) plant due to serious poverty and hunger. The harsh Okinawan economic situation in the 1920s and the 1930s, so-called *Sotetsu Jigoku* (Sago Palm Hell), accelerated Okinawan emigration (Tomiyama 1990: 39, 76–82). The living conditions of Okinawan settlers in Davao were much better than in Okinawa. Thus, Okinawan females residing in farm villages wished to marry males who had already settled down in Davao, these marriages often being arranged by their parents (Kin-chô-shi Hensan Iinkai 1996: 129). As a result, Okinawan issei could bring their wives from Okinawa as "a summoned wife" generally without much difficulty.

Another barrier preventing Okinawans and other Japanese from intermarrying was their racial bias against native Filipinos. In the Davao Okinawan community, marrying a Filipina was not recommended because it was not so honorable for their families, and was understood to be a disadvantage for their accumulation of wealth.[19] One Okinawan issei's narrative clearly shows this: "Before my departure for Davao, I was advised by all my relatives that I should not get a Filipino wife because, once I married, almost all my savings would be spent on my Filipino wife's many relatives."[20]

The third factor in the low intermarriage rates was local Filipinos' ethnic prejudice toward Okinawans. The Okinawans were distinguishable from mainland Japanese due to their somewhat different appearance and culture. They were called *Otro Hapon* (the other Japanese) by Davao's Filipino residents.[21] The Filipinos had the impression that the Okinawans were "bearded and hairy of body," and "uneducated and coarser in language and behavior" (Cody 1959: 174). The Bagobo thought Okinawans were *matapang* (brave) and *masungit* (morose). They usually wished to intermarry with mainland Japanese rather than with Okinawans.[22] In pre-war Japan, mainland Japanese had a strong tendency to look down on or discriminate against Okinawans, partly due to the Okinawan cultural differences and lower economic status. This trend existed even in the Japanese migrant communities abroad (e.g., Peru; Ropp 2002: 279–95). In the Davao Japanese community, there was not such strong discrimination or direct insults by mainland Japanese against Okinawans because some Okinawan settlers – such as Kôzô Ohshiro, Vice-President of Ohta Development and the first President of the Davao Japanese Association – were very influential in the business and activities of Japanese associations.

Nevertheless, it is hard to deny that there was a tendency for mainland Japanese settlers to regard Okinawans as second-class Japanese citizens. Okinawa was a quasi-colony and the poorest prefecture within the Japanese nation-state before the war. The mainland Japanese recognized that Okinawan issei living standards were generally lower than their own.[23] Indeed, many Okinawan immigrants (together with Filipino workers who migrated mainly from the Visayas) worked as employees or laborers of Okinawan-managed *abaca* plantations. The behavior of Okinawan laborers, such as walking barefoot and eating food with their hands, was not so different from that of Filipino laborers.[24] The majority of pre-war overseas Okinawans were simple laborers, and in many host countries ranked socially between white colonizers and mainland Japanese immigrants and native people (Ishikawa 1987: 95–7). In this way, the Okinawans in Davao were not exceptional.

As a consequence, there were almost no marriages between Okinawans and mainland Japanese in Davao and the other areas in the Philippines.[25] Some Okinawan settlers chose native women from the Bagobo, Visayan, and Moro communities as their wives. However, fewer Okinawans intermarried than did mainland Japanese.[26] An Okinawan male marrying an Okinawan female was the norm in pre-war Davao.

The ambiguous citizenship of *mestizo* nisei

According to a census survey conducted by the Philippine government in 1939, nationwide there were 874 Filipinas who had a Japanese husband. The total number of *mestizo* children under twenty years old with Filipino mothers was 2,358. Among these *mestizo* nisei, 1,618 were reported to be "citizens of the Commonwealth of the Philippines" and 740 were reported to be "citizens of Japan" (Philippines Commission of the Census 1941: 398, 465). In Davao Province, 487 out of 754 *mestizo* children (64.6 percent) were reported to be Filipino citizens, whereas only 66 out of 189 *mestizo* children (34.9 percent) were reported to be Filipino citizens in Mountain Province (ibid.). Pre-war Philippine citizenship law and Japanese nationality law stated that children of Japanese male and Filipino female parents should be Japanese nationals as long as their parents' marriage was legal. So why were the majority of *mestizo* nisei considered to be Filipino citizens by the Philippine government?

The problem of citizenship is probably related to the land issue. In Davao, many issei intermarriers did not register their marriages at the local civil registry even after their attendance at a tribal marriage ceremony. Some scholars, such as Goodman (1967: 107) and Hayase (1984: 222), have argued that the reason for this was that Japanese husbands did not wish their Filipino official wives or common-law wives to lose their Philippine citizenship and thereby lose their rights to possess or purchase public lands. Indeed, pre-war Philippine citizenship laws stipulated that upon a Filipina's marriage to a foreigner, by virtue of the laws of her husband's country she acquired his nationality.[27] Non-registration of marriage was also attractive for Filipino wives married to Japanese who preferred not to lose Philippines citizenship, and more importantly, landownership rights. If a couple did not register their marriage, their offspring was considered an illegitimate child with Philippines citizenship. Therefore, many issei intermarriers, especially *abaca* cultivators, refrained from registering their marriages. Conversely, many issei seem to have registered their marriages in Mountain Province where the majority of the intermarried were non-farmers who did not have strong interests in holding land.

Japanese journalists (and a researcher) who visited Davao in 1935 and 1936 wrote that there were around 1,000 children of mixed Japanese and Filipino parentage in Davao (Furusawa 1936: 92; Tôa Keizai Chôsa-kyoku 1936: 219). These *mestizo* nisei comprised one-sixth or one-seventh of all children of Japanese settlers in Davao (Ôgimi 1935: 158; Tôa Keizai Chôsa-kyoku 1939: 182).[28] For the issei, education of the nisei became an important issue after they decided to stay on in the Philippines as permanent residents. The majority of issei wished to educate their children in the same manner as Japanese pupils in Japan. They had national pride, and wished to prevent nisei assimilation with Filipinos, whom the issei considered to be inferior.

Each Japanese association established and funded a Japanese elementary school in each major city after 1917. *Mestizo* nisei were also enrolled in each Japanese elementary school. In May 1935, all principals of each Japanese school gathered in Manila, and adopted *Wakon-hisai* (Japanese spirit and Philippine knowledge) as their educational principle.[29] Moreover, they decided to use mixed-blood children to foster "national virtue" and to make them superior to the Filipinos (Ôgimi 1935: 210–11). In accordance with this policy, Japanese teachers made efforts to educate all nisei – including *mestizos* – to be leaders in future Philippine society.

As of June 1939, a total of 1,899 pupils were studying at twelve Japanese elementary schools in Davao. Among them, 208 pupils were *mestizo* (Hattori 1939: 26). Unlike American nisei who studied at private Japanese schools for only a few hours after their schooling at American public schools, Philippine nisei pupils studied at Japanese elementary schools full-time every weekday, and did not go to Filipino schools at all. At Baguio Japanese Elementary School, the majority of pupils were *mestizo* nisei since the school opened in 1925 (Kojima 1996: 85). It was quite difficult for many *mestizo* nisei to study at Japanese schools initially due to their Japanese language deficiency, having grown up with Japanese-Filipino mixed cultures and languages. Japanese teachers prohibited *mestizo* pupils from speaking Filipino languages at school. The students had been inculcated with *Yamato-damashii* (the Japanese spirit) by studying the same subjects as those taught at schools in Japan, and reciting *Kyôiku-chokugo* (the Imperial rescript on education) frequently.

However, the "Japanization" of *mestizo* nisei was problematic. Takeo Nakamura, one of the Japanese consulate staff in Davao, claimed that "those who got Japanese nationality formally are few" (Nakamura 1939: 7). He made this passing comment in a Japanese magazine in 1939, and was of much consequence to *mestizo* nisei because they had been educated as subjects of Imperial Japan even without "formal Japanese nationality." Why did Japanese schools approve the enrolling of many such children? This was explained by Ryôzô Hattori, then principal of Davao Japanese Elementary School, in a Japanese magazine. Hattori stated that *mestizo* children were "treasures of Japanese pioneers who advanced into savage lands at the risk of their lives, fought febrile diseases, and cultivated in the front line with an indomitable spirit, living together with savage tribes" (Hattori 1939: 26).

Although Nakamura did not explain the background of their nationality problem, it probably originated from issei intermarriers' neglecting to register the birth of their *mestizo* children at the Japanese consular office. Intermarried issei probably feared that their children would lose their rights to gain Filipino citizenship and inherit their mothers' land if they were to register their children's birth at any government office. When U.S.–Japan relations worsened after the Manchurian Incident in 1931, and the Japanese forces advanced into northern French Indochina in 1938, the Philippine government ordered all foreign residents to register at local immigration offices. In June and July 1941, all Japanese residents, including *mestizo* children, were registered and given alien certificates by the Philippine government. Nevertheless, many *mestizo* nisei did not yet formally hold Japanese nationality because illegitimate children were usually not entered on their fathers' family register, which was kept at the local municipality office in Japan. This was a major cause of problems between Filipinos and Nikkeijin.

Consequences of collaboration with the Japanese forces

Manila was occupied by the Japanese military between January 1942 and February 1945. At that time, almost all issei and mature nisei were mobilized as soldiers. Immediately after their occupation, the Japanese military administration ordered all Japanese civilian residents to collaborate fully. Davao was used as a food supply base for Japanese soldiers due to the presence of the large number of Japanese civilian residents. A Japanese military detachment ordered Japanese *abaca* planters to convert their improved lands into crop farms, and engage in constructing airfields and other military installations. Consequently, the *abaca* industry in Davao had been almost devastated by 1944 (Furukawa 1956: 335).

The nisei's relationships with local Filipino communities were also significantly affected. For example, most *mestizo* nisei who had studied at Filipino schools were transferred to Japanese schools because they were considered to be subjects of Imperial Japan. It was expected that they would later join the Japanese military.

Many issei intermarriers were conscripted to help pacify local Filipinos due to their strong community connections. Many nisei were also conscripted as telephone operators, cooks, housekeepers, and so forth. Bilingual *mestizos* who could speak Japanese and native languages became useful interpreters and some of them were ordered to work as interpreters for the Japanese military police. *Mestizo* nisei had to demonstrate their loyalty to the Emperor by their collaboration. However, the Filipinos hated the military police because they arrested so many suspected of being anti-Japanese, and tortured or executed them without trial. As a result, *mestizo* nisei collaborators were also hated, and one of them was executed by the Manila Tribunal after the war.[30] Some *mestizo* nisei collaborators were executed by anti-Japanese guerrillas, whereas others were tortured and even executed by the military police when suspected of spying for guerrillas.[31]

Davaokuo ended with the conclusion of the war. Thousands of Japanese civilian residents, many of whom had been conscripted into the Japanese forces, died during World War II. Other surviving issei and nisei raised by two Japanese parents were repatriated back to Japan. However, the United States occupation forces did not have a firm policy on repatriation of issei's Filipino wives and their *mestizo* children. They let them choose between remaining in the Philippines and going to Japan. Some Filipino wives went to Japan with their children due to concerns for their children's safety and education, and to avoid Filipino racial hostility against the Japanese. However, the majority of Filipino wives chose to stay in the Philippines because many of them had already lost Japanese husbands by the end of the war, and wished for their relatives' assistance in taking care of themselves and their children. Even Filipino wives whose husbands survived the war were generally reluctant to go to Japan, an unknown country for them and thought to be too cold for them to live in winter. They thought their hometown was a better place to bring up their children.

In Davao, some *mestizo* nisei who fought as soldiers for the Japanese forces hid in the mountains or on isolated islands after the war, fearing revenge by Filipino guerrillas. There was no information in these areas about the Allied Forces' repatriation program. As a consequence, the majority of *mestizo* nisei and an estimated twelve orphans of Japanese parentage remained in the Philippines (around 3,000 in total) after the war[32] and had to contend with local Filipinos' harassment and discrimination. To conceal their Japanese ancestry, many changed their Japanese last names to Filipino names, and abandoned any documentation that could prove their ancestry. As a result, until recently, the Japanese government denied them status as either Nikkei or Japanese nationals.

Mestizo nisei and war orphans of Japanese parents have organized associations in Iloilo, Baguio, Davao, and other major cities in the Philippines since the 1970s.[33] They came to be known as "Nikkeijin" by Japanese visitors and residents, and have called themselves so since the 1980s. Their associations were united into The Federation of Nikkeijin-kai Philippines in 1992. The federation claims that there are now over 20,000 Nikkeijin in the Philippines and has recently argued that the remaining *mestizo* nisei and Japanese war orphans are "displaced Japanese," and have submitted requests to the Japanese government for such things as payment of pensions for nisei veterans and bereaved families, the right to search for their Japanese relatives, and the granting of Japanese nationality to Nikkeijin applicants. Today, *shû seki* (the entering of one's name on the Japanese father's registry, or the creation of one's own name through legal proceedings) is a popular movement among aged *mestizo* nisei and Japanese war orphans who wish to gain or regain Japanese nationality. These movements have occurred in parallel with massive emigration of sansei and yonsei to Japan as unskilled laborers since the early 1990s. Currently, the main mission of the Philippine Nikkeijin associations is to locate the family registries of their members' Japanese ancestors, making it possible for young Nikkeijin to work in Japan and earn enough money to take care of even their Nikkeijin parents who suffered from poverty for so long after the war.

Conclusion

During World War II, the Allies and the Japanese fought fierce battles throughout the Philippines. As a result, the Philippines suffered some of the greatest economic and social losses of any country in Southeast Asia. The number of Filipino war dead was 1,111,938 (*Manila Times* 1951, cited in Zaide 1957: 369), whereas the number of Japanese war dead in the Philippines was about 518,000 (Ohno 2000: 68). It was natural for Filipinos to consider the Japanese as invaders and destroyers after the war. Issei collaboration, willing or unwilling, with the Japanese military undid many years of effort to develop good Japanese–Philippine relations. The *mestizo* nisei who have remained in the Philippines have taken the brunt of the blame for atrocities against Filipino guerrillas or innocent civilians by the Japanese military.

Since the war, Filipino war trauma has gradually healed, and their perception of Japan and the Japanese has changed dramatically since Japan's economic development. Japan provides the most economic assistance to the Philippines of any country in the world. The conditions of *mestizo* nisei have also vastly improved. Thus, Philippine Nikkeijin now proudly proclaim their Japanese ancestors' great contributions to this neighboring nation as shown on occasions such as the centennial celebration mentioned above. On the other hand, they are pursuing redress – demanding compensation for their confiscated properties, and being recognized as descendants of Japanese by the Japanese government. These identity politics have no doubt been influenced by actions of other overseas Japanese remaining in Asia (such as the Japanese orphans left behind in China). However, attempts to "regain" Japanese nationality are rare, since it means abandoning their Filipino citizenship.

Many *mestizo* nisei have unforgettable, bitter memories of their ethnic segregation. They failed to assimilate with local Filipino communities and behaved as Japanese citizens during the war. Today, aged *mestizo* nisei wonder if they should seek to acquire Japanese citizenship and give their children and grandchildren Nikkei status – a qualification to work in Japan regardless of whether they have Japanese nationality. On the other hand, they expect their descendants to be a successful "model minority" in Philippine society in the near future, like other Nikkei (such as Japanese Americans). Their choice will be subject to economic and social conditions in both Japan and the Philippines – the country to which they once belonged and the country where they will remain until the end of their lives.

Notes

1 The 100th anniversary celebration of the entry of Japanese Benguet migrants was reported in many Philippine national and local newspapers such as *The Philippine Star* (February 21, 2003), the *Baguio Midland Courier* (February 23, 2003), and the *Skyland News* (February 23 to March 1, 2003). The most influential nationwide newspaper, *Philippine Daily Inquirer*, also carried an article, which commemorated the contribution of Japanese workers in the construction of Benguet Road (March 12, 2003).
2 The centennial celebration of the arrival of the first Japanese immigrants in Davao was reported on the front pages of many local newspapers such as the *Mindanao Times* (August 25, 2003), the *Mindanao Daily Mirror* (August 26, 2003), and the *Sun Star Davao* (August 26, 2003). The *Mindanao Times* and the *Sun Star Davao* published Japanese centennial editions on August 17, 2003 and August 25, 2003, respectively.
3 I use the term "Nikkeijin" instead of Nikkei in this chapter because Japanese descendants in the Philippines call themselves "Nikkeijin." *Jin* means *people* in Japanese. The term "Nikkeijin" came to be commonly used in Nikkei communities in the Philippines after Japanese visitors and residents introduced this term in the 1970s.
4 Davao centennial events were reported in various Japanese mass media. The nationwide TV broadcasting system, NHK, reported the Davao events and the Philippine Nikkeijin's hard life histories in its nightly news program on August 29, 2003. Japanese nationwide newspapers such as *Asahi Shimbun* (August 27, 2003) and *Mainichi Shimbun* (September 2, 2003) also reported the events and the Philippine Nikkeijin problems in Davao.
5 Paul Spickard (1989: 20) defines "intermarried" and "intermarriers" as people who have married others not of their own ethnic group. The terms "*mestizo*" and "*mestiza*" are Spanish words. During the Spanish colonial period, these terms were introduced to the Philippines by the Spaniards, and have been commonly applied to people of native-foreign parentage. I use the term "*mestizo* nisei" in order to distinguish them from other Japanese nisei that are composed of mainland Japanese nisei and Okinawan nisei. The overwhelming majority of the nikkei in the Philippines are *mestizos* or *mestizas*.
6 Hemp's hard fiber (which does not absorb water) was the best material for vessel ropes before the end of World War II. In the Philippines, it began to be produced for export to the United States after 1820 when American naval officers took back a sample to the United States. After that the United States became the principal importer of Philippine *abaca*, which came to be known to the world as "Manila hemp" (Furukawa 1956: 483–7; Constantino 1975: 117–18).
7 *Population of the Philippine Islands in 1916* reported that the number of Bagobo was only 9,350 (Beyer 1917: 38). The Philippine government in 1997 estimated that the number of Bagobo was 231,351 in Davao City and 60,236 in the southern neighboring province, Davao der Sur. A survey conducted in 1986 revealed that there were about seventy-three cultural minority groups with a total population of over 5.7 million on Davao whereas there were eight major groups in the Philippines in general (Luna 1990: 192–7). Mamitua Saber, a Filipino sociologist, classified the Filipinos into three groups, namely the Christian Majority, the Muslim Minority, and the Isolated Tribal (Pagan or Animistic) Minority (Saber 1975: 22–3). The majority of Filipino women who intermarried with issei males belonged to the third group.
8 A Bagobo female is called Bagoba just as a Filipino female is called Filipina.
9 The term "tribe" was frequently used for non-Christian ethnic groups during

100 *Shun Ohno*

the American colonial period. Recently, that changed, and those groups are referred to as "cultural minorities" or "cultural communities" by the Philippine government. "Moro" was the derogatory name for all Muslim ethnic groups by Spanish colonizers. During the American colonization period, Muslim Filipinos were still called Moro by Americans and Christian Filipinos. In recent years, Muslim Filipinos began to call themselves Moro in order to unite all Muslim Filipinos against Christian Filipinos.

10 The Visayas is a vast area in the central part of the Philippines. The native people or the native language of the Visayas is called Visayan.
11 The term "Igorot" has often been used to designate the majority of non-Christian inhabitants of northern Luzon. Otley Beyer, an American anthropologist, estimated that the number of the Igorots was 61,308 as of 1916 (Beyer 1917: 19–24; Beyer 1921: 933).
12 Interview with Keisuke Matsuo in Okayama City on January 24, 2003.
13 Interview with Yoshitaka Ute, the second son of Yasutarô Takamori, in Davao City on August 21, 2003.
14 Yoshiroku Shirota mentioned in his book one Japanese settler who married a granddaughter of a Bagobo datu and acquired 24 hectares of homestead land in his wife's name. Homesteading was one method used by Filipinos and Americans to acquire public land for cultivation (Umehara 1976: 63–4; Shirota 1985: 150).
15 When an influential Bagobo datu was interviewed by a Filipino legal advisor for Japanese cultivators, he said: "The Japanese are all good. We like them very much" and "If we lease to [Christian] Filipinos, we would be deprived of our land" (Shibata 1942a: 284–5).
16 Marriage gifts are called dowry by the Clata Bagobo, one of the subgroups of the Bagobo. In their communities, slavery was common before World War II. Keisuke Matuo's father gave two slaves as a dowry when he married a Clata Bagoba (interview with Ceaser Matsuo, a nisei of Japanese and Bagobo parentage, in Davao City on September 24, 2002).
17 According to a Japanese government survey of 1934, there were 20,834 Japanese residents in the Philippines and Guam (Japan Gaimushô Ryôji Ijû-bu 1971: 166–7). In the same year, the number of Japanese residents in Guam was recorded as only forty-three (United States Governor of Guam 1934).
18 In the Japanese community of Davao, Okinawans constituted 52 percent in 1928, 49 percent in 1936, and 53 percent by 1943 (Kamohara 1938: 179; *Manila Shimbun*: January 23, 1943).
19 *Ryûkyû Shinpô*, the Okinawan local daily newspaper, reported on January 10, 1912 that Japanese who intermarried with Bagobo women were "oddball fellows." This view seems to be a reflection of Okinawans' racial prejudice against indigenous cultural minorities in the Philippines.
20 Interview with Kin'ei Ikehara, an Okinawan issei returnee, in Kin-cho of Okinawa Prefecture on October 18, 2001.
21 In many host countries and colonial territories, Okinawan immigrants were distinguished from mainland Japanese by native people. For example, they were called *Japan pake* in Hawaii, and *Japan kanaka* in Micronesia (Arakaki 2002: 300).
22 Interview with Santos Idal, a Bagobo male, aged 69, in Davao City on September 24, 2002.
23 Interview with Tatsuo Uchida, a mainland Japanese nisei, aged 74, in Davao City on August 29, 2002.
24 Interview with Yasuto Namisato, a male Okinawan nisei, in Naha City on October 15, 2001.
25 Toyoko Arasato, a female Okinawan nisei born in Davao in 1928 states, "the

Origin of Philippine Nikkeijin problems 101

Okinawans drew the line between themselves and the mainland Japanese, and the relationship between the two groups did not go well" (interview with Arasato in Davao City on August 26, 2002).

26 This view was shared by all fourteen Okinawan Davao issei and nisei returnees whom I interviewed in Okinawa in October 2002. This view differs from some scholars' views on Japanese intermarriages in pre-war Davao. Cecil Cody, Josefa Saniel, and Shinzo Hayase indicate that intermarriages between Okinawans and Bagobo were common (Cody 1959: 184; Saniel 1966: 118; Hayase 1984: 221).

27 A Filipino woman did not ipso facto lose her Philippine citizenship or nationality merely by intermarrying. Under U.S. law a foreign woman married to an American citizen did not ipso facto acquire American citizenship (Aruego 1954: 472–3). Japan's old nationality law (1899–1950) states that a foreign wife gains Japanese nationality after she marries a Japanese male. Thus, a Filipina who legally married a Japanese male should acquire Japanese nationality.

28 The number of *mestizo* nisei residing in Davao seems to have been around 1,000 before and during the war. According to a survey of the Philippine Nikkeijin Kai (PNJK) based in Davao City, the number of nisei who are registered as PNJK members (including the number of dead) was 927 as of June 2003.

29 In pre-war Japan, *Wakon-yôsai* was an educational principle at schools, which encouraged Japanese children to study Western knowledge and nurse Japanese spirit. *Wakon* means the Japanese spirit, and *yôsai* means Western knowledge in Japanese. *Wakon-hisai* is a term copied from *Wakon-yôsai*. In Japanese, *hi* means the Philippines and *sai* means knowledge.

30 Takuma Higashiji, a nisei of Japanese and Igorot parentage and an interpreter for the Kempeitai, was hung as a war criminal along with Tomoyuki Yamashita (commander of Japan's 14th Army) and Sei'ichi Ohta (commander of the Kempeitai in the Philippines) on February 23, 1946. At that time, Philippine newspapers reported that Higashiji was a "civilian interpreter" but did not mention his ethnic background (*Manila Chronicle* 1946: February 24).

31 Carlos Teraoka, a *mestizo* nisei of Japanese and Filipino parentage, lost his two elder brothers who had been conscripted in Baguio during the Japanese occupation. His eldest brother was executed by the military police after he was suspected of spying. The other brother was killed by Filipino guerrillas (interview with Teraoka in the province of Pangasinan on July 8, 1995).

32 According to the survey of Japan's Ministry of Foreign Affairs of 1995 on "Firipin Zanryû Nipponjin" [Japanese Left Behind in the Philippines], 1,748 nisei were alive and 377 nisei were already dead in the Philippines as of 1995. Among the 2,125 remaining nisei, there were only twelve "pure" Japanese nisei (so-called Japanese war orphans), and the other nisei were all Japanese *mestizos* (Firipin Zanryû Nipponjin Tokubetsu Chôsa Iinkai 1995: 3).

33 The first Philippine Nikkeijin association – the Japanese Orphans Organization of Iloilo City – was organized by *mestizo* nisei and Japanese war orphans in 1973. A bigger association, the Japanese Filipino Association of Northern Luzon (currently the Japanese Filipino Foundation of Northern Luzon), was organized in Baguio City in 1974. The other large association, the Philippine Nikkei-Jin Kai, was organized in Davao City in 1980 (Ohno 1991).

6 Constructing Japanese Brazilian identity

From agrarian migrants to urban white-collar workers

Nobuko Adachi

How did the social and economic conditions of the early Japanese migrants to Brazil determine their geographic location? And how has the location of these settlements affected the ideology and personal identity of today's Japanese Brazilian community? The answers to these questions guide us to a fuller understanding of the complexities of today's multifaceted and dynamic Japanese Brazilian community.

Currently, more than a million and a half people of Japanese descent live in Brazil, the largest congregation of Japanese living outside of Japan. Their ancestors first arrived in 1908 when contract workers came to fill coffee plantation labor shortages. By 1941, when the breakout of World War II strained relations between Japan and Brazil, causing all immigration to cease, some 180,000 Japanese[1] resided in the country (Lesser 1999; 91: 6; Lone 2001: 71, 101).

In the pre-war period, two forms of Japanese emigration to Brazil took place: an influx of migratory coffee plantation laborers who planned to work in Brazil for only a short period purely for economic purposes, and those who migrated to establish farm villages under the auspices of Japanese government sponsorship. Although these Japanese immigrated in the same short period of time, from the same Japanese geographic areas and social classes, to the same Brazilian region – the states of São Paulo and Paraná still today having the largest Japanese Brazilian concentration – their differences in motivation for emigrating to Brazil have influenced the character of Japanese Brazilian communities found today.

Although the differences in distribution and settlement patterns are quite varied, they have been closely associated and influence each other through interwoven social and economic structures (see Fujimura 1970). The founders of these Japanese communities have formed narratives to establish their identities and to provide explanations for their presence and geographic distribution in Brazil.

While the populations of Japanese migrant communities in Brazil were closely integrated before World War II began, after the war they split over differing beliefs about the war's outcome. As the majority of Japanese migrants and their nisei children did not understand Portuguese well enough to follow world events in the news, the result was actually ambiguous. Some settlers accepted Japan's defeat gracefully, realizing that their futures – and loyalty – now lie in Brazil. Others could not believe Japan had lost. These immigrants still longed for their ancestral homeland and regarded anyone who believed the news of Japan's defeat to be a traitor. For many of these "non-believers," this was reason enough for violence; they often attacked Japanese Brazilians who had resigned themselves to the war's outcome, and numerous people were killed in bombings or riots.

Such actions – and the way many Japanese Brazilians remained in denial about Japan's defeat – caused later generations of Japanese Brazilians to feel shame, not only due to their rural upbringing and lack of Portuguese fluency, but also because of their parents' and grandparents' ignorance. In an effort to leave these old ways behind and a desire to enter mainstream Brazilian society, many young people left their Japanese communities to seek higher education in the cities. Once they began associating with non-Japanese Brazilian elites at the universities, many came to view physical labor, including farm work, as belonging to the lower classes – a notion brought over from Europe by the Portuguese aristocracy (Maeyama 1981). In addition, as there were more job opportunities for college graduates in cities than on the farms, they often chose to stay in the cities after graduation. Consequently, today urban Japanese Brazilians and rural Japanese Brazilians have developed different views of Brazilian society, images of Japan, and notions of what it means to "be" Japanese in Brazil.

To comprehend more fully how these two very different views evolved requires a context and I begin by reviewing the history of the Japanese in Brazil, and locating them in the political, social, and economic structure of Brazilian society. I then look at the formation of three different types of Japanese immigrant settlements. Each type of Japanese community reflects different aspects of experiences in Brazil, and I explore ethnographically how each lifestyle developed in particular social and physical environments. I then investigate how Japanese Brazilian society changed following the ideological confrontations concerning Japan's defeat in World War II, and explore how this conflict contributed to the social and political marginalization of Japanese in Brazilian society. I argue that race and ethnicity have influenced how Japanese Brazilians spatially constructed their communities, and have determined their ability or desire to assimilate and acculturate into mainstream Brazilian society. However, the evolution of what it means to be Japanese Brazilian today has been a long journey, and the Japanese Brazilian sense of self is complex, versatile, and many-sided. Japanese Brazilian personal identity and Japanese Brazilian group identity are not always synonymous, and it is the dynamic interplay between the two that gives this particular diasporic community its unique character.

Life on the coffee plantations

The majority of Japanese migrant workers came to Brazil, sight unseen, as contract workers. They signed their contracts through *imin-gaisha* (emigration agencies) in Japan, which often actively recruited workers in prefectures that were suffering from poor economies. Once they arrived in Brazil, however, it did not take them long to realize that making any real money would be difficult. Since 1900, plantation owners had faced economic calamity due to over-production of coffee beans, and had been reluctant to replace their old trees with expensive (young and initially unyielding) new ones. Japanese, therefore, harvested from old trees that produced significantly fewer coffee beans than they were promised in Japan. *Fazendeiros* (plantation owners) also tried to weather the depression by saving money on labor costs wherever they could. For example, they paid wages to farm-hands in the form of credits to plantation general stores, which meant that workers had to buy their necessities at highly inflated prices, reducing their effective purchasing power (Handa 1970: 58).

Since coffee had become almost 60 percent of Brazil's national income by 1880 (Graham 1993: 115), the coffee crisis was extremely serious for the national economy. The Brazilian government tried to help the fazendeiros by recruiting cheap labor from overseas, even changing the immigration law of 1889 that prohibited Asians and Africans to immigrate to Brazil. Previously only European workers had been invited. However, after finding out how bad the physical conditions were on the plantations and how hard the work was, European workers often ran away, seeking protection from their consulates to let them break their contracts (Imin 80-nen-shi Hensan Iinkai 1991: 33).

Instead of risking a diplomatic rift with European nations over the issue of contract labor, Brazil opened its doors to Asians. Fazendeiros requested Japanese to come with at least three family members.[2] Tomô Handa, who migrated to a coffee plantation in 1917 with his parents at the age of eleven, recalled those days and told that escaping from a plantation with all the family members at once was harder than for a single man alone who could fade away in the middle of the night (Handa 1970; personal communication, 1992).

Simply put, life for the early Japanese immigrants was difficult at best. Japanese immigrants faced not only economic hardships, but also social and cultural tensions in their daily lives on the plantation. Since the first European arrival in 1500, only slaves had done physical labor in Brazil, and slavery had only been abolished twenty years prior to the arrival of the first Japanese. Elite Brazilian attitudes toward plantation laborers had not yet evolved to seeing workers as modern, capital wage laborers rather than as slaves. Work conditions for the Japanese migrant workers were hardly different from those of the slaves, and both former slaves and migrant farm-hands worked side-by-side, living in the very same simple primitive quarters, and sharing outside kitchens and bathrooms with each other. There were schools on the *fazendas* (large plantations) that all the children of plantation workers attended, but Japanese parents worried that their children were only associating with children of former slaves, whom they saw as socially and culturally inferior. Food and fauna was strange, and Japanese immigrants were discouraged from practicing their native religions, Buddhism and Shinto. In addition, the heavy demands of farm labor soon became intolerable, physically and psychologically, for many Japanese plantation farm-hands (Imin 80-nen-shi Hensan Iinkai 1991: 33).

Discovering that making money within a short period was almost impossible, many Japanese workers decided to stay in Brazil longer than they had originally planned. They also, however, wished to be free from the slave-like conditions on the plantations. Consequently, the migrants' immediate goal became to leave the plantations for places where they could farm with their own people. Immigrants who had family members with them in Brazil made such decisions sooner than those who had left their families back in Japan (Handa 1970: 216–17).

The social structure and geography of three types of Japanese Brazilian communities

When the Japanese first began immigrating to Brazil in 1908, most settled in the farming states of São Paulo and Paraná. At least three types of Japanese communities may be identified there. After finishing their contracts as coffee plantation workers, some Japanese left the plantations individually to rent or own fields near concentrations of other Japanese. I will call this first settlement pattern a "Japanese neighborhood." Others followed a charismatic personality who led people – often based on some philosophy or ideology – to start a new life in a new location. I will call this pattern a "leader-based district." Third, some Japanese immigrants moved into settlements built or established by Japanese governmental or quasi-private agencies. I will call these communities "sponsored districts."

The Sankaku Minasu neighborhood

By the end of the 1910s fazendeiros who were not able to hold on to their plantations any longer started renting or selling off their land piece by piece. As soon as they had finished their contracts and paid off their debts to their employers, Japanese workers rented small plots of land[3] or pooled their money together with relatives, people from the same Japanese prefecture, or with people who came over on the same ship, and purchased small plots of farmland. Since Japanese migrants often moved in where other Japanese already were, in some areas the Japanese population grew rapidly.

One such area was the Sankaku Minasu neighborhood. After a few Japanese families migrated to Conquesta City (located near the Rio Grande River in Minas Gerais) in 1916, many other Japanese families followed. This area spread out toward the cities of Igarapava and Uberaba, with over 400 Japanese families living there by 1919. Since these three cities – Conquesta, Igarapava, and Uberaba – formed a triangle, this Japanese neighborhood was called Sankaku Minasu (The Triangle Cities of the Minas State) by the immigrants.[4]

Handa (1970: 222) explains that part of this rapid growth was due to the natural environment. Since the area of the Sankaku Minasu was not fit for coffee trees, Brazilian landlords happily leased out large tracts of mostly unused land to the Japanese settlers; this area was perfect for wet, Japanese-style, rice cultivation. The majority of Japanese immigrants had not previously been familiar with coffee trees before arriving in Brazil anyway, but their families had been rice farmers for generations. Many either rented farmlands from fazendeiros, subleased fields from other Japanese, or worked directly for Japanese who had already rented farm fields. By renting land from Japanese, these subleasers could avoid legal paperwork and negotiating in Portuguese.

Among Japanese who rented land directly from Brazilians, some chose to be *parceiros* (tenant farmers), who paid 25 percent of their total harvest to their landlords. Others chose to be *empreteiros*, who simply paid a fixed rental fee. The parceiros opened up forests for their farm fields, built their living quarters in the area, and bought their own crop seeds. Empreteiros, however, had their fields and housing provided for them by fazendeiros. Thus, although it was harder for Japanese to be parceiros, without knowing Portuguese in an unfamiliar country, the relationship between landlord and parceiro was more equitable than that with the empreteiros. Both parceiro farmers and landlords shared the same goal of having a good harvest, and the local Brazilians were business partners with the Japanese rather than with their supervisors.

Immigrants in the Japanese neighborhoods had fled from the oppressive plantation environment. Although such people were hesitant about dealing with Portuguese speakers, they did not intentionally segregate themselves from local people. They formed Japanese ethnic neighborhood communities for the sake of economic, social, and psychological security, but they located themselves in mainstream activities in Brazilian society.

Another distinctive feature of Sankaku Minasu was that the majority of these settlers continued to be tenant farmers even after they made enough money to afford their own small plots. According to Handa (1970: 214–24) the Japanese in the Sankaku Minasu were homesick for their homeland, and they were reluctant to buy land in the host nation. To do so would be a public admission that Brazil was no longer a workplace, but a new second home. Raising rice – which was the quintessential symbol of

Japanese culture (Ohnuki-Tierney 1993) – reminded them constantly of home. Many of them probably could not – or would not – commit themselves to seeing Brazil as their future.

This, as we will see later, has important implications in the debate over Japan's defeat in World War II. To admit that Japan lost the war was also an admission that their imagined homeland was no longer there for them. Their manipulation of what "home" is, is what gave them their sense of what it meant to be Japanese. Unlike people of the leader-based districts and sponsored districts (which I discuss below), people of Sankaku Minasu, then, longed for their home in Japan. They felt they were in Brazil only temporarily – however long that might be – and were waiting for the day when they would return home.

Thus, the residents of Sankaku Minasu did many things to maintain their ties to their homeland. For instance, when family members died in Brazil[5] they made *ihai* (Buddhist mortuary memorial tablets) as portable graves so that the survivors could relocate without feeling they were leaving behind the souls of their departed ancestors (see Maeyama 1997: 143, 145). They founded Japanese schools for their children and initiated the Nihonjin-kai (Japanese Community Organization). The Nihonjin-kai organized celebrations for the Japanese Emperor's birthday and New Year's festivities in the Japanese school yards. While the Sankaku Minasu neighborhood grew rapidly prior to World War II, the Japanese gradually vanished from the vicinity after the war. The post-war economic depression in Brazil forced many to sell their farmlands, and tenant farmers were forced to move on.

The Hirano leader-based district

Some Japanese migrant workers left their plantations as a group, with a Japanese leader. These people pooled their money and purchased farmland. It was easier for Japanese immigrants to follow a leader who was able to negotiate with Portuguese speakers, and who would handle all legal documents with Brazilians, than it was for them to organize their life in a new area by themselves (Handa 1970: 221). Many made long-term commitments as farmers but still wished to return to Japan someday (Handa 1970; Saito 1976; Maeyama 1996), and large numbers of them did not apply for Brazilian citizenship[6] (Saito 1983: 221).

The Hirano district is one such leader-based district. Umpei Hirano and his followers founded it. Hirano was one of the five interpreters who came to Brazil with the first immigrants in 1908. Unlike most other interpreters who could only speak Spanish or English, Hirano was fluent in Portuguese and could communicate well with Brazilians. Because of his language ability, soon after his arrival in Brazil he was hired to be a manager on the Guatapará plantation. After working there for seven years he bought a sizable parcel of land of about 19.7 square kilometers

(7.6 square miles) located by the Dourados River in Caferândia township – about 370 km (230 miles) northwest of the city of São Paulo (see Map 6.1).[7] In 1915, Hirano and some twenty young men from the families who wished to migrate with him opened up the area before the other settlers moved in. Unlike Japanese neighborhoods (such as Sankaku Minasu), communities founded as leader-based districts were usually located in a forest or a hinterland as they chose cheap land where a large group of Asian families could relocate. Consequently, trailblazers had to go in with machetes and axes to clear the newly purchased land for settlement. Such expeditions were dramatic experiences for Japanese migrants. Thus, leader-based districts usually celebrated their founding anniversaries on the day of the group's first arrival in the area. The Hirano community is no exception. People today still celebrate the date the first vanguard reached the Dourados River on August 3, 1915.

Within a year, over eighty Japanese families had moved into the area. There was an abundance of water from the river, and the soil was rich, ideal for wet rice cultivation. However, soon after the start of the Brazilian rainy season in January, people began to develop high fevers. By August, 1916 – just a year after the foundation of the settlement – almost eighty people had died of malaria (Hirano Shokumin-chi Nihonjinkai 1931). Hirano had excellent command of the Portuguese language but knew

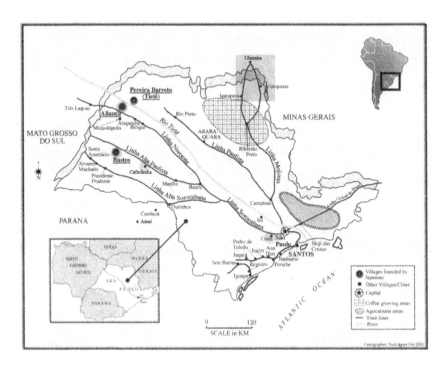

Map 6.1 Japanese settlements in São Paulo State.

little of living in the tropics. The graves of those who died from the malaria epidemic were indicated by temporary wooden markers, stating the victim's name, date of death, and which prefecture he or she was from.

In February 1919, Umpei Hirano himself died of malaria. Soon after his death, the people remaining moved several miles away from the river to avoid the mosquitoes. After moving into this area the survivors named the new settlement the *Hirano Shokumin-chi* (the Hirano Community). By 1930, the settlers had organized a Buddhist congregation and in 1934 they built a temporary temple, despite the fact that the Japanese government prohibited the practice of Buddhism in Brazil. The Japanese government was very aware of the ideology of *embranquecimento* (the "whitening" of society movement) deeply entrenched within Brazilian society at this time, especially among the elites (Normano and Gerbi 1943: 31). At first, Asians were not even allowed to enter Brazil as migrant workers due to these fears of miscegenation. The Japanese government did not want its people in Brazil to face the kind of racial discrimination they encountered in North America, and tried to avoid any potential cause for conflicts with Brazilians (Adachi 2001). Conversion to Catholicism was encouraged. However, it was more important for the Hirano survivors – who faced great adversity in establishing their community – to build a temple and to bury their family, friends, and comrades following Japanese customs, than it was to worry about racial discrimination (yet they did not build the permanent temple until 1950, the oldest Buddhist temple in Brazil).

In 1995, I attended the eightieth anniversary of the founding of the community, which was held next to a statue of Umpei Hirano in front of the Buddhist temple. A golden bust of Hirano is also to be found inside the temple. The villagers worship Hirano as their Guardian Deity. Only the name of Umpei Hirano was referred to during the ceremony, even though he was with them for less than four years and his family left the settlement soon after his death. Other names of leaders and founders who remained in the Hirano community for the last eighty years were not even mentioned.

Many stories of Umpei Hirano – both apocryphal and true – are still told by Japanese Brazilians. For instance, it is often repeated that Hirano was the only Japanese who ever became a manager of a plantation (as these positions were usually assigned only to European immigrants). The story of the settlement's founding is also well known: When Hirano discovered that plantation owners were selling migrant workers daily necessities at outrageous prices in the plantation store, he went to a store in town (using the horse provided to him as a manager) and bought items on behalf of the workers. According to witnesses at the time, when Hirano decided to leave the plantation and establish a farming community on his own, 200 Japanese immigrant families asked to go with him. When some settlers contracted malaria, he visited them every day for over three years until his own death. When things were initially difficult in the new settlement and Hirano suggested they might wish to return to the plantations, no one left, saying that as long as Hirano stayed they would too (Hirano Shokumin-chi Nihonjinkai 1931).

As these narratives demonstrate, Hirano has become a legend and a folk hero, and the settlers were his loyal followers. The ideology of the Hirano residents, therefore, became one based on the loyalty and bravery of the original people, who did not abandon their hero in time of need. In other words, they were not just poor economic refugees or temporary immigrants, but were people who were loyal followers and worked hard to maintain the community founded by a legendary leader. Settlers in leader-based districts create legends based on their leader's personality and character, repeating stories of their heroic exploits or past accomplishments, and every year they reconfirm the community's identity through a celebration of the settlement's foundation.

As mentioned above, in the case of Hirano this reinforcement takes place near a statue of Umpei Hirano, the symbol of the community, in a Buddhist ceremony led by an ordained Buddhist monk.[8] However, although the Hirano residents are more geographically and culturally isolated than the neighborhoods discussed above and do maintain many of their Japanese customs, they also respect Brazilian culture and values, and encourage their children to receive a Brazilian education, hoping for them to successfully establish themselves in mainstream Brazilian society. Although many educated Nikkei have left the district seeking lives outside the farm community, many return to attend the founding anniversary ceremonies.

This respect toward both nations, Japan and Brazil, was imparted to them by Hirano himself, who established his position in mainstream Brazilian society while also devoting himself to the plight of poor Japanese immigrants. The sense of being "children" of this heroic character who worked in both Japanese and Brazilian societies today gives them a dual Brazilian and Japanese identity. This seems typical for most leader-based districts. Unlike the Japanese in the neighborhoods, residents of leader-based districts had more opportunities to develop a community ideology, which gave them the confidence and ability to form a personal identity within mainstream Brazilian society without giving up their Japaneseness. This dual identity, then, is not a hybrid product of two ethnic cultures; instead, their identity is very dynamic and contingent – that is, dependent on venue, social context, and personal motivation – as reflected by how they see themselves.

This type of duality can easily be seen in their children's religious practices. Although the majority of Hirano issei were Buddhists and they passed this on to the next generations, they also encouraged them to visit the cathedral as often as the temple: to practice Catholicism to demonstrate their being good Brazilian citizens, and to practice Buddhism to reify their being Japanese. Thus, today, the young people of the Hirano community partake in both Brazilian and Japanese Brazilian social and cultural activities with little ethnic strife or conflict.

As might be expected, there was also generally less tension in the leader-based districts concerning Japan's defeat in World War II (though no Japanese Brazilian community was completely immune from violence). Even though some communities were more isolated than the neighborhoods, and reliable news was harder to obtain, because of this dual identity as both Japanese *and* Brazilian, residents had less invested in a Japanese victory.

Government-sponsored districts: Bastos and Aliança

The so-called Four Settlements (*Yon Ijûchi*) of Aliança, Bastos, Tiete, and Assai (see Map 6.1) were founded – and operated – by a Japanese government emigration project. Unlike most plantation migrant workers who came to Brazil to earn money to take back to Japan, most residents of the Yon Ijûchi villages came to Brazil with the intention of staying for a long time and establishing new lives.

There are several conflicting reasons why historians believe the Japanese government established Japanese communities in Brazil and other foreign countries. Tajiri (1991: 87–8) believes that this was really a domestic and economic issue, an attempt to ease a perceived overpopulation problem[9] (see Stanlaw, Chapter 2, and Dresner, Chapter 3, this volume). Saito (1976), however, argues that the reasons were largely international and political. Japan wished to have overseas territories and colonies of its own in developing countries to demonstrate its political power and influence to the rest of the world. The Japanese government, then, had a great stake in the success of the Japanese settlements in Brazil, and could not afford to see its people causing trouble by abandoning their contracts or returning to Japan.

The Emigrant Association of Japan – in an effort to insure the safety of the emigrants in tropical areas of Brazil – instituted a set of regulations for the establishment of new, sponsored districts in 1925: First, the size of the village should be at least twenty-four square kilometers (6,000 acres or about nine square miles) and should be located within forty kilometers (twenty-five miles) of a train station; second, the area had to be at least 450 meters (1,476 feet) above sea-level and have good drainage and rich soil; and third, the area had to be free of tropical diseases. The soil requirements indicated that the Japanese government was planning on having the immigrants cultivate coffee trees. Brazil was facing a coffee crisis at the time, and yet coffee remained the most important commodity produced in Brazil. In addition, in order to avoid the Hirano tragedy, the government decided that coffee – instead of wet rice cultivation (grown in areas with higher malaria prevalence) – should be the crop of choice.

These requirements were announced after the Aliança area, the first government-sponsored district, was purchased, and it was found that the land was less than satisfactory. The area of Bastos, the second government-sponsored district, did fulfill these requirements. The government purchased the 120.8-square-kilometer (46.6-square-mile) piece of land located along the Paulista railway line, 580 kilometers (360 miles) from São Paulo City in 1928. The government then set up the Brazilian Colonial Association[10] in 1929 to supervise each sponsored district. Generally this association is known by its acronym, BRATAC,[11] among Japanese Brazilians.

Already by 1930, BRATAC had provided many facilities and factories in Bastos, including a Japanese school, a hospital with a Japanese doctor, a pharmacy, an oil refinery, an ice plant, rice-cleaning, coffee selection, cotton-carding, lumber, silkworm, silkworm egg, and silk mills. BRATAC successfully helped settlers continuously until World War II broke out, when BRATAC was cut off from Japanese government support.[12]

BRATAC not only set up facilities and factories, but it also provided an agricultural philosophy of living for the migrant farmers. This was called the GAT (G̲ozar A̲ T̲erra, or "Love the Soil") movement. This doctrine taught respect for farm work and said that people should "love nature and settle down on the farm" (Cotia Sangyô Kumiai Chûô-kai Kankô Iin-kai 1987). It also taught that people should not strive for economic achievement. For example, Shigeshi Nagata, a leading figure in the Aliança district, was one of the most influential leaders among Japanese Brazilians. His famous slogan was "*Kôhî yori-mo hito o tsukure*" (Cultivate humanity rather than coffee). Such teachings encouraged Japanese Brazilians to stay on in the farming hinterlands instead of moving to the cities – until after World War II when the younger generations began to move to the urban areas for higher education.

The initial responses to Bastos were lukewarm. Even though it was a well-prepared settlement with an established infrastructure, only sixty-eight families migrated to Bastos from Japan in the first year, 1928, and only fourteen families re-migrated from coffee plantations. Even the following year, the district received only ninety-six families. The reason for this was the manner of its promotion in Japan. Unlike Aliança, established by the governments of three prefectures – Nagano, Toyama, and Tottori – which actively recruited their own people to emigrate, Bastos was a national undertaking. Thus, no specific prefecture was responsible for signing up recruits. In addition, the Japanese government did not at first encourage workers leaving the plantations to re-migrate to Bastos because it was originally intended to reduce population pressures in Japan. However, after having difficulty enrolling people from Japan, Bastos started actively taking in re-migrants in the third year. Consequently, unlike Aliança where the majority of people came directly from Japan, about one-third of the settlers of Bastos re-migrated from coffee plantations.

In contrast to the neighborhood and leader-based Japanese communities, the sponsored districts were established deeper in the interior forests (as was the case for these four villages). Seeing the stability and growth of these communities, many non-Japanese Brazilians also migrated there looking for work. One of the major jobs for such non-Japanese Brazilian migrant workers was that of the daily-paid farm-hand, the *camarada*. Migrant camaradas were given living quarters by their Japanese employers. When Brazilian towns grew up near the Japanese villages, Japanese also started providing camaradas with transportation between their houses in the towns and the farm fields every morning and evening. These conditions remain largely the same today.

These patterns of residence and employment have had important consequences in the way these villages developed. Unlike the Bastos settlers, the Aliança settlers have shared geographical space with Brazilians throughout their existence. However, they generally do not share social space or time. For example, even now in Aliança, if both Japanese Brazilians and their camaradas work in the same fields, Japanese Brazilians return home to have lunch while the camaradas usually stay in the fields to eat and to take a nap in the shade before starting work again in the afternoon. While Japanese Brazilians play baseball, local non-Japanese Brazilians play soccer. Like other areas of Brazil, in Aliança very few Japanese Brazilians, if any, play soccer, and few camaradas play baseball.

In the case of Bastos, however, the villagers went to great lengths to maintain their social and physical distance from non-Japanese Brazilians, and separated their residential areas from non-Japanese Brazilians in the village. Since the 1950s the poultry business has grown tremendously there, and the villagers have come to depend on the labor of the camaradas. Bastense provide living quarters instead of transportation, and hire whole camarada families including their wives and children. Upon seeing the rapidly increasing numbers of camarada children in public schools, many Bastense moved their residences to the downtown area and built a private school for their children. Today they also have an exclusive hospital and a social club downtown.

Residents of the government-sponsored districts have always held the economic, social, and political power in their villages. Nonetheless, as mentioned above, the Japanese government required that the first residents should not practice Buddhism. The majority of Nikkei were thus baptized in the Catholic Church, though many Japanese settlers had (and still have) Buddhist altars in their homes. But because Japanese are religiously quite eclectic there was actually little conflict or resistance, and most Japanese saw no contradiction in following both Catholic and Buddhist practices.

These government-sponsored district communities were among the most geographically isolated of the three types of Japanese settlements found in Brazil. They *chose* to segregate themselves from non-Japanese Brazilians rather than integrate into mainstream society. They had been conspicuously sponsored by the Japanese government, and helped by its various agencies such as BRATAC. They perhaps had a more vested interest than either of the other two types of Japanese communities in maintaining a homeland connection. Indeed, they created their community ideology and personal ethnic identity through fostering these close ties with Japan. As might be expected, then, many residents of government-sponsored districts were reluctant to accept the reality of Japan's defeat in World War II.

Kachi-gumi and Make-gumi violence: the formation of a postwar Nikkei identity

By the onset of World War II, the vast majority of Japanese migrants were living in the farming areas of the interior of Brazil,[13] and many owned their own fields. Regardless of which of the three types of migrant communities they came from, everyone still generally thought of themselves as *Nihonjin* (Japanese).[14] Some sent their children back to Japan to visit their grandparents and receive a Japanese education. New immigrants from Japan continued to arrive regularly. Japanese Brazilians maintained contact with each other through communal activities such as baseball, kendo (Japanese fencing), and judo matches. There was a strong ethnic and community consciousness.

However, in 1942 when Brazil declared war against Germany and Italy – but not yet Japan – Japanese officials nonetheless left Brazil, and many of the remaining migrant workers felt abandoned by their home country's government (Miyao 1991: 150). Furthermore, while Japanese communities in Brazil were closely linked to each other prior to the war, Japanese Brazilian society subsequently fractured over differing interpretations of Japan's World War II defeat. An important example of such an incident is the so-called Kachi-gumi–Make-gumi conflict. In many ways this incident proved to be a defining moment for the current social conditions of Japanese Brazilians.

Brazil's authoritarian president Getúlio Vargas, in his nationalization project of 1923, limited the number of new immigrants to 3 percent of those who had arrived in the previous fifty years (Tajiri 1991: 100). This percentage was changed to 2 percent after the immigration reforms in the United States and Canada in 1924 reduced their Japanese immigration even more. Because Japanese were relatively new immigrants, they – along with Arabs and Jews – were affected by these immigration quotas more than were European migrants, whose history was longer (Lesser 1999: 130; Kinshichi *et al.* 2000: 140). Vargas also banned the teaching of foreign languages in 1938, and newspapers and magazines written in foreign languages became subject to strict censorship in 1939.

Furthermore, after Brazil joined the Allies in their war against Germany and Italy in 1942, Vargas ordered the relocation of Japanese residents from the Santos international seaport and the Japantown area in the city of São Paulo, the ostensible reason being the threat of Japanese sabotage. Although the government selected the Amazon area for the relocation of these 1,500 Japanese, they voluntarily moved to the hinterlands of São Paulo state where they could join the Japanese farm communities already long established in the area (Miyao 1991: 150). Although the number of people being relocated was small compared to that of North America – and the majority of Japanese Brazilians already lived in the geographically isolated interior – we should not dismiss the impact that these acculturated, urbanized Japanese might have had on rural Japanese Brazilian society. No doubt their views on farm work and manual labor influenced the post-war generation of young people. Indeed, immediately after World War II ended, Japanese Brazilian society split into two factions over beliefs about who had won the war.

The Kachi-gumi, or the "Victory Group" – disregarding official pronouncements by the Brazilian government and the media – believed that Japan had won the war. The core of the Kachi-gumi were members of the Shindô Renmei, or the "League of the Subjects of the Emperor," who had been against Vargas' nationalization policies since the 1930s (Lesser 1999: 138). They saw Vargas' Brazil as an enemy both of the nation of Japan and the local Japanese Brazilians. By 1945 they had dismissed all official announcements by the Brazilian government as pure propaganda, including the news that the Allies had won the war.

The Make-gumi, or the "Defeat Group," consisted of those who eventually came to accept the fact that Japan had lost the war. At first, as many Japanese Brazilians were hoping for a Japanese victory, large numbers believed the Shindô Remmei, rather than the news they were hearing. A majority of Japanese migrants at this time still longed to return to their home in Japan some day (Handa 1970), even if it was becoming increasingly obvious that this was never going to happen. They identified themselves through their ancestral homeland, and it was hard for them to accept an American occupation of Japan without feeling a great psychological burden. Gradually, many Japanese Brazilians started to realize that Japan had truly lost, but the Kachi-gumi viewed such persons as traitors to both Japan and the Nihonjin (the Japanese in Brazil). They felt justified in attacking these "defeatists," and mobs sometimes burned homes and beat people in the streets. Bombs were planted – the first one killing a man in his home in Bastos in March 1946 – and soon the death-toll was rising, eventually reaching several dozen. Kachi-gumi terrorist activities increased, and in July alone seventeen bombs killed ten people and injured seven. For the most part the Make-gumi did not retaliate at first, but eventually they fought back, causing large-scale disruption. For a while there was at least one violent incident somewhere every other day.

In late 1946, while fighting between the Kachi-gumi and the Make-gumi continued, Kachi-gumi terrorism spread to non-Japanese Brazilians. In Oswaldo Cruz, a village about 20 kilometers from Bastos, a local Brazilian, disgusted with the violence, shouted at some Japanese to leave town. After the quarrel escalated into a fight, the local Brazilian was killed by a Japanese man, and anti-Japanese protests and continued conflict led to a riot involving the whole town. The Brazilian army was dispatched a week later and finally established order after much destruction and bloodshed.

How did such violence start, and who is to blame? Part of the reason was the inability of Japanese settlers to get regular and reliable news. They were not able to read Japanese-language newspapers during the war – including those that had been published in Brazil before being closed down – so many had to rely on hearsay. The vast majority of settlers, and many of their children, were not able to attend Brazilian schools because of their isolation. No Brazilian teachers wished to live among the Japanese migrants in the hinterlands. Children of Japanese migrants, then, only received a Japanese education in the villages – there were teachers from Japan in the BRATAC-sponsored areas and migrants who had some education taught their children in other Japanese Brazilian communities.[15] Consequently, few were fluent enough in Portuguese to adequately understand the regular news. Some Japanese settlers, however, heard news from Japan on hidden short-wave radios that had escaped detection by police. But they caught this news only sporadically, and what they heard was often just Japanese government propaganda; even the Japanese in Japan did not know how badly the war was going for them and were unprepared for their defeat. Handa (1970) recalls that in the beginning the majority of Japanese Brazilians believed in a Japanese victory, and very few accepted Japan's loss. Although their Brazilian neighbors told them of an impending Allied victory, many could not dismiss the news they were hearing on the radio.

Furthermore, until the current Emperor (who assumed the throne in 1989), the Japanese sovereign never spoke in public in the daily vernacular. Thus, when the Emperor spoke to the nation to announce the surrender, a majority of the people even in Japan did not immediately comprehend what the language of his statement meant. It is little wonder, then, that Japanese Brazilians were confused when they heard Japanese news. The confusion of Japanese Brazilians at this time is well described by Handa's eye witness account:

> One day we were told that Japan was defeated by the Allies. Although we knew the news of the Japanese government had to be a little exaggerated, we could not believe that everything they told was a lie. It just could not be true. Regardless of what Brazilian newspapers were saying, we tried to understand what the Emperor said to the Japanese through his radio broadcast of August 14, 1945. After consulting with

each other, [many of us thought that] what the Emperor said was ... Japan had been defeated by the Allies. Yet when some people said, "That's right, that's right. We won!" even though we felt something was wrong, we started to believe in the victory of Japan.

(Handa 1970: 644–7)

The Kachi-gumi–Make-gumi conflict, then, was due to a lack of accurate information rather than to any special allegiance to Japan or rejection of assimilation into Brazilian society, at least in the sponsored areas. In a sense, these immigrants were victims of the political agendas of both nations. The Kachi-gumi–Make-gumi conflicts were greatest in the neighborhood districts, as they housed the greatest numbers of those who still harbored deep attachments to Japan. No incidents of violence were reported in the leader-based districts, as the charisma of the individual leaders kept their communities united. Nonetheless, many Japanese Brazilians believe today that the conflict was due to the ignorance of Japanese migrant farm-hands and their children, neither of whom received a proper education in Brazil.

Conclusion

Being foreign migrant workers, when the Japanese arrived in Brazil they were marginalized politically, economically, and socially. Arriving on the coffee plantations during a deep depression, Japanese immigrants experienced more discrimination than new migrants usually did, as all of the marginal groups competed for dwindling resources. Japanese were treated little better than former slaves, unlike most European migrants – such as the Italians, whose Catholicism, white skin, and native language close to Portuguese helped them adapt to Brazil relatively easily. Japanese had to argue with Brazilian government officers on the docks over their eligibility to even enter the country; they were "colored" people, with "strange" Asian customs, speaking a totally different language. Indeed, the similarities between the experiences of Japanese and those of the earlier African slaves were striking. With the sole exception of Umpei Hirano, neither Africans nor Japanese could ever rise to be plantation managers (unlike the Italian immigrants who managed much of the farm land in Brazil). Experiencing the same marginalization as that of former slaves on the plantations, Japanese migrant workers chose to form their own communities where they could at least survive economically and improve their social environment. For these immigrants who experienced plantation labor, the homeland was more than just the place they were *from*. As Handa (1970) and Saito (1983) tell us, the majority of Japanese thought that someday they would return – an attitude so common in immigrant communities that it has even been given a name: the "Myth of Return" (Watson 2004: 898). This idea of returning to the homeland some day no doubt provided these immigrants with hope and motivated them to persevere as they struggled with their difficult new life in Brazil.

Nikkei people in the neighborhood districts practiced their Nihonjin-ness – and constructed their identity – among themselves, in contrast to their daily association with local Brazilians. On the other hand, Nikkei people in the leader-based districts formed their Nihonjin-ness and identity in contrast to other Japanese communities. Nikkei people in the sponsored districts formed their Nihonjin-ness and identity within their Japanese villages in Brazil with the support of the Japanese government.

It was only natural that it took time for some Japanese Brazilians to accept Japan's defeat in World War II. If the homeland was no longer a strong or healthy nation, how could they hold on to the anticipation of a triumphant return, which supported them for decades during the hard and long hours of working in the fields (see Watson 2004: 897; Dresner, Chapter 3, this volume)? In addition, as Handa (1970) – one who lived through this difficult period – points out, because many did not want to think of the homeland suffering after the war, they tried to convince themselves that the news they were hearing from Brazilians was mere wartime propaganda. As his recollections suggest, the majority of Japanese in Brazil were emotionally on the side of the Kachi-gumi at first, even though politically they had no vested interest in the outcome of the war either way.

Besides this emotional reluctance to let go of a long-held vision of their homeland, which had sustained many during their years in Brazil, we also need to consider the negative impact which the Kachi-gumi–Make-gumi conflict caused in Japanese Brazilian society. Because the conflicts were perceived to be among rural farmers, farmers in general lost status – not only among local Brazilians, but also among their own children and grandchildren. The events were considered too shameful to talk about, and soon became banished from conversation. Without a deeper understanding of the dynamics of their parents' and grandparents' situation – living in remote areas, viewed as peripheral to mainstream society, clinging to pride in the old country and its traditions, and perhaps to the idea that it would always be there for them, and not wanting to recognize that they had been abandoned by their homeland – many young Nikkei felt sad and ashamed of being the sons and daughters of "ignorant" immigrants.

Younger Japanese Brazilians, then, decided they needed an education so as not to be the same ignorant farmers their parents and grandparents were (who could not even speak Portuguese well). Seeking a higher education was something Japanese people sought in the late nineteenth and early twentieth centuries, even back in Japan. Japan at this time was in the middle of a tremendous period of Westernization and industrialization, and education was thought to be a road for both personal social mobility and national growth and development. This was the period when the first immigrants were arriving in Brazil, and they carried this respect for learning with them. Consequently, many Japanese Brazilians – if financially able – sent their children back to Japan for schooling, in spite of their ties to farming and land.

Now, as Japan was in the middle of post-war reconstruction, Brazilian higher education became more attractive (as national universities such as those in São Paulo were free). For the new generation, higher education meant studying in Brazil instead of "returning" to Japan to study. These young people had every intention of going back to the farms after they finished school. However, once they were exposed to the bourgeois lifestyles of the Brazilian middle and upper classes, they came to see manual labor and farming as unattractive. Instead of following the GAT teachings and clinging to farming, they now wanted to enter white-collar occupations (Handa 1970; Maeyama 1981; Saito 1983).

In the Brazilian cities, these Japanese Brazilians formed close associations with other Japanese communities. While associating with different ethnic groups, this new generation of urban Japanese Brazilians came to identify itself as Nihonjin (Japanese) within Brazilian society. For them the "homeland" was not Japan, but the rural communities from which they came. Living in a Portuguese-speaking social environment, they are losing their Japanese language. However, unlike many Japanese in North America, Brazilian Nikkei have experienced fewer problems over their Japanese ethnicity and social identity.

Yet, when many Japanese Brazilians went to Japan during the start of the dekasegi movement in the 1980s, they rediscovered their Japanese roots, and their ethnic identity started to change dramatically. In Chapter 12 of this volume, for example, Tsuda describes the experiences of many dekasegi migrant laborers who have returned to Brazil after working in Japan. Being discriminated against by local Japanese, and being viewed as "foreign" workers in the nation of their ancestors, Japanese Brazilians in Japan also rediscover their Brazilness. For them, Brazil is now becoming the homeland, and many young Japanese Brazilians find synergy in concepts that blend both societies into a new identity, still Japanese, yet within a more fully realized Brazilian context.

Notes

1 There were also Japanese re-migrants from Peru, Bolivia, and Paraguay to Brazil, and it is very hard to specify how many Japanese re-migrated from these countries. Westney (1983: 201) claims 200,000 Japanese migrated to Brazil during this period, while Kimura (2004: 6) estimates 179,321, citing Japanese government emigration records. Thus some 20,000 people may have re-migrated from neighboring countries.
2 Children under the age of twelve were not counted as persons.
3 They were usually between 0.25 to 0.50 square kilometers (sixty-four to 128 acres).

4 This was different from the local Brazilian's triangle, Triângulo Mineiro (Minas Triangle), which was a much greater area, i.e., between the Rio Grande River and Paraíba City.
5 Many Japanese died of tropical diseases, such as malaria and typhoid, in the early days of immigration to Brazil.
6 For example, when I conducted my fieldwork in the 1990s, the majority of the first-generation Japanese in a Japanese commune in Aliança, São Paulo (about one hundred people) still did not have Brazilian citizenship.
7 Today, it takes about five and a half hours to travel by bus along the Noroeste Railway to reach this area from the city of São Paulo.
8 A Buddhist monk from the *Jôdo-kyô* sect has now settled down permanently in this district.
9 This type of state-sponsored project was not unusual for the Japanese government. For example, in the 1960s Japanese migrated to Bolivia, the Dominican Republic, and the Amazon area of Brazil under the government project, and in the 1970s and 1980s many elderly people bought their houses in tropical nations such as Cuba and the Dominican Republic because of the government campaign promoting their inexpensive daily cost and nice weather for pensioners. It is said the government wished to reduce the domestic population.
10 The *Burajiru Takushoku Kumiai* in Japanese and the *Sociedade Colôniadora do Brasil Limitada* in Portuguese.
11 BRATAC stands for *Brazil Takushoku Kumiai* (the Brazilian Colonial Association).
12 After the war, the financial department of BRATAC split off and changed its name to *Banco do America do Sul* (the Bank of South America). Today it is one of the biggest banks in Brazil. Although it is reduced in size and influence, BRATAC is still active in the São Paulo area. However, the only major remaining business of BRATAC is a silk factory.
13 According to Tajiri (1991: 113, 127), 87 percent of Japanese migrants (over 175,000 people) were engaged in farming in the hinterlands of São Paulo state, and 2.4 percent of them (4,875 people) were in the city of São Paulo.
14 This contrasts with the common term the settlers used for Japanese in Japan: *Nihon no hito* (lit. Japanese person).
15 By 1939 there were 486 Japanese elementary schools in Brazil and some 30,000 children were studying there (Tajiri 1991: 117).

7 A stone voice
The diary of a Japanese transnational migrant in Canada[1]

Keibo Oiwa

A brief history of Japanese Canadians

The first Japanese immigrant is believed to have arrived in Canada in 1877. Before the end of the nineteenth century, Canadian passenger ships regularly plied the transpacific route, bringing nearly 5,000 Japanese immigrant workers to Canada. Some of these Japanese remained in Canada to try and create a better future for themselves, their families, and descendants. Their history may be divided into two periods, with the outbreak of World War II on December 7, 1941, as the dividing line. The first is, by and large, the history of the issei (those born in Japan who immigrated as adults), and is "above all, a history of a racial minority struggling to survive in a hostile land" (Ichioka 1988: 1). I will present a brief history of Japanese Canadians and explore why they have been seen as "quiet." I will do so by looking at the extraordinary wartime diary of a rather ordinary issei woman, Kaoru Ikeda.

The pre-World War II period

Before World War II, nearly 95 percent of Japanese immigrants and their descendants were concentrated in a small area of southwest British Columbia, no more than a dot in the corner of the huge map of Canada. Immigrant workers from Japan participated in the early settlement of this young province and soon became an essential part of the fishing, mining, and lumber industries.

The early Japanese settlements, which consisted almost exclusively of male migrant workers, were temporary and unstable in nature. In the second decade of the twentieth century, when "picture brides" (Makabe 1995) began arriving *en masse* from Japan to join their prospective husbands, the Japanese Canadian population grew to form permanent communities (see Adachi (1976) for more details).

Constrained by both formal and informal racial discrimination, the Japanese Canadian community constituted a small, largely self-contained society within British Columbia. Not unlike immigrants of Chinese and

Hindu origin, Japanese Canadians were deeply resented by white society. Throughout the pre-war period, the British Columbian government made great efforts to curtail both the numbers and the civil liberties of the Japanese Canadian population. Most whites found it simply unacceptable that Asians should be regarded as equals. The animosity reached a climax in 1907 when as many as 5,000 whites went on the rampage in the Japanese and Chinese quarters of Vancouver.

From that time until the end of World War II, there was no significant decrease in popular anti-Japanese sentiment – the difference between Japanese and Japanese Canadians was considered inconsequential. An anti-Japanese platform would always help local politicians get elected. Sanctions against the militaristic government of Japan and discriminatory laws against Canadian citizens of Japanese descent were never logically differentiated. As the political relationship between Japan and North America deteriorated (until finally Japan's attack on Pearl Harbor ignited the war in the Pacific), prejudice and suspicion of Japanese immigrants became ever more intense.

In the pre-war years, Vancouver was home to nearly 40 percent of the Japanese Canadian population, of which the great majority was concentrated in the small area along Powell Street, forming an ethnic enclave known as Japantown, or "Little Tokyo." Political, economic, educational, and religious institutions – and organizations with an almost exclusively Asian clientele – thrived along with a great number of commercial establishments. The community boasted Japanese bathhouses, Japanese-language newspapers, a Japanese-language school, a judo club, Buddhist and Christian churches, gambling parlors, restaurants, and stores offering an assortment of Japanese foods. Smaller communities were also formed throughout the province: Steveston and other fishing villages, sawmill towns along the Pacific coast and on Vancouver Island, and agricultural communities in the Fraser and Okingan valleys.

According to census data, in 1941 the entire Nikkei population in Canada was 23,149. Of this figure, the ratio between issei and nisei (the children of immigrants who were born in the host nation) was about two to three (Adachi 1976: 414). According to Shinpo (1986), in 1934 those over the age of twenty constituted approximately 12 percent of the Nikkei population, and this increased to 36.5 percent in 1941. The birth rate peaked in 1929. Thus, during the pre-war years, only a small proportion of nisei came of age; for most, this began during the wartime and post-war years.

The war period

The second period of Japanese Canadian history covers the years during and immediately after the Pacific War. The setting shifts to include all of Canada, as the Japanese became scattered across the 5,000 kilometer-long Canada–United States border.

Immediately after the Pearl Harbor attack on December 7, 1941, all persons of Japanese descent, even Canadian citizens, were branded as "enemy aliens." Within hours, about forty Japanese nationals suspected of being "dangerous elements" were detained. Other measures quickly followed, all in the name of security. The entire fleet of about 1,200 Japanese Canadian fishing vessels was impounded. Automobiles, radios, and cameras were confiscated and a night-time curfew was imposed. All Japanese and Japanese Canadians were required to register with the newly established British Columbia Security Commission, which was in charge of all matters pertaining to the Nikkei. They were also now required to carry identification. By the end of February 1942, the government had decreed that all Japanese Canadians residing in the "protected area" of coastal British Columbia – that is, about 21,000 persons or more than 90 percent of the entire Japanese Canadian population – were to be relocated. In the prevailing climate of hysteria, the War Measures Act was enacted and used to justify anti-Japanese racism.

By the end of October that year, all Japanese Canadians throughout coastal British Columbia were thoroughly uprooted. Those living outside the Vancouver area were first herded into the Hastings Park Exhibition Grounds, which was converted into a temporary transit center. After weeks or months of humiliating imprisonment in buildings that had previously housed livestock, they were sent to so-called relocation camps in the interior of British Columbia and elsewhere. About 12,000 were sent to old ghost towns in the mountains, or to shanty towns hastily built by Nikkei work crews. Of this group, nearly 5,000 were concentrated in the Slocan Valley, British Columbia, forming separate camps at Slocan City, Bay Farm, Popoff, Lemon Creek, and other locations (Adachi 1976: 415). About 4,000 families were sent to the Prairie Provinces where they worked on sugar beet farms under harsh conditions. Approximately 700 men were detained in prisoner-of-war camps in Ontario, first at Petawawa, then at Angler. Most of those imprisoned were accused of disobeying and resisting the authorities (or planning to do so), and were called *gambari-ya* (diehards) by fellow Japanese settlers and their children – sometimes with admiration, sometimes in mockery.

While a similar process was going on in the United States, in some ways the persecution of the Japanese Canadians was even harsher than that of the Japanese Americans. By quickly liquidating confiscated homes, businesses, farms, and other personal possessions, and by prohibiting them from returning to the coastal area until 1949, the federal government (led by Prime Minister Mackenzie King) fostered the destruction of pre-war Japanese immigrant society. It is evident that even after the war anti-Japanese racists in British Columbia did not give up their dream of getting rid of all "Japs," not only in their own province but also across Canada.

Toward the end of the war, while 120,000 Japanese Americans had been permitted to return to their homes on the West Coast, the great majority of Japanese Canadians still remaining in the interior camps were given a choice: move themselves east of the Rockies, or sign papers renouncing their Canadian citizenship and agree to be repatriated (i.e., deported) to Japan. As public support grew for their right to stay in Canada, the government's deportation policy was finally cancelled, but not before approximately 4,000 people were sent to Japan. Under the order to relocate again – and this time to disperse themselves throughout Canada – many Nikkei chose to try their luck in eastern Canada (Canada 1947).

Post-World War II life

In the 1950s some Japanese Canadians began to move back to the coastal area of British Columbia and formed the basis of today's thriving community. Discrimination was supposed to have ceased, but this was not always so in practice. A considerable number of those who had been deported to post-war Japan began to return to Canada. They were referred to as *kika* (resettlers). To add to these demographic changes, a trickle of new Japanese immigrants began to arrive in the 1960s as Canada reopened its doors.

In 1977, Japanese Canadian communities scattered throughout Canada celebrated the 100th year of Japanese Canadian history. It was an occasion with much symbolic significance, for until that time Japanese Canadians, by and large, had kept a low profile, almost as if they deliberately tried to avoid attracting attention to themselves. The 100th anniversary was probably their first major attempt since World War II to reintroduce themselves to mainstream Canadian society and to seek their place as an ethnic minority within the rapidly changing Canadian mosaic. At that time, Canada began to embrace pluralism and multiculturalism as new national principles, and ethnic and racial minorities were actively engaged in tackling discrimination and asserting their rights.

According to Kobayashi (1989: 23), the Japanese Canadian population in 1986 totaled 54,505. Of this number, those who immigrated from Japan before 1950 represented only 3.2 percent of all Japanese Canadians (ibid.: 57). The issei population is rapidly disappearing and their children, the nisei, are growing old. The memory of the wartime experience imprinted on Japanese Canadian history is quickly fading.

On September 22, 1988, the Canadian government announced the Japanese–Canadian Redress Settlement for wartime mistreatment. This historic agreement was signed with the National Association of Japanese Canadians (NAJC), the nucleus of the national movements for redress. The agreement included the government's formal apology to Japanese Canadians and symbolic payments for surviving individuals and communities. For the members of the NAJC and its supporters, the settlement was a great achievement in the struggle for justice and human rights, and was an inspiration to native people and Canada's other ethnic minorities. Thus one could argue that Japanese Canadians are experiencing a turning point in their history. The third period of Nikkei history – following the pre-war, war, and post-war periods – has now begun.

Breaking silence

It is curious that most of the writings on Japanese Canadian history have characteristically been a history in the passive voice – a history in which a people, instead of being the main actors and thinkers, were the objects of other people's action and thought. It is as if they had never played a creative role in their own history – that it was simply fashioned by others. In the pre-war, wartime, and immediate post-war years, Japanese Canadians almost always appear in history as victims of discrimination, facing uprooting, incarceration, and dispersal. It is as if the history of the persecuted could be reduced to what their persecutors did. We rarely encounter firsthand accounts of what the persecuted felt, thought, or wished to do (or failed to do). We hear little of the meanings they attached to their thoughts and actions.

It is not that there has been no discussion about this voice; it has usually been identified as silence. North American issei have often been characterized as reticent and quiet people who say nothing about their wartime experiences even to their own children. While the idea of the quiet Japanese Canadian has become an ethnic stereotype, few serious attempts have been made to access the depths of this socio-psychological phenomenon. The Japanese Canadian poet Joy Kogawa opened her novel about her own wartime experience, *Obasan*, with an unforgettable passage about silence. To quote just part of it:

> There is a silence that cannot speak.
> There is a silence that will not speak.
> Beneath the grass the speaking dreams and beneath the dreams in a sentence sea. The speech that frees comes forth from that amniotic deep....
> If I could follow the stream down and down to the hidden voice, would I come at last to the freeing word? I ask the night sky but the silence is steadfast. There is no reply.
>
> (Kogawa 1981: ii)

Kogawa was actively involved in the redress movement in the 1980s which sought to let Japanese Canadians face their own past. Their unwillingness to remember, their fear of talking, their tendency to blame themselves, and even to justify the injustice done to them as a blessing in disguise, all constituted large obstacles. They needed to address their own silence. The success represented by the redress settlement has no doubt encouraged and inspired many to begin to deal with their past experiences.

In no way meant to blame the victim, it is necessary to mention "self-censorship" among Japanese Canadians. It has contributed to the silence and blank spaces in their history. I believe it was just after the redress settlement in 1988 when small pieces of issei oral history appeared in a local community newspaper. One nisei man approached the editor to ask how some issei dared to say they had felt excited about Japan's military advance in the early part of the Pacific War, and that they had felt sad at the news of Japan's surrender. "Since when are we allowed to say something like that?" he asked. For him, the statements of these issei were an embarrassment.

As in any community, there are always embarrassing things that insiders prefer to keep hidden from outsiders. During and immediately after the war, the main sources of embarrassment for many Japanese Canadians were those who refused to follow government orders even though, in every interior camp and settlement, there were those who held similar sentiments. Between the so-called pro-Japan and pro-democracy groups, conflicts were common. A good many people, especially issei (who could not completely give up the idea that Japan might be victorious) felt deeply ashamed at the end of the war.

It is common to feel embarrassment or even shame about the past, whether one's own or someone else's, especially as it is embodied in the lives of one's parents or grandparents. On many occasions I have heard issei talk of their own (or their children's) embarrassment about being Japanese before, during, and immediately after the war. Young people would often feel self-conscious about their poor English-speaking issei parents and their traditional Japanese customs, rituals, and manners. As Joy Kogawa (1990) recalls, children wished they had been born a *hakujin* (white person). It is not difficult to imagine that such sentiment, akin to self-hatred, was the product of many years of racial prejudice and discrimination experienced by the Japanese settlers and their descendants in Canadian society. At the same time, it is hard to overestimate the importance of their wartime experiences in shaping their psychological and social identity. The entire Japanese Canadian history continues to revolve around the wartime experience of uprooting, incarceration, and dispersal. In this chapter I attempt to touch the core of that experience.

To restore the lost pages of history is not an easy task. Language has been a barrier, especially for the Japanese-speaking issei. After the war, when assimilation and dispersal became the order of the day, the Japanese language went underground. The linguistic gap between generations began to widen. It became difficult to distinguish what the issei did not want to talk about from what they wanted to talk about but could not express. The linguistic barrier between generations often coincides with cultural and social discontinuity. As Kogawa says, "There is a silence that cannot speak."

Several years ago, I began to try to penetrate this silence. Instead of an unwillingness to talk, I discovered shyness, humility, and a sense of resignation. Many individuals I spoke with maintained they did not have anything interesting to say, that they were just simple and ordinary folk; they were very sorry to be so boring. When I insisted that I wanted to hear "simple and ordinary" stories about their lives, they slowly began to talk. I then realized that their reluctance to speak might stem from a pessimistic feeling that they would not be understood. *Hakujin* would not understand them, not only because of the language barrier, but also because in the minds of the issei they belonged to a different class. Younger Japanese Canadians would not understand them either, because of the linguistic, cultural, and social distance between generations.

Finally, there is a sentiment that they, the issei, cannot be understood by Japanese in Japan because there has been a general lack of concern in Japan for those who left for another country. The other side of this sentiment is the tendency to want to defend the Japanese. The issei would say, "*Shikata ga nai*" (It cannot be helped), adding, "Japan has different traditions and customs." The issei seem extremely patient, not only with the native Japanese, but also with the Canadians who surround them. They do not blame others for their lack of understanding; they seem somehow to have managed to go beyond this.

The anthropologist Barbara Myerhoff (1980: xv) once characterized our species as *Homo narrans* (humans as story-tellers), implying that culture is a "story" we tell about ourselves. The following story is a very revealing part of Japanese Canadian culture.

The Slocan journal of Kaoru Ikeda

Kaoru Ikeda's memoir and diary offer a rare picture of daily life in a relocation camp as seen from one woman's point of view. It demonstrates how the women, with their networks of mutual support, coped with the unfamiliar and often harsh environment so that life became not only tolerable, but meaningful and even enjoyable. With the shortage of desirable Japanese foodstuffs, they were most resourceful in cultivating gardens, gathering berries and mushrooms, and inventing ways of food preservation – as well as new recipes to replace traditional dishes. Besides providing food, they grew flowers (often exchanged as gifts), organized classes to learn useful skills, and joined religious, recreational, or artistic clubs (such as the *haiku* poetry group in which Kaoru Ikeda participated). They continued observing both traditional and Western festivals and rites of passage, and invented substitute garments for the children. It was a highly creative period.

Kaoru was born in 1875 in Niigata Prefecture in Japan. After marrying Arichika Ikeda (1864–1939), a man from the same prefecture, she came to Canada in 1914. Arichika is known as one of the Japanese pioneers of North America. He arrived in the United States in 1890, and was part of the colonization of northern California. He joined the Klondike Gold Rush in the Yukon, spent time in Alaska, and later moved to British Columbia and began mining for various minerals. Today there is even a bay on the British Columbian coast that bears his name.

After her husband died in Vancouver in 1939, Kaoru Ikeda, who was already a naturalized Canadian by this time, remained in Canada with her children and grandchildren until she died shortly after World War II. When Japan attacked Pearl Harbor on December 7, 1941, she was sixty-six years old. In June of the following year Kaoru was forced to abandon her house and move with the family of her daughter, Chisato, to the interior of British Columbia. She spent three years at the Slocan Relocation Camp and then another year in a camp at New Denver, British Columbia. While waiting to resettle elsewhere she became sick and died in the spring of 1946, less than a year after World War II ended.

The following two sections are excerpts from a journal – originally written in Japanese that I have translated here – which Kaoru Ikeda kept over a two-year period from December 1942 until December 1944. The first one-third of her 120-page journal is a memoir written in December 1942, looking back at events of that year. The remaining two-thirds of her journal is a diary of daily life in the relocation camps. Even these few selected glimpses weave a revealing tapestry.

Memoir

As Kaoru Ideka recalls the days immediately after Pearl Harbor, feelings of pride in her heritage conflict with confusion, anger, and disbelief as events unfold:

> The 7th of December [1942]! What bewildering and confusing days we have been living in since Pearl Harbor. With its great mission to establish world peace, Japan is fighting with great success, amazing the rest of the world ... we feel proud of our country and pray that our advances continue until our final victory.
>
> The year before last, after Canada joined the war in support of England, we Japanese in Canada contributed all the resources we had, like buying Victory Bonds and making donations for the national defense and to the Red Cross. Even our children at school saved their allowances to buy savings stamps, while housewives found the time ... to sew and knit for the Red Cross. We did all we could to prove that we were loyal Canadian citizens. How did the authorities respond to our efforts? They carried their vigilance to extremes, confiscating all firearms owned by Japanese Canadians and outlawing the use of gunpowder even for industrial purposes, drawing up a registry of our names, and taking our fingerprints. They began to treat us with increasing harshness. Once Japan joined the war ... executives of

firms that had direct ties with Japan were arrested and jailed. The number of arrests increased, and later, I hear, there were many arrests among those who refused to go into the camps.

All Japanese Canadian fishermen had to hand over their boats to the government. On land, car, camera, and radio ownership or operation was forbidden, and these were confiscated. Beginning on the night of the 7th [December 1941] ... blackouts went into effect along the Pacific Coast.... Mobs harassed the [local] Japanese and I even heard they set fire to homes and beat people up....

The federal government['s] ... orders keep changing.... The recklessness and confusion displayed while confiscating our fishing boats demonstrated especially well how shocked they were by the first air attacks and how they feared the Japanese. Was this the behavior of a great country? There have been many stories of this kind, silly enough even to make an old woman like me burst into laughter.

According to Prime Minister King's original announcement from Ottawa, only those with Japanese citizenship would be removed from British Columbia, while nisei and naturalized citizens would be allowed to stay. However, a faction of British Columbian politicians ... persistently urged the government to revoke our business licenses, take away our lands and property, and imprison us as enemy aliens.... As a result, Ottawa gave the British Columbia Security Commission full powers to have all Japanese Canadians relocated to a minimum of 100 miles inland. Our community foundation, created by more than half a century of our pioneers' sweat and blood, was destroyed. The lands, property, and businesses that we 22,000 compatriots had achieved after many years of hard work were taken from us, and we were herded to the interior of the province.

Actions of the government became harsher still in the days before removal:

> Our men who had been working in factories, lumber camps, and other places were all dismissed and exiled from Vancouver. They were sent to work on road camps in Ontario, Alberta, and the interior of British Columbia. They were separated from the women, children and older people unable to work.... [In Vancouver] there was so much confusion in the Powell Street area that you would have thought it was the scene of a fire. In the beginning of March, K-san was sent to a place called Hope. A curfew was imposed ... forbidding any Japanese to be outside between seven in the evening and seven in the morning ... we have not a single weapon to defend ourselves. As enemy aliens we could not claim the protection of the law and even if we were kicked around we could do nothing but grit our teeth, swallow our tears, and obey orders.

[My son Arimoto] was finally sent away to a road camp, a place called Taft, on April 13th.... Wealthier people were given certain choices as to where they could live, using their own resources. They were allowed to take all of their household goods with them, but the burden was still a heavy one because they had to pay all moving and living costs. Naturally, most people [like us] cannot afford it.

Each of the church denominations was co-operating with the Security Commission on behalf of its followers, and tried to rent plots of land to be moved to.... I could not help feeling grateful and happy (to the point of shedding tears) to see hakujin missionaries work devotedly to help the Japanese. The necessary arrangements for places to live (and fuel) were to be handled by the Commission. The only thing we would have to pay ourselves would be the cost of food. This way the expenses would be quite low.

Catholics were going to Greenwood, Anglicans to Slocan, the United Church people to Kaslo, and the Buddhists to Sandon.... Decades earlier they had been prosperous mining towns, but the mines had been abandoned and the buildings, large and small, were now decrepit and deserted.... I couldn't imagine what sort of places they would be. In May we were finally leaving for these camps.

An agent took charge of the house, and all our business matters were to be entrusted to him. We were told that the house rent was to be kept by the government and we were not to receive it. We sold off most of the furniture, but since the buyer took advantage of our situation we got very little for it. I was mortified, but there was no point in complaining when almost every Japanese was in the same position. All our possessions – house, land, and store – were listed and handed over to the government custodian. All we could do was to grit our teeth, hold back our tears, and head for the interior.

Departures were heart-rending and life in exile brought many difficult adjustments:

On Wednesday, June 3rd, one hundred and forty people, including us, were assembled and sent to Slocan, British Columbia. Two trains had gone at the end of May, and this was the third one.

The day before departure I cut as many flowers from the garden as I could and went to visit the family graves. I offered the flowers to my dead husband, my son Ken, and my older brother, and bid farewell to them all....

We took rice to T's house, cooked it and made many rice balls to stuff in our lunch boxes. We also packed our bags with bread, butter, roast chicken, canned goods, and fruits to take with us on the long trip. This was enough food for about three or four days. Soon my daughter's family came to join us for a farewell dinner.... Although

Mrs. T's home cooking was always delicious, that day the miso soup and the boiled food was especially tasty.... I wondered if the day would come when we could again share a meal. My heart was heavy....

At six-thirty we boarded the train. The Mounted Police examined each of us and checked our names off against a registry. Every passenger was handed a dollar to pay for a meal on the train. I again tried hard to control my tears and be silent while experiencing such humiliation. I kept repeating to myself, "We are no longer Canadian citizens; we are Japanese taken prisoner in an enemy country. Behind us stands the national dignity of the great nation of Japan. One day we will again have our dignity."

[As] the train slowly pulled out, I felt hollow as I was being driven away from the place where I had lived for nearly thirty years. At rail crossings here and there, crowds of Japanese gathered to wave and call out their good wishes. On a bluff near the outskirts of town the T family was sadly waving goodbye. All of us were moved to wave handkerchiefs out the windows until we could no longer see each other....

Surrounded by dark green hills and a mirror-like lake, Slocan has some fine scenery. It's just like a summer resort and the water is so clean that it runs through the pipes that go directly into the kitchens. We must think it lucky to move to a place like this, since there are said to be camps where water is not in such abundant supply....

When I arrived there were about five hundred of us, but I heard there were plans to bring in four to five thousand people. There were about three hundred or so hakujin settlers already living in the area. Officials at the Commission office were kind enough, but what gave us unexpected pleasure were the smiles and friendliness of the local hakujin. It relieved my fears somewhat and I began to think that living in exile would not be as bad as we thought it would be.

We stayed in a big hall on the outskirts of town for exactly one week, until Tokunaga and the others had the luck to find an empty house.... A mile or so into the mountains to the southeast of Slocan there were the remains of a silver mine. There were a number of abandoned buildings, large and small, but since no more than five or six years had gone by since they had been used they still looked new. The main building was large enough to be divided into apartments and over twenty Japanese were working hard as carpenters to make the building suitable for the evacuees.

The small building at the foot of the hill was assigned to us. It was the former mine office. Its light brown paint was still in good condition and it had many large windows that let in a lot of light. The five people in our family were given one house to live in together. This was a fortunate exception, which caused envy and jealousy among others.[2]

132 *Keibo Oiwa*

> Tokunaga acquired some scrap lumber from the nearby mill and made shelves. The rest of us were also busy putting plates, food, and other small things in order. We began to clear the land around the house and made a garden. We planted lettuce, radishes, and beans although it was a bit late in the season. We also transplanted the chrysanthemums, trefoil, and coltsfoot that we had uprooted in such a hurry the morning we left Vancouver. There were so many tough thickets, dead trees, and a network of bracken roots that a spade wouldn't even break through ... it was dreadful backbreaking labor for Tokunaga.
>
> The 21st was the anniversary of my husband's death.... His photograph, enlarged and framed, was hung on the kitchen wall. Since there were plenty of little lilies blooming behind our house, I picked some, put them in a small empty bottle, and left them as an offering on the makeshift altar that Tokunaga had nailed together from a piece of board.... With some leftover flour and red bean paste we made dumplings and boiled some fiddleheads we picked on the mountain. We put these dishes in front of [the] photograph as an offering and we humbly shared a meal with him. I am sure my deceased husband must have been surprised to have this service in such unfamiliar poor surroundings. It made me think of how he loved fiddleheads. Every year we had gone to the woods near Burnaby to pick them.
>
> In order not to create unemployment problems the Commission tried to supply work for as many Japanese as possible: carpenters and skilled craftsmen, people to collect firewood from the forests, others to transport and chop it, warehouse hands, truck drivers, janitors, bath house workers, stovepipe cleaners, sales people in shops, hospital attendants, busboys and waitresses in restaurants. There were over a thousand people in all....
>
> Wages were as small as they were in the road camps, but since we did not have to pay for housing we made enough to buy food. The old and the sick that could not work or did not receive any money from family members working in road camps were given government assistance.

By August of 1943, Kaoru Ikeda, her family, and friends were resigned to their circumstances and found creative solutions to meeting the challenges of life in Slocan:

> Fortunately I was extremely healthy. I had completely recovered from the hay fever that I suffered so much with in Vancouver. In my old age I was unable to be much use in the household and felt sorry for my daughter and her husband to have a burden like me on their shoulders.... I prayed I could maintain my health until peacetime would come again. Also I prayed my whole family would be kept safe.

We found huckleberry bushes everywhere in the woods. In August when the berries became dark red and ripe, we picked and ate them with sugar and milk – they were so delicious. After having heard that the local people gathered bushels of them to make jam, we too went to pick and make jam two or three times. Both the color and the taste were first class. Everyday, however warm it was, I put on a sweater and two pairs of socks as protection against the mosquitoes, and wandered off into the mountains. Chisato would see me off, making fun of my outfit and wishing me luck on my quest.

The fall scenery of Slocan was especially fine. From the mountaintops we could see the clear water of the lakes down below. The mixed yellows of the willows and deciduous trees against the deep green of the mountains and the red maples composed a beautiful canvas. When the berry season had passed we began to gather pinecones and dead twigs. Some of the cones were extraordinarily large.... And they were filled with so much sap; they burned extremely well in our morning fire. Searching for mushrooms was also fun. The mountains being so full of pine, one would expect matsutake mushrooms[3] to appear. On Sundays there were many people who went hiking in search of [them], but we could not find any. Anyway, where ever one lives offers unique pleasures.

Waking on the morning of October 31st, we were all amazed to discover a blanket of pure white snow. Although previous mornings had been cold and frosty, no one could have imagined that we would have snow so soon. Looking at each other, somebody said what we were all thinking: "We should have known better, Slocan is not Vancouver!" That night was Halloween but how could it mean anything in this place? Mariko discovered a few fireworks that were left over from the year before. After dark we divided some apples and fireworks with the children across the way until they had two or three each. Then to everyone's delight we set off a display.

There were about 5,000 Japanese in the general area of Slocan, in various communities. As their first year in exile passed, some tried to continue life as normally as possible, while others began to show the effects of enforced restrictions.

The Japanese there [in a nearby community] have formed an association called Hakko-kai[4] and the women have their own group. I hear that there are many brave women who don't hesitate to take their demands and grievances right to the Commission. They are quite ready to shout and pound the table until they are heard.

I hear a school is being built, but because there is a lack of construction materials the work goes very slowly. It may not be so bad for the little ones, but for high school-aged kids it's not so simple. With nothing to do they won't learn anything good except to run loose and play around. Children whose parents keep a close eye on them will be all right, but there are, I hear, plenty of the other kind whose parents have money enough to be extravagant and have a good time gambling. Of course the young people will imitate them. Some, they say, will stake a bundle at gambling. There are also many ugly stories going around about the hoards of wild young kids who are out at the movies and dance halls all night.

Even among the workingmen there are said to be those who slack off and fool around during working hours, saying that it's stupid to work seriously for such low wages. When I think how relentlessly we were driven into these circumstances it is understandable how some of us can lose heart and give up trying. But considering our position as displaced Japanese, shouldn't we try and keep a little more self-respect? Let's not despair over our fate. There will be a day when peace is restored to the world. Concerned people knit their brows in worry about what is happening to our young people. When the time comes they will have to form a second wave of pioneers and create a new Japanese Canadian history....

Until now I have been a firm believer that Japanese are diligent, honest, humble, and kind. I have always been proud of my people. However, since coming to this place I have heard many stories that portray our people as capable of every kind of wickedness. Of course I realize these are only partly true. But still ... it hurts me so much to hear that Japanese people can be so base. Whatever our lot in life may become we must not despair; we must strive for a better future without ever losing our sense of gratitude.

As their second year in Slocan begins, and shortages of all types increase, the people do their best to celebrate the holidays.

The recent shortages of goods in this country are unbelievable. Last year aluminum products were restricted, next it was rubber; gas rationing goes without saying. Similarly there are severe shortages of steel, and glass products, shoes and other leather goods. Synthetics have replaced cotton, and among foodstuffs sugar was rationed first so there is hardly any candy available. We manage to buy a few sweets for Christmas, but jams and canned fruit are almost completely out of stock.

Time is passing so quickly; the year is almost over. There was a Christmas concert at the church and the children from Sunday school and kindergarten received some presents. Mariko was baptized on the Sunday of Christmas week. Despite a shortage of ingredients, Chisato managed to make a delicious Christmas cake and baked lots of cookies. We sent my son Arimoto cake and cookies as well as a leather half-coat. He was so pleased with his gifts that he sent a letter of thanks by special delivery, which arrived on Christmas Eve. I was most relieved to know that he was celebrating Christmas in good health.

Ayako and Mariko went into the mountains to find a small Christmas tree. Sadly their many Christmas ornaments were left in Vancouver, but they are imaginative enough to make their own. They waded through the snow and picked heaps of red berries they found thrusting up from the ground. Then they threaded them alternately with balls of cotton into 5- to 6-inch-long pieces, and with these draped over the tree's branches, with some store-bought silver "icicles" sprinkled on, we had first class decorations – quite lovely. Here and there we placed three or four birds I made from rags.

We had a wonderful dinner of delicious roast chicken that Chisato cooked in place of turkey.... Then a whole crowd of kids from the other building descended upon us to admire our Christmas tree. Each of them was very happy to receive the cookies and apples wrapped in paper and the little cloth birds and pin cushions that we divided among them. Later in the evening the older kids played cards exuberantly and were pleased when we served them Christmas cake and cocoa. Thus, our Christmas turned out to be an unexpectedly merry time.

Now we are at the end of the year. In this wandering life of ours, there isn't much we can do to prepare for the New Year. Knowing that the children long for kuri-kinton (sweetened chestnut) I substituted peas for chestnuts and managed to make mame-kinton (sweetened beans). I chopped fruits into the leftover gelatin, which made for a nice dessert. I cooked the few black beans that we had received from Mrs. M and been saving for this occasion. Chisato baked some cupcakes and made udon noodles, which took her a long time. She cooked the chicken and made spaghetti, which was everyone's favorite. This is the whole list of our New Year's feast.... Thus the year 1942 has come to a close at last.

Diary

Following her memoir of events immediately preceding Japan's entry into the war and the months after, the diary section of Ikeda's journal offers rare snapshots of life and attitudes in the detainment areas.

March 13, 1943
It's been raining for days; the snow is now almost all gone. Spring is in the air. The long winter of hibernation is slowly coming to an end. However for us Japanese spring still seems far away. The other day there was an announcement that the land, houses and other properties in B.C. owned by Japanese would all be disposed of by the

Custodians. I know there are people whose boats and cars have already been sold. One person whose car cost nearly one thousand dollars had it sold for seventy-five, and after the Custodians took their handling and transportation fees the man got next to nothing. This situation is causing panic among those with property.

On the other hand I hear that Canada's shortage of manpower is becoming a serious problem. There are government people who want to send the Japanese to farms in Eastern Canada. They are trying to do it but they can't agree on a policy. The Japanese are sick and tired of the government and the Commission wavering, and feel they cannot trust them. As Japanese we are not willing to accept the idea of going east, there is a rumor that the government will use force. They say after the work in the winter finishes those who were working for the Commission now will have no jobs. They say that they will never give us unemployment relief. This implies that there is no other way than to move east.

Thus, young bachelors, who have few responsibilities, have begun to move. But middle-aged men, with a family to support, well ... it is not so easy. They are worried about having to do different labor than they are used to. It is almost a year since [we left Vancouver] last spring and we are finally settling into our simple life, and now they are talking about moving us again. So the women here are disturbed and spend a lot of time anxiously discussing what will happen. I also hear rumors that the young people working on the road camps will also be forced to move to sugar beet farms. I am very worried about my son. Right here my son-in-law will be able to work in the office for the time being, but in the future we don't know what will happen. Chisato is worried.

The Japanese Committee is said to be planning to appeal to the Ottawa government to overturn the decision to dispose of our personal property. I doubt very much that such an appeal will do anything. Now we are prisoners of the war, living in an enemy country. They will do whatever they want to do. The politicians in the province of British Columbia are determined to uproot the foundations that the Japanese had managed to lay. I pray that the strength of our nation will shine over us one day....

Construction of the school is finished, so children can now start going to school in April.

The other day Chisato made tofu, which she learned from Mrs. Kawabata from across the way. It was very delicious. I had believed that we didn't have the necessary ingredients for tofu, but according to Mrs. Kawabata we can substitute Epsom salts. Camp life has its own merit. Because we are here we are learning certain ways to survive.

These days the price increases are outrageous. There are shortages of almost everything. The lack of vegetables is especially serious. A cabbage the size of a baby's head costs from thirty to fifty cents, a bunch of celery from fifty to eighty cents, spinach is twenty-five cents a pound, apples sixty cents a dozen, oranges are eighty-five cents a dozen, and canned goods are practically nonexistent.

Now that the snow is gone everybody is working hard to make their own vegetable gardens. Digging gardens in this country is hard because of the stumps, rocks and trees. But everyone works hard, making nice borders of wood, and the gardens all look pretty. In my family we are also very busy digging and planting gardens. An acquaintance from town gave me bulbs for various flowers so I decided to make a small flower garden just in front of our house. I found last year's pansies and snapdragons still alive after the long winter, so I transplanted them into my new garden.

Another fall arrives.

September 27, 1943
It's cold in the mornings and evenings. I hear that the vegetables were damaged by frost in Bay Farm and Popoff. Therefore, everyone is putting cloth sacks and newspapers over their gardens. Since we don't have much in our garden we don't have to cover it, except the chrysanthemums, which are beginning to bloom.

I learned from a friend how to make pickled plums as a substitute for Japanese umeboshi pickles. So we bought green plums. Luckily we have some shiso (red beef-steak plant) leaves planted in the garden which we added to the pickled plums.... Here shiso is very rare, so I gave several friends some of the precious leaves. I hear those without shiso would use beets for red coloring. People made me promise to give them seeds so I will try to extract as many shiso seeds as possible.

Fuki (coltsfoot) is also very precious. People are asking me for even a small root of it. I was told that it is best to replant fuki in the fall and cover it with compost so that next spring good sprouts will come out. I asked my son-in-law to do the job. He found that the roots were strong and long, so I could give some to my friends.

Mariko was accepted at the Slocan high school and is now commuting. There she still gets a correspondence course, but being in a school environment is better for her. The Catholic Church opened a high school that many attend, and the Anglican Church just opened a high school, too, and many of Mariko's friends are now going there. Both schools only go up to grade eleven, so as a twelfth grader Mariko had to go to the Slocan high school.

Our chrysanthemums have small yellow flowers. These are the ones my grandchildren received in New Denver as Easter presents. Thanks to my son-in-law who took good care of them, they are doing well.

October 14, 1943
Clear and sunny. Feeling better I finally got up. The last few days suddenly became cold and this morning the ground was completely frozen and it spoiled our garden. Everybody is busy salvaging whatever they can from their gardens. Our chrysanthemums withered. In the afternoon I walked into the mountains for a short walk. Probably because the summer was too dry, or too many trees have been cut down, the mushrooms are not good this year.

I hear that the Canadian government decided on a policy of "selective service" in which young bachelors are forced to go east for work. These are Canadian-born young people. How can the government treat these Canadians in the same way as they treat us – as enemy aliens? The government deprived them of their simple human and civil rights and herded them off to unfamiliar places. Although stripped of their rights, the Japanese Canadian men are still expected to live up to the obligations of being Canadians when the Government sees fit. How unreasonable! I know well that there is no point in resisting but I can't control my anger.

November 18, 1943
The Spanish consul came to visit and at the Bay Farm camp he had a meeting with the Japanese Committee. According to the consul, Spain is limited to trying to protect Japanese nationals and they are not concerned with nisei or naturalized Canadians. This statement caused much agitation among the Japanese here. The Canadian government has taken everything not only from the Japanese nationals but also from the nisei and the naturalized Canadians. Thus, we all ended up together in the interior. But if the Japanese and Spanish governments thrust us aside as Canadians then what will we do? No protection from anybody. Some are upset, some are depressed. It's a big mess.

More thoughtful people say that Japan won't give up on us. It is rather understandable for the Spanish to officially take this position. The Japanese government and people must know how we are treated by Canada. For instance, some Japanese, including nisei and naturalized Canadians, have already gone back to Japan through prisoner exchange programs. They are sure to have reported what is going on over here.

The Canadian government is so hypocritical. On the one hand they deprive us of the right to be Canadian and on the other they regard us as Canadian when they need our manpower. Their so called selective service is now being challenged by many people so the government is shifting its position and have now begun to allow some young people to work within the province of B.C. More and more young people who are eager to work are going to logging camps. Then again those parents whose sons had been sent east are complaining that it's not fair that others are allowed to remain in B.C. to work. I hear that there was an incident where these people with complaints demonstrated at the Commission office making a large scene. I think everything stems from the government's lack of definite direction.

Entering their third year in exile:

December 24, 1943
In the afternoon on this Christmas Eve day we were surprised to see the Mounted Police go into the mountains and come back with a big radio receiver on a sled. We heard that somebody informed the Mounties that Mr. K, who lives above us, had a short wave radio. They raided his house and confiscated the radio. Deep in the mountains without much entertainment would it be so harmful for someone to listen to the radio? I'm shocked at the narrow-mindedness of the Mounties and the existence of a Japanese informant who will sell-out his own people. I cannot help feeling hateful. I feel sorry for Mr. K.

January 30, 1944
Clear and sunny, very cold. Today there was distribution of care packages from Japan at the Bay Farm school. I saw the people from across the street going with empty buckets to pick up their packages. My daughter and Tokunaga also went during the morning. One bottle of soy sauce per person, one pound of tea per family and half a pound of miso per family.

Sitting looking at this gift, which has traveled across the world, sent by my compatriots, I can barely restrain my tears as the memories well-up. At lunch we gathered to drink some of the tea, appreciating its beautiful scent, good quality and rich taste.

At first there were many conflicting opinions as to how to distribute the care packages. I hear the Committee members spent a lot of time discussing the possibilities. According to some people these packages were sent as gifts for the Japanese nationals and were not supposed to be distributed to the nisei and naturalized Canadians. But then others argued that everybody here is herded together as enemy aliens, so we should not discriminate. People were divided about whether to distribute to each individual or each household. They even debated whether a small baby should be considered as a person to receive goods. At the end they concluded that even a baby should be treated with equal rights.

It was announced that the empty soy sauce barrels would be sold ... we all ended up drawing lots. Fortunately we were lucky enough to buy a barrel. The care packages were distributed to every camp where Japanese Canadians have been relocated. There was an article in *The New Canadian* about the trouble concerning the distribution of the care packages. A group of young nisei in eastern Canada insisted that they were Canadians with no relationship whatsoever to Japan. To distribute care packages to them, they argued, was an insult to them as Canadians. Using strong words they refused the package and again protested to the Ottawa government asking to be recognized as Canadian citizens.... For an old person like myself this behavior was far beyond my comprehension.

Those young people born in this country grew up and received their education here. Now they have settled in the east and are trying their best to be accepted as true Canadians. Considering all this, their actions are understandable. But the real problem is that even though they repeatedly try to prove their loyalty to Canada, Canadians are such traditionally strong racists that they refuse them equal treatment. For the time being because of the wartime shortage of manpower, Canada is trying to make the best use of Nikkei labor, but when the time comes they will flip their attitudes to the other side. We have seen Canada's true nature through our recent experiences. What is democracy? Who can talk about it? Who has the right to accuse Japan of invading other countries? Isn't Britain the champion invader? The last several centuries of British history are full of invasion after invasion. Since they can be neither Japanese nor Canadian, I wonder what the future of the nisei youth will be? Deprived of civil rights these young people are in a sad situation. I just hope that their efforts will lead to a positive solution.

May, 1944
I've been seriously ill since midnight of the twelfth. The doctor came to examine me and said I had to go to the hospital.... I was told that I had an ulcer of the intestine. It was very painful and I was often nauseous. I couldn't swallow anything, including medicine. They had to inject me with the medicine and put an intravenous in my arm for nutrition. For a while they said I was in critical condition, but after four days the pain began to lessen and I was able to take in a small amount of medicine and orange juice. The doctor assured me that I would recover.

December 7, 1944
This day is back again. It has been three long years since Pearl Harbor. What is happening in my native country? The Americans have been joyfully boasting of the bombing of Tokyo. But also I hear that Japan is doing very well on many battlefronts that the Americans haven't talked about. I can only pray for good results. The news from radios and newspapers that we get access to is full of propaganda.

The diary of Kaoru Ikeda tells us of conflicts among different Japanese Canadian factions, the bureaucracy and betrayal of the Canadian government, and the state of the war in which Japan was increasingly in crisis. Despite Kaoru's anger toward the Canadian government, her sympathy for the nisei generation who insisted on their Canadian citizenship grew. On the one hand she accepted her fate as an enemy alien with resignation, while on the other, she quietly wished for a better future for the younger generations and their recovery after the war. At the end of 1943 she wrote this tanka poem:

> I thought
> it would only be temporary
> In this Mountain country
> another year passes
> as snow deepens

The following year, 1944, her health deteriorated. On her birthday in November, she wrote: "I was afraid that I would not be able to live until this birthday, but I am grateful to have made it." The last entry of the diary is December 7, which is the third anniversary of Pearl Harbor. The last two sentences describe her thoughts about the war:

> The difference between reality and propaganda is now hard to distinguish. I cannot believe everything that is reported. Because we cannot hear the news from Japan we are in a constant state of anxiety.

Notes

1 A different and longer translation of this diary and memoir was published in *Stone Voices: Wartime Writings of Japanese Canadian Issei* (Oiwa 1991). Parts of the original Japanese text may be found in Ikeda (1990: 77–101).
2 The five family members were the author herself, her daughter Chisato, Chisato's husband Tokunaga, and their daughters Junko and Mariko.
3 *Matsutake* mushrooms, which grow in pine woods, are a favorite Japanese delicacy.
4 *Hakko* (the whole world) evokes Japan's mission of uniting the world under its leadership. It was a key propaganda word in wartime Japan.

8 The Japanese of Peru
The first-century experience and beyond

Daniel M. Masterson

The Japanese community of Peru is the oldest and most well established of all Asian communities in Latin America. People of Japanese ancestry have been residing in Peru for more than a century where they initially made productive lives as merchants, tradesmen, shopkeepers, mechanics, and cotton farmers. In more recent decades their descendants have become doctors, dentists, lawyers, accountants, and successful businessmen. Of course, in the most prominent example of political success, Alberto Fujimori served as Peru's president for a decade after his election in June 1990. As the Nikkei of Peru move beyond their first century of experience, the younger generations face many of the same challenges in this century as their forbears in Peru confronted in the first years of the twentieth century. Younger Japanese Peruvians are migrating to their ancestral homeland in search of the secure and comfortable lives that have eluded them in Peru. Before I discuss these issues, let me briefly examine some of the distinctive characteristics of the Japanese Peruvians in order to place their experience in the context of the broader Japanese diaspora in Latin America (Masterson and Funada-Classen 2004: 11–86).

The mainly male workers who migrated from Japan to work in the sugar cane fields of coastal Peru were the first Japanese immigrants to establish permanent residence in Latin America. Arriving in 1899, they were able to accomplish what a small contingent of Japanese contract laborers that traveled to the Mexican state of Chiapas in 1897 could not do: create new lives in a very difficult environment. The Japanese colony in Chiapas failed after less than eighteen months due to harsh working conditions and inadequate support from the Japanese immigration company that sponsored them. The vast majority of the Chiapas immigrants returned to Japan. It was in Peru where the Japanese established a permanent presence when 780 contract laborers arrived during the last year of the nineteenth century.

Japanese sugar workers in Peru were expected to fill the void left by African slaves, freed in the 1850s, and Chinese bonded laborers who abandoned the plantations amid much violence in the 1870s and 1880s. The most immediate difficulties confronting the Japanese workers were disease and overwork. Cholera took a heavy toll during their first three years. Other major problems included inadequate food and housing, underpayment by plantation management, and the sometimes violent hostility of the local native population (Gardiner 1975: 40–70). Anti-Japanese feelings may have been enflamed by the local press in the communities near the sugar plantations of Peru's central coast. In mid-1899 one such newspaper, *El Nacional*, carried the banner headline "Death to the Japanese!" The primary cause of this hostility seemed to be the perception that Japanese sugar workers were being paid higher wages than their Peruvian counterparts. Violent confrontations resulted, and the Peruvian police were rarely inclined to protect the newly arrived Japanese migrants (Sakuda 1999: 97–107). These conditions forced many Japanese laborers to flee the plantations and to seek a more tolerable lifestyle in the metropolitan Lima-Callao region. Summing up conditions on the sugar plantations for the first Japanese immigrants to Peru, immigration agent Teikichi Tanaka lamented, "The plantation [in Peru] is a country unto itself into which national law does not enter; the owner is a potentate; and punishment a matter of course. Even life and death are at the will of the plantation" (Irie 1951b: 447). These first refugees from the cane fields established a pattern that would set them apart from their Japanese counterparts throughout the rest of Latin America. From the beginning of the twentieth century to the present day, they have been highly concentrated in Peru's capital and its environs. Unlike in the rest of Latin America, and particularly in Brazil, most Japanese Peruvians chose to make their living in urban commerce and services rather than in the agricultural sector. The Japanese immigrant family emerged during the second decade of the immigrant experience in Peru, largely as a result of the *yobiyose* system that was quickly initiated during the first decade of the twentieth century. Strong family unity has been the focus of the Japanese Peruvian cultural solidarity that has helped the immigrants and their descendants meet the challenges of World War II and the guest worker migration of the younger Nikkei to Japan after 1990.

Another way in which the Japanese Peruvians are unique is their recent involvement in national politics. A relatively small number of Japanese Brazilians have held local and state political offices. But nowhere else in Latin America or, for that matter, anywhere else in the world outside of Japan, has a person of Japanese ancestry been elected to the presidency of their nation. The Alberto Fujimori phenomenon in Peru is today the focus of much scrutiny and debate. The Peruvian nisei broke the pattern of abstention from politics that has been so characteristic of the Japanese in Latin America. Significantly, many Japanese Peruvians opposed Fujimori's original candidacy for the presidency in 1990. Some were worried that a failed or disgraced Fujimori presidency would call dangerous attention to a Japanese community that had suffered many decades of anti-Japanese sentiments that only began to abate during the 1960s. Memories were still vivid among the aging issei and some of their children of the destructive May 1940 anti-Japanese riots in Lima that forced many issei to abandon their homes and businesses and return in poverty to Japan. Even more painful were the memories of the deportation and internment of nearly 2,000 Japanese Peruvians who were rounded up by Peruvian authorities at the behest of the Roosevelt Administration and imprisoned in camps in the southwestern United States during the years 1942 to 1947. Very few of these internees returned to Peru, and most were again deported from the United States to a devastated Japan during the last days of the war and its immediate aftermath (Gardiner 1981: 25–160).

When Fujimori announced his candidacy for the presidency in 1990, most were proud to have a successful nisei contend for the nation's highest office. But others were loath to have the historically low profile of Peru's Japanese community raised to a level where political attacks and open acts of violence might threaten the well-being of the Japanese community. His spectacular initial successes in the war on terrorism and economic stability gained Fujimori widespread praise in Peru as well as abroad. Ultimately, however, after nearly a decade in office, the scandal-plagued collapse of the Fujimori administration and his self-imposed exile to Japan in 2000 brought Peru's Japanese community the notoriety it abhors. Fujimori's experience may well have affirmed the wisdom of the apolitical outlook of the region's Japanese. Indeed, until the appearance of the Fujimori phenomenon, the Latin American Nikkei could be called the region's "unknown immigrants." But after Fujimori's departure to Japan, Peru's Japanese have been left in a state of great unease. After struggling against strong anti-Japanese sentiments for much of the past century, Peru's Japanese are once again on the defensive. How will Peru's Nikkei confront the post-Fujimori era in Peru, at the same time facing an even greater dilemma – the migration of thousands of sansei and yonsei to Japan since 1990 in search of the economic security that is very difficult to attain in Peru? These questions are best initially addressed by providing a brief social and historical profile of Peru's Japanese community.

A Japanese Peruvian community profile

As the twenty-first century began to unfold, the Japanese Peruvian community approached approximately 58,000. This is a conservative projection based upon the results of a census conducted by the Japanese community in 1989 and built upon the earlier findings of a similar 1966 survey that, while very useful, was not as sophisticated or as comprehensive as the later survey. Since 1989, Peru's Japanese community by this estimate has grown at a rate of less than 900 per year. Significantly, the projected 58,000 for 2003 does not take into account the Japanese Peruvians who have migrated to Japan over the past decade or more. It is very difficult to determine the exact number of these migrants, but estimates place them as high as 20,000 to 30,000. I am choosing to include these migrants within the Japanese Peruvian community because it is not yet certain how many of these sojourners will become permanent residents of Japan (Morimoto 1991: 211).

How the 1989 census defines "Japanese" is addressed primarily by social and institutional criteria. Accepting that certainty regarding race mixture or *mestizaje* is nearly impossible to ascertain, the directors of the census used the following criteria to arrive at their estimates. Arguing that there were certain social institutions that were established by nisei in Peru which heavily discouraged membership by those who married non-Japanese partners, the census established a "social nucleus" of the Japanese population of approximately one-third or 32 percent. Another 28 percent were "familiar" with the networks. Another 40 percent had no connections with these organizations at all. Question number 20 of the 1989 census asks specifically about marriage with non-Japanese partners. As one would expect, the highest rate of intermarriage was among the sanseis. The 1989 census showed that the issei generation was rapidly passing away in Peru. Those issei between the ages of 75 and 79 comprised the largest single age group in Peru, or 538 of 2,311 (23.3 percent) (Morimoto 1991: 73).

With very little post-World War II immigration from Japan, Peru's issei presently number less than 5 percent of the Japanese Peruvian population. Thus the leadership role of the issei of Peru passed long ago to the nisei and sansei generations. Peru's sansei comprise half of all Nikkei. The Nikkei, who have held a prominent leadership role since the 1950s with Fujimori being the most outstanding example, now comprise less than one-third of Peru's Japanese. The yonsei and gosei make up 14 percent and less than 1 percent respectively. It is the sansei and yonsei that have migrated to Japan in the greatest numbers as a result of the political turmoil and limited economic opportunities of the past two decades in Peru. As indicated earlier, the vast majority of the nation's Nikkei reside in the Lima-Callao metropolitan area, and today more than 80 percent of Peru's Nikkei reside and work in the nation's largest urban setting.

With the possible exception of Mexico's Japanese, who were relocated to the nation's Federal District during World War II, Peru's Nikkei are one of the most highly centralized communities anywhere in Latin America. The very concentrated nature of their community aided Japanese Peruvians in the creation of schools, fraternal and business associations, and cultural activities. Peru's influential Central Japanese Association, for example, was frequently consulted by Japanese diplomatic officials regarding immigration questions and policies that affected the Japanese community. In addition, the Japanese community's internal communications networks, and most particularly its newspapers, were facilitated by the cohesive nature of Japanese cultural patterns in Peru. Some of Latin America's first Japanese-language newspapers were published in Peru including *Nipponjin* (which appeared in 1909), *Andes Jihô* (first published in 1910), and *Nippi Shimpo* (which appeared in 1921) (Sakuda 1999: 153–4). On the other hand, the concentration of the Japanese in Lima and Callao made them far more visible and an easier target for anti-Japanese activity. It is no coincidence that far more Japanese Peruvians were deported during World War II than Japanese from other Latin American countries.

The economic activities undertaken by Peru's Nikkei have undergone some significant changes over the course of the past eight decades. Traditional occupations in commerce and the service industries have remained relatively stable. However, the number of Japanese engaged in agriculture declined from 28 percent in 1930 to less than 6 percent during the 1990s. More Japanese are employed in the service industries (38 percent) and commerce (29 percent) than in any other occupation. This has been true since the first years of the Japanese presence in Peru. Only after the first two decades of settlement did the first issei begin to drift into agriculture, and this was primarily in cotton growing in the Chancay Valley near the town of Huaral. The first commercial and service enterprises operated by the issei were cafés, small merchandizing shops, dry-cleaning establishments, barber shops, and photography stores. Today, small Japanese-owned establishments such as these can still be frequented in Lima and its immediate suburbs. With the growing prosperity of Peru's Nikkei, more than 10 percent have made careers in industry, with many in management positions. Smaller numbers make their living in construction, the health industries, and education (Morimoto 1991: 177–82).

For those Japanese who work in the professions, most are engineers, accountants, physicians, and dentists. High school and university teaching are also popular occupations. Careers in the professions grew steadily but slowly from the mid-1960s to the late 1980s, but terrible economic and social conditions during the early 1990s and the resulting limited opportunities for professionals in Peru have clearly reversed this trend over the past decade. Just as in Brazil, many highly trained and well-educated Nikkei left their chosen professions for much more highly paid manual labor jobs in the factories of Japan. It should be noted that the number of Japanese in the professions in Peru has always been a relatively small component of the Japanese community, despite the high level of education of Peru's Nikkei. Whether this is reflective of lingering prejudice against the Japanese or rather a continued preference for the established vocations among the Nikkei is still not clear.

It will be useful to take a brief look at the diet, dress, and cultural rituals of Japanese Peruvians, as some examples will be helpful in gaining a better understanding of Peru's Nikkei. As of the last decade, Japanese Peruvians usually combined at least one Japanese meal per week with the native food of their nation. As one might expect, rice and vegetables are the main staples of their diet. On festive occasions, *mochi* (rice cake) is served. The people of Okinawan origin primarily eat soup with rice and pork. Also popular with the Okinawans of Peru is a rice drink known as *on* that is consumed on a daily basis. The Japanese of Peru dress in Western style, but the kimono and two types of sandals known as *zôri* and *geta* are worn. The Japanese Peruvians are impeccable in their personal habits. The public bath is still as popular for men as it is in Japan (Fukumoto 1997: 399–509).

Many Japanese Peruvians still engage in rituals regarding birth and coming of age. This adherence to Japanese traditions is interesting considering that over 90 percent of the respondents to the community census of 1989 listed their religion as Roman Catholic. This conjunction is often during marriage and funeral ceremonies; for example, a Catholic wedding is often marked by the serving of saké and *mochi*. This practice is also often followed at funerals. A very popular festival among the Okinawans is called *Shiimi-sai* or festival of the dead. *Shiimi-sai* is celebrated during the third moon of the year. Traditional Japanese music as well as dance and song are also especially important to the Japanese Peruvians. Children are taught Japanese songs in school and adults sing them on special occasions. Some traditional folk dances are performed on special occasions. These are often performed to the accompaniment of such musical instruments as the *shamisen*, a type of banjo, and the *shakuhachi*, a flute made of bamboo (Fukumoto 1997: 420–2).

With the migration of many Japanese Peruvians to Japan over the past decade, an important question arises. What will the cultural impact of long-term residency in Japan be for the Peruvian Nikkei and their children, some of whom were born in Japan? If these sansei and yonsei return to Peru in significant numbers will they have greater adherence to Japanese cultural traits, or will they maintain the usual distance from the attitudes of their parents and grandparents? Furthermore, what will be the consequences for the Japanese Peruvian community if large numbers of its young people remain in Japan? Partially deprived of its future leaders, the prospects for Peru's Nikkei would indeed be grim. In order to understand the significance and historical context of the dilemma confronting the Japanese Peruvian community, I will provide a brief overview of the evolution of the Japanese Peruvian community.

Evolution of the Japanese Peruvian community in Peru

Two individuals, one Peruvian and the other Japanese, were responsible for bringing the first Japanese contract workers to Peru: Teikichi Tanaka, an official of the Morioka Emigration Company, and Augusto B. Leguía, a prominent sugar planter and later president of Peru, drafted the four-year contract bringing the 790 immigrants to Callao aboard the Japanese vessel *Sakura-maru* in April 1899. These workers were to be paid twenty-five yen or approximately US$12.00 per month. The immigrants' expenses were to be taken out of their wages up to a total of ten yen per month. Many workers hoped to save as much as 720 yen during their four-year contractual obligation. This would leave them with the substantial sum of $320 when they prepared to return to Japan. Since Japanese workers in Japan earned less than half of the Peruvian wage scale, most of the first Japanese workers who migrated to Peru felt that the substantial risks they were taking were worthwhile as they ventured to a strange land.

Few of these workers, however, who came from Japan's prefectures of Niigata, Yamaguchi, Hiroshima, and the separate Ryûkyû Islands (Okinawa), ever earned even a fraction of the 720 yen they hoped to save. From the beginning the Okinawan immigrants made up a sizable component of the migrant population to Peru. Often viewing themselves as culturally apart from the *naichi-jin* or home island Japanese, the Okinawans established their own prefectural organizations soon after the first group of thirty-six immigrants arrived in Peru in 1906. By the end of the 1930s, which marked the end of all substantive Japanese immigration to Peru, approximately 10,300 Okinawans had settled in Peru. Okinawans thus comprised more than half of Peru's Japanese population by the beginning of World War II in December 1941. For their part the *naichi-jin* in Peru tended to keep their distance from the Okinawans and this reflected a cultural pattern that was emulated in other Japanese communities throughout Latin America (Tigner 1956: 582–600).

During the first decade of the twentieth century more than 6,000 Japanese migrated to Peru. Only 230 of these migrants were women and they were mainly the wives of contract laborers brought to Peru before 1906. Peruvian plantation owners clearly preferred single male contract laborers. Indeed, prior to 1910 only 184 of the Japanese were free immigrants. At the end of the first decade of the twentieth century, 80 percent of the 6,000 Japanese were still living in Peru. Death, mainly from diseases such as cholera and typhoid, claimed the lives of 481 of these first issei pioneers. Among this group, 241 were able to transmigrate from Peru primarily to Mexico, Bolivia, Chile, and Argentina (see Amemiya, Chapter 10). A small number were able to find the financial means to return to Japan (Fukumoto 1997: 122–42).

From the early twentieth century until 1930, Peru remained relatively politically stable. With the Depression, however, economic hardship, mass politics, and increasing anti-Japanese sentiment emerged in Peru. Anti-Japanese riots occurred at the beginning of the 1930s during the administration of army colonel Luis M. Sánchez Cerro (1930–3). This anti-Japanese sentiment may be attributed in large part to the frustration and anger of the nation's hardship-ridden working- and lower-middle-class elements who wrongly blamed the Japanese, whose businesses remained viable, for a good part of Peru's economic woes. Enflaming the anti-Japanese feelings was the stridently nationalist leftist party called the *Alianza Popular Revolucionaria Americana* (American Popular Revolutionary Alliance (APRA)) party. APRA leaders continued to play the anti-Japanese card throughout the 1930s and the World War II years, in an effort to gain national legitimacy as a prelude to achieving full political power (Masterson 1991: 67–8). After Pearl Harbor, however, APRA's efforts were neutralized by the conservative President Manuel Prado y Ugarteche (1939–45) who participated fully in Washington's efforts to deport and detain as many Japanese Peruvians as possible in U.S. internment camps.

By 1940, 17,598 Japanese were residing in Peru. Of this total, 5,853 were women, and thus a significant gender imbalance existed even after four decades of Japanese settlement. In 1940 Peru's Japanese population was by that time overwhelmingly centered in the Lima-Callao metropolitan area. Few among the first Nikkei in Peru had the opportunity to own land, but because of their continued success in urban commerce and the service industries, an increased influx of female migrants, and the success of the *yobiyose* system, the foundations of Peru's Japanese community were well established during the two decades before World War II.

For those Japanese immigrants still laboring on the sugar plantations, the decade following 1910 brought significant change. Loss of traditional markets hastened the demise of Japanese contract labor in the sugar industry. Thus some issei left the failing sugar plantations to begin small-scale ventures in increasingly profitable cotton production. The Chancay and Cañete Valleys near Lima were the centers of Japanese cotton production, and the city of Huaral in that region became the agricultural and cultural heart of a rising Japanese elite in the cotton trade. By the end of the 1930s Nikamatsu Okada, who came to Peru as a contract laborer in 1903, was one of the most prosperous cotton producers in the Chancay Valley. Sadly, due to his prominent place in the Japanese Peruvian community, he would be deported and interned during World War II (Gardiner 1981: 15).

The prosperity of Japanese commercial interests in Lima-Callao, and their success in the cotton trade despite the economic rigors of the Depression, compounded by growing fears of Japanese militarism following the occupation of Manchuria and the beginning of the Sino–Japanese war, intensely strained relations between Japanese and Peruvian nationals. Adding to this tension were strong feelings against Japanese cultural insularity in Peru. Also troublesome for Peruvian nationalists was the decision of the vast majority of Peru's issei not to seek Peruvian citizenship and the exclusivity of the Japanese school systems and trade associations (Ciccarelli 1982: 116–25). As one Japanese immigrant described it to me, the Japanese community was a "nation within a nation." This insularity assured a common bond among the Japanese in Peru, which was necessary for their mutual assistance programs. On the other hand, it produced ill-founded and often completely false beliefs about the Japanese and their activities among the non-Japanese that could not easily be dispelled.

The anti-Japanese movement and World War II

As previously noted, the May 1940 riots, which arose due to false rumors regarding Japanese military activities in northern Peru, were extremely damaging to the Japanese community. Two days of rioting and looting cost the lives of ten Japanese and injury to hundreds more. Damage in Lima and Haural, where rioting was less intense, involved 600 homes and businesses. The Japanese consul in Lima estimated the damage at approximately US$7 million in 1940. Peruvian police did not attempt to stop the rioting on the first day, and only after the Japanese Embassy lodged a strong protest with the Peruvian government did police use tear gas to end the rioting and looting (FBI 1942: 14). The May 1940 riots were a prelude to an even greater affront to Peru's Japanese community. At the behest of the Roosevelt Administration, which felt the need to assure the protection of the Panama Canal and the west coast of South America from Japanese attack after Pearl Harbor, more than 1,800 Japanese Peruvians were detained by Peruvian authorities and deported to the United States for internment. These deportations were supposed to target only Japanese community and business leaders on a "proclaimed" or so-called black list. In reality they involved the haphazard round-up of any Japanese males that Peruvian police could easily apprehend. The deportations began in early 1942 and continued until mid-1944. The wives and children of many of the deportees later joined their husbands in the camps in the southwestern United States. A significant majority of the more than 1,800 Japanese deportees and those from other Latin American nations were repatriated to Japan while the war still raged. This assured these unfortunates continuing sacrifice and social dislocation for many years after World War II. Only a few hundred were permitted to remain in the United States after their case was championed by the American Civil Liberties Union. Eventually, the Peruvian government allowed a mere fifty of its former Japanese residents to return. In the final analysis strong anti-Japanese prejudice and economic motivation prompted the Peruvian government to cooperate enthusiastically with the deportation program. Raymond Ickes, sent by President Roosevelt to the region to evaluate the deportation and internment program, concluded in mid-1943 that "attempts have been made to send lots of Japanese to the United States because Peruvians wanted their businesses and not because there was any evidence against them" (OSS 1943: 1). The Peruvian government of President Prado was rewarded by Washington for its cooperation with generous lend–lease aid and economic development loans, the most important of which was used to construct Peru's first steel-making facility at Chimbote in northern Peru (Gardiner 1981: 52–173; Higashide 2000: 88–213).

The May 1940 riots and the deportation of Japanese from Peru and other Latin American nations was the low point of the Japanese experience in Latin America. However, it must be remembered that more than 80 percent of Peru's Japanese remained in the country during the war, struggling to survive in the face of a hostile government and a largely antagonistic populace. They were, however, not interned as were their counterparts in the United States, and there were a good number of examples where Peruvians, ignoring the tide of anti-Japanese feeling, helped the Japanese Peruvians to hold on to their land and businesses by serving as interim managers during the war. These examples are the bright side of a very dark episode in Peruvian race relations. They are rarely mentioned in the accounts of the deportation and internment process, but their principled kindness should not be forgotten. Also worthy of attention are Peru's wartime nisei who were frequently presented with the task of maintaining their parents' businesses that were transferred into their names in order to prevent confiscation. The vast majority of Japanese Peruvians who were not deported survived by living very low-profile lives, or they fled to Argentina or Brazil where anti-Japanese prejudice was less pronounced. Heads of families, particularly those on the "proclaimed list," were forced to go into hiding or bribe Peruvian officials on numerous occasions to avoid detention. Despite these many hardships, most of Peru's Japanese were able to rebuild their lives after World War II, but many were forced to start over again, and some began in middle age in entirely new occupations. Such was the case with Alberto Fujimori's father Naoichi, who lost his successful tire repair business during the war and never fully recovered economically in the post-World War II years (Kimura 1998: 13–15). How his family's hardships during and after the war influenced the still quite young nisei, is still open to question, but clearly the younger Fujimori was fully aware of the need to overcome past prejudices against the country's Japanese. While campaigning for the presidency in 1990, Fujimori, who was often called *Chino* (the Chinese) by the Peruvian masses, sought to identify more with the nation's dark-skinned majority than Peru's highly educated coastal elite, who found the novelist Mario Vargas Llosa a candidate more to their liking.

Rebuilding the post-war Japanese Peruvian community

Post-World War II Peruvian governments were unwilling to address the problems of their Japanese Peruvian constituents until the regime of Fernando Belaúnde Terry (1963–8). General Manuel A. Odría (1948–56) reinstated diplomatic relations with Japan in 1952, but nevertheless continued to bar Peruvian citizenship to Japanese who sought naturalization under terms dictated by immigration legislation passed in the early 1930s. Over the course of the next half century, Japanese immigration to Peru was negligible. Thus the second largest Japanese community in Latin America behind Brazil grew very slowly. The self-census in Peru, conducted in 1966, listed the population of the Japanese immigrants and their descendants at 32,002 persons. With very few post-World War II issei establishing new lives in Peru, the nisei, sansei, and yonsei generations became the main focus of the Japanese community's economic and cultural activities. Third- and fourth-generation Japanese were increasingly inclined to marry native Peruvians, although the rate of intermarriage was still low compared with other immigrant groups in Peru.

As they sought to establish stable lives during the post-war era, the Peruvian Nikkei gained strength through collective support. Just as mutual aid societies were the backbone of the Japanese community before World War II, they remained so throughout the latter half of the twentieth century and beyond. The Okinawan Mutual Aid Society, for example, was formed in 1948 to help the Okinawan population of Peru as well as the devastated people of their war-torn homeland. Japanese cotton farmers in the Chancay Valley who survived the war, regrouped and formed the *Asociación Fraternal de Japonesa de Valle de Chancay* (Japanese Fraternal Association of the Chancay Valley). As a social and cultural center for the large Japanese population of Lima-Callao the *Centro Cultural Peruano-Japonés* (Japanese Peruvian Cultural Center) was one of the most important of its type in Latin America. Significantly, the land upon which the cultural center was built in the Lima barrio of Jesus María was donated to the Japanese community by the government of Fernando Belaúnde Terry in partial compensation for the expropriation of Japanese properties and the deportation of Japanese nationals during World War II. Although the compensation was minimal given the amount of suffering involved, it represented the first attempt by any government in the Americas to address the question of reparations for wartime mistreatment of their Japanese residents. The pattern for the Belaúnde administration's reparations was established in 1954, when the Japanese community in Peru was able, with obvious diplomatic assistance from Tokyo, to have the Odría administration enact legislation that called for compensation by the Peruvian government for some of the larger Japanese properties seized by the government during World War II.

Despite these measures, Peru did not encourage, nor did it appeal to, Japanese immigrants during the two decades following World War II. Only 800 Japanese immigrants entered Peru between 1952 and 1970 and the very restrictive immigration laws passed during the 1930s remained largely intact. Thus Brazil, Argentina, Bolivia, and even Paraguay were far more inviting for Latin America's new issei than the nation that became home to the first large contingent of Japanese immigrants at the beginning of the twentieth century. As the Japanese economy began to prosper in the 1960s, successive Peruvian governments sought better relations with Tokyo. In 1960 the Peruvian government announced it was willing to allow the relatives of Japanese Peruvians to emigrate to Peru. Nevertheless, only 150 Japanese immigrants were subsequently admitted under this new legislation. Very likely, few Japanese (given the strengthening economy in Japan) saw better opportunities in Peru than at home. Peru's Nikkei, however, even as Japan's economy was rapidly recovering, still remained committed to bettering their lives in Peru. It is true that the favorable immigration laws which opened Japan's doors to Latin American Japanese in the late 1980s had not yet been enacted. Still, Peru's Nikkei were mainly concerned with rebuilding their lives, especially the social and economic networks that had ensured cultural solidarity in the past. This was particularly true at the local and regional level where Nikkei associations had not previously been strong. For example, the *Sociedad Mutualista Japonesea de Libertad* (Mutual Society of the Japanese of Liberated) in northern Peru was created in 1951 and remained a very active organization through the mid-1990s. Similar fraternal organizations were also established in Chiclayo, Huancayo, Tarma, Cañete, and Callao over the course of the next decade.

Peru's Japanese-language newspapers had been closed during World War II, but new ones appeared in the war's aftermath. Newspapers and magazines such as *Peru Shimpô, Sakura, Nikkô,* and *Juventud Nisei* – and later *El Japón, El Dia, El Nisei, Fuji,* and *Puente* – were publishing regularly and provided much needed community and economic news, thus helping to re-establish community bonds that had been so badly strained during the trauma of war. Increasingly, however, these periodicals and others came to be published in Spanish because the nisei and sansei readership lacked the necessary Japanese language skills (Rocca Torres 1997: 261–74).

Not being conflicted by the sojourner mentality of their parents, the nisei, like their counterparts elsewhere in the Americas, spoke the native language of their country, ate the food of their homeland, and accepted most aspects of the life of their native country. In some cases the nisei chose to have their children educated in the elite foreign community schools such as the Abraham Lincoln School, the Roosevelt School, and the British Primary School. Almost all attended Peruvian universities instead of traveling to Japan. Some students were sent to the United States or Europe to complete their education. Thus the issei's earlier practice of sending their children to Japan to complete their education all but ended. For most parents there was little choice, since their children lacked sufficient Japanese language skills to adjust to living and studying in Japan.

As the Japanese economy began its prolonged boom in the late 1960s, Peru benefited from expanded trade with Japan, but still remained tied to established patterns. Thus Peru traded primary products such as copper and zinc while importing Japanese heavy machinery and automobiles in ever-increasing numbers through the early 1980s. Because Peru's political situation remained unstable, foreign debt became increasingly burdensome, and Japanese businesses were disinclined to invest significantly in the Peruvian economy. Official government assistance to Peru during this period was another matter. In 1983, Japan provided 39 percent of the total economic assistance Peru received in that year (Berrios 2001: 4–5). However, as terrorism increased, instigated primarily by *Sendero Luminoso*, and Peru's economy faltered to the extent that President Alan García (1985–90) felt compelled to suspend payments on Peru's foreign debt, Japan suspended public assistance loans. It is from this troubled setting that Alberto Fujimori emerged as a relatively unknown candidate for the presidency in April 1990.

During this era Peru's Japanese achieved a place of prominence in their society as a result of Japan's growing economic importance, the need of the government to depend more heavily on Tokyo's economic assistance, and ultimately the election of Alberto Fujimori to the presidency. During the two decades before his surprise election, they began to quietly rebuild their lives and achieve modest levels of prosperity even while the Peruvian economy was in steady decline. With Fujimori as president and the promise of substantial Japanese aid and investment and closer ties with the second largest economy in the world, many native Peruvians began to see the Japanese community as an avenue for easing the crushing poverty in Peru. Just as importantly, during his first term in office (1990–5) Fujimori, as the first in a number of "elected dictators" in Latin America during the 1990s, accomplished what few expected. He badly weakened Sendero Luminoso, quickly privatized state-owned corporations, and brought raging inflation under control, thus stabilizing an economy that had been in utter chaos.

As the twentieth century closed, Alberto Fujimori made significant achievements in reducing further the cycle of violence in Peru, continuing to improve the nation's economy, rebuilding the country's infrastructure, and resolving a long-standing border dispute with Ecuador. In some important ways, Fujimori was one of the most successful Peruvian presidents of that century. But he was tarnished by some of the most common flaws of modern Latin American political leaders, including *personalismo*, the need to replace institutional democracy with the cult of personality. He seemingly had little regard for human rights in his quest for national security and, predictably, demonstrated a tolerance for corruption on a massive scale among his closest government associates. Fujimori ruled like a typical Latin America *caudillo* (strong and personalistic leader) with the confidence and resolve of the leaders who transformed Japan during the Meiji era. But his forceful and often questionable legal methods, the rampant corruption in his administration, and his penchant for *continuismo* (continuing in power) eventually led to his downfall and self-imposed exile in Japan after a decade as president (Sakuda 1999: 409–97).

The Japanese Peruvian community, despite welcoming the success of Fujimori during his first term in office, remained ambivalent regarding his presidency. Ultimately their fears proved to be correct. Still, the most pressing challenge to the Japanese community in Peru was not the anti-Fujimori backlash that arose in the late 1990s, but rather the exodus of so many young Nikkei to Japan during the last decade of the twentieth century.

As of the late 1990s, the Japanese Association of Peru has experienced a significant drop in membership. This is very likely due to the exodus of many young Nikkei to Japan, and the lack of relevance the association has for a generation that tends increasingly to identify more with native Peruvians than with the Nikkei community. Still, one in four members of the Japanese population in Peru regularly attend its meetings and functions. Where regional associations of Nikkei exist, such as in the Department of Lambayeque and particularly in the city of Chiclayo, the Nikkei tend to be even better organized (Rocca Torres 1997: 261–74).

The Japanese of Peru are so well organized that they have been able to host conventions of the Pan American Nikkei movement. At the 1995 Pan American Nikkei convention in Lima, for example, President Fujimori addressed the plenary session and expressed his views regarding people of Japanese descent in the Americas. The Peruvian president claimed that

> Two feelings are combined inside the hearts of those who belong to the Nikkei communities in our countries: The respect for the cultural traditions of our parents and the deep love for the land that welcomed them and where they were born. Between the respect and love for our ancestors and the spiritual and material roots taken in our countries, we have built our homes and forged our professions in which our hard work and the honesty of our values have always distinguished us. I belong to the melting pot of these values.
>
> (Fujimori 1995: 4)

While somewhat hyperbolic, Fujimori's characterization of the Japanese experience in Peru and elsewhere in the Americas was largely accurate. What he did not mention was the emerging frustration in the mid-1990s of Peruvian, Brazilian, and other young Latin American Nikkei with the limited economic opportunities in Latin America, and their decisions to follow the sojourner impulse of their parents and grandparents and seek a better life in Japan.

Japanese Peruvian migration to Japan

Conditions of civil unrest, endemic poverty, and severe inflation in the late 1980s and early 1990s made Peru one of the most unstable and dangerous countries in Latin America. Japan, on the other hand, was viewed very favorably by the Peruvian Nikkei. A survey was conducted in 1989 by Amelia Morimoto and her associates. In a sampling of 5,000 Peruvian Nikkei, Japan was selected by four out of ten respondents when asked to name their "ideal country." These responses were consistent through the four generations included in the survey. People of Japanese heritage in

Peru viewed Japan as having strong moral and cultural values, including a very positive work ethic, good citizenship, and social solidarity. But some negative opinions of the Japanese people were also voiced, characterizing the Japanese as "mechanized and cold," living in a society that was too "competitive and perfectionist" (Morimoto 2002: 144–5).

In 1991, soon after the arrival of the first wave of Japanese Latin Americans to Japan, a Japanese Immigration Cooperation Agency (JICA) study was conducted. Involving interviews with over one thousand migrants from Brazil (62.4 percent), Peru (21 percent), Argentina (10 percent), Paraguay (3.2 percent), and Bolivia (2.2 percent), it offered valuable early impressions of the migrants' lives in Japan. The informants ranged in age from sixteen to sixty-seven, and the average age was thirty-one. Males outnumbered females by almost two to one. Okinawa was the prefecture of ancestral origin of the majority of these so-called guest workers. Quite significantly, four out of ten of these Nikkei migrants were university educated; yet at the time of the survey eight out of ten were employed in Japanese factories. Clearly, the faltering economies of Latin America were offering little hope for the underemployed Nikkei and, like their forebears, they sought a better standard of living, if not a better professional lifestyle in Japan. At the beginning of the 1990s this group of informants from the JICA study was earning an average of US$3,319 per month for males and $2,032 for females. Even considering the very high cost of living in Japan, these wages ensured a far better lifestyle than could ever be possible in Peru or the rest of Latin America. Indeed, these monthly wages represent one of the highest pay scales for common laborers in the world. As for their intentions concerning returning to Latin America or staying in Japan, two out of every three of the JICA informants stated that their intentions were to remain in Japan for as long as possible. Thus the pattern of low repatriation rates that characterized their forebears' emigration to Latin America was being repeated in reverse.

The near collapse of Peru's political and economic structures in the early 1990s very likely led a significant number of Nikkei migrants to Japan to seek permanent relocation if possible. After all, many non-Japanese native Peruvians were doing the same in the United States and Europe. At the very least, the new Japanese sojourners were seeking to emulate the pattern of the first Nikkei pioneers to Peru in the early twentieth century; that is, to better their lives and those of their children in any way possible. Even as the Japanese economy began its long decline during the early 1990s and Peru's internal political and economic conditions significantly improved under the iron-fisted leadership of Fujimori, the tide of Nikkei emigrants from Peru to Japan did not lessen. The precise number of these "new sojourners" in the period 1989 to 2003 is in dispute. Mary Fukumoto (1997) claimed that by the mid-1990s the number of Japanese Peruvians who had registered to travel to Japan approached 40,000. This would have been nearly 80 percent of the entire Japanese community in Peru based upon careful projections of the 1989 census. The actual number may well have been increased by the so-called Nikkei *chicha* (false Nikkei) – those non-Japanese Peruvians who held forged papers or who went to extraordinary lengths to have their facial features surgically altered to appear Asian. These fraudulent immigrants numbered as many as one in three among migrants to Japan before Tokyo made the immigration laws far stricter. Many of these Nikkei *chichas* were deported when the Japanese economy began to falter badly in the late 1990s.

The impact on the Japanese community in Peru of this massive migration of Nikkei was dramatic. The Okinawan associations in the Peruvian provinces, and important Japanese associations such as the *Centro Nikkei Estudios de Superiores* (Center of Superior Nikkei Studies) and the *Asociación Nikkei de Callao* (Nikkei Association of Callao), suffered severe drops in membership. Attendance at Japanese primary and secondary schools as well as Peru's universities declined significantly as young people abandoned their courses of study in favor of "quick money" in Japan. Japanese marriages in Peru became very difficult as potential partners declined for both genders. Often social events such as dances, team sports, and the like were abandoned for lack of participants. One young Japanese, when interviewed in 1992, characterized the young Nikkei community in Peru as "paralyzed because all of our people have gone to Japan" (Fukumoto 1997: 359).

Ironically, the migration of Peruvian Nikkei to Japan was occurring during the administration of the only person of Japanese heritage to be elected chief executive of any nation other than Japan. In spite of impressive achievements, his overreaching personal ambitions culminated in his ultimate flight and self-imposed exile in Japan. Together with Fujimori in Japan are thousands of his fellow Peruvian Nikkei, who face the twenty-first century with a great degree of uncertainty.

Peruvian Nikkei face decisions about where they should live for the rest of their lives and what culture they will now embrace. Speaking at the plenary session of the 1995 Pan American Nikkei Conference in Lima, Japan's ambassador to Peru, Morihisa Aoki, made remarks that foreshadowed the dilemma of the Japanese Peruvians at the beginning of the twenty-first century. The ambassador urged the Japanese of Peru and all of Latin America to "leave the Japanese culture to the third and fourth generations, which are the Nikkei generations of the world, and, to cooperate so that the third and fourth generations can move from being simple Nikkei to become Nikkei of international transcendence" (Aoki 1995: 5). Clearly, the ambassador was referring not only to Japanese Peruvians maintaining strong cultural ties with their Japanese heritage, but also to their acceptance of a cultural cosmopolitanism that will allow them to embrace the values both of their native land of Peru and the heritage and values of Japan. Given the difficulties that many nisei, sansei, and yonsei have had adjusting to Japanese society, it appears that "international transcendence" will be a great challenge. Thus, after more than a century of the Japanese experience in Peru, its younger people of Japanese heritage are faced with many of the same decisions as their forebears. Can they find the economic security they seek for themselves and their children? Will their children be educated with a concern for both their Peruvian culture and that of their new Japanese homeland? Will they continue to suffer the slights of cultural discrimination that their parents and grandparents suffered in Peru while trying to make new futures for themselves in Japan? And for those Nikkei who remained in Peru, what will their future be against the immediate backdrop of the disgraced Fujimori regime?

Current evidence presents a mixed picture. Tsuda's (1999b) careful studies of Japanese Latin American guest workers in Japan suggest that, despite initial discrimination, these workers, and especially their children, demonstrate a tendency to extend their stays in Japan indefinitely while contemplating permanent residence there. Tsuda believes these guest workers are generally having success assimilating into Japanese culture and are accepting Japan as their permanent home. He arrives at this conclusion despite reports (among the most virulent reactions by native Japanese against the guest workers) evoking characterizations such as "weirdos" and "fake Japanese" as well as referring to them as a "virus" that is invading the "pure" bloodstream of the Japanese people (ibid.: 700–23). Funada-Classen, who worked in Osaka Prefecture with the schoolchildren of Japanese guest workers from Peru and Brazil in the mid-1990s, is less optimistic about the future of the Latin American Nikkei in Japan. Noting that very young Nikkei from Latin America are losing or have never attained Spanish or Portuguese language proficiency, she suggests they would have a very difficult transition if their families were required to return to Latin America. It should be understood that under Japanese law, the children of these migrant workers do not necessarily attain Japanese citizenship. Moreover, Funada-Classen suggests that those Japanese Latin American migrants who began their schooling outside Japan will have very difficult challenges when taking the highly competitive exams for admittance to Japan's finest universities. Most particularly, their lack of Japanese language proficiency will always be an impediment to their social and professional progress in Japan (Masterson and Funada-Classen 2004: 259–60).

Unquestionably, the future of the Japanese Peruvians both in Japan and their home country is uncertain, but what is quite apparent from the historical social and cultural patterns of the Peruvian Nikkei is that they will confront their future with courage and resolve. It is clear from their past experiences in Peru that they will work together to forge a better future for themselves and their community whether that be in Japan or Peru.

9 Japanese Latin Americans during World War II
A reconsideration

Lane Ryo Hirabayashi and Akemi Kikumura-Yano

C. Harvey Gardiner is one of the pioneers in the study of Japanese in Latin America. In a widely cited book, *Pawns in a Triangle of Hate: The Peruvian Japanese and the United States* (1981), and in a subsequent article titled "The Latin-American Japanese and World War II" (1986), Gardiner offers a very detailed and disturbing portrait of different aspects of this topic.

In this chapter, after summarizing a number of Gardiner's points, we synopsize various case studies based on data from *The Encyclopedia of Japanese Descendants in the Americas* (Kikumura-Yano 2002) in an effort to supplement his seminal contributions. Almost every chapter of the encyclopedia was written by insiders working together collectively to represent their own community's histories and experiences.[1]

Our thesis is that individually and collectively these community histories paint a somewhat different overall picture of Japanese Latin American experiences than the one portrayed by Gardiner. At one level, this may be because Gardiner's actual focus is not Japanese Latin Americans per se – despite the title of his 1986 article – but specifically those Japanese Latin Americans who were kidnapped from their homes in Peru and to a lesser extent in Panama.[2] These individuals and families were then incarcerated in special camps in Texas and New Mexico operated by the U.S. Immigration and Naturalization Service during World War II. And although Gardiner does not cite Michi Weglyn's book, *Years of Infamy: The Untold Story of America's Concentration Camps* (1976: 54–66), Gardiner thoroughly documents the fact that the U.S. federal government was interested in using these Japanese Latin Americans as a "barter reserve."

In sum, we will argue that when one considers the experiences of Japanese Latin Americans in the Americas during World War II as a whole, they were much more diverse than Gardiner indicates. Although further primary research, both in terms of oral histories and archival work, will be needed to fill in the overall picture, we offer an outline of the variations for Argentina, Bolivia, Brazil, Chile, Cuba, Mexico, Paraguay, and Peru. We also offer a preliminary analysis to account for how and why individual Latin American countries responded differentially to their Japanese and Japanese Latin American residents.

C. Harvey Gardiner's thesis

In his well-known article "The Latin-American Japanese and World War II," C. Harvey Gardiner gives a concise summary of his previous research.[3] His basic claim is that persons of Japanese descent in Latin America suffered egregious treatment and endured profound suffering during this period.

Gardiner's primary focus is on the 2,264 Japanese Latin Americans who were arrested and deported from twelve different Latin American countries during the war. These people were brought into the United States and "experienced the violation of their civil and legal rights, both by their country of residence and by various branches of the American government" (Gardiner 1986: 142). Although the original target of deportation and incarceration was supposedly Japanese diplomatic personnel, Gardiner notes that ordinary persons were swept up as well in some Latin American countries.[4]

In addition, in terms of trying to explain differential treatment, it is pertinent to note that, although he does not address variation explicitly, he does offer a brief analysis of why differences in the treatment of Japanese Latin Americans occurred. Gardiner basically argues that those Japanese in Latin American countries which faced the Pacific Ocean (i.e., countries between Mexico and Chile) had to deal with a general climate of "ignorance, prejudice, hate, fear, and disregard for legal norms" (Gardiner 1986: 142). According to Gardiner, those who lived in countries along the Atlantic, such as Brazil and Argentina, did not. The assumption here is that it was natural that Japanese immigrants would tend to concentrate in the Pacific Coast countries and that, in case of war, Japan would be most likely to invade those countries. Thus the climate for anti-Japanese sentiments would be more conducive there.

After noting the important, if little known, role of Panama and the United States in developing a policy of arrest in Panama, and incarceration in the United States, Gardiner notes that Costa Rica, Colombia, Ecuador, Peru, and Bolivia quickly followed suit.[5]

Beyond this, even though twelve Latin American countries eventually sent persons of Japanese ancestry to the United States for internment, Gardiner focuses most of his attention on Peru. This is probably because the 1,800 incarcerated Japanese Peruvians account for almost 80 percent of all Japanese Latin Americans incarcerated in the United States. One must realize, however, that – depending on which demographic estimates are used – this action impacted upon, at most, only 10 percent of the total population of people of Japanese descent in Peru at the time, and perhaps even as low as 6 or 7 percent.[6] Even so, Gardiner argues convincingly that the Peruvian government's interests in deportation were largely economic and sociocultural as opposed to military (for example, Japanese language schoolteachers, rather than potential saboteurs, were particularly targeted). In the end, as interesting and important as the Japanese Peruvian case study is, we think that, overall, it entails an unusual and thus atypical case.

In the final section of his piece, Gardiner discusses the United States' use of the Japanese Latin Americans as barter exchange. In other words, in the end, the United States wanted Japanese Latin Americans in order to exchange them for U.S. citizens overseas who were stranded or captured in the Pacific after the United States entered the war. The overall picture Gardiner presents is accurate and thus distressing. In short, Peruvian and American authorities conspired to kidnap select Japanese (legal) residents and Peruvian citizens of Japanese ancestry, confiscate their papers, and forcibly incarcerate them. Subsequently, after the end of the war, in many cases these persons were denied their right to return to Peru.[7] Concomitantly, they were also not allowed to apply for U.S. citizenship. The effect on individuals could be traumatic, as Gardiner relates in the case of a thirty-seven-year-old merchant from Lima, Taiichi Onishi, who tried to commit suicide no less than four times during his first two weeks in Texas (Gardiner 1981: 31). He was finally committed to an asylum but not before pertinent agencies tried to deny responsibility and wash their hands of Onishi's case. In this sense, we totally agree with Gardiner's analysis that, if mass incarceration was difficult for Japanese Americans, it must have seemed even more irrational and bewildering for the Japanese Latin Americans:

> Their countries were not fighting Japan; they were interned in a foreign land whose language and laws were strange to all of them; and their camps, never publicized, drew neither public scrutiny nor the attention of humanitarian agencies.
> (Gardiner 1986: 144–5)

That much said, we would like to cite details presented in individual chapters of *The Encyclopedia of Japanese Descendants in the Americas* (Kikumura-Yano 2002) and then reconsider the data in a larger comparative framework. We argue that, while pioneering and seminal, Gardiner's emphasis on the Peruvian and Panamanian cases cannot be taken as paradigmatic for the experiences of Japanese Latin Americans as a whole, especially in terms of the experiences of those who remained at home during the war years.

The evidence for variation: selected case studies

As mentioned above, we have drawn largely from Kikumura-Yano's *The Encyclopedia of Japanese Descendants in the Americas* (2002) in order to marshal case studies to document our thesis about intragroup diversity. She commissioned teams of scholars from local universities, museums, and historical societies to write chapters expressing Nikkei points of view about Nikkei experiences in seven different Latin American countries. We will also add data about what happened to issei and nisei in Cuba because, although not included in the encyclopedia, this case represents yet another important variation.[8] One of the striking things about these chapters, to us, is that when viewed comparatively they document that Nikkei had a fairly wide range of experiences in these countries between 1940 and 1945.

Argentina

In Argentina by 1938, there were approximately 6,000 Nikkei living in a country with a population of about six million (Laumonier 2002: 77; see also Stanlaw's table 2.2, Chapter 2, this volume). In terms of anti-Japanese sentiment Argentina had no systemic record. Importantly, although subject to some pressure by the United States (Gardiner 1981: 17–18), Argentina remained neutral during most of the war. Only in 1944 did that country cut off trade with both Germany and Japan, and it was only on March 27, 1945, when it was completely clear who was going to lose, that Argentina finally declared war on the Axis powers.[9]

Certainly, as in many of the other cases we will summarize below, Japanese Argentines did endure various restrictions. For example, some businesses were seized, newspapers and Japanese language schools were closed, and community meetings were forbidden (Laumonier 2002: 78). Comparatively speaking, however, the Japanese Argentines did not suffer during the war years and by 1947 all of these restrictions were lifted.

Bolivia

The case of Bolivia is a bit different. Although there are some variations in the published statistics, there were probably somewhat more than 500 persons of Japanese descent living in that country when the United States entered the war.[10] Bolivia terminated its formal relations with Japan in the month after Pearl Harbor and then declared war on Japan. Although the overall population of Japanese descendants was small, at the request of the United States' government, the Bolivian authorities kidnapped and sent at least twenty-nine Japanese Bolivians to the United States (Amemiya, Chapter 10, this volume; Kunimoto 2002), about 6 percent of the total Japanese Bolivian population. Compared to the massive dislocations experienced in North America, this was a relatively small number and percentage of the total.

Again, restrictions were placed on the remaining Japanese Bolivians, and their small businesses, apart from restaurants and barber shops, were shut down. Small farmers, on the other hand, pursued their businesses freely, and the remaining population seems to have been essentially left alone (Kunimoto 2002: 102). Thus the overview statement for this chapter asserts that "World War II had little impact on the lives of Nikkei residents in Bolivia, especially since the government did not adopt anti-Japanese measures" (ibid.: 95).

Brazil

Brazil is an interesting case because it had, during World War II, and still has today, the largest number of people of Japanese descent in all of the Americas. Brazil accommodated almost 190,000 persons of Japanese descent by 1941 (Mizuki *et al.* 2002: 145, table 4.1). They were notably concentrated in São Paulo and Paraná, the southern regions of Brazil.

Japanese Brazilians along the coast and in other "sensitive" areas such as downtown São Paulo were forced to move inland (Ninomiya 2002: 155). There were, however, no mass removals, and certainly no mass incarceration, of Japanese Brazilians. Nor did Brazil send any Japanese diplomats, nationals, or Japanese Brazilian citizens to the United States, even though there is evidence that anti-Japanese sentiments had been extant both before and after the war (Ninomiya and Moniz 2002: 127). Interestingly enough, the key dynamic that evolved was a dramatic split between those who believed that Japan was winning or had even won the war (called *Kachi-gumi* by Japanese Brazilians), and those who did not (called *Make-gumi* by Japanese Brazilians) (Ninomiya 2002: 120-1). What is remarkable about this split was its intensity inside the Japanese ethnic community; after the war, believers started attacking – and even assassinating – non-believers. This split caused the deaths of almost a dozen Japanese Brazilians and, when the conflict spread, causing the deaths of non-Japanese Brazilians, riots between Japanese Brazilians and non-Japanese Brazilians broke out that had to be quelled by the army. Although such divisions occurred in other Latin American countries the passions of the believers reached their peak in the Brazilian setting, generating a number of accounts of this unusual phenomenon (Maeyama 1979).

Chile

Japanese Chileans' experiences during the war years were generally benign. To begin with, by 1940, Japanese Chileans were a relatively small population of just under 1,000 persons (Hirose *et al.* 2002: 199, table 6.2). Despite the fact that the United States tried to pressure Chile to send Japanese Chileans up north, there was no record of significant prejudice or discrimination against persons of Japanese ancestry. What is more, there were sectors of Chilean society that were neutral or even pro-Axis from the start (Takeda 2002: 184). Although there was some prejudice in evidence after Pearl Harbor, and some Japanese Chilean businessmen did suffer closure and appropriations, these were neither widespread nor systematic. Only months before the end of the war did Chile finally declare war on Japan. The overall record, then, indicates that, from the perspective of Japanese Chileans, the majority of their compatriots gave them few problems.

Cuba

In Cuba, the number of Japanese immigrants was small. Many intermarried and did not experience prejudice. There was one key pre-war concentration of farmers on the Island of the Pines (*Isla de Los Pinos*) (Ropp and Ropp 2002: 131–2).[11] Following Pearl Harbor, the Cuban government decided that it was best to intern *all* adult men of Japanese descent (some 300 Japanese issei and nisei) on that island, essentially leaving their wives and children on their own (www.greatleap.org/cuba/obon.html). These men lived in a special prison under the watchful eye of the Cuban government. By 1946, everyone had been released. After the Cuban Revolution, Castro eventually decided to turn the island into an international youth center, and it was renamed Isla de La Juventud. Some 200 persons of Japanese or part-Japanese descent continue to reside there today (ibid.: 132).

Mexico

The case of Japanese Mexicans is a mixed one. There had been both anti-Chinese and anti-Japanese sentiments during different periods of Mexican history (Hu-DeHart 1980; Akachi *et al.* 2002: 210). In part because of its ties to the United States, as tensions between the United States and Japan grew, so also did the tensions between Mexico and Japan. Following Pearl Harbor, Mexico ended all diplomatic relations with Japan and declared war (Akachi *et al.* 2002: 213). In terms of Japanese Mexicans, their financial assets were frozen and many issei were subject to suspicion and temporary detention.

Japanese Mexicans in the interior were basically left alone. Those on the coast (e.g., Baja, Ensenada) and on the border (e.g., Tijuana, Mexicali), however, were commanded to move to one of Mexico's two largest cities: Mexico City or Guadalajara. Together with Japanese Mexicans from the states of Sonora, Sinaloa, and Coahuilla, some 2,800 persons were forced to relocate (Akachi *et al.* 2002: 214). While most were not confined, others joined camp-like settlements, most notably Texixco, an agricultural area located near the Federal District.

Paraguay

The case of the 500 to 600 Japanese Paraguayans by 1940, as represented by the scholar and community activist Emi Kasamatsu, entails yet another variation. Although Paraguay had severed ties with Japan as early as February 1942, a treaty between Paraguay and Japan that was signed in 1919 was cited by Paraguayan authorities as a basis for defending the rights of Japanese Paraguayan residents (Kasamatsu 2002: 252–3). As in previous cases, some of the operations of civic and educational organizations were suspended (ibid.: 233). In any case, Kasamatsu reports, there were no attacks on the dignity or rights of persons of Japanese descent, nor were there expropriations of any kind.

Peru

Finally, in the case of the Japanese Peruvians, there is ample evidence of anti-Japanese sentiment in Peru, historically speaking. Tensions increased during the 1930s due to U.S.–Japan tensions, but also because the Japanese Peruvians were perceived as: (1) having a large concentration in visible places such as Lima; (2) being too competitive; (3) being too successful; and (4) being separatists (Morimoto 2002: 252). Animosities eventually built up into an anti-Japanese riot in Lima in 1940. With the outbreak of war, a host of restrictive prohibitions were passed limiting economic activities. Japanese language schools were forced to close and properties were confiscated. Within months, the Peruvian government kidnapped and forcibly sent approximately 1,800 people of Japanese ancestry – non-citizens and Peruvian citizens alike – to the United States. As Gardiner and others indicate, this was one of the most egregious cases of victimization in Central and South America (Hagihara and Shimizu 2002).

Variations and variables

Even with synoptic accounts of selected Latin American case studies the variations are fairly clear. These include very traumatic cases involving partial removal, and mass incarceration, such as the 1,800 people first taken from Peru to the United States. Only a small percentage of Japanese Peruvians, however, were singled out and incarcerated in this fashion. Thus the experiences of the vast majority of Japanese Peruvians would differ from those who were deported. Cuba would also fit into this category: while the wives and children of the Cuban issei and nisei must certainly have suffered due to the loss of their husbands and fathers, only Cuban Japanese men were actually incarcerated.

There were intermediate cases as well. One example would be Mexico, where Japanese Mexicans were not incarcerated per se but some were forced to move to one of two key Mexican cities if the authorities felt they were living in proximity to sensitive and/or strategic areas. We can hypothesize that the 2,800 persons who were forced to move from the coast and northern states to Guadalajara and Mexico City suffered more intensely than those who were left in place. Similarly, Japanese Brazilians were not incarcerated, but some had to move away from the coast and downtown São Paulo and all were subject to various restrictions.

In yet other cases, the chapters from *The Encyclopedia of Japanese Descendants in the Americas* (Kikumura-Yano 2002) as well as our first-hand interviews with leaders of the Japanese Argentine and Japanese Chilean communities indicate that, at least in terms of popular perceptions, little trauma or even stress occurred. In addition, we note that these countries each face either the Atlantic or Pacific Ocean, which refutes one of Gardiner's explanations of differential treatment. In place of that explanation, we would like to offer a preliminary analysis to address the kinds of variables that would help to account more fully for the differences described above.

First, what is central is a given Latin American country's position in World War II with regard to either favoring the Allies, favoring the Axis, or basically staying neutral for all intents and purposes. For example, our understanding of the situation in both Argentina and Chile was that, while remaining neutral in practice (in the sense of not being directly engaged in the war), both countries had influential sectors that favored the Axis powers. As a partial index of this fact, in Argentina especially, when we asked about Japanese descendants' suffering during World War II, to our surprise it was almost as if the question failed to register. The Latin American countries that immediately supported the United States when it entered World War II, such as Panama, were willing to arrest and deport select persons of Japanese ancestry in an effort to cooperate with the United States and thus with Allied war efforts.

Second, and concomitantly, the degree to which the American government could either influence or put pressure on a given Latin American government and influence their public policies in regard to Japanese descendants had a noticeable effect. For example, when the United States entered the war, given the Peruvian authorities' support for the Allied cause, Peru was one of the governments that quickly complied with the United States' requests for the arrest and deportation of seemingly suspicious and/or seemingly dangerous Japanese Peruvians. The policies of other Latin American countries that were less attendant to the United States and the Allies' cause were nowhere as drastic or as punitive vis-à-vis the Japanese descendants.

Third, the extent to which there was a systematic anti-Japanese/anti-Asian movement in the country in question is relevant as well. In the case of Chile, there were few immigrants (only 1,000 by the onset of war) and the first-generation issei tended to intermarry with Chilean women. As a result there was a preponderance of *mestizos* among the second-generation Chilean Japanese. In the case of Peru, on the other hand, while intermarriages occurred from early on, there was a history marked by perceived competition and threat. Evidence of an anti-Japanese movement can be verified by "yellow journalism" dating back to the 1930s (Araki 2002: 81).

This grew so intense that in May 1940 there was an anti-Japanese demonstration so violent that some 500 Japanese Peruvians fled their homes in fear of their lives (ibid.: 82). A great deal of Japanese Peruvians' property was also destroyed by mobs.

There are other possible variables that might feasibly enter the mix, but these would have to be examined on a case-by-case basis. For example, if one considers the small numbers of Japanese Chileans, most of whom were married to Chilean women if they were married at all, it is easy to understand why the Chilean authorities may not have considered these men to be much of a threat. We could conjecture that critical mass, or the lack of it, might have been operant in some cases. By "critical mass" we mean the relative percentage of Japanese Latin Americans in a given country or area. This figure is quite variable, both within and between nations. For example, while the critical mass of Japanese Brazilians might be a small percentage compared to the country's total population, it can be very high depending upon the state, region, or district. Unfortunately, to date, little research has been conducted which specifically compares critical mass with such variables as the degree of anti-Japanese sentiment in a venue, types of community-building, or amount of political empowerment.[12]

To what extent did the local populace play a role in advocating for or subsequently supporting efforts to deport Japanese Latin Americans? We have not seen much on this topic, although it has been well documented in the United States (e.g., Daniels 1970; CWRIC 1982). Perhaps the clearest case where future researchers might look for evidence would be that of Peru. Because of economic competition and tension, we hypothesize that – along with the deportation of Japanese diplomats, and suspect community elements such as teachers – the seizure of property and capital was an operant variable in targeting those Japanese Peruvians who were selected for deportation.[13]

One wonders, since it is not explicitly discussed in the literature that we have seen, about the role of naturalization and citizenship during this period. Our preliminary inquiries with colleagues who contributed to *The Encyclopedia of Japanese Descendants in the Americas* (Kikumura-Yano 2002) indicate that, unlike the situation in the United States, issei immigrants to Latin American countries before the war did not necessarily make an effort to naturalize, even though this opportunity may have been available to them. Why? We aren't certain, although sensibilities about race, Japanese racial purity and racial superiority may have been at play here.[14] On the other hand, it is clear that, in countries such as Peru that had anti-Japanese movements before the war, neither governmental authorities nor the public at large were committed to the protection of their "citizens' rights" when issues of national security were seemingly at hand.

Conclusion: Examining the Nikkei experience beyond the Japanese American perspective

A couple of lessons come to mind when taking a comparative perspective on the Nikkei, using Latin America as a unit of analysis within the larger context of the Americas as a whole. Given that Japanese and their descendants in the United States are the primary focus of the scholarly literature on Nikkei in the Americas, we must clearly eschew the projection of this particular dimension of the Nikkei experience on those Nikkei in Central and South America. In fact, once the Americas as a whole is adopted as the unit of analysis, the theme of variation in and of Nikkei experiences takes pride of place.

This said, we hope we have clearly made the point that pioneer scholar C. Harvey Gardiner's path-breaking account of the Japanese Peruvians who were forcibly taken from their homes and deported to the United States needs to be put into the larger context of what happened to the Japanese Latin Americans who remained at home. There was more variation, in this regard, than Gardiner's cases would suggest.

Moreover, although Gardiner was probably right that we will never know how many people bribed their way out of deportation, or relied on political influence to escape the dragnet, there are still many facts we should be able to find out to give us a fuller, more nuanced understanding of the "wartime experiences of the Japanese [who] remained in Latin America" (Gardiner 1986: 145).

Gardiner was right to be cautious, of course, insofar as many of the authorities' key decisions were not documented. Documents on the part of all parties involved may well have been destroyed, any extra-legal arrangements are bound to have been hidden, and aggressors were certainly not going to keep accounts of what was taken from their victims. Yet the individual chapters in *The Encyclopedia of Japanese Descendants in the Americas*, written by scholars in collaboration with community-based historical societies, museums, and organizations, indicate that there is still a great deal of light that can be shed on what happened to Japanese Latin Americans from the perspective of those who actually lived the experience.[15]

In conclusion, we have just started the process of the comparative analysis of Nikkei experiences, and even in terms of the 1940s alone there are many fascinating questions that have yet to be addressed. For starters, how important is "collective historical trauma" vis-à-vis subsequent efforts for redress (Ross 1997)? In the case of Peruvians, does trauma have to do with salience of Japanese Peruvians in the Japanese Latin American redress movement (Hagihara and Shimizu 2002)? When we compare the Japanese Peruvian kidnappings, say, to the removal of Japanese Mexicans from the coasts or the border to Mexico City and Guadalajara, it is understandable why the Japanese Peruvians would be more resentful if not angry about their treatment. Or is it merely a matter of the relative critical mass of Japanese Peruvians taken to the United States as compared to the very small number of incarcerated Japanese Latin Americans from other Central and South American countries?

Another question has to do with the Japanese Cubans. The men were incarcerated and then, partly for economic reasons, the post-war response on the part of the community was one of dispersal and then general assimilation. Following the Cuban Revolution, there are indications that the Japanese Cubans assimilated further into the larger society. Was this a reflection of either dedication to the principles of the subsequent socialist state, or perhaps an understanding that the country under Fidel Castro's leadership was trying to evolve beyond a society divided by class, ethnicity, race, and religion (Ropp and Ropp 2002: 139–40)? Were the Japanese Cubans willing to let bygones be bygones given such a utopian vision (Hiura 2000; Nakagawa 2000)?

In terms of Brazil, while there is literature on the Kachi-gumi phenomenon, we have not seen a convincing analysis of why, although extant, the Kachi-gumi/Make-gumi split was not such a powerful dynamic in other parts of the Americas. Could critical mass, along with the fact that while there were restrictions in Brazil they were not traumatic for the group as a whole, again have had some kind of effect?

In any case, while a foundation is taking shape, it strikes us that there is plenty of research to be done on the histories of the communities of Japanese descendants in specific countries in Latin America. As this research base is being solidified and extended, however, it also strikes us that the real richness of this work will be that it allows broader comparisons that might help us to understand more fully the variations and differentiations that so clearly characterize Nikkei experiences in the Americas.

Acknowledgment

We would like to thank Nobuko Adachi, James Stanlaw, Harumi Befu, and especially Roger Daniels, for their comments. We know it is not easy to coordinate panels at a national conference and then produce a book, so all of us who were involved in this project are grateful for their efforts. We are also grateful to Yoko Nishimura and Robyn Hamada Gilmore for research assistance on the demographic data presented herein. We alone are responsible for the contents of this chapter, however.

Notes

1 We acknowledge that the chapter on Bolivia was not written by an insider but rather by a Japanese scholar, Iyo Kunimoto. Her work, however, was done in collaboration with members of the Federación Nacional de Asociaciones Boliviano Japonesas.

2 In this sense, we think that it might have been more accurate to title his article "The Latin American Japanese Forcibly Taken to the United States During World War II," because that is its primary focus.
3 This was apparently a summary originally prepared for a conference (personal communication with Roger Daniels, December 2003). The "Biographical Note," on page 145, however, indicates that it is also based on a full range of Gardiner's prior publications in English and in Japanese.
4 In his book *Pawns in a Triangle of Hate*, for example, Gardiner offers a useful, detailed analysis of the backgrounds and occupations of the Japanese Peruvians who left Peru on the ship *Shawnee* (Gardiner 1981: 42–6).
5 It is interesting that, in doing so, Panama and the United States were essentially replaying an agreement that resulted in Germans being detained and sent from Panama to the United States during World War I (Gardiner 1986: 142).
6 We were not able to resolve clear differences in population estimates, especially given the fact that the criteria for defining and counting "Japanese Peruvians" have apparently changed over time and depending on whether Peruvian, Japanese, or Japanese Peruvian authorities have been in charge of a given census. On page 144 of his essay, for example, Gardiner indicates that the general estimate of the total number of persons of Japanese descent in Peru was in the order of 25,000. Hagihara and Shimizu (2002: 206) cite the 1940 population to be 26,000, of whom some 9,000 were Peruvian citizens. Basing her estimate on the National Census of 1940, a credible Japanese Peruvian scholar puts the total number of Japanese Peruvians at more like 17,598 (Morimoto 2002: 273; also table 9.2). In any case, the 1,800 Japanese Peruvians who were kidnapped and deported to the United States were a minority, comprising about 10 percent of the total Japanese Peruvian population.
7 According to Gardiner, fewer than 100 Japanese Peruvians were allowed to return home, largely because they were either citizens and/or they were married to Peruvian citizens.
8 Although Stephen Masami Ropp is a member of the larger International Nikkei Research Project, neither he nor his wife are of Cuban or part-Cuban descent. Rather, they were able to extensively interview Mr Francisco Shinichi Miyasaka, President of the Asociación de La Colonia Japonesa de Cuba, about the Japanese Cuban experience. It is this interview that we draw from here. See also the articles on Miyasaka's goodwill visit to California by Hiura (2000), and Nakagawa (2000).

For the record, we note that Cuba was not included in *The Encyclopedia of Japanese Descendants in the Americas* (Kikumura-Yano 2002) because the International Nikkei Research Project advisors decided to prioritize those countries in the Americas with Nikkei populations of over 1,500 persons.
9 This late arrival of Argentina into the war may account for some of the relatively good treatment and acceptance experienced by Argentinian Nikkei that community leaders reported to us in the field.
10 Kunimoto and Wakatsuki (1985), for example, indicate that there are three basic estimates: (1) Tigner, who gives a total of 506 in 1941 (cited in Kunimoto and Wakatsuki 1985: 30); (2) Kamo, who calculated 526 in 1943 (cited in Kunimoto and Wakatsuki 1985: 30); and (3) official Japanese government figures of 240 in 1940 (cited in Kunimoto and Wakatsuki 1985: 31). According to Yoko Nishimura, the discrepancy may be explained by the re-migration of Japanese Peruvians to Bolivia during this period (personal communication with Yoko Nishimura).
11 It should be noted that the number of Japanese Cubans has always been small. The Ropps cite Mr Francisco Miyahara's estimate that even today there are only some 1,300 persons of Japanese or part-Japanese descent, and that the community has as many as five generations (Ropp and Ropp 2002: 132).

12 For a general overview of the Japanese diaspora and some of these cases, see Daniels (2000) and Gardiner (1986).
13 It would also be interesting to discover which Peruvian individuals, companies, or governmental officials benefited financially from these expropriations.
14 See the fascinating study of these issues in the immediate post-war period by Yukiko Koshiro (1999). Koshiro notes a strong sense of racial superiority on the part of post-war Japanese immigrants to Latin American countries. It is understandable how such sentiments might impact upon the decision to naturalize, especially when Japanese citizenship became such an advantage to Japanese Latin Americans during the 1980s and 1990s (see Lesser 2003).
15 In terms of the Peruvian Japanese who were taken to the Immigration and Naturalization Service camps, Grace Shimizu is the founder and director of the Japanese Peruvian Oral History Project that is continuing to document the experiences of the Japanese Peruvians imprisoned in Texas and New Mexico during the war. Thus it is not inconceivable to us that there may yet be more information available over time about the secret histories that Gardiner believed would never come to light. For more information on this project, interested readers may contact the JPOHP at P.O. Box 1384, El Cerrito, CA 94530 or by email at jpohp@prodigy.net.

Part III
Constructing identities in the Okinawan, Nikkei, and permanent resident diasporas

10 Four governments and a new land
Emigration to Bolivia

Kozy Amemiya

It takes national governments to implement large-scale immigration projects. The ways in which the governments are involved not only determine where and how the immigrants are settled but also affect how the immigrant communities grow. The case in point is Japanese immigration in Bolivia. In its 100-year history, their community has shaped a unique pattern of compartmentalization. It is separated vertically in terms of time and horizontally in terms of physical location into components that are distinct from one another. Vertically, it is separated into the pre-World War II group of spontaneous immigration and the government-sponsored post-war group. Horizontally, the pre-war group is divided between the Amazon region and the old Andean cities, with little contact between them. The post-war immigrants settled in the Santa Cruz region. They established Colonia Okinawa, comprising immigrants from Okinawa and their offspring, and Colonia Japonesa San Juan, made up of those from mainland Japan.[1] Such compartmentalization is a distinctive feature of the Japanese Bolivians as compared to other groups of Japanese ancestry in the Americas.

The separation of the Japanese Bolivian community in the Amazon region from the rest of Bolivian society is due primarily to geographical isolation. On the other hand, the almost complete disjuncture between pre-war and post-war immigrants and the two separate post-war settlements has more to do with the active intervention of governments than with mere physical distance or different times of immigration. Unlike the pre-war immigration that took place spontaneously on an individual basis in pursuit of personal goals, in the post-war era the four governments of varying degrees of power and status – Japan, Okinawa, Bolivia, and the United States – organized, sponsored, or encouraged the immigration programs of mainland Japanese and Okinawans to Bolivia. The eastern lowlands of Bolivia were isolated and undeveloped, but fertile, and awaited immigrants to populate and cultivate them. At the same time, Okinawa and Japan pushed emigration in the hope that it could solve serious domestic problems of overpopulation and political instability.

Active government intervention in the flow of Japanese immigrants into

Bolivia made the post-war immigrants shape their communities separately from those of pre-war immigrants. First, the Ryûkyûan[2] government prepared a settlement under the auspices of the United States. A few years later the Japanese government set up theirs. Each government was responsible for and took charge of aiding immigrants in its respective settlement until 1967, when Colonia Okinawa also came under the administration of the Japanese government. Each government of Japan, Okinawa, and the United States had its own interest and purpose in the immigration projects with consideration given to domestic issues and international geopolitics. How did the interests and purposes of these governments interact with others to shape the Okinawan and Japanese immigration programs? And how did these programs affect the condition and destiny of the immigrant communities? This chapter explores these questions; but first, let us examine how the pre-war immigrant communities developed, in order to highlight the difference between pre-war and post-war immigration.

Pre-war immigrants in Bolivia: spontaneous migration

Japan and Bolivia established diplomatic relations in 1914. Neither before nor after that pact did the Japanese encounter any barriers to entering Bolivia. The Bolivian government encouraged immigration from overseas in the first half of the twentieth century, but no immigration on a large scale took place from any country. The Japanese government took an interest in sending its immigrants to Bolivia for the first time in 1936, after Japanese immigration into Brazil had come under severe restriction a few years earlier and Japan needed alternative sites. However, government-organized Japanese immigration never took place because, as Japan's invasion in China developed into all-out war in East Asia (see Guelcher, Chapter 4, and Tamanoi, Chapter 13, this volume), the government needed more manpower (Nihonjin Boribia Ijûshi Hensan Iinkai 1970: 90). Japanese pre-war immigration in Bolivia thus remained individually based, spontaneous, and small.

Japanese immigration to Bolivia originally began with re-migration of Japanese from Peru. Although there is disagreement among present Japanese Bolivians as to whether those migrants should be considered the first Japanese immigrants into Bolivia (Amemiya 2002a: 96), there is no question that the ninety-one men plus two Japanese supervisors who entered Bolivia from Peru's sugar plantations in 1899 were among the first Japanese to set foot in Bolivia (Kunimoto 2000: 105–8). They were among the 790 men who went to Peru initially as contract workers on sugar plantations, but left their employment after only a couple of months due to the harsh working conditions. They did not settle initially in Bolivia, hence the disagreement about whether they were refugees or migrant workers. Nevertheless, their arrival in the northern Amazon region of

Bolivia is significant in setting the pattern of early Japanese immigration into Bolivia (Kunimoto 2000; Nihonjin Borivia Ijûshi Hensan Iinkai 1970: 23–58). Most Japanese migrated to Bolivia from Peru, while some came directly from Japan in the 1900s and 1910s. All went to the northern Bolivian Amazon region of Pando and Beni Departments[3] due to the rubber boom (see Okihiro, Chapter 11, this volume). Still, the number of such migrants was not large, nor did they have any protection extended by the Japanese government since Japan and Bolivia did not establish diplomatic relations until 1914.[4]

Extremely isolated from the rest of Bolivia, and having no contact with other Japanese or Japan, most of these men remained in the region, married local Bolivian women, and produced progeny. Unable to retain any semblance of Japanese culture, they were in large part absorbed by the local Bolivian community. Only a few of their offspring were conscious of their Japanese ancestry or were interested in preserving or restoring their heritage – until around 1990, when they found that their Japanese ancestry had become a valuable asset. Proven legitimate, it would give them a special status, allowing them to work in Japan as *dekasegi* and earn more money than they had ever dreamed of (Amemiya 2001: 1–3; Ikuno 2000; see also Ohno, Chapter 5, and Tsuda, Chapter 12, this volume). However, this has not inspired these Bolivians of Japanese ancestry to form a distinct ethnic group; nor have they established close contact with other Japanese Bolivian groups. Thus, although they are now the largest in terms of numbers (close to 10,000 in the late 1990s) among all the Japanese Bolivian groups,[5] they remain isolated and dispersed and have no impact as an ethnic group upon Bolivian society.

Around 1920 the rubber boom began to decline rapidly, and some of those who had worked in the rubber industry in the Amazon region migrated to La Paz and other cities. Many such re-migrants ran general stores, grocery stores, restaurants, and the like in the cities. A few were engaged in trade with Japan and became quite successful. In 1939, as Japan's war in China spread, Japan began importing various Bolivian ores necessary to expand production of military equipment since the supply of ores from China had stopped. This boosted the Bolivian economy. Major Japanese trading companies set up offices in La Paz. Japanese capital and Japanese immigrants in La Paz grew rapidly. They joined Bolivia's economic and social activity, and shaped a distinct Japanese Bolivian community. Some have called the year 1940 the "golden period" for the Japanese in La Paz (Furuki 2000: 135–6).

However, the number of Japanese in Bolivia never exceeded 900 in total, and their economic and social bases were so precarious that their role in Bolivian society was crushed at the onset of the Pacific War. Japan and Bolivia severed diplomatic relations in 1942, and Bolivia (under pressure from the United States) froze the assets of Japanese Bolivians and rounded up twenty-nine Japanese residents in Bolivia to be interned in a concentration camp in the United States (Furuki 2000: 137). Although the Japanese Bolivian community did not suffer the anti-Japanese treatment that Japanese Peruvians had to endure, its progress in Bolivian society was halted.

Japanese immigrants before World War II received no assistance from either the Japanese or Bolivian government to settle and begin new lives in their adopted land. In contrast, post-war Japanese immigration into Bolivia involved a dramatic change, having been organized and financed by Japanese, U.S., and Ryûkyûan governments as planned projects. The resulting Japanese Bolivian communities developed quite differently from those of pre-war immigrants.

The post-war Bolivian situation and the United States

When the Pacific War broke out, Japanese migration to Bolivia was suspended. Japan's surrender to the Allied Powers in 1945 led to the occupation of both Okinawa and Japan, separately and differently, by the Supreme Commander of the Allied Powers (SCAP) led by the United States. Faced with the same problems of population pressure and acute shortages of food, housing, and jobs, interest in overseas emigration rose in both Japan and Okinawa. However, under the SCAP occupation, emigration was firmly restricted. Moreover, the former host countries were suspicious of Japanese immigration.[6] With the signing of the San Francisco Peace Treaty in 1952 and regaining sovereignty, Japan was able to start negotiating the possibility of emigration programs with various countries. However, the United States continued to occupy Okinawa by keeping the government of the Ryûkyû Islands (GRI) under control. The High Commissioner denied the GRI the power to negotiate with foreign countries directly and it had to rely on the United States.

Bolivia became the first country that not only accepted but also welcomed immigration from Japan and Okinawa. The revolution in 1952 led by the *Movimiento Nacionalista Revolucionario* (MNR), or the Nationalist Revolutionary Movement, and with wide popular support of farmers and miners, brought about profound social change in Bolivia. Bolivia was – and still is – poor. At the time of the revolution, its per capita GDP of US$118.60 was the second lowest after Haiti in the Western Hemisphere, its life expectancy was the lowest in Latin America, and its infant mortality rate the highest. Seventy percent of the population were illiterate, and were hence disenfranchised due to a literacy requirement. Bolivia's economy depended on tin, which was owned by three tin barons, referred to as the Big Three. Tin accounted for 95 percent of its foreign currency, the major buyer being the United States. Bolivia had a small population (about three million in 1950) in a huge land area (the size of Texas and California combined), and yet could not feed itself, importing 40 percent of its food supplies (Klein 1992: 319; Lehman 1999: 100). One of the causes of low productivity was that land distribution was bound by the *latifundia* system, to which the majority of the indigenous peasants were tied. With holdings of more than 1,000 hectares, a mere 6 percent of landowners controlled 92 percent of all cultivated land (Klein 1992: 228; Lagos 1994: 53). In 1952, the MNR set out to nationalize the tin mines, enfranchise farmers and miners (most of whom were indigenous) by eliminating the literacy requirement, and undertook agrarian reform by abolishing haciendas, redistributing land, and distributing government-owned land.

The United States, at the height of the Cold War, was dubious about nationalistic movements and the possible spread of communist influence in Latin America. When a left-wing, communist-backed government proposed a similar revolutionary agenda in Guatemala at about the same time, the United States launched a covert operation to overthrow it in order to protect its security and economic interest in that country, namely the United Fruit Company. In Bolivia, however, the United States no longer needed Bolivia's tin, and therefore had no major economic interest at stake. Moreover, the Truman administration's officials saw at the core of the MNR a group of pragmatic social reformers, led by Victor Paz Estenssoro, who became Bolivia's president. They not only found the MNR revolution acceptable but concluded that it would be beneficial to support the MNR government on the grounds that its failure would increase communist infiltration in Bolivia and its surrounding regions and pose a greater threat to U.S. security. The MNR at first took an anti-U.S. stance, but in desperate need of U.S. aid in order to achieve its goals and hence ensure its survival, it came to terms with the United States. The Eisenhower administration sent massive aid to Bolivia – US$13.4 million in 1953 and $18.4 million the following year – while it spent about $20 million in covert operations to overthrow Guatemala's government, which led to Guatemala's long and tragic civil war (Blasier 1971: 61–5; Klein 1992: 227–45; Uemura 1992; Lehman 1997, 1999: 91–113).

The key to Bolivia's economic development, and therefore its social stability, was the development of the eastern lowland of Santa Cruz, which was a sparsely populated vast flatland of rich soils. From 1949 to 1952, the United States conducted an extensive USAID (United States Agency of International Development) study (Maeda 1986: 34) which confirmed the region's potential as Bolivia's bread-basket. With the United States prepared to pour massive aid into developing this region, the MNR regime encouraged domestic migration from the highland to the Santa Cruz area (Stearman 1985) and welcomed immigration from overseas. It was in this context that Japanese immigration occurred. It took the effort and persuasion of MNR member Alcibiades Velarde Cronenbold, who served as Governor of Santa Cruz and Minister of Agriculture, to gain Bolivia's acceptance of immigration from Okinawa and Japan. Velarde was from Santa Cruz and was well acquainted with Japanese immigrants in that region, who reportedly extended their help to him in 1949 when MNR members were suffering political repression. In addition, Velarde was familiar with the achievements of Japanese immigrants in Brazil and reportedly had a high regard for them (Maeda 1986: 45–6, 221–3).

The Okinawan immigration project

Okinawa was the only prefecture in Japan where fierce battles were fought on land in World War II. After Japan's defeat, Okinawa was separated from mainland Japan by the Allied Powers for strategic reasons and was occupied by the United States military. While Japan experienced wide-ranging political and social reforms and regained its sovereignty in 1952 with the San Francisco Peace Treaty, Okinawa remained separate from Japan under U.S. military occupation and strict control until 1972. The authority of the Okinawan government, the GRI, was tightly circumscribed by the power of the U.S. Civil Administration of the Ryûkyû Islands (USCAR). USCAR could exercise, in whole or in part, full authority in the Ryûkyûs, "if deemed necessary for security reasons" (Yoshida 2001: 62–3). The Okinawan emigration project was no exception. GRI had no power to negotiate with foreign governments and could not implement emigration without the approval of, and financial and political assistance from, the United States. In addition, Okinawans were "stateless," having neither Japanese nor U.S. passports. USCAR issued identity cards for Okinawans, which served in place of passports, but these were not accepted by all countries.

Okinawa's post-war problems were enormous. Shortages of food, housing, and jobs were exacerbated by acute population pressure due to a large number of repatriated former colonists and soldiers plus high birth rates. The problems were intensified by the expropriation of large areas of the most fertile cultivated land by the U.S. military. Lacking control over their own lives, and with a long tradition of migration, Okinawans sought solutions in emigration and re-established the Okinawa (renamed Ryûkyû shortly afterwards) Overseas Association. However, most would-be emigrants in the prefecture that was the poorest both in pre-war and post-war Japan needed financial support. Those post-war Okinawans who could afford to finance their own transportation or had relatives in the host country who would send for them were limited. Neither the GRI nor the Ryûkyû Overseas Association had resources to finance the travel costs of individual emigrants. Hence they remained dependent on U.S. assistance.

Initially, USCAR was indifferent to either Okinawa's population problems or Okinawans' desire for emigration. Its most positive response to Okinawans' pleas was to offer a domestic migration program to the southernmost islands of Yaeyama. However, the Yaeyama Islands were notorious for malaria and the area was so small that this program elicited little enthusiasm. As the United States began expanding its military bases in

Okinawa in 1950, expropriating more land and driving Okinawan farmers out of their homes and ancestral lands, Okinawans' discontent deepened. Driven out of their own farmlands, Okinawans were squeezed into small and crowded areas, having little prospect of a better future for themselves or their children. USCAR feared their discontent would fuel social instability and create a hotbed for communist influence, even threatening the military occupation of Okinawa. In this tense political situation, USCAR started touting overseas emigration as a solution to Okinawa's population problems (Amemiya 2002b). Thus, the United States endorsed overseas emigration as a way to ease discontent. As far as the United States was concerned, Bolivia was an ideal destination that would allow it to kill two birds with one stone. It could help the new MNR government in Bolivia in developing the Santa Cruz region, and at the same time provide Okinawans with the possibility of overseas emigration. The Pacific Science Board of the National Research Council, commissioned by the U.S. government, sent James Tigner, a PhD candidate in Latin American history at Stanford, to Latin America in 1952 to survey Okinawan communities in various countries, including Bolivia.

Originally, the idea of post-war Okinawan immigration to Bolivia emerged in 1949 among pre-war Okinawan immigrants in Riberalta in the Amazon region, who were concerned about the plight of compatriots in their devastated homeland. Joined by other immigrants from the cities of La Paz and Santa Cruz, they appealed to the GRI to permit the immigration project. Meanwhile, they selected a settlement site for the future immigrants, forty-five miles east of Santa Cruz de la Sierra, and purchased 2,500 hectares adjacent to government land that the MNR regime was to grant for cultivation. Tigner had been informed of all these activities of the pre-war immigrants, and it appears that by the time he arrived in Santa Cruz de la Sierra, the United States had decided to promote the emigration of 12,000 Okinawans to Bolivia over a period of ten years. This was considerably more than anything the pre-war immigrants had envisioned, and Tigner had to persuade them to join this grandiose project (Amemiya 1999, 2002b).

As Bolivia was formally selected as the destination for the Okinawan emigration project, the new elite in Okinawa, Ichiro Inamine of the Ryûkyû Overseas Association and Hiroshi Senaga of the GRI, made a survey trip to Bolivia in February 1954. Inamine, along with the Chief Executive of the GRI, Shûhei Higa, lobbied U.S. officials and politicians for financial aid to the Okinawan emigration project. Inamine contacted and solicited help from the Republican Congressman from Minnesota, Walter Judd, who was concerned about the spread of communism in East Asia and was most cooperative. This is the same Judd who, in 1949, proposed the Judd Bill that was to make first-generation Japanese Americans eligible for U.S. citizenship (Koshino 1999: 142–3). Someone in the U.S. State Department sympathetic to the plight of Okinawans suggested bringing them to the

United States, but such a suggestion was dismissed for domestic political reasons (National Archives 1956).

The bill to fund Okinawan immigration to Bolivia was passed and the emigration project rushed forward without either sufficient surveys of the land and its surrounding conditions, or sufficient preparations for receiving new immigrants. The Japanese government obtained some knowledge about the proposed settlement site for the Okinawans and issued a warning about its isolated location and bad roads, which would likely lead to difficulties in farming and to "escapes" of immigrants from the settlement to other regions and other countries (National Archives 1954). The Japanese government was concerned not so much about the new Okinawan immigrants' welfare and destiny as about the reputation of Japanese immigrants in Bolivia, since Japan was planning to send its own immigrants to Bolivia at a site in the Santa Cruz region.[7]

However, given the limited supply of land in Latin America for a large-scale Okinawan immigration project, the United States was worried about Japan's emigration plans. James Tigner, who played an instrumental role in turning the Okinawan immigration plan into a reality, paid a visit to the Ministry of Foreign Affairs in Tokyo in 1952, on his way to Okinawa, to see how far Japan had come with its plans for emigration to Bolivia. He noted in his report a concern in the United States that "the progress of the Japanese Government in developing South American colonization will thwart the USCAR's efforts to introduce Ryûkyûans in this area unless similar steps are taken by our Government" (National Archives 1952).

In an incredibly hurried manner, 400 Okinawans, selected from 4,000 applicants, many with families, arrived in two groups in 1954 at the settlement site that the pre-war Okinawan immigrants had purchased and named Colonia Uruma. The housing was incomplete, and wells had not yet been dug when they arrived. Unfortunately, the Japanese government's warning turned out to be all too true. A mysterious disease took fourteen lives and put the majority, regardless of age, into sick beds within eight months of their arrival. Moreover, simultaneously with the disease, a tremendous flood assaulted Colonia Uruma in February of the following year and made the immigrants' situation intolerable. Isolated from outside contact in a new and threatening land, the new Okinawan immigrants were so distressed that they decided to move to another site.[8] However, they were forced to move again due to a dispute over the ownership of the land, and finally settled in the current Colonia Okinawa. Immigration resumed in 1956 and continued until 1965, but the total number of immigrants reached only 3,200, far below the original target of 12,000.

The Japanese immigration projects

During the occupation between 1945 and 1952, SCAP took various measures for political reorientation and social reorganization to democratize

Japan. No such measures were applied to Okinawa. The U.S. occupation's different treatment of mainland Japan and Okinawa was manifested in its view of and approach to population problems and emigration. In Okinawa, USCAR paid little attention to population issues until the expropriation of land for expansion of its military bases provoked serious social protest around 1950. Then USCAR touted overseas emigration as a solution to population pressure, considered primarily as a safety-valve to pacify Okinawan discontent over land issues. In Japan, on the other hand, SCAP regarded Japan's population problems with great alarm from the very beginning of its occupation and saw the agrarian land issue as the heart of the problem. Hence, SCAP enforced stringent land reform, which never took place on Okinawa.

SCAP was concerned that Japan's post-war population pressure might, as it had done in the 1930s, once again trigger Japan's expansion overseas or might be used to justify it. To investigate and explore solutions, SCAP consulted U.S. demographers. These specialists concluded that emigration would do little to ease Japan's population pressure as long as Japan's birth rates remained high, and recommended the dissemination of birth control (SCAP 1996: 117).[9] At the same time, Japanese birth control activists from the pre-war era, such as Tenrei Ota and Shizue Kato, were pressing for liberalization of abortion. In 1948 they made a breakthrough with the passage of the Eugenic Protection Law, which replaced the National Eugenics Law of 1941 that had restricted abortion.[10] With further revisions in 1949 and 1952, legal abortion became available practically on demand. Individual Okinawans sought overseas emigration for a better life, rather than a solution to population problems in their military-occupied homeland. Likewise, Japanese emigrants sought a better future for themselves and their children. To respond to such popular interest in emigration, private supporters set up an overseas emigration association in 1947. SCAP, however, viewed post-war Japan's interest in overseas emigration as "a remnant of Japan's imperialistic expansionism" and tried to suppress it.

Japan had to wait to take up emigration projects until it recovered its sovereignty in 1952. As soon as the occupation ended, Japan established the Bureau of Emigration within the Ministry of Foreign Affairs, and began sending out feelers about possible settlement sites for new emigrants. Peru was out of the question with its still strong anti-Japanese feelings. In August 1953, the Japanese government sent an official to Bolivia to inquire about the possibility of Japanese immigration. The Bolivian government responded positively. Bolivia, like other Latin American countries, had hoped for European immigrants, but that was not happening. Hence they decided to accept immigrants from Japan and Okinawa as cheaper alternatives (Wakatsuki 1987: 285–6).

Diet Representative Tadasuke Imamura, encouraged by the Bolivian officials' acceptance of Japanese immigration, paid a visit to Bolivia in

November 1953, where he met Minister of Agriculture Velarde, who was already enthusiastic about accepting Japanese immigrants. With Imamura's urging, the Japanese government sent a survey mission to Bolivia in February 1954, which happened to coincide with the survey trip of the Okinawan Emigration Mission to Bolivia. Although none of the documents of these missions mentions the other's presence, it is implausible that neither knew of the other's activity. As I noted earlier, Tigner voiced U.S. concern in his report about the contest between the United States and Japan for colonizing sites in South America. Bolivia was the only destination the United States could arrange and was willing to finance for Okinawan emigration. If the GRI and the USCAR can be faulted for sending Okinawans to Bolivia with insufficient surveys of the land and inadequate preparations, thus causing greater suffering than necessary, the Japanese government did no better for its immigrants.

Representative Imamura made his second visit to Bolivia in October 1954, the same year that Okinawans began arriving, accompanied by an official from the Ministry of Foreign Affairs and the Chairman of the Japan Overseas Associations Federation. On this occasion, Japan and Bolivia reached a tentative agreement to allow ten to fifteen Japanese families to immigrate immediately as an experiment and eventually to bring in a thousand families. Before that idea went to a planning board, however, an entrepreneur named Toshimichi Nishikawa had entered Bolivia in August with the intention of setting up a sugar-processing plant with the assistance of the Foreign Ministry. He founded the Santa Cruz Agricultural Development Cooperative in October, and in November he met up with Representative Imamura, and together they looked for a site for this enterprise. They selected a site, about eighty miles northwest of Santa Cruz de la Sierra, at the present location of San Juan, and decided to purchase 500 hectares, adjacent to 13,000 hectares of public land to be granted for cultivation in the future. Shortly after the decision was made, however, Representative Imamura began to have doubts about the appropriateness of the site. He now insisted that it was too far from anywhere and that another site should be selected that was much closer to the city. Nishikawa was distressed and immediately wrote to the Foreign Ministry that a change of site would be unnecessary, claiming that construction of a road was already underway that would soon connect San Juan to Santa Cruz in about two hours of travel time.

Unfortunately, Representative Imamura died suddenly after returning to Japan, leaving no one else to raise an objection. The exchange between Imamura and Nishikawa was thus suppressed. The immigration plan went ahead without further investigation of the site. Much later, officials at the Foreign Ministry admitted that the site was not selected after thorough research and good planning. In fact, it was ten years before the road was completed, and San Juan was initially just as inaccessible as the Okinawans' first settlement. The immigrants themselves ridiculed the site as one "not even a dog would pass through" (Nihonjin Borivia Ijûshi Hensan Iinkai 1970: 90–2).[11]

Thus, in 1955, before Japan and Bolivia had signed a pact on immigration, eighty-seven Japanese immigrated into Bolivia. Although the number of immigrants was much smaller than that of the Okinawans who had arrived a year earlier, the conditions awaiting them were just as poor. Housing was incomplete, no food was in store, no roads were open to the settlement, and no land allotment had been made. Conditions were so bad, with the immigration pact still pending, that the Foreign Ministry halted the departure of a second immigrant group. The sugar-processing enterprise itself was so ill-conceived and poorly organized that it was abandoned in August 1956 even before it got started, leaving the new immigrants in the jungle with no assistance from outside (Nihonjin Borivia Ijûshi Hensan Iinkai 1970: 98–9; Maeda 1986: 45–6). This immigration, planned and executed by private enterprise, is commonly called the Nishikawa Immigration to distinguish it from the government project that followed.

The Japanese government took over the immigration project, signing a formal agreement with Bolivia. It first set up a consulate in La Paz in November 1955 and began negotiations with the Bolivian government in February 1956. At the beginning of the negotiations, the idea was to send as many as 50,000 Japanese families, or 200,000 persons, in the course of twenty years. Eventually, both governments agreed on a greatly scaled-down project of 1,000 families, or 6,000 persons in six years, and signed the pact in August 1956, only four days before President Paz Estenssoro's term in office ended (Nihonjin Borivia Ijûshi Hensan Iinkai 1970: 98–9; Maeda 1986: 36–7).[12] It was the first immigration pact that Japan signed with any country.[13] However, even this plan was not fulfilled, as was the case with the earlier Okinawan immigration, and only 1,600 Japanese emigrated to Bolivia.

One administration over two communities and beyond

Both of the post-war immigration projects – one for Okinawans and the other for mainland Japanese – were launched with insufficient preparation. The governments that organized these projects, Okinawan and Japanese, were first and foremost preoccupied with sending out a large number of people. Support of these immigrants was secondary, and was not confined to Bolivian emigration. In an attempt to respond to popular enthusiasm for overseas emigration and faced with limited areas to send immigrants to, in the 1950s the Japanese government frantically sought to sign up countries that would accept Japanese immigrants. Although the Japanese government sent missions to prospective host countries, as it did to Bolivia (as did the GRI), in order to determine whether the places were suitable for immigration, the investigations were perfunctory, and were only designed to establish that the sites had been inspected. Yasuo Wakatsuki, chief advisor to the

Federation of Japanese Overseas Associations for San Juan from April 1959 to March 1962, maintains that the investigations were unbelievably sloppy and the worst in Japan's emigration history, and that the way in which officials at the Ministry of Foreign Affairs selected the sites was irresponsible (Wakatsuki 1987: 172–5).

As if to compensate for this failure, the Japanese government began in 1957 to provide Colonia San Juan with financial and technical aid through a public corporation, the Japan Overseas Associations Federation (JOAF). Another organization called Emigration Promotion Ltd. handled loans to immigrants.[14] Under these aid agencies the situation in San Juan began to improve in 1960, although the economic and social situations were still far from stable. To explore diversification of crops, mechanization, and technological improvement, the JOAF founded an experimental farm in Colonia San Juan in 1961, which played a pivotal role in helping the immigrants succeed in diversified farming (Maeda 1986: 178–82). Toward the end of the 1960s, San Juan finally began to stabilize.

Okinawan immigrants benefited rather more than their counterparts in San Juan at the initial stage of their colonization, in spite of the tragic beginning, thanks to U.S. sponsorship that provided them with more onetime monetary aid and more heavy equipment. However, this benefit was short-lived, since the new immigrants desperately needed technical assistance and long-range financial aid, which they never received from the United States. The consequent disparity between Colonia Okinawa and San Juan became evident around 1958, and was recognized both by Japanese diplomatic representatives and the Okinawan immigrants themselves. The Ryûkyû Overseas Association set up its office in Santa Cruz in 1959 to provide the Okinawan immigrants with assistance, but the Okinawan government was severely limited under the United States occupation.

In December 1962 a young Japanese Bolivian nisei from Riberalta, Pedro Shimose, wrote in *Presencia*, a daily newspaper in La Paz, a series of reports on the Okinawan and Japanese immigrant settlements, noting a sharp contrast between the two. In Colonia San Juan, he was met by children with smiling faces and was impressed by the immigrants' hard work. In Colonia Okinawa, he bemoaned, "*¡Cuánta diferencia existe, entre esta colonia y la de San Juan!*" (What a difference between this colony and that of San Juan!). In Colonia Okinawa, Shimose saw suspicious children and exhausted adults. He interviewed some immigrants who told him that the North Americans were in charge of their welfare, but "they do not have much interest in us. They visit us every now and then, but do not understand our struggle. In fact, they have abandoned us." The Okinawan immigrants told Shimose they would like to receive the same treatment from the Japanese government as the San Juan immigrants were getting (Okinawa Prefectural Archives).[15] In order for that to happen, Okinawan immigrants had to get their residual Japanese citizenship restored and come under the Japanese government's protection.

Japanese Acting Ambassador to Bolivia, Eiji Kawasaki, who took up the post in 1961, informed Tokyo of the plight of Colonia Okinawa and made several recommendations to improve the situation. He learned that the Bolivian Minister of Agriculture, appalled at the disparity between San Juan and Colonia Okinawa in late 1962, publicly opposed the U.S.–Bolivia Immigration Pact then under consideration regarding Okinawan immigration, and he called on the Japanese government to also oppose it. However, since Okinawa's reversion to Japanese rule was not yet on the public agenda, the higher officials at the Foreign Ministry were reluctant to take issue with the United States over the treatment of Okinawan immigrants. Acting Ambassador Kawasaki was instructed to refrain from taking any adverse actions in Bolivia.

The situation changed in 1965. Mr. Kawasaki, now Ambassador to Bolivia, received information that the U.S. government was about to sign a pact with the Bolivians regarding the Okinawan immigrants. The pact was similar to that between Japan and Bolivia, except that it included two conditions: (1) the Okinawan immigrants were to take Bolivian nationality, and (2) the Bolivian government was to be responsible for protecting them. These conditions meant that the Okinawan immigrants would be permanently deprived of their residual Japanese nationality and that the United States would be relieved of any responsibility for them. This time, Ambassador Kawasaki succeeded in winning Tokyo's approval to intervene in stopping the U.S.–Bolivia pact. He was called back to Tokyo in November of that year, but he continued to speak out about the predicament of Colonia Okinawa. As the Okinawa reversion movement was gaining momentum, the Japanese government decided to bring up the issue at the Japan–U.S. committee discussions in May 1966. There it was agreed that the Japanese government would be responsible for protecting Okinawans overseas, that the Japanese government and Japan's Overseas Emigration Agency would handle Okinawan overseas immigration, and the Japanese government would issue Japanese passports to Okinawans for overseas travel. In Bolivia, the new Japanese Ambassador Ken Usui negotiated with the Bolivian government and the U.S. Embassy, and succeeded in October 1967 in having Okinawan immigrants included under the Japan–Bolivia Immigration Pact (Nihonjin Borivia Ijûshi Hensan Iinkai 1970: 143–5).

Thus, the two post-war colonias finally came under the single administration of the Japanese government. As Japan became more prosperous, the amount of foreign aid increased. These settlements depended on the Japanese government's aid for major public works, social services, and the education of children, as the Bolivian government lacked the resources to provide adequately even its native citizens with such works and services. Over the years of devastating hardships and failures, the majority of the original immigrants in both settlements had left, either to return to their places of origin or to re-emigrate to other countries in the Americas. Those who remained at last established themselves, with the Japanese government's substantial assistance, as a prominent ethnic community in Santa Cruz, by then the most economically vibrant region of Bolivia.

Conclusion

U.S. policy during the Cold War era kept Okinawa separated from Japan, leading to the creation of Colonia Okinawa, which contributed to the horizontal disjuncture in the Japanese Bolivian community. Bolivia is the only country in the world in which Okinawan immigrants have established their own settlement community, distinct and separate from other Japanese. Having their own self-contained community has fostered a strong Okinawan identity, without them feeling marginalized. At the same time, due to close contact with the Japanese government, they identify themselves as Japanese instead of Bolivian. When they were still under the administration of the U.S. government, they were keenly aware of the benefit of having their Japanese nationality reinstated. For one, they would receive financial and technical aid from the Japanese government, which was vital for the survival of Colonia Okinawa. For another, they would shed their stateless status.

This did not weaken the ties which the Okinawans in Bolivia had with their homeland. The Ryûkyû government kept its office in Bolivia and, even after Okinawa's return to Japan in 1972, Okinawa Prefecture kept sending aid to Colonia Okinawa. This still continues today. Moreover, exchange between Okinawa and Bolivia and Okinawa and Japan has increased, as witnessed in the celebration of the fiftieth anniversary of Okinawan immigration to Bolivia in August 2004 (Amemiya 2004), and is cultivating in Bolivia an Okinawan identity (Arakaki 2002). The Okinawans have established a good reputation among Bolivians, for whom Okinawa and Japan are synonymous.

There is another consequence of the immigration projects organized by the three governments in the post-war era. It kept communities of immigrants from both Okinawa and Japan reliant on the Japanese government far more than on the assistance provided by pre-war immigrants, and reinforced the vertical disjuncture from the pre-war Japanese Bolivian community. Both the colonias of Okinawa and San Juan in Santa Cruz, having made remarkable progress in agricultural production, are now among Bolivia's leading producers of soybeans, wheat, rice, and other produce. They have established themselves as a distinct ethnic group. In contrast, the descendants of Japanese immigrants in the Amazon region in Bolivia have been largely ignored by the Japanese government and, being widely dispersed and deeply rooted in Bolivian society, are not distinguishable, culturally and economically, from most poor Bolivians. Hence, these three groups – Colonia Okinawa, Colonia Santa Cruz, and Amazonian Japanese Bolivians – exist not as a unified ethnic group but in parallel without intersections with one another.

Another by-product of Japan's support of post-war immigrants is the isolation of immigrants from Bolivian society; that is, the immigrants who have remained in the colonias did not need to mix with other Bolivians, except for business transactions. Now that both post-war immigrant communities are not only financially secure but also prospering, it is anticipated that aid from Japan will diminish in the not too distant future. Already, the Ministry of Foreign Affairs closed the Bureau of Overseas Emigration in 1999. The post-war immigrants and their offspring now face the new challenge of taking an active part in Bolivian society.

Acknowledgment

This study was made possible thanks to the generous support of the Japan Foundation and the Japan Policy Research Institute.

Notes

1 I will refer to this Japanese settlement as Colonia Japonesa San Juan, or simply San Juan, regardless of the time frame (even though it underwent several name changes).
2 Okinawa is also called Ryûkyû.
3 The Department is a political, administrative unit of Bolivia equivalent to a state without much political power delegated from central government. Bolivia consists of nine departments.
4 Five hundred and seventy-four Japanese were counted in 1917 (Nihonjin Borivia Ijûshi Hensan Iinkai 1970: 27).
5 Estimates by the Federación Nacional de Asociaciones Boliviano-Japonesas in the pamphlet of the centennial of Japanese immigration to Bolivia. No systematic census has been taken of the descendants of Japanese immigrants in the Amazon region.
6 Peru, in particular, held a strong anti-Japanese sentiment for many years even after World War II.
7 This also reflects on the Japanese government's general discriminatory perception and treatment of Okinawan immigrants. For example, the Ministry of Foreign Affairs of the Japanese Government banned Okinawan emigration to Brazil, along with that from Kagoshima, from 1913 to 1916, claiming (incorrectly) that they had fled their work sites before completing their contracts (Yabiku 1987: 38).
8 Tigner notes, "Following the outbreak of a disease to which the local population had become immune, and an unseasonal period of drought, it was decided to move the colony to another site" (1963: 224). However, he vastly underplays the enormity of the disaster and the impact of the disease (hantavirus).
9 These population specialists included Warren S. Thompson, Pascal K. Whelpton, Irene B. Taeuber, and F. W. Notestein.
10 The Eugenic Protection Law eviscerated the criminal abortion clause that has remained in the Penal Code untouched up until the present.
11 It is not clear when Imamura's complaint was uncovered.
12 Maeda (1986) analyzes the enormous size of the immigration plan at the initial stage as the reflection of the desire of both Japanese and Bolivian

governments. That is, Japan hoped to duplicate in Bolivia the pre-war experiences of sending 15,000 to 18,000 emigrants per year overseas, and Bolivia wanted a large population of hard-working immigrants in order to fulfill the ideal of the 1952 Revolution.
13 Japan signed the immigration pact with Paraguay in 1959, with Brazil in 1960, and with Argentina in 1961 (Maeda 1986: 46).
14 In 1963, the two organizations merged into the Overseas Immigration Agency, which developed into Japan International Cooperation Agency (JICA) in 1974.
15 These reports were translated into Japanese by the Director of the Colonia Okinawa in Bolivia, and sent to the Chief of the Economy Bureau of the GRI. English translation is mine (Okinawa Prefectural Archives, R000538508).

11 Acting Japanese

Gary Y. Okihiro

> Fifty years gone by
> After I left Izumo
> Clouds roll over Mount Rainier.
> My heart turns among them,
> Restless and forlorn.
>   Genji Mihara, 1958
>   (Ito 1973: 723)

The older I get, the more sentimental I feel. New York's weather doesn't help – the gray skies, the icy winds, endless winter, no patch of green. And that's dangerous for an historian, whose very life-blood must course with detachment and objectivity. Emotion constricts the scholar's arteries and veins. Despite my training and discipline, age and art draw me to cemeteries, both figuratively and literally, in a yearning for community, for continuity, for certainty. There, on stone, an economy of words bears the burden of lifetimes, however brief, of thought and activity. "Ichiro Fujii, September 15, 1918, died at 33." "Isokawa, 25 years." "To meet together in one place," the grave marker reminded – the past on common ground.

> Graves of Japanese
> Record the strife and struggle
> Of all immigrants.
>   Akebono
>   (Ito 1973: 883)

The Japanese experience is, of course, the story of all immigrants, all sojourners on this planet called Earth, for we are all wanderers, no matter how rooted. There are no natives, no foreigners. We are mere visitors to the land and sea, which sustain us in our ceaseless quest for home. There is no permanence, no forever. And history is in the crossing – the middle passage – and not in the destination – the landing. There is no teleology, no finality. There are only turnings and struggles and the sacred sea and Earth.

Row upon row of government-issued gravestones face busy Claremont Road in Carlisle, Pennsylvania. In the middle of this well-tended plot grows a weeping cherry tree whose trunk is encircled and embraced by prayer cloths, strings of shells and beads, and small bundles of sage and sweet grass. The stones, the selfsame stones that bear soldiers' names in U.S. national cemeteries, tell the story of American Indian children who died at the Carlisle Indian Industrial School: "Abe Lincoln, Son of Antelope, Cheyenne, January 17, 1880," "Maud, Daughter of Chief Swift Bear, Sioux, December 13, 1880," "Lucy Prettyeagle, Sioux, May 9, 1884," and "Unknown." Established in 1879 by a U.S. Army officer and "Indian fighter," the Carlisle School held children, in part, to guarantee the docility of their parents in the yet resistant Far West, and sought to "Americanize" them. In the founder's words, "Kill the Indian and save the man" (Archuleta *et al.* 2000: 16). Escape and freedom, no doubt, were on some children's minds. When I made my pilgrimage to Carlisle, someone had thoughtfully placed sneakers at the foot of Lucy Prettyeagle's gravestone, perhaps (I'd like to think) to aid her in swift flight, and carry her home.

On a hill overlooking another school for natives, the Foreign Mission School in Cornwall, Connecticut, sits the grave-site of Henry Opukahàia. Like the Indian children at Carlisle, Opukahàia was far away from home. Carried on board an American ship from Hawaii to New York City, Opukahàia was the inspiration for the founding of the Foreign Mission School in 1817 and the mission to Hawaii in 1819. The school's purpose was to train, in the words of the historical marker, "young men of many races to act as Christian missionaries among their peoples."[1] On June 1, 1825, there were fourteen American Indian students, six Hawaiians, four Chinese, a Portuguese, and "one Jew from England."[2] Although slated to accompany the first missionary company to his land of birth, Opukahàia died on February 17, 1818. His large tombstone, distinguished for its size and horizontal lie, reads in part:

> He was once an Idolater, and was designed for a Pagan Priest; but by the Grace of God and by the prayers and instructions of his pious friends, he became a Christian. He was eminent for piety and missionary Zeal. When almost prepared to return to his native isle to preach the Gospel, God took to himself. In his last sickness, he wept and prayed for Owhyee but was submissive. He died without fear, with a heavenly smile on his countenance and glory in his soul.[3]

In July 1993, Opukahàia's family and friends took his remains from Cornwall to Kona on the island of Hawaii. But his tombstone, with leis, seashells, and a piece of sandalwood on it, endures the inevitable New England winters.

I feel a kinship with Japan like the one I hold with the spirits of American Indian children and Hawaiians along the coast where I now reside. It wasn't always so. In Hawaii, some of my earliest recollections included the comforting circle of nuclear family and a rather large extended family, my maternal grandparents having reared five daughters and four sons, all of whom married and had children of their own. We were "Japanese," as far as I knew, as opposed to my fishing buddy who was "Chinese" and the neighbor girl, with braces on her polio-afflicted legs, who was "haole." It later dawned on me that my father was Japanese and my mother Okinawan, and my sister and I were thus *hapa* or "half" and "Japanese, but not quite." My darker skin and hairy legs hinted at my "not quite" status. But for practical purposes, I was Japanese pure and simple.

In the Ethnic Studies Oral History Project, one man, Choki Oshiro, recalled how a Japanese assistant *luna* (field overseer) treated the Okinawan sugar plantation workers "like cats and dogs." "I was taught we Okinawans were also subjects of Imperial Japan," he remembered (Ethnic Studies Oral History Project and United Okinawan Association of Hawaii 1981: 406). By the 1950s – my own childhood, or "small kid time" in the island – sentiments such as those experienced by Choki Oshiro were relics of the past. By the time I came of age, Imperial Japan was no more, and I was Japanese.[4]

It never occurred to me that being Japanese was an acquired taste that might have changed with time and circumstance. I thought of it as a biological fact, an inheritance, and a birthright. The Japanese government once considered all those born of Japanese fathers to be Japanese citizens, and the Imperial Rescript on Education promulgated by the Meiji Emperor in 1890 declared:

> Our Imperial ancestors have founded Our Empire on a basis broad and everlasting and have deeply and firmly implanted virtue; Our Subjects ever united in loyalty and filial piety have from generation to generation illustrated the beauty thereof. This is the glory of the fundamental character of Our Empire, and herein also lies the source of Our education.
>
> (Ichioka 1988: 201)

In the United States, the scientist Harry H. Laughlin advised the House Committee on Immigration and Naturalization in its authorship of the 1924 Exclusion Act that sought to protect the United States gene pool from pollution and degeneration by southern and eastern Europeans, Koreans, and Japanese.[5] Like prisons for criminals and asylums for the insane, Laughlin held, immigration laws must protect the nation from invasive and biologically inferior stock (Kevles 1985: 103–4). And the former publisher of the *Sacramento Bee* and Director of the Associated Press, V. S. McClatchy, testified in favor of the 1924 Act:

> The Japanese, he warned, are less assimilable and more dangerous as residents in this country than any other of the peoples ineligible under our laws.... With great pride of race, they have no idea of

assimilating in the sense of amalgamation.... They come here specifically and professedly for the purpose of colonizing and establishing here permanently the proud Yamato race. They never cease being Japanese.

(Daniels 1970: 99)

I was Japanese, and that was that. The problem was, I might have looked Japanese but I didn't speak, dress, or walk like a Japanese. We all knew, having grown up in Hawaii, that "real Japanese" couldn't distinguish "r" from "l," the men were all skinny and wore their pants high up their waist, and the women took short steps and didn't stride. We could spot them a mile off, those Japanese. When I went to California, I was shocked to see Japanese speak like haoles. If you closed your eyes, you'd swear a white person was talking. Even the old people spoke English instead of Hawaiian pidgin English. I began to entertain doubts about my membership in "the proud Yamato race."

In the 1960s, with the U.S. war escalating in Southeast Asia and the movement for civil rights spreading in the United States, I developed a "Third World consciousness," an imagined solidarity with people of color in their struggles for self-determination and liberation. We were the children of the migrant workers, Filipina/o and Chicana/o. The words and deeds of revolutionaries in Cuba, Algeria, China, and Viet Nam broadened our minds and sharpened our resolve, and we nurtured kinships across racialized divides and national boundaries. Of course, those communities were imaginary, and even as we strove to include we also chose to exclude. We reinstalled hierarchies of race, gender, sexuality, and class, despite our stated efforts to dismantle them, and our analyses of oppression and resistance were reductive and often misguided, despite our best efforts to expose lies and seek truths. Assuredly this was not the golden age.

Still, I shall never forget the months I spent in South Carolina in the fall of 1968, staying a few days in the home of an African American sharecropper and his family and teaching biology at an African American high school. I can still see the low morning sun filtered by trees and moss, backlighting a student's feet in too large and much worn leather shoes. His wasn't a statement of fashion but of necessity. And I am still angered by the memory of my friend's dead baby in Molepolole, Botswana, in 1970, and the white physicians at the hospital who dispensed pills with "NTO" for "native treatment only" inscribed on them. My four years in Africa were some of the best years of my life. Decades later I renewed the solidarity I had imagined in my youth during my visit to Viet Nam in the spring of 1999. The warm, moist air, the countryside, the people, were all familiar to me courtesy of the media coverage of the American war that had devastated the people and poisoned the land. In the heartfelt embrace in Hanoi of a Vietnamese colleague, who had lost his brother to an American bomb, I felt an intimacy of life and death, of family and home.

Those kinships we conjure are complicated and changeable to be sure. And they don't depend upon blood or culture or citizenship alone. My identities and communities, imaginary though they may be, defy those categories and fences. And with age, I have come to appreciate my various sequential and simultaneous incarnations as Japanese, Okinawan, *hapa*, Asian American, person of color, a member of the Third World, and so forth. I thus resist notions of "the Japanese" in Japan and in the diaspora, as if there exists a root and "homeland," a singular source of authenticity, and its offshoots and their varieties bred on "foreign" soil, strange sites of deviance from the original. Instead, we know Japanese to be a creation situated in time and place. Japanese is historical, and has a history. And yet we seem to persist in the mistaken belief of a primal, pure, and unchanging tradition at the center, and its degeneration and contamination at the edges. The irony is that tradition may be found instead at the margins. My mother learned from her parents Meiji Japanese, and when she visited Japan during the 1980s, the Japanese found her speech oddly rural and perhaps quaint and old-fashioned. Modern Japan failed to recognize one of its ancestors.

But I am not pursuing that line of argument because I believe it to be incorrect, the inversion of core and periphery. What I am suggesting instead is that there is no margin, no mainstream, no authentic, no fake. When considering the Japanese, there are multiple centers and identity creations enacted by individuals in and across time and space, despite attempts by the state, society, and individuals to define and police a singular identity and culture. European Orientalism, of course, is one of those hegemonic discourses. Japan's Orientalism, both imposed and resisted, was not only of its Asian others, but also of itself (cf. Tanaka 1993; Kelsky 2001). And like all identities, although but a script, Japanese gains form and currency through theory and practice. In the recording and enactment is the reality.

In June 2003, my family and I stayed for a week with relatives in Okinawa. It would probably be the last visit for my eighty-five-year-old mother, and my former wife and I wanted to have our sons to gain an appreciation of their Okinawan ancestry. My older son and I had briefly met some of those kin some five years earlier through the kindness of Hojun Kakinohana, a law professor at the University of the Ryûkyûs, who heard from my lecture there that my maternal grandparents were from a village outside Naha. But we hadn't met all our kin nor had we stayed with them. My mother made that possible. Her cousin, Kazuo, opened his spacious, two-story house to us, and his wife, Haruko, cooked us sumptuous meals and washed our mounds of sweaty clothes. Every day, relatives from the surrounding hills of Osato-mura dropped by for a visit, and on the weekend, the extended family of nearly a dozen men and women and their children rented a bus and hired a driver to take us on an all-day excursion along Okinawa's fabled coast. That family gathering and the great kindness shown us, whether out of obligation or in anticipation of reciprocation, established and reinforced bonds of kinship. And I could feel my *Chinen* grandmother's presence on her family farmland, and recognized the cane fields that still surround the houses and the papaya and banana trees and the orchids that grow in profusion. In that recognition, the islands of her birth, Okinawa, seemed close to the islands of her death, Hawaii.

This encounter in Okinawa among those defined as kin surely has its counterpart in other places, in the intimacy of neighborhoods and at work, and in shared experiences of joys and sorrows where identifications and identities have formed beyond the bounds of blood. Having plaited the twine of kinship, we can certainly suture other strings of solidarity across the fissures of ethnicity, nation, culture, gender, sexuality, and class. This is no doubt true for all peoples, and the Japanese sojourn in the Americas, of course, reveals the verity of this contention. But although a common language and citizenship – as well as anti-Japanese hostility in host nations abroad – may have held them together as Japanese, there is ample evidence pointing to adaptations and alliances that produced newly expanded ways of being Japanese.

Kikuko Saiki described her love for Mexico. Her husband, Mario, had been in Mexico for decades and had married and lost two previous wives, the first a Mexican and the second a Japanese. They met in Osaka, and within a month were married. Mario, she explained, was an insistent suitor. Although she had studied Spanish in Japan and had planned to go to Latin America, Saiki was disappointed when she first arrived in Mexico. The land, she said, seemed so barren. But Mario's children from his former marriages and their grandchildren brought joy to her life, and they tried to teach her to become Mexican. She began cooking Mexican food, and learned to make Japanese dishes with Mexican ingredients. "I experienced alternately the joy and disappointment of creation," she recalled playfully. She made pickled vegetables, *miso* paste, and tofu, and used a Mexican purple bean to make the fillings for Japanese sweets. She satisfied her craving for *nattô* (fermented soybeans) by wrapping beans in the dried cornhusks used to make tamales and placing the bundle in a warm place. The husks, she explained, helped to ferment the beans. Her cooking, Saiki reported, alternated between chilis and tomato sauce and soybeans and soy sauce. And then she began craving *pansita* and spicy Mexican foods, and eventually contributed recipes to a Mexican cookbook intended for the Japanese. Their son, Saiki declared proudly, married a Mexican woman who, on her visits with her, asked to learn to cook Japanese food. "I am truly happy to have moved to Mexico," she concluded. "Mario! Thank you so much!" (K. Saiki 1996: 93–105; M. Saiki 1996).

During the period 1900 to 1915, the rubber industry was the principal instigator of Japanese and Okinawan migration to Bolivia, and its demands rose and fell with the worldwide market for rubber from the Amazon Basin. Japanese companies, such as Morioka Emigration Company and Meiji Colonization Company, supplied most of those migrants and many came to Bolivia from Peru (see Amemiya, Chapter 10, this volume). In all, during the first two decades of the twentieth century, less than 500 Japanese and Okinawan men and ten women labored in eastern Bolivia. The American Rubber Company hired the majority of that group, although Bolivian, German, and Swiss rubber companies also employed Japanese and Okinawan workers. After the collapse of the rubber boom, some returned to Japan and Okinawa, others went to Peru, and those who remained in Bolivia moved to towns such as Riberalta and Trinidad in the eastern part of the country. There, they opened grocery stores, barber and tailor shops, and bazaars, and a large number went into small farming, producing garden crops for the local market (Tigner 1963).

The life of a rubber gatherer or *seringero* was arduous and lonely. The day normally began at 4 a.m. when the *seringero* started his round of eighty to 150 rubber trees. He placed cups on the trunks to collect the sap, gathered wood to make a fire and the nuts that made the white smoke needed to cure the rubber, and cooked the milky fluid while taking care to prevent rain-water from diluting and thus spoiling the batch. *Seringeros* commonly stayed in the forest for three or four months at a time before returning to outposts to deposit their accumulation of crude rubber and restock their provisions of food, ammunition, utensils, and other supplies. They lived in one-room huts made of logs and thatched with leaves, and usually planted gardens for their vegetables and hunted and fished for their meat. During the heavy rainy season from November through April, most *seringeros* left the forests for the towns where they worked on nearby farms (Tigner 1963: 210–11).

Okinawans and Japanese worked together with Bolivian *mestizos* and Indians for the rubber companies. Many of them married Bolivians, Pedro Shimose recalled, and worked to gain the respect of their fellow Bolivians. By 1952, 76 percent of Okinawan men and 83 percent of Japanese men had married Bolivian women (Tigner 1963: 214). Shimose's father worked for the railroads, and taught him, despite hard times, to "always look forward." During World War II, Bolivians vandalized German and Japanese property, and Shimose was ashamed to be the child of a Japanese man. But his father persisted in his love for Bolivia, and Shimose pointed to the symbolism of names that combined Japanese and Spanish as indicative of the formation of singular, harmonious identities as Japanese and Bolivians (Nihonjin Ijû 100 Shûnen Hensan Iinkai 2000: 47–9).

Yoshiko Toma's family arrived in Bolivia after sunset. Although an earlier group of immigrants greeted them, remembered Toma, "I still recall feeling so lonely." She gathered branches and leaves to make beds for the family, and fended off the swarms of mosquitoes that attacked them. As the children slept, Toma reflected on their decision to leave

Okinawa. "I really regretted coming to such a remote country ... deep in the forest," she admitted. "I sighed and sighed." And although exhausted from her long journey, Toma could not sleep (Bolivia Colonia Okinawa Nyûshoku 25 Shûnen Hensan Iinkai 1979: 89–91, 146).

Masako Tamashiro recalled: "We came full of hope to this unknown country, but it was in the middle of a jungle and I got all sorts of skin problems. It was like hell." Tamashiro and her husband cleared fields from the forest, and returned drained. "It was such a tough life that I could not remember how many times I cried." Things got more difficult when her baby was born because she had to work in the fields and tend to the baby at the same time. "I kept my spirit up, saying to myself, 'it is not only me who is suffering; everyone endures the hard life,'" she noted. Besides the rigors of work, Tamashiro missed her mother and brothers and sisters, and felt alienated from everything around her. "I felt unbearably lonely," she declared (Bolivia Colonia Okinawa Nyûshoku 25 Shûnen Hensan Iinkai 1979: 146, 164).

Despite these estrangements and struggles, the Okinawan colonists persisted and built a community in Bolivia's Santa Cruz region. They erected a school for their children, established a Women's Association, and reclaimed the forest from the monkeys, snakes, armadillos, ant-eaters, and deer. It was like "a war," observed Yoshiko Toma, but also immensely satisfying to win the fruits of their labor. In fact, she declared, all of their difficulties helped to bequeath "strong minds" to the second generation. And she summed up her years of toil and sorrow: "It is strange, but even though my house is in the middle of nowhere, I now feel no pain because I consider it my home" (Bolivia Colonia Okinawa Nyûshoku 25 Shûnen Hensan Iinkai 1979: 147).

Peru's arid coastal area allowed for agriculture and fishing, and mainly whites, with their enslaved Africans, *mestizos*, and Asians settled the region after the Spanish wars of conquest in the eighteenth century. Indians predominated in the Andean mountains with their minerals and pastures for livestock, and along their eastern slopes, which form the head-waters of the Amazon River with its dense stands of tropical trees and their products. Peru's need for labor placed divergent racial groups in similar company insofar as they constituted a subordinate class to their white owners. Beginning in 1849, in anticipation of slavery's end in 1855, Peru's government approved a series of actions that would result in more than 100,000 Chinese indentures entering the country between 1850 and 1883.

Following this period, Peru's government then initiated the recruitment of Japanese for the country's coastal landowners who had relied successively upon enslaved Africans and indentured Chinese to supply their chronic need for cheap, efficient workers. The first Latin American nation to establish diplomatic relations with Japan in 1873, Peru instructed its agent to promote trade and migration that would assist in the development of Peruvian agriculture. The envoy had been prompted by the *María*

Luz incident of 1872, in which Japan charged the Peruvian ship, anchored in Yokohama harbor, with slave trafficking, and freed all of its cargo of Chinese coolies.

Peru's 1876 census reported fifteen Japanese in the country, and in 1889 Korekiyo Takahashi formed the Japan-Peru Mining Company to mine silver in Peru. The venture soon collapsed, however, and only after 1898 did Japan send migrant workers to Peru. The initiative began when Augusto Leguía, a sugar industry leader and later Peru's president, invited Teikichi Tanaka, Leguía's friend from college days in the United States and an agent for the Morioka Emigration Company in Brazil, to visit Peru to discuss supplying laborers for that country's cane fields. Japan approved Morioka's petition to send migrants to Peru in 1898, and Morioka arranged a contract with plantation owners that bound the worker to four years at a monthly wage of £2.10 (about twenty-five Japanese yen, or US$12.50) for ten-hour workdays in the fields and twelve-hour days in the mill. Planters provided for travel costs, housing, and medical needs, and Morioka supplied laborers with work clothes, shoes, and a hat. It should be noted that around 1900 in the United States, agricultural workers received about a dollar a day. Thus, what the plantation owners in Peru were offering was less than half the going rate on the United States mainland, and even substantially less than plantation workers made in Hawaii. But this was a little higher than the Japanese average salary of the period (which was about twenty-one yen per month).

On February 28, 1899, 790 migrants sailed from Yokohama to Callao on the *Sakura-maru*. The ship arrived in port on April 3, and the next day it followed Peru's coastline, stopping to unload its cargo of laborers at eleven plantations. Barely three months later on June 29, Morioka's Tanaka wired Japan's minister in Mexico: "Feeling against immigrants strong. Contracts broken on flimsy grounds. Many have returned to Callao. Have been clashes with Peruvians. Situation out of control" (Irie 1951a: 445).

Investigations by Japanese agents revealed that the planters felt that the Japanese got "angry about little things," were "lazy," failed to obey regulations and orders, and regarded supervisors and plantation officials as "dogs and horses." Japanese workers objected to the monopoly of plantation company stores, preferring to buy from Chinese merchants, and refused to work under overseers who were abusive, threatened them with whips, and treated them like slaves. Some planters saw Japanese protests as "uprisings" that set a bad example for Indians, and Japanese staged work slow-downs in response to perceived injustices. By August, the number of Japanese who had fled or been expelled from plantations reached 321, and they gathered in Callao, sought alternative employment, or stayed in town where some native workers, who saw the Japanese as competitors, shouted abuse and threw stones at them. Labor protests and runaways continued, and by the end of October 1900, due to disease and poor working and living conditions, 124 of the original group had died. (For a detailed accounting of these early years, see Irie 1951a: 437–52; Irie 1951b: 648–64.)

Despite the trials of the first contingent and the desire of many from that group to return to Japan, the Morioka Emigration Company continued to ship laborers to Peru. By the end of 1909, of 6,295 migrants, 5,158 remained in Peru, 481 had died, 414 returned to Japan, and 242 remigrated to other countries (Irie 1951b: 651–2). Contract terms and some working conditions improved in response to workers' complaints, but labor strife and protests continued and desertions were a common feature of this period. Keiichi Ito, a Japanese official in Lima, summed up the status of Japanese workers in Peru in 1909: "In this country, there are over 5,000 Japanese. Although ten years have passed since the first group arrived, I must say that, all things considered, they have made no success worthy of mention. In some respects, things have almost ended in failure" (ibid.: 653).

In truth, the situation was more complicated than this gloomy estimate. A few Japanese workers had managed to save, despite their near-subsistence wages, enough money to rent small plots of land for tenant farming, and others sent remittances back to families in Japan. Apparently, not all of the workers' earnings reached their destinations. Both the Meiji and Morioka companies were accused of swindling migrants of remittances given to the company in trust. Instead of passing on the sums, according to a bank investigation, Morioka officials skimmed off part of the total, claiming that the shortfall was due to the rates of exchange. Further, the company delayed payments so that it could deposit the remittances into its account to bolster its credit rating and derive interest from the investment, and sent the money only after repeated inquiries by the laborers and their relatives (Irie 1951b: 659–60). Some emigration companies, thus, in their recruiting efforts deceived migrants about the prospects for labor and profit in Peru, and cheated them, once in the country, out of a portion of their hard-earned savings.

Japanese Peruvians, according to Shizuko Abuso, looked down with contempt on Chinese Peruvians, and in turn, Ginyu Ige reported, Chinese Peruvians distributed anti-Japanese leaflets and exhibited an intense dislike for Japanese Peruvians (Kin-chô-shi Hensan Iinkai 1996: 367–8, 394). And although Japan's attack on China in 1937 prompted a distinction in Peru between Japanese and Chinese and fueled anti-Japanese sentiment (see Titiev 1951: 238–9; Higashide 1993: 105–12), the proximate position of Chinese and Japanese in the social formation is clear, along with their kinship with their enslaved African predecessors. European conquerors and settlers brought all of them, racialized as inferior peoples, to Peru to employ them in labor useful for and profitable to the white rulers and owners. And, despite the divisions of race, ethnicity, class, and nation, which were both induced by Peru's rulers and enacted by the subject peoples, the relatedness of African, Chinese, and Japanese within Peru's social formation cannot be denied and should never be forgotten.

This brief, idiosyncratic reflection upon self and the Japanese experience in the Americas argues for the contingency of the category "Japanese." Kikuko Saiki's family of Mexicans and Japanese were as genuinely Mexican and Japanese as any from among the "pure" types. They were simply different, and they expanded the meanings of the identities of Mexican and Japanese. After Saiki (and others like her), to be Mexican and Japanese included alternating between chilis and tomato sauce and soybeans and soy sauce, and craving *pansita* and *nattô*. Race and nation are never pure or static, and are complexly constituted and constituting. Bolivia's Okinawan and Japanese rubber workers and their Bolivian wives formed unions that were both Bolivian and Japanese (or sometimes Bolivian and Okinawan), despite the fractures of race and war. Pedro Shimose, as his name reveals, is Bolivian but also Japanese. And the Okinawan settlers in Bolivia's eastern regions staked their claims upon the unremitting land, and, with labor and love, called the place their home. Bolivia and Okinawa are equally the homelands of Okinawan peoples. Peru's African, Chinese, and Japanese, although separated by racializations, were related by class position in the social formation. A new consciousness of solidarity and of Japaneseness might have developed upon that same field of engagement.

Our subject matter – Japanese and Japanese Americans – must have no borders. It will soon, if it hasn't already, lose its racialized moorings because of out-marriage and reproduction. It never was the homogeneous entity Imperial Japan liked to claim (and scholars too often assumed), whether in Japan or the Americas, but was always differentiated by region, ethnicity, gender, class, language, religion, and politics. Similarly, Japanese language and culture were always receptive, to varying degrees, to winds of change generated both within and without the islands that eventually comprised the nation of Japan. A state of mind and an enactment, being Japanese traverses the social formation of race, gender, sexuality, class, and nation, at the intersections and interstices of time and space and the turnings and struggles of our restless crossings.

Notes

1 This is taken from a plaque placed on the site of the Foreign Mission School in Cornwall, Connecticut.
2 From the same plaque mentioned in n. 1.
3 Cornwall Cemetery on Cemetery Hill Road, Cornwall, Connecticut.
4 See Amemiya (Chapter 10, this volume) for the status of Okinawa and Okinawans in the Japanese empire.
5 The Chinese had been excluded already by the Chinese Exclusion Act of 1882. See Daniels (Chapter 1, this volume).

12 Crossing ethnic boundaries
The challenge of Brazilian Nikkeijin return migrants in Japan

Takeyuki Tsuda

Internationalization at home and abroad

Kokusaika, or internationalization, has become one of the most pervasive ideologies in Japan today. Despite its efforts to become more visible and influential abroad, however, Japan's record of internationalizing on the domestic front is much more mixed. The most problematic aspect of Japan's domestic internationalization is its reluctance to accept foreign peoples, despite its wholesale importation of foreign popular culture and English words.

Although Japan suffered from periodic labor shortages in the 1970s, the country continued to insist on its ethnic homogeneity and refused to accept any unskilled foreign workers, preferring instead to attempt to optimize domestic labor productivity and supply in order to meet its labor needs. By the late 1980s, however, Japan's labor shortage became so acute that it finally began to succumb to the pressures of global migration. Yet, even when faced with increasing levels of immigration, the country's population of immigrants is still minuscule compared to Euro-American countries.[1]

I will examine how the Japanese have reacted to the largest and most prominent group of immigrants, the Latin American Nikkeijin, who began "return" migrating to Japan in the late 1980s in response to a severe economic crisis in South America.[2] Most of these Nikkeijin are Japanese Brazilians, whose immigrant population is currently estimated at around 280,000 and continues to grow despite the prolonged Japanese recession. Although the Brazilian Nikkeijin are relatively well educated and mostly of middle-class background in Brazil, they still earn five to ten times their Brazilian salaries in Japan as unskilled factory workers. An open Japanese immigration policy toward "ethnic Japanese" (up to the third generation) and well-established transnational labor recruitment networks between Japan and Brazil have increased the migrant flow.[3] Most Japanese Brazilians originally migrated to Japan with intentions of working only for a few years and then returning to Brazil with their savings, but many have now brought their families to Japan and the process of long-term immigrant settlement has begun (see Tsuda 1999b). The vast majority of immigrants are of the second and third generations (*nisei* and *sansei*) who were born and raised in Brazil, do not speak Japanese very well, and are culturally Brazilian.

At first glance, the Brazilian Nikkeijin may not seem to be the most appropriate immigrant group with which to assess future Japanese responses to foreigners since they are "ethnic Japanese." However, because they are among the largest group of migrants, and particularly because it might be expected that their ethnic affinity would make them easier to incorporate into Japanese society, they provide an early indication of Japan's ability to accommodate other foreign immigrant groups. In addition, the presence of a large immigrant minority group of culturally Brazilian Nikkeijin can challenge restrictive definitions of Japaneseness by causing the Japanese to realize the cultural diversity that exists among Japanese descendants. This contrasts with culturally *and* racially different non-Nikkei foreigners who have no personal ethnic relevance to the Japanese, and are therefore less capable of forcing the Japanese to reconsider and loosen rigid ethnic boundaries. In other words, if the Japanese Brazilians cannot be incorporated successfully into Japanese society and produce a more ethnically inclusive national identity, the chances that this will happen with other types of foreign workers in the future are quite slim. Judging from the current status of Nikkeijin return migrants in Japan, the prospects for the domestic internationalization of Japan in the age of global migration seem rather bleak.

The social marginalization of Japanese Brazilians in Japan

As Brazil's oldest and by far largest Asian minority (population over 1.2 million), the Japanese Brazilians are socially well integrated into Brazilian society but continue to feel quite culturally "Japanese" and assert a rather prominent Japanese minority ethnic identity. In general, they are well regarded by mainstream Brazilians for what are perceived to be their positive Japanese cultural attributes, their relatively high socio-economic and educational status, and their affiliation with the highly respected country of Japan. In turn, the Brazilian Nikkeijin take pride in their Japanese descent and cultural heritage, and identify rather strongly with positive images of Japaneseness, actively reinvent and re-enact traditional Japanese festivities and cultural activities within their communities, and generally distance themselves from what they perceive negatively as "Brazilian." As a result, in Brazil their Japanese ethnic consciousness continues to remain stronger than their national Brazilian identities (Tsuda 2003b: ch. 1).

When the Japanese Brazilians return migrate to Japan, they often anticipate being ethnically accepted, if not welcomed, as Japanese descendants, and look forward to congenial relationships with the Japanese. In Japan, however, they confront a narrow Japanese ethno-national identity that defines Japaneseness not only by Japanese descent, but also by complete Japanese linguistic and cultural proficiency. As a result, the Brazilian Nikkeijin discover that although they felt quite Japanese culturally in Brazil – and are reminded of the fact of their Japaneseness in various subtle and institutional ways – they are generally not accepted in Japan as Japanese because they appear culturally foreign, not only for their lack of Japanese language proficiency, but also for their perceived Brazilian behavior. The remarks of one local Japanese resident in Oizumi town (which has the highest concentration of Nikkei immigrants in Japan) were quite representative of this general reaction:

> There's a lot of *iwakan* (sense of incongruity) towards those who have a Japanese face but are culturally Brazilian. If they have a Japanese face, we interpret this to mean they are Japanese, so we initially approach the Nikkeijin this way. But then when we find they are culturally different, we say they are *gaijin* (foreigners).

Therefore, although the Japanese Brazilians were always called *japonês* in Brazil, when they go to Japan they are suddenly labeled *gaijin*. At the factory (which I will call Toyama) where I conducted participant observation, the Brazilian Nikkeijin were often addressed as *gaijin-san* (Mr. or Mrs. Foreigner), although personal names were usually used in more informal situations. The Japanese Brazilians are also referred to as *gaijin* outside of the workplace, especially when they speak Portuguese in restaurants, stores, and trains.

The status of the Japanese Brazilians as foreign outsiders in Japan is further reinforced by the social exclusion and marginalization they experience as an ethnic minority and the general tendency of most Japanese to keep their distance from unfamiliar foreigners.[4] Many Japanese Brazilians feel socially estranged from the Japanese, even when they work in the same factories and live in the same towns and apartment buildings. Social interaction between the two groups is minimal in most cases. At Toyama, the Nikkeijin and Japanese workers always remained apart during break and lunch-hours, sitting in separate rooms or at different tables and conversing only among themselves. Sometimes, if a group of Japanese Brazilians were sitting at a certain table during break, the Japanese would avoid that table (even if there was room), complaining that the Nikkeijin were "taking over" their break areas. Interaction was limited at most to brief smiles or greetings in the morning, and short exchanges of a few words or simple questions. On the factory assembly lines, general conversation between the two groups was kept to a bare minimum and was usually limited to work instructions. A number of times, I witnessed Brazilian Nikkeijin and Japanese workers performing the same task together on the same machines for hours without exchanging a single word.

Outside the workplace, the social alienation of the Japanese Brazilians is also quite notable. Only a few have sustained social relationships with their Japanese co-workers outside of the factory. Few of the Brazilian Nikkeijin have contact with their Japanese neighbors or participate in local community activities. Even though the Japanese Brazilians do not live in geographically segregated immigrant enclaves, there is still a certain amount of residential segregation – a large number of them live in apartments where a notable proportion of the residents are other Nikkeijin.[5]

Interactions between Brazilian Nikkeijin and Japanese outside of the factory are generally limited to clerks and workers at local stores, banks, and municipal offices. According to one research survey, 44.3 percent of the Japanese Brazilians report that they have almost no social contact with the Japanese and 15.8 percent have only minimal contact. This does not mean that the other 40 percent are necessarily well integrated into mainstream Japanese society: only 14.5 percent report having active relationships with the Japanese (Kitagawa 1996), and even fewer have active contact with their Japanese relatives.[6] In fact, the only Brazilians who seem to interact with the Japanese to any notable degree are those who work as bilingual liaisons in local government offices or in Japanese companies and brokerage firms that employ Nikkei workers. Despite their large numbers and their ethnic affinity to the Japanese, intermarriage between the two groups remains very rare and considerably lower than intermarriage between Japanese and Americans in Japan.[7]

This does not mean that there have been no attempts by the Japanese to establish closer relationships with Brazilian Nikkei immigrants and socially incorporate them into their local communities. Small- and medium-sized businesses in the manufacturing sector (where most Japanese Brazilians are employed) obviously welcomed their Nikkei workers (especially since many would not be able to stay in business without them) and generally held favorable opinions of them. The Japanese employers who I interviewed advocated more open immigration policies and even favored granting permanent residence to foreign workers. Some worked to actively promote smooth relationships between their Japanese and Nikkei employees and encouraged them to socialize outside of the factory.

Local governments in cities with large Nikkeijin populations[8] have also been receptive to the Japanese Brazilians, providing many services for them including national health insurance, Japanese language classes, guidebooks in Portuguese, counseling and other personal services, as well as assistance with alien registration and even job placement. In order to promote ethnic interaction and understanding in local communities, a number of them have established international exchange offices which organize special events, festivals, and cultural activities that bring Japanese and foreign residents together. Kawasaki (which is the most proactive city in its immigrant integration policies) has even offered limited local government representation to its foreign residents.[9]

Nonetheless, most of my Brazilian Nikkei informants felt quite alienated from the Japanese and very few reported being socially accepted in Japan (Tsuda 2003a). The causes of their social marginalization and isolation are rather complex and are not simply the product of a restrictive ethno-national identity that defines them as culturally alien foreigners. Since a majority of the Brazilian Nikkeijin cannot speak Japanese effectively, language is a significant barrier. Their social separation, however, is also a reflection of Japanese group dynamics, where any means of social differentiation seems to produce mutually exclusive social groups constituted according to insider/outsider distinctions. It was also evident that the ethnic avoidance behavior of the Japanese is sometimes motivated by latent prejudice toward the Nikkeijin that is based on both negative preconceptions of their migration legacy and social status and unfavorable opinions of their "Brazilian" cultural behavior (see Tsuda 2003b: ch. 2). Indeed, some Japanese Brazilians claim that their Japanese relatives look down on them because they are seen as having returned to Japan as impoverished migrants, despite the fact that their parents or grandparents "abandoned" Japan decades ago with intentions to succeed economically in Brazil (cf. Ishi 1992: 70).

The social exclusion of the Brazilian Nikkeijin is also a function of their marginal position in the Japanese labor market. Since most of them are informal, temporary contract workers who are borrowed from outside labor broker firms, they do not belong to the companies where they work and therefore remain socially separated from regular Japanese employees. Since they are not employees of the company, they are usually not invited to company outings and other events with Japanese workers. In addition, as a casual and disposable workforce, they are constantly transferred from one company to another by their labor broker depending on changing production needs. As a result, most of the Japanese Brazilians at Toyama did not stay in the factory for more than a few to several months. Few Japanese workers bothered to associate with such transient outsiders who constantly circulated in and out.

The Brazilian Nikkeijin respond to their ethnic rejection by actively withdrawing into their own social groups and isolating themselves in acts of self-segregation, thus contributing to their own social marginalization. Most of the Nikkeijin do not actively seek out relationships with the Japanese, mainly because the Japanese do not seek out relationships with them. In addition, although the Japanese Brazilians are beginning to settle long term or permanently in Japan (see Tsuda 1999b), many continue to view themselves strictly as sojourners who intend to return to Brazil in a few years after accumulating sufficient savings. As a result, they have little incentive to integrate themselves into Japanese society and to establish long-term, meaningful relationships with the Japanese.

The performance of Brazilian nationalist identities

Not only do Japanese Brazilians feel ethnically excluded and segregated as foreigners in Japan; they also become acutely aware of their Brazilian cultural differences, experience ethnic discrimination, and recognize many of the negative aspects of Japanese cultural behavior. In response, many of them experience a resurgence of Brazilian national sentiment in Japan as they distance themselves from the Japanese and assert their Brazilian cultural differences as a form of opposition. In this manner, the dislocations of migration can produce a form of deterritorialized nationalism where national loyalties are articulated outside the territorial boundaries of the nation-state (see Tsuda 2003b: ch. 3).

A common way in which the Nikkeijin display Brazilianness to the Japanese is through dress. Although their manner of dress is normally different from the Japanese, some deliberately wear distinctive Brazilian clothes to capture Japanese attention. The effectiveness of clothing as a marker of Brazilianness has actually increased the demand for Brazilian clothes in Japan. Of course, some Japanese Brazilians wear Brazilian clothes in Japan purely out of physical comfort or habit, but for others it is a prominent ethnic display of cultural difference, if not defiance. The manager of a Brazilian clothing store explained that the clothes she sells have distinctive designs, fashions, and colors that cannot be found in Japanese department stores. Jeans have colorful ornamental features, and those for women tend to be tighter around the hips. Shirts are in bold colors and may have mosaic patterns, while T-shirts with the Brazilian flag, national colors, or the country's name displayed prominently are also popular.

The expression of Brazilian counter-identities in Japan also involves the use of language and greetings. For instance, Martina, a sansei woman, mentioned that although she speaks Japanese well, whenever she walks into a store she makes a point of speaking Portuguese loudly enough so that the Japanese will notice. "I don't want to be confused as Japanese," she said, "so I always show them I am Brazilian." Similarly, the tendency of some Nikkeijin to greet each other loudly and affectionately in public by embracing or kissing is a display of Brazilian behavior that is completely incongruous with Japanese culture.

Some individuals take their ethnic resistance further by exaggerating their Brazilian behavior in a rebellious, exhibitionist manner, purposefully acting more Brazilian in Japan than they ever did in Brazil. Others engage in much more subdued expressions of their Brazilian identity. This is especially true among the more acculturated Nikkeijin, who are more accommodating toward Japanese expectations and feel more pressure to conform. Such concerns are most salient among those Nikkeijin who speak fluent Japanese and who are the most likely to be mistaken as Japanese due to their cultural and linguistic abilities and their unwillingness to display overtly Brazilian behavior. Therefore, they sometimes find subtle ways to differentiate themselves as Brazilians and avoid being held to the same social standards as the Japanese.

In this manner, there is considerable variation in the conscious expression of ethnic resistance among Japanese Brazilians. The enactment of Brazilian nationalist counter-identities in Japan occurs not only in individual behavior, but in collective ritual performances as well. The most important example is the samba parades that the Japanese Brazilians organize in local communities with high Nikkeijin concentrations. Although most Japanese Brazilians never participated in samba in Brazil and even scorned it as a lowly Brazilian activity, they find themselves dancing samba in Japan for the first time in their lives. However, since they have insufficient cultural knowledge of this national Brazilian ritual, their ethnic performance in Japan is not structured or regulated by preordained models of samba, but is a spontaneous form generated by them in the context of enactment. The samba parade I observed in Oizumi town was an improvised, haphazard, and casual performance. The "samba costumes" worn by the Japanese Brazilians were randomly chosen, and ranged from simple swim-suits, clown outfits, festival clothes with Brazilian national colors, to T-shirts and shorts. Apparently, few of the Nikkeijin knew how to design or construct any real samba costumes or had the resources to do so. In addition, most did not seem to know how to dance samba properly and, even if some of them were familiar with it, almost no one had the experience or will to execute it properly. Instead of properly schematized body movements, most of the participants seemed to be moving and shaking their bodies randomly, some in a lackadaisical manner. The general result was a pot-pourri of costumes and individuals moving their bodies randomly without any of the pattern, definition, or precise rhythm of Brazilian samba.

Because of this lack of proper knowledge about samba and the random nature of the costumes and choreography, the Nikkeijin samba performance was culturally structured only on the most general and rudimentary level. Therefore, participation is less an enactment of a pre-established cultural schema than the creation and active generation of a new one. Nonetheless, it was seen as very Brazilian because of its distinctiveness in Japan. This process of cultural authentication was also supported unintentionally by the presence of attentive Japanese spectators, who showed active interest in the unusual and different festivities of another nation.

Nikkeijin return migrants and Japanese ethno-national identity

So how do the Japanese respond to the presence of an immigrant minority of Japanese-descent Latin Americans and how does it influence their own ethno-national identity? The presence of a new Nikkei immigrant minority can potentially challenge essentialist notions of Japanese ethnic identity, in which those who are "racially" Japanese (i.e., of Japanese descent and therefore have a "Japanese face") are assumed to be "culturally" Japanese as well (see also Kondo 1986). This assumed correspondence between race and culture is the result of Japan's ideology of ethnic homogeneity in which all Japanese are seen as the same race and are all perceived as culturally similar in thinking and behavior (cf. Yoshino 1992: 120).[10] Such thinking was exemplified by the comments of one neighborhood doctor to whom I spoke:

> When you live in Japan, you come to take this for granted. Everyone looks Japanese and we all think and act in more or less the same way. So when we see someone who has a Japanese face, we end up thinking that they are like the Japanese – that they will speak and behave like the Japanese [i.e., be culturally Japanese].

Because the Japanese Brazilians are racially Japanese but culturally Brazilian, they are ethnic anomalies (cf. Kondo 1986) who defy classification by transgressing the traditional ethnic boundaries between "Japanese" and "foreigner." A number of my Japanese informants specifically described the surprise and personal disorientation they felt when they first encountered the culturally different Nikkeijin, who so blatantly contradicted their previous ethnic assumptions and expectations. A freelance journalist spoke the most clearly about the ethnic incongruity of the Japanese Brazilians:

> When we first set eyes on the Nikkeijin, our spontaneous reaction is one of confusion and shock. We think they are really strange. We assume they are Japanese, so we talk to them, and then wonder why they don't understand us and cannot communicate in Japanese. They look Japanese, but speak in a strange tongue. Most Japanese do not have a concept of a Nikkeijin. So we say, "who are these guys?" We always expect those with a Japanese face to have a certain level of Japanese culture. But the Japanese are now changing this attitude.

The Japanese Brazilian immigrants' cultural differences disrupt and disassociate the assumed correlation between race and culture that is the foundation of Japanese ethno-national identity, thus potentially leading to new ethnic attitudes (cf. Murphy-Shigematsu 2000: 211). Those on the margins of society reveal the basic assumptions and categories by which a society operates (see also Valentine 1990: 50) and frequently have more of a transformative impact on collective identity than do complete insiders or outsiders.[11]

Despite the transformative potential of the Japanese Brazilians, however, it has not yet caused the Japanese to expand their exclusive definition of Japaneseness to include those who are racially Japanese but culturally different. Most of my Japanese informants clearly indicated that the Japanese Brazilians would never be ethnically accepted as Japanese until they completely assimilated into Japanese culture and became fluent in the language. Most of these Japanese interviewees were quite disappointed if not disillusioned by how culturally Brazilian the Nikkeijin are (cf. Yamanaka 1996: 84). Although some Japanese felt that this loss of Japanese culture was more or less natural, many of them had expected the Nikkeijin would retain the Japanese language and culture to a much greater extent abroad and expressed their reactions by such words as *gakkari* (disappointed), *kitai hazure* (did not live up to expectations), and *shitsubô* (disappointing, disillusioning). Such sentiments were clearly expressed by a young Japanese woman in Oizumi:

> The nisei and sansei are disappointing. Because they are the children of Japanese, we want them to maintain Japanese culture, although we feel that it's also natural that it weakens. It all depends on appearance – if they were mixed-blood, we don't expect this, but if they look Japanese, we think that the ability to communicate in Japanese is obvious. Therefore, we feel betrayed.

Nowhere is this unfavorable perception of Japanese Brazilian behavior more evident than in the workplace. The Japanese employees on the assembly line at Toyama generally gave the Brazilian Nikkeijin rather low marks for their work ethic and ability, and saw them as lazy, slow, irresponsible, and careless on the job (Yamanaka 1996: 84). Most made rather negative comments, such as the following from a young male worker at Toyama:

> The Nikkeijin don't work very well, so the Japanese workers are forced to pick up the slack. They don't do all the required procedures and sometimes skip machines if the assembly line starts moving faster. Even a stupid Japanese would not do these things. They don't share the Japanese perception of work.... It is because of their different culture and upbringing. Sometimes we even wonder if they have the ability to do even simple work.

The negative assessments by the Japanese of the cultural attributes of the Nikkeijin were not only limited to the workplace, but also occurred outside of the factory. Some Japanese residents held unfavorable opinions about the Japanese Brazilians in their neighborhoods. The most frequent complaint from local residents was that the Japanese Brazilians were a disturbance (*meiwaku*) because they make excessive noise in their apartments, turn up their stereos too loud, and party until late at night on weekends (see also Watanabe *et al.* 1992; Japan Institute of Labor 1995).

The behavior of the Nikkeijin in the streets also creates some negative impressions. Even in the town of Oizumi, where the residents have become used to constantly encountering foreigners in the streets, some still do not like to see Nikkeijin walking around in groups, dressed in a strange manner, speaking loudly in Portuguese, and otherwise behaving in ways that seem alien.

Among my Japanese informants, perceptions of the Nikkeijin as culturally alien foreigners seemed to increase awareness and appreciation of their own distinctive national cultural qualities, thus causing a restrictive narrowing of ethno-national identity. They realized the importance of the cultural aspects of being Japanese to a much greater extent, having previously taken them for granted as a natural consequence of being "racially" Japanese. In this manner, although the encounter with the Nikkeijin *de-essentializes* Japanese ethnic identity by problematizing the assumption that shared racial descent is the fundamental determinant of who is Japanese, it may produce a more restrictive definition of Japanese identity based on an increased cultural nationalism. One Japanese worker spoke very clearly about such ethnic reactions:

> After encountering the Brazilian Nikkeijin, I have become more conscious of my Japaneseness. This is something you ordinarily don't think about when you are just with other Japanese, but when I am with Nikkeijin, although we are of the same blood, I see how different they are from us – in thinking, attitudes, the ways they talk and dress – and I recognize what is Japanese about myself, my special Japanese cultural traits. I realize that I am a real Japanese, whereas they are not.

Indeed, it was quite notable how a majority of my Japanese informants engaged in homogenizing discourses of Japaneseness when reflecting upon the negative ethnic differences of the Japanese Brazilians, characterizing the Japanese as more diligent, formal, quiet, polite, and restrained compared to the Nikkeijin.

Just as the Japanese Brazilians increase their consciousness of their Brazilian national differences when they encounter the culturally different Japanese, most Japanese also experience an increased awareness of their distinctive Japanese national characteristics and identity when confronted by the cultural differences of the Nikkeijin. Instead of identifying with each other across the borders of ethnic difference, both migrants and their hosts seem to be hardening mutually exclusive ethnic boundaries in their cultural encounters.

When asked about the future prospects of increased immigration to Japan, virtually all of my Japanese informants stressed the importance of Japan as an ethnically homogeneous nation, and believed that the disruption of this mono-ethnicity through immigration would have negative consequences because the restrictive nature of Japanese society makes it difficult to incorporate large numbers of foreigners. Not only did the presence of the Japanese Brazilians and other immigrant foreigners cause most of my informants to increasingly value the perceived ethnic homogeneity of their nation, they also predicted dire future consequences for Japan if the country was forced to accept massive numbers of immigrants, including ethnic discrimination, serious anti-foreigner backlashes, increased crime, and ethnically segregated immigrant ghettos.

The nationalist consequences of transnational migration

The return migration of the Japanese Brazilians and the possible resurgence of national identity among their Japanese hosts have important implications for the study of transnationalism and for the continued salience of the nation-state in the global ecumene. By asserting a Brazilian nationalist identity, actively displaying their Brazilianness in Japan, Nikkei immigrants seemingly resist Japanese ethnic hegemony by challenging Japan's nationalist project of assimilating culturally incongruous minorities under an ideology of national homogeneity. In this manner, a number of scholars have claimed that transnational migrants subvert and undermine the power of nation-states by maintaining strong transnational ties to their homeland and not developing any allegiance to their host country. In other words, through a type of "antinationalist nationalism" (Clifford 1994: 307) and a refusal to assimilate to the dominant culture of the host country, they escape the nation-state's hegemonic agenda. As a result, Basch and colleagues (1994: 290) interpret global migration as an act of resistance and opposition by individuals to the state, while Appadurai (1996) associates it with the emergence of "postnational imaginaries" which produce new forms of transnational allegiance that hasten the decline of the nation-state.

Undoubtedly this is one reason (among others) why countries that value ethnic homogeneity discourage, if not prohibit, large-scale immigration. Indeed, the massive influx of ethnically different foreigners has been strongly perceived by the Japanese government as a threat to social stability and national integrity (cf. Lie 2001: 49). One of the most prominently cited reasons among Japanese immigration policy-makers for why Japan should not accept unskilled foreign workers has been the fear that public order will be disrupted by increased ethnic conflict and discrimination caused by ethnic diversity (Nojima 1989; Liberal Democratic Party 1992; Ministry of Labor 1991, 1992; Ministry of Justice 1994, interviews with government officials). Although the migration of the "ethnic Japanese" Nikkeijin was initially seen as an exception, the government's opinion seems to have changed recently. They were unprepared for the explosive influx that resulted, and did not realize that so many would bring their families and settle in Japan (see also Kajita 1994: 168). In addition, the Nikkeijin were more culturally Brazilian than expected and have not assimilated smoothly.

However, transnational migration has various unintended consequences and may not be as serious a challenge to the Japanese government's attempt to promote national unity through an ideology of ethnic homogeneity as it believes. My analysis indicates that the massive influx of Nikkei immigrants, by shifting the definition of Japaneseness from race to culture, may produce an intensification of cultural nationalism and create a greater awareness among Japanese of their distinctive cultural homogeneity (cf. Douglass and Roberts 2000: 26, 30), thus implicitly revitalizing their sense of national allegiance.

Conclusion: the future of Japan as a country of immigration

How the Japanese will react to *non*-Nikkei foreign workers in the future is still an open question. Will they be even less tolerant and accepting toward immigrants who are *both* culturally and racially foreign? Or do some Japanese find non-Nikkei immigrants more socially acceptable, and thus are more likely to reconsider and reduce the country's restrictive ethnic barriers in response to them? Do the Japanese react in a more negative and ethnically exclusionary manner to the foreignness of the Nikkeijin precisely because they are Japanese descendants and were expected to be more culturally similar?

My interviews with Japanese informants seemed to indicate that this was not the case. Although many Japanese react negatively to the Japanese Brazilians, most of my informants felt a certain amount of ethnic affinity *with* them due to their Japanese descent and clearly preferred them to foreigners of non-Japanese descent, who are completely alien. Of course, this is especially true of Japanese Brazilians who could speak some Japanese. Even toward the Nikkeijin who had become culturally foreign, there was a strong sense among my informants that they could somehow be culturally comprehended because of their shared descent. Many of the Japanese I spoke with even referred to them as *dôhô* (brethren) or *miuchi* (companions of the inner circle). For example, this type of general sentiment was expressed by a Japanese factory worker in Oizumi:

> Discrimination and disparagement is less toward the Brazilian Nikkeijin because they have a Japanese face. This creates a feeling of commonality with them as our brethren. Since we see them as people who were originally Japanese, we feel closer to them than other foreigners. There is much more discrimination toward the Korean Japanese.

Some of my informants felt safer and more at ease with the Japanese Brazilians than with other foreign workers. According to one local Japanese business owner:

> At least with the Nikkeijin, we feel their blood ties as part of the Japanese group and a sense of commonality and security, in contrast to other foreign workers whom we approach with caution because some of them look scary and are a source of fear. I tend to relax more and feel safer with Nikkeijin because of this sense of affinity.

A number of informants also noted that they held less prejudice toward the Brazilian Nikkeijin because they had very little knowledge of Brazil and thus had no reason to actively dislike the country, given its lack of historical contact or conflict with Japan. Although the general perception of Brazil as a poor, underdeveloped, and crime-ridden country prevailed, it also evoked rather cheerful and bright images associated with soccer, samba, carnival, and music, as well as the country's natural beauty and resources. For such reasons, those Japanese who actively disliked foreign workers in general and wished they would promptly leave Japan mentioned that they could at least tolerate the presence of Nikkei immigrants and learn to live with them if necessary.

However, even with the Nikkeijin, serious conflicts with Japanese are not unknown. Several years ago, complaints from local Japanese residents toward Japanese Brazilian residents in the Homi public housing complex of Toyota City (Aichi Prefecture) over improper garbage disposal, noise, theft, and vandalism triggered a campaign by a right-wing group to expel the Nikkeijin from the neighborhood, leading to an incident where a campaign vehicle was set on fire. There was a serious threat that the tension between the Japanese and Nikkeijin would escalate into violence and retaliation before the situation was defused partly with the deployment of police officers (Sellek 2001: 215–16).[12]

Nonetheless, there was consensus among those Japanese whom I interviewed that there was much more prejudice and discrimination toward Korean Japanese because they are not of Japanese descent, even though most of them were born and raised in Japan and are culturally assimilated. Others cited previously low images Japan had of Korea and Koreans, as well as the historical antagonism that has existed between the two countries caused by Japan's colonial past and wartime atrocities. My informants also claimed that discrimination was greater toward mixed-descent Nikkeijin (*konketsu*), who were seen as more foreign in contrast to Nikkeijin of pure Japanese descent. In this manner, my informants' ethnic preferences were based on perceived degrees of racial closeness. Indeed, a number of them indicated that they are very wary of racially different, non-Caucasian foreigners. Even in a place like Oizumi where foreigners of all types have become a common sight in the streets, Japanese residents still actively avoid approaching or talking with them or sitting near them on trains, especially at night and especially if the foreigner is dark-skinned. Non-Nikkei Brazilians of darker complexion in Japan report that they experience more discrimination and are sometimes mistaken for Pakistanis or Iranians. It is also quite apparent that the level of socioeconomic marginalization of foreign workers in the Japanese labor market closely follows this racialized hierarchy of ethnic preference (cf. Mori 1994). The comments of one Japanese employer are quite illustrative:

> When it comes to hiring foreigners, there are clearly several levels based on like and dislike. We feel [ethnically] the closest to the Nikkeijin, so they work at the best firms with the best wages. Then come the Chinese and Koreans, whom we find less preferable and therefore they work in less desirable jobs. At the bottom are Bangladeshis and Iranians, who work in the smallest companies that pay the lowest wages. We avoid interacting with Middle Easterners the most, so they get the worst jobs. It really shouldn't be this way, but it just is.

If Japan is currently having trouble accepting and socially integrating its own Nikkei descendants, its ability to do so for other, more alien immigrants in the future is seriously in doubt. Not only are such immigrants likely to remain both ethnically and socio-economically segregated, they may become targets of anti-immigrant, nationalist sentiment if there is a massive expansion of the foreign population, as has happened in other immigrant societies. Are my Japanese informants correct in predicting nativist backlashes and public protests, and even violence against foreigners in the future (*à la* Germany)? Indeed, in the late 1980s and early 1990s, when immigration was a contentious social issue in Japan, there were already demonstrations and propaganda by Japanese right-wing groups against immigrants, and a large number of neo-Nazi flyers were posted and distributed, urging Japan to expel immigrant foreigners (*Asahi Shimbun*, April 7, 1993; *Japan Times*, October 16, 1989). This is troublesome especially because the immigrant population in Japan is still much smaller than in Euro-American countries. However, Japan has always had vocal and prominent right-wing extremist groups that have sometimes resorted to violence to promote their ends. As in the case of Germany, even if the general public remains tolerant and restrained, violent reactions from a small minority of extremists are enough to create a general social crisis. Although concern about the foreign worker problem has abated at all levels in Japanese society due to the decade-long recession and stabilization of the immigrant population, the Japanese media have continued to publish prominent articles about illegal immigrant smugglers, Chinese "snakeheads," and alleged increases in foreigner crime. Indeed, 46 percent of the Japanese public already wants the government to more seriously crack down on illegal workers (up significantly over ten years) (Prime Minister's Office 2000).[13] If such signs are any indication, Japan's eventual transition to a tolerant and inclusive multi-ethnic society will indeed be quite difficult.

Notes

1 Only 0.75 percent of Japan's population is foreign-born, in contrast to most Euro-American countries where the percentage of foreign-born ranges from a few percent to over 10 percent of the population.
2 This chapter is based on over twenty months of intensive fieldwork and participant observation in both Japan and Brazil. Nine months were first spent in Brazil (1993–4) in two separate Japanese Brazilian communities in the cities of Porto Alegre (in Rio Grande do Sul) and Ribeirão Preto (in São Paulo). During my one year's stay in Japan (1994–5), I conducted fieldwork in Kawasaki (in Kanagawa Prefecture), and Oizumi and Ota cities (in Gunma Prefecture), where I worked for four months as a participant observer in a large electrical appliance factory with about 10,000 workers, of which 1,000 were Japanese Brazilians. Close to one hundred in-depth interviews (in Portuguese and Japanese) were conducted with Japanese Brazilians, Japanese workers, residents, employers, and officials.
3 For an analysis of the causes of Japanese Brazilian return migration, see Tsuda (1999a).
4 For a detailed analysis of the social segregation of the Japanese Brazilians in Japan, see Tsuda (2003a, 2003b: ch. 3).
5 Only 12.7 percent of the Nikkeijin live in apartments with only Japanese residents; 33.6 percent live in apartments where over 25 percent of the residents are other Nikkeijin (Kitagawa 1997). The proportion is higher in communities where they are highly concentrated. Although the reasons for this residential segregation are complex (see Tsuda 2003b: ch. 2), there is a certain tendency for Japanese residents to move out of apartments when the Nikkeijin move in.
6 Only 11.6 percent have active contact with their Japanese relatives whereas 56.7 percent have almost no contact and 17.2 percent have occasional contact (Kitagawa 1997).
7 In 1993, there were only 771 marriages between Japanese and Brazilian nationals (almost all of whom are Nikkeijin) compared to 1,625 intermarriages between Japanese and Americans. This is especially notable because the population of Americans in Japan was only a quarter of the Brazilian population at that time, and linguistic, racial, and cultural barriers are much greater between Japanese and Americans than between Japanese and Brazilian Nikkeijin.
8 These include Oizumi and Ota cities in Gunma Prefecture, Hamamatsu and Toyoha cities in Aichi Prefecture, and Kawasaki and Fujisawa cities in Kanagawa Prefecture.
9 See Pak (2000) for an analysis of local government policies toward immigrants and the emergence of a type of "local citizenship."
10 In this manner, when race and culture are seen as correlated, they tend to be conflated (Medina 1997).
11 Rosaldo (1989: 207–9, 215–17) claims that those who live in the border zones of gender, race, ethnicity, or nationality are frequently most capable of creativity and change through transcultural blending. According to Rutherford, the margin is a place of resistance which threatens to deconstruct dominant and hegemonic forms of knowledge (1990: 22).
12 The most serious incident between Nikkei residents and Japanese occurred in 1997, when a gang of Japanese youth randomly assaulted more than ten Japanese Brazilian youth in a park near Komaki station (Aichi Prefecture) as an act of revenge. A fourteen-year-old Nikkei youth was kicked, beaten, and stabbed, dying three days later.
13 See Tsuda and Cornelius (2004) for a more detailed analysis of Japanese public opinion toward immigrants.

13 Overseas Japanese and the challenges of repatriation in post-colonial East Asia

Mariko Asano Tamanoi

In 1965, Japanese journalist Magoroku Ide accepted an invitation from the government of the People's Republic of China to visit the country. Still seven years before the resumption of diplomatic relations between Japan and China, travel to China was restricted to those officially invited and even they were subject to state surveillance. Among the places he and his fellow Japanese journalists visited was the city of Anshan in northeast China. Having boarded the train to return to Beijing at the conclusion of their visit, they heard the clear voice of a woman saying, "Please take care of yourselves, goodbye," in Japanese. Not visible from their train window in the crowd of Chinese who came to bid farewell, Ide and his colleagues were stunned to hear the voice of a Japanese woman. Although they wondered whether it was possible that Japanese were living in Anshan in 1965, they could not make the connection between her and the approximately 10,000 Japanese who were then living in northeast China, much less to the Japanese imperial past (Ide 1993).

Ide's confession of his ignorance of "overseas Japanese" in northeast China suggests that in the mid-1960s such a category of people was an anomaly. We must remember, however, that in the early 1940s, more than 1.5 million Japanese lived in Manchuria (Kôsei-shô 1997: 32). On August 9, 1945, these overseas Japanese encountered Soviet troops as Japan capitulated (finally surrendering six days later). With Japan's capitulation, these overseas Japanese – who were citizens of the Japanese Empire – lost the protection of the Japanese state. The Japanese government vacillated about their fate, first wanting to leave them in Manchuria, at other times requiring them to return home, "even though [according to the Ministry of Foreign Affairs] the welfare of the Japanese in Japan proper would be sacrificed [by the repatriation of these overseas Japanese]." They were finally ordered to return (Wakatsuki 1995: 48–50).

Thus, for the overseas Japanese in Manchuria, the meaning of home changed drastically in 1945. Before, they had tried to make their home in Manchuria. After Japan's capitulation, they had to return to Japan to seek the protection of the Japanese state once more, becoming once again Japanese of the heartland (*naichi*), rather than the peripheries (*gaichi*).

By the 1960s, the distinctions between *gaichi* and *naichi* had faded, as the Japanese nation came to see itself as a single ethnicity or race (Yoneyama 1999: 4; see also Oguma 1995, 2002).

The Japanese woman who bade farewell to Ide in Anshan, then, had been "homeless" since the time of Japan's capitulation. She should have returned home after Japan's surrender, following the Japanese government's instructions. Since she did not, she lives in China, a country to which she does not really belong. The Japanese public in the mid-1960s did not remember people such as her, who were mostly children at the time of Japan's surrender. Many were orphans while others had been separated from their relatives. They were raised by Chinese adoptive parents, grew up speaking Chinese, later married Chinese citizens, and made their own families in China; they made *homes* in China. Consequently, when belated repatriation finally began in the early 1980s, they were seen as "overseas Chinese" by much of the Japanese public. In Japan, it was possible that they might merge with the increasing number of Chinese immigrants, both legal and illegal, who were coming to Japan to work as semi-skilled laborers.

In this chapter, I will discuss these "overseas Japanese" in northeast China, and describe how they can potentially challenge conventional ideas about Japanese and Chinese identities. The chapter consists of three sections. The first is a brief overview of Japanese colonialism in northeast China and of the conditions leading to the orphans' abandonment. The second is an overview of their repatriation to Japan. The third section considers relationships among returnees, Japanese society, and the Japanese government in contemporary times. In conclusion, I will critically examine the notions of ethnicity, race, nationality, and citizenship, which have been challenged by the presence of these overseas Japanese.

This chapter is based on my long-term ethnographic research in Japan between 1984 and 2001. From 1984 to 1996, I conducted research in rural Nagano in central Japan, which sent more than 37,000 farmers to Manchuria in the 1930s (Young 1998: 329).[1] In Nagano, my informants were those who managed to return to Japan between 1946 and 1949. In 1998 and 2001, I shifted my fieldwork to Tokyo, where large numbers of those who had been left in China have settled since the early 1980s. In addition to ethnographic research, I have also examined the history of Japanese imperialism in northeast China, and been informed by the autobiographies written by Japanese repatriates from Manchuria.

Overseas Japanese in Manchuria in the age of empires

Japanese migration to Manchuria began a few decades before the Russo–Japanese War (1904–5), and by the early 1930s about 240,000 Japanese had moved there (see Guelcher, Chapter 4). In 1932, Japan officially established the territorial colony of Manchuko, "a separate state under Chinese leaders who took their orders from Japanese officers and civilian officials" (Duus 1989: xxiix). The exact number of Japanese in Manchuria at the end of World War II is unknown. yet it is believed that about 1.5 million Japanese were stranded there on the eve of Japan's surrender. Among these were a large number of agrarian settlers. Most came after World War I, or were encouraged to resettle during Manchuko colonization. While most never intended to make a vast fortune, these agrarian colonists thought they could live adequate and comfortable lives on the Asian mainland. To give some idea of their hardships during repatriation, consider the oral narrative of Harue, a survivor whom I met in Nagano in 1988. She lost not only her "paradise" in Manchuria, where her husband aspired to become a large-scale landowner; she also lost her two children to epidemics.

> In the middle of January [1945], several months before Japan's capitulation, my husband was drafted by the [Japanese] military. Well, he was eventually taken as a POW to Siberia. Soon after Japan was defeated, the Manchurian [local] bandits attacked our settlement. We were robbed of cows, horses, and clothes. We sought refuge at a nearby building ... and lived there collectively for a while. When the bandits returned the second time around, I saw them killing many of my fellow settlers. I really feel sorry for those who were murdered then. Since we [the survivors] did not know when the bandits would return, we decided to go our separate ways. At that time, we received a notice that we would be able to return to Japan in September [1946]. But, at the shelter [for Japanese] in Harbin, epidemics erupted and spread like wildfire.... To escape the epidemics, my children and I left the shelter momentarily, but two of my kids died only two days apart from each other. Having lost them, I did not know whether I was sad or not. In retrospect, I guess I was in a state of total confusion, of total shock.

Why, in the wake of Japan's surrender, did Harue and other agrarian colonists in Manchuria encounter such a terrible fate? Why were some of them left in China for so long? And why are several hundred of them still believed to be in China today?

The simple answer to these questions is that they were destined to suffer once the Japanese Empire collapsed. In sending agrarian colonists to Manchuria, the Japanese military placed them near the border with the Soviet Union for purely strategic reasons. Without knowing the military's intentions, agrarian colonists planned to settle in the region to help create a Japanese Empire. By the end of the 1930s, the Japanese state began targeting village youths, men whose ages ranged from fourteen to twenty-one, as future agrarian colonists. They were to be incorporated into the Patriotic Youth Brigade, a paramilitary group inaugurated nationwide in

1938. While this process was underway, the Japanese army began its systematic draft of able-bodied men – husbands and fathers of the families of agrarian settlers. They were mobilized to protect South and Southeast Asia against the United States. This mobilization eventually became "bottom-scraping" (*nekosogi* in Japanese), and radically altered the human geography of each colony. Those who were left behind were largely the young Brigade members, women, children, and the elderly. Instead of protecting civilians, my informants now believe the Japanese army used them to create a buffer zone in northern Manchuria against an imminent Soviet attack.

As the army correctly predicted, the Soviet Union did invade Manchuria in 1945. The young Brigade members became "the first line of defense ... and many died in Manchuria" (Young 1998: 406). The women, children, and elderly were thus left without much protection. Their husbands, fathers, and sons, if not yet drafted by the Japanese military, were taken by the Soviets to Siberia. The local peasants, who were once themselves displaced by the Japanese settlers, turned their rage against Japanese colonists. The civil war between communist and nationalist forces in China, who both tried to use Japanese civilians for their own benefit, created more confusion among the Japanese stranded in Manchuria. The severe winters and poor hygienic conditions caused malnutrition, epidemics, and other diseases. In order to save the lives of their children, as well as themselves, some agrarian colonists were forced to, in their own words, "leave," "give up," "abandon," "sell," or "entrust" their loved ones to Chinese families.

In post-war Japan, these children are called *zanryû koji* (the orphans who have remained behind). Since they were raised by Chinese adoptive parents and were no longer thought to be culturally Japanese children, the term "orphan" attracts special attention. In 1998, I interviewed Mr. Yamamoto, the chief of the Chûgoku Zanryû Koji Taisaku-shitsu, an "office to deal with the orphans who have remained behind in China," within the Japanese Ministry of Health and Welfare. He pointed out several characteristics of *zanryû koji*. First, they were born of Japanese parents. Second, they were orphaned or separated from their families in the wake of the Soviet invasion of Manchuria and Japan's capitulation. Third, they are defined as those who were younger than thirteen at the time. Fourth, they have remained in China since then. Last, but perhaps most important, they are unsure or ignorant of their identity (or *mimoto*, a primordial notion that literally means "the roots of a person's body").

Mr. Yamamoto, however, acknowledged several problems with this official (and media) definition of *zanryû koji*. First, *zanryû koji* naturally grew up. Second, they were raised by Chinese adoptive parents and have Chinese names and Chinese nationality. Third, until 1993, the government did not include in the category of *zanryû koji* the Japanese women who were older than thirteen at the time of Japanese capitulation. Although many of these women eventually married Chinese men, the

Japanese government deemed these women to be old enough (at the time) to decide their own life courses. Consequently, until 1993, the government ignored them. In September of that year, twelve such women returned to Japan from northeast China. Since they arrived on Sunday, all government offices were closed. Without money and anyone to rely on, they spent a night in the airport lobby with a banner attached to their piled-up luggage. It read: "Dear Prime Minister Hosokawa, please let us die in Japan, signed *zanryû fujin.*" These women changed *koji* (orphans) to *fujin* (women) to indicate their female gender and older age.

Since then, Mr. Yamamoto said, the government has been paying for the return trips of these women, as it has done for the orphans since 1981. Although the government still distinguishes "women" from "orphans," I deny the difference between them, and use "orphans" for all. In so doing, I suggest that, regardless of their age and gender, orphans were forced to stay behind in northeast China.

While the life trajectories of these orphans vary greatly, they have one thing in common. They were once abandoned by their Japanese parents and the Japanese state, but were adopted by Chinese parents and became Chinese citizens. Yet, due to the special circumstance at the end of the war, they have been compelled to search for their often unverifiable *mimoto* (deep identities). However hard they try to belong to a single family and a single nation, they are still, and will always continue to be, in a state of non-belonging (or, more strictly speaking, belonging to multiple families and nations, none of which overrides the others). Hence, repatriation does not necessarily solve their identity problems. Rather, for these orphans the state of forlornness has continued since the time of separation from their families. These feelings linger for a number of reasons. It is true that war everywhere causes the breakup of families, but the case here is special in several respects. The first factor is the economic discrepancy between China and Japan, both before and after World War II. Before the war, the Japanese came as colonists and occupiers; after the war, the Japanese economy came to dominate East Asia and much of the world. The children of this legacy are hardly just *any* orphans; in an area that was – and is – relatively poverty-stricken, a shadow of economic undertones is always present both for the adoptive parents and adoptee children. Second, some of the older children no doubt had lingering memories of their lives as Japanese, as opposed to the Chinese they had become. Finally, from both sides of the Sea of Japan are notions of race, language, and culture – of what it means or *be* Japanese (apart from mere nationality or citizenship).

Memories, imagined and real, of overseas Japanese in the age of global capitalism

In 1988, I met Hisayo, another repatriate from Manchuria, in Nagano. Remembering her ordeal of repatriation, she said:

> I covered the face of my son with a scarf. As the soil was completely frozen, my neighbor could not properly bury him. But later I wondered, and I still wonder, whether he might have been still alive then, and whether he is still alive today somewhere in China.

Her son died of the typhoid that spread quickly among the children at one of the temporary shelters for Japanese. Nevertheless, Hisayo still hoped to be reunited with her son. Such odds might be quite slim. In contrast, those who "gave up" their children to the custody of Chinese couples have more hope of discovering them. We should also remember that, if the children of agrarian settlers are still alive, they may not have forgotten their parents either. While the parents remember their children in Japan, some children may remember their parents in northeast China. Yet, being separated by time and space, they are yet to meet.

In the early 1970s, these parents finally brought the memories of their loved ones to the attention of the Japanese public. Urged by them, in 1974 the Asahi Newspaper, one of the leading national newspapers in Japan, published a partial list of the orphans still stranded in northeast China.[2] Entitled "The Record of Those Who Parted Alive from Their Loved Ones," the article consists of two sections. One section, "Tracing Memories from China," introduces memories of the orphans remaining in China who are searching for their relatives in Japan. The other section, "Tracing Memories from Japan," offers narratives of Japanese repatriates remembering their loved ones whom they believe are still alive in China. What follows are two entries from the section "Tracing Memories from China."

> *Guilan Wu* (Female): Although I do not remember when and where this happened, my mother and I boarded a freight train and arrived at Fushun. There, we lived in a big garage of a house with a huge gate. A Chinese man later arranged an adoption for me so that I began to live with Qinglin Wu. In the spring of the following year, when my mother was about to return to Japan, my neighbor, a Chinese lady, hid me in the closet bureau [at her home]. My mother frantically searched for me, but could not find me and returned [to Japan] alone. I am now 34 years old. I live with my adoptive father. According to his memory, the current age of my mother is probably between 59 and 61.

> *Yuhua Zhang* (Female): My Japanese name is probably Kazuko Aihara. I think I was born in 1940 but do not remember my birthday. After

the war's end, my aunt took me to Changchun where we lived in a concentration camp. Around the summer of 1946, I was entrusted to Fan Qingwen, who ran a tailor shop in Changchun. I was wearing a *kimono* then, and had bobbed hair.

The memories of orphans are necessarily vague due to their ages at the time of separation. To verify their Japanese nationality, they must rely on the memories of many others, including their adoptive parents, neighbors, and friends in China. Both of the above entries, then, are in reality representative of the experiences of many people.

If one entry in "Tracing Memories from China" matches another entry in "Tracing Memories from Japan," it becomes possible for the orphan to discover his or her deep identity. The entry below (from "Tracing Memories from Japan"), however, demonstrates that such a match could be extremely difficult to obtain. The entry begins with the names of the missing orphans. The numbers in parentheses are their ages at the time of separation in Manchuria.

Hiroe Yamamoto (age 5), Takashi Ihara (age 18), Satomi Ihara (age 14), Sumiko Ihara (age 10), Yoshie Nonaka (age 9), Fumiko Nonaka (age 7), Kuniaki Takama (age 13), Setsu Ihara (age 4), Kiyoko Tanaka (age 15), Kôichi Andô (age 6), Kimiko Andô (age 3), Kazuko Ihara (age 8): In May 1945, as the last group of agrarian colonists from Japan, those from the county of Achi in Nagano prefecture, settled in the province of Heilongjiang. However, because of the Soviet invasion of Manchuria, they moved to another farm colony named Sado in the prefecture of Boli in the same province. There Soviet soldiers attacked them, and many [if they survived the attack] were dispersed. In October of the same year, those who had survived returned to their agrarian settlement of Sado, but they were attacked again, and the Soviets captured all the Japanese men and took them as POWs. All the women [who had been left behind] had to survive one entire winter working for Chinese farmers. During this time, many [of these] women gave up their children to Chinese families.

In these entries, the Japan–China Friendship Commission speaks of the memories of those who have been searching for their loved ones,[3] since the reopening of Japanese–Chinese relations, particularly since the 1980s. Their entries show how the Japanese agrarian colonists suffered enormously after Japan's capitulation. In the last entry, Jishô Yamamoto, the teacher of these students, searches for them, including his daughter, Hiroe. One of them, Kazuko Ihara, sounds almost identical to "Kazuko Aihara," the Japanese name for Yuhua Zhang. Their biographies overlap substantially, raising the hope of discovery of *mimoto*, the deep identity of Yuhua Zhang. Yet some gaps in information given by Zhang, Jishô

Yamamoto, and the relatives of Kazuko Ihara were undeniable. In this particular case, Zhang could not find her biological parents.

Between 1974 and 1981, on sixteen occasions, the Asahi Newspaper published biographies and photos of orphans still in China. Finally, in 1981, the Japanese government extended an official invitation to the first group of forty-seven orphans to visit Japan. Since then, in collaboration with the Chinese government, the Japanese government has made efforts to locate more orphans in China. By 2003, the government had invited 2,133 orphans. In addition, about 650 more orphans managed to travel to Japan without the government's assistance and reunite with their relatives.[4] These orphans visit Japan on the government's assumption that they are Japanese. Once in Japan, they are expected to prove their "Japaneseness" by locating their Japanese relatives, thereby proving not only their individual-primordial identities but also their collective-national identity in the modern system of nation-states. Note here that these numbers do not include several thousand Japanese women who, as we have seen, had little means to return to Japan until 1993 (Ogawa 1995: 235).

Although the orphans are said to have been deprived of their deep identities, they have in fact multiple identities, none of which they have chosen of their own will, and each dependent upon whether viewed from the Chinese perspective (including that of the Chinese state) or the Japanese perspective (including that of the Japanese state). Nonetheless, the Japanese media seem to have focused on only a few such identities.

Reporting on the orphans, the media always presented them with tremendous sympathy as innocent victims, because they were then powerless children, incapable of making decisions. They were indeed *rekishi ni honrô sareta* (tossed around by the waves of history). On the television screen, the orphans always looked poor and uneducated, suggesting the difficulty of these repatriates from rural China ever fitting into a modern, affluent Japan. After all, they did not speak Japanese, nor did they have knowledge of Japanese customs. Scenes of the volunteer workers teaching them Japanese songs or plays surely made them look like children. The government and media's insistence on the continuous use of the word "orphans" seemed only to corroborate these screen images.

Whereas the Japanese media freely appropriate images of human misery, the true voices of the orphans who have suffered barely reach the Japanese audience. Because of the language barrier, direct communications between the orphans and their Japanese relatives are extremely difficult, if not impossible. Consequently, in the past, the Japanese public has tended to assume that all of these orphans suffered *in China*. The following logic underlies this reasoning, though it does not necessarily apply in every individual instance.

- At the time of Japan's capitulation, the orphans were small children.
- They grew up in a country that was alien to them.

- They grew up in a poor, rural region of northeast China.
- They did not learn their mother tongue (Japanese) or have forgotten it.
- They did not learn their own culture or have forgotten it.
- They suffered from various kinds of discrimination in China because they are not Chinese; this suffering was particularly acute during the time of the Cultural Revolution.
- They have been deprived of the love of their birth parents.
- They were forced into a life that they would not have chosen had their parents not immigrated to Manchuria.
- They lost not only their homes but also their homeland, Japan, and they have been deprived of their Japanese nationality.
- Though usually Chinese citizens by default, they have been deprived of the universal human right to a nationality and are therefore unable to find their place in the system of nation-states.[5]
- As a result of all of the above, they do not know their deep identities.

Accepting all of the foregoing to be valid assumptions, it logically follows that there is only one way to redress the suffering of the orphans: restoring to them their Japanese nationality, thereby enabling them to live permanently in Japan with their Japanese relatives. Predictably, this is the solution to which the Japanese state has adhered since 1981.[6] However, we need to listen to the genuine voices of orphans rather than be consumed by these media images of them in post-colonial Japan. Thus, in 1998, I recorded the following narratives of two orphans in Tokyo, whom I call Takashi and Toshio. Since they spoke in Chinese, volunteers, who were then teaching them Japanese, translated their stories for me. Here are summaries of what they said.

> *Takashi*: I was about two when I was separated from my family, so that I hardly remember what happened. Many years later, I found out that my father had died soon after his arrival in Manchuria. [After Japan's capitulation,] I was dying of malnutrition so my mother entrusted me to my adoptive parents in exchange for food. My adoptive parents did not have children of their own. They were very poor and made me work once I regained my health. But they let me attend a school when I was about seven. When I was eleven or so, my adoptive father died. My adoptive mother remarried, but my second adoptive father soon died in 1961. I knew I was Japanese since I was seven because the kids at my school called me "a little Japanese" all the time. However hard I pressed my adoptive mother, she did not tell me anything about my parents. In 1960, I married a Chinese woman and we later had four sons and one daughter. A few years after 1972, two Japanese women in the village where I lived returned temporarily to Japan. They were sisters, and older than I was. While in Japan, these two sisters received

a visit from my mother and elder sister. I wanted to return to Japan badly, but my adoptive mother pleaded with me not to leave her. In the end, I waited until she passed away. It was 1988. The following year, I returned to Japan with my wife and fourth son. My mother lives in Wakayama with my sister and her family. She also has three sons, all of whom are married. They are all good to us, but we decided to move out of my mother's house to Yokohama. We did not want to rely on them, and this way, I was able to find a job.

Toshio: I was about four when Japan surrendered. This is what I later learned. I am a survivor of the collective suicide that took place in the colony of Hataho. My mother, two brothers, and a sister all died there. As my father had been drafted, he was not with us. My elder sister and I survived this ordeal. Later, a Chinese man took me to his home, while someone else took my sister to his home. My adoptive parents were poor. I remember they had five or six children of their own but they died one after another, except for one daughter. I guess they needed a boy. I worked very hard. When I first went to school, I was already ten years old. I knew I was Japanese. My friends called me "a little Japanese" and often ridiculed me. In 1960, I married a Chinese woman and we had two daughters and one son. Soon after, I met a Japanese woman who was able to speak and write Japanese. [After 1972] I wrote many letters and asked the Japanese government to search for my relatives in Japan. When, in 1980, a group of Japanese visited our village to pay respects to the Japanese who had died there, I asked them to search for my relatives. In 1982, to my great surprise, I received a letter from my father. He was remarried to a woman who had lost her husband in Manchuria. She already had three children from her previous marriage. Later, my father had two more boys with her. I visited my father in 1982 and told him that I would like to return to Japan, but his wife, that is, my stepmother, adamantly opposed my return. My father told me that I would have nothing to inherit from him. I guess it was his wife who made him say so. But after 1982, both my father and stepmother died. Finally, in 1986, I returned with my wife and three children to Hiratsuka [a city in Japan]. My children quickly learned Japanese and now have good jobs. But they have left us. I worked at a small factory for more than ten years, and now live on my small pension. My wife is still able to work. When she stops working, I wonder whether we may have to ask the government for livelihood assistance.

The narratives of Takashi and Toshio reveal several common elements of the life histories of orphans. They have many "families," but each of them suffered from forces rooted in the system of nation-states at war. The families to which they were born were shattered in the aftermath of the

Soviet invasion of Manchuria and Japan's capitulation. While the situations of families into which they were adopted varied greatly, the adoptive families were, generally speaking, poor. Thus, in post-colonial Japan, two mutually opposing images of the Chinese adoptive parents co-exist: the benevolent parents who sacrificed their own lives to raise and protect their children, and the poor parents who exploited the labor of adopted children for their own survival.

Both are media creations and are, perhaps, untrue; yet both Takashi and Toshio told us that, even though most adoptive parents were poor and sometimes strict, they "saved our lives and made us live," for which they are grateful. Lastly, the families raised by the orphans in China also suffer(ed) from the inevitable forces originating in the system of nation-states. When the orphans decided to return to Japan, some of their family members opposed the idea. While Toshio returned with his entire family, Takashi returned with only his wife and fourth son. For some orphans, then, returning home meant severing ties with the parents that brought them up and their Chinese relatives. When this happens, it is usually the adoptive parents who suffered most, not only from a financial loss but also from an incalculable social loss.[7] In addition, the Japanese state has monitored which orphans are entitled to return to Japan, and which members of their families are able to return with them.[8]

While in China, these orphans were on the margin of Chinese society. Those that have returned to Japan are generally on the margin of Japanese society. Indeed, for quite some time after 1975, the Japanese state regarded them as "aliens." Even though some were able to locate their family registers (*koseki*) where their names are recorded in Japanese, they still had to carry certificates indicating their alien status while in Japan. Hence, for many orphans, restoring their Japanese nationality has become the top priority after their return to Japan. However, their children and grandchildren do not necessarily wish to become naturalized Japanese. In such cases, *zanryû koji* (who must prove their Japanese nationality) and their family members must live with two distinct nationalities in a Japan that does not allow its citizens to hold dual nationality. Orphans and their families must struggle with the systems of nation-states whether they are in China or in Japan, and the repatriation to Japan in itself hardly eliminates that struggle.

The passage of time makes it difficult for the orphans to discover their true identities. Their parents may well have died, aged, and if they survive, they may have become emotionally distant. Relatives may have only vague memories of the orphans and be reluctant to acknowledge their relationship with the newly arrived relatives from China. Many opt to ignore them. The reasons vary. Some fear entangling obligations to support blood relatives whom they have never met and who do not speak a common language. Some do not want to associate with the orphans, who do not look like or act Japanese. Others worry about their meager inheritance.[9] Some prefer not to acknowledge their children legally or emotionally because they have remarried and have chosen to forget their past.[10] Chinese adoptive parents have also aged and some are no longer alive. Aging adoptive parents often choose not to reveal the identities of their adopted children for fear of losing them and the lifeline of support in their old age. Without relevant information coming from parents, some orphans were doubtless forced to give up the idea of discovering their deep-seated identities altogether.

These circumstances forced the Japanese government to change some of its original policies on the repatriation of orphans. For example, until 1989, orphans could not return permanently to Japan without the consent of their Japanese relatives. Since the government originally regarded orphans as dependants of their Japanese relatives, they had no choice but to settle down with them in Japan. In that year, the government implemented a new institution called the special sponsor system, where orphans whose Japanese nationality has been proved are able to return home as long as they have special sponsors. In theory, any Japanese national may apply to be a special sponsor. In reality, however, the Japan–China Friendship Commission has been the primary sponsor.

The passage of time since Japan's capitulation also means that many of the aged orphans, most in their late sixties or older, cannot return to Japan without one or more of their children to help support them. Yet, until 1992, most orphans had no other choice but to return alone: while in the eyes of the Japanese government the orphans are Japanese, their family members are foreigners. In 1992, the Japanese government implemented a policy that allowed disabled orphans to return with their immediate families. Two years later, the government adopted the same policy for any orphan over sixty-five years of age; in 1997, the government lowered this to sixty. As a result, many of those who are already in Japan have invited their Chinese family members to join them. Since the early 1980s, more than 6,000 families, or about 20,000 orphans and their relatives, have returned to Japan,[11] not including the Japanese wives of Chinese citizens who, since 1993, have also been returning with their families (or with the families of their children).

Returnees, the Japanese government, and society

The former agrarian colonists in Manchuria who returned to Japan in the second half of the 1940s and the orphans who remained in China reflect several sets of oppositions: the classical age of nationalism versus the global age of nomadism, colonialism versus post-colonialism, and colonization versus globalization (Hall 1997). Yet, if generational differences are ignored, one may easily miss seeing the tensions between the colonists and the orphans, as well as how these various oppositions play out. In this global age of nomadism, it is the Chinese and the Japanese orphans who have reversed the earlier route established by the Japanese colonists. However, there is nothing celebratory in the lives of most of these

Chinese-Japanese; although they often receive tremendous sympathy from the Japanese public, particularly their Japanese relatives, they also suffer the difficulties associated with having to remake their lives in an unfamiliar culture at an advanced age, problems exacerbated by the discrimination they face after returning to Japan. The government's solution – to offer them Japanese nationality (but not necessarily full citizenship) – often backfires for them; while they are allowed to legally stay in Japan, their lack of full benefits causes economic hardships, perpetuating the stereotype of them being poor Chinese. Another solution that some orphans employ is to become perpetual nomads, moving back and forth between Japan and China, seeking to access the advantages of global capitalism.[12] However, this solution is open only to those who can afford it. Moreover, these perpetual nomads must move within a system of nation-states that often restricts their freedom of movement.

How do Japanese repatriates from Manchuria who returned to Japan in the late 1940s react to the resurgence of colonial racism based on Japanese concepts of racial supremacy? One option is to simply join mainstream Japanese society and become, once again, the bearers of colonial racism, not only toward the ex-colonized, but also to their own children whom they gave up to Chinese families half a century ago. Another option is to live with profound guilt, recognizing that "we caused the suffering of our children," but advocating at the same time the restoration of their Japanese nationality – the Japanese state policy since the early 1980s. Yet another option is to challenge the colonial legacy by listening to the genuine voices of orphans and their family members. Doing so could enable them to challenge the meaning of ethnicity, race, nationality, and citizenship in the context of an East Asia caught in the wave of global capitalism.

In Nagano, most of my informants have chosen the second option; that is, prompted by both empathy and guilt, they turned their emotion into action as volunteer workers. They assist orphans in their search for their deep identities. For example, they provide information they have discovered about lost children in China to the Japanese government, thereby facilitating communications between the orphans and their Japanese relatives. They also offer the orphans moral support by visiting them during the difficult period of identity verification. The villages in Nagano that sent large numbers of agrarian colonists to Manchuria often invite orphans to spend some time in the Japanese countryside. Once the orphans arrive, these volunteers offer various practical forms of assistance. They teach the orphans not only the Japanese language, but also how to apply for welfare programs, how to shop at a grocery store, how to install a home telephone, how to open a bank account, and most importantly, how to restore their Japanese citizenship or obtain it for their spouses and children.

These volunteers, however, tend to accept only one kind of orphan – those who are willing to restore their Japanese nationality. They have little sympathy for those orphans who wish to keep their Chinese nationality after repatriation to Japan. For example, in 1998, I met Mr. Takahashi, a volunteer worker for the orphans. He was a Brigade member in Manchuria during the war. In 1945, he was arrested by the Soviets and sent to labor camps in Siberia: he could not return to Japan until 1949. In 1998, he introduced me to Mr. Wang, who told me: "My father had me retain my Chinese nationality, while my brother took Japanese nationality. This is good for us as we plan to start a taxi company in China in the near future after we earn enough money here in Japan to do so." Mr. Wang's father is an orphan, a child of Japanese agrarian colonists in Manchuria. Yet Mr. Wang has never met his father's Japanese relatives. Although he returned to Japan at the Japanese government's expense, he has retained his Chinese nationality and name because, he said, "my father does not remember his Japanese name anyway." While his father lives on a pension, Mr. Wang has been leading a busy life in Tokyo with his brother. A former elementary schoolteacher in northeast China, he now works six days a week, thirteen hours a day, in a small factory to earn the money that will allow him to start his own business in China.

Since China joined the World Trade Organization, an increasing number of orphans and their children have opted to keep their Chinese nationality. Instead of returning permanently to Japan, they combine Japanese and Chinese nationalities to achieve various economic goals. Mr. Wang's story suggests the emergence of orphans as active agents who make the best out of often adverse circumstances. Yet it is precisely people such as Mr. Wang whose citizenship decision is problematic for Japanese volunteers such as Mr. Takahashi (and the Japanese state), who believe that the orphans who return from China must become Japanese citizens. As long as orphans wish to attain both Japanese nationality and Japanese citizenship, they are ready to help them as much as possible.

Indeed, in the summer of 2001, Mr. Takahashi and other volunteers helped about six hundred orphans and their families stage a protest march, and walked with them from Tokyo Station to the busy commercial district of Ginza.[13] Some of these orphans were holding white and yellow banners with messages reading: "We are orphans from China," "Assure us our post-retirement security," and "Please do not forget us." Even if an orphan worked for ten years after repatriation to Japan, Mr. Takahashi said, he or she would only be eligible for a monthly pension of about 50,000 yen (about US$440) after retirement. Since this is by no means enough to live on, such retirees inevitably receive welfare assistance, inviting criticism from the Japanese public. In this march, the orphans criticized the Japanese government for offering them Japanese nationality, but not full Japanese citizenship.

The following year, this group of orphans initiated a lawsuit before the Tokyo Metropolitan Circuit Court against the Japanese government. Helped by Japanese volunteers and lawyers, the 637 plaintiffs claimed the following. First, the Japanese state had deserted them in Manchuria after World War II. Second, in 1974 the Japanese state changed their status from "missing" to "dead" in Japanese household registries without due investigation. Third, since repatriation the Japanese state has not provided orphans with adequate assistance. Therefore, each plaintiff claims compensation from the Japanese state in the amount of 33,000,000 yen (about US$300,000).[14] In this lawsuit, which has not yet been concluded, the orphans question the gap between the Japanese nationality that they have and Japanese citizenship (that they believe they do not have). By so doing, they have transformed the gift from the Japanese state – Japanese nationality – into the basis for demanding full citizenship.

Does this mean that none among the Japanese repatriates (who returned to Japan in the late 1940s) has chosen the third option? That is to say, is no one ready to challenge the colonial legacy in Japan by listening to the genuine voices of orphans whether they may be Japanese or Chinese? In concluding this chapter, I will describe one incident that took place first in Tokyo, and later in Liutiaogou in northeast China. This incident suggests the realization of the possibility of another option – by together remembering the Chinese people who were in northeast China, the two generations of Japanese repatriates can communicate better with each other.

Conclusion

In 1998 I was introduced to Mr. Yamada, another repatriate from Manchuria who assists returnee orphans as a volunteer worker. When I visited him at his home in downtown Tokyo, he showed me some fifty tiny figurines of Jizô, placed neatly in a box. Jizô, one of the most important Buddhist deities in Japan, is believed to aid the souls of dead children while simultaneously comforting their mourning parents. Jizô statues are found throughout Japan, and the deity is "perhaps the most ubiquitous, popular, and widely loved in Japanese religion" (Ivy 1995: 144–5; cf. Schattschneider 2001).

Mr. Yamada makes these little figurines. He starts by collecting tiny stones on the beach or by the roadside. Using his artistic skill he polishes the surface of each stone, paints a child's face on it, and transforms the stone into a Jizô figurine. Each figurine represents an immigrant child who died in Manchuria, as well as the sorrow of the child's parents. According to Mr. Yamada, however, each Jizô also represents an immigrant child who survived in China, as well as the devotion of his or her Chinese adoptive parents. While the post-war Japanese government counted the orphans as dead, Mr. Yamada resurrected their lives in tiny stones. That same day, Mr. Yamada took me to a gallery near his home. Located in the posh Roppongi district of Tokyo, the small gallery attracted many young women and men. There Mr. Yamada displayed his figurines –

called Manshû Jizô (Manchurian Jizô), and sold them to gallery visitors. The money he made went to fund another project: to build a stone monument in China to express gratitude to the Chinese adoptive parents of Japanese orphans. Indeed, by then, the project was already well underway. A well-known cartoonist, himself a repatriate from Manchuria, was then building a monument to a family of three – a pair of Chinese parents and their adopted son, a child of Japanese agrarian colonists in Manchuria.

In 1999, Mr. Yamada and his group finally completed this grand project. What surprised me greatly when I read a newspaper article reporting this event was that they built the monument in Liutiaogou, the very site of the Japanese incursion into Manchuria on September 18, 1931. In addition, they held a ceremony celebrating the completion of the monument inside the September Eighteenth Museum, a venue that is known for its displays condemning Japanese imperialism. The monument, then, represents more than the suffering of the orphans. It also embodies the pain of their adoptive parents, and by extension, the pain of the people of China who suffered not only the pain of their adopted children leaving for Japan, but also the Japanese invasion during World War II. Representing the orphans, Mr. Tanaka, one of the members of Mr. Yamada's group, spoke at a ceremony to an audience of about two hundred, including his eighty-four-year-old adoptive father. Mr. Tanaka now lives in Japan as a Japanese citizen, but has never forgotten the adoptive parents he left behind in China. He said: "After the resumption of diplomatic relations between Japan and China, my adoptive father saw me off to Japan while crying.... My adoptive parents let me eat steamed rice every other day while they ate only corn and kaoliang."[15]

Many who attended this ceremony remembered the suffering of the Chinese people, but the orphans belong to both groups: the Japanese (the former colonizers) and the Chinese (the formerly colonized). If we cling to traditional notions of race, ethnicity, nationality, and citizenship – and the idea that a single ethnicity invariably corresponds to a single nationality and a single citizenship – we lose sight of a space where the orphans live both in Japan and in China, that is the space of multiple, often disorganized, identities (Ching 2001: 175). Yet the wisdom of people such as Mr. Yamada gives us hope that a resurgence of colonial racism in Japan can be prevented, not by endorsing the Japanese state policy (and the identity politics of some orphans as well as Japanese volunteers), but by critically addressing the history of Japanese imperialism in northeast China.

Writing on children growing up in an era of global capitalism, Sharon Stephens (1995: 3) asks a series of poignant questions:

> What sorts of social visions and notions of culture underlie assertions within international-rights discourses that every child has a right to a cultural identity? To what extent is this identity conceived as singular

and exclusive, and what sorts of priorities are asserted in cases where various forms of cultural identity – regional, national, ethnic minority, or indigenous – come up against one another?

Stephens is interested in the "complex globalizations of the once localized Western constructions of childhood," and the impact of those constructions on the everyday lives of children in the contemporary world (ibid.: 8; cf. Scheper-Hughes and Sargent 1998). I believe that the Chinese-Japanese war orphans equate with Stephens' children growing up in a multicultural setting, and argue that the orphans (and their children and grandchildren) have a right not to be constrained within an exclusionary Japanese cultural identity, and "not to have their bodies and minds appropriated as the unprotected terrain upon which cultural battles are fought" (Stephens 1995: 4). These cultural battles are often imposed upon the orphans. Furthermore, such battles have been taking place largely in their absence – among the Japanese government, media, society at large, and the parent generation of Japanese repatriates from northeast China. Unless we find better ways to approach the orphans there is a serious danger that they will be consumed in these cultural battles, their voices left unheard.

The commemoration of the monument in Liutiaogou makes us reconsider the meaning of both the overseas Japanese and the overseas Chinese. When we examine critically the stories and memories of those who became both overseas Japanese (in China) and overseas Chinese (in Japan), we then understand that the notions of ethnicity, race, nationality, and citizenship in East Asia today are more multifaceted than we would normally imagine. Yet, at the same time, we also understand that the system of nation-states, which is still unable to accommodate flexible citizenship along with flexible ethnicity, race, and nationality (Ong 2002), has made the life of overseas Chinese-Japanese miserable in both locations. However, more and more of these "orphans" – both in terms of parentage and nation-state – have developed, and will continue to develop, their own strategies and understandings of family, ethnicity, race, nationality, and citizenship.

Notes

1 According to *Nagano-ken Manshû Kaitaku-shi* [The History of Colonization of Manchuria by the Agrarian Colonists from Nagano Prefecture], about 20 percent of the agrarian colonists had been drafted into the Japanese military prior to Japan's capitulation. Among them, 78 percent returned home safely as they were protected by international agreement. In contrast, only about 40 percent of civilians – women, children, and the elderly – returned to Japan (Manshû Kaitaku-shi Kankô-kai 1984: 719).
2 Asahi Newspaper, August 15, 1974.
3 These repatriates of the parent generation were being greatly helped by Nitchû

Yûkô Kyôkai, the Japan–China Friendship Commission (hereafter the JCFC). Founded in 1950, the JCFC served as a liaison between China and Japan during the time when the two governments did not have diplomatic relations. Although the JCFC played a major role in realizing the repatriation of Japanese from China, the group suffered from factionalism due mainly to the worsening relationship between the Chinese and the Japanese communist parties. In 1966, one faction severed its relationship with the Japan Communist Party while another continued to maintain its party relationship. It is the former that inherited the group name the JCFC, which eventually became an interest group for Japanese repatriates from China. The organization not only collaborates with the Japanese government in locating orphans in China; it also demands that the government facilitate their naturalization.

4 See "Koji Kankei Tôkei Ichiran" [Statistical Data on the Orphans] at http://www.kikokusha-center.or.jp.

5 For this argument, the media often rely on Article 15 of the Universal Declaration of Human Rights, which reads: "Everyone has the right to a nationality. No one shall be arbitrarily deprived of his nationality nor denied the right to change his nationality." See http://www.un.org/Overview/rights.html.

6 Indeed, in 1988 the Japanese government built twenty centers called Chûgoku Kikokusha Jiritsu Kenshû Sentâ [Center to Assist the Independence of the Returnees from China]. At these centers, former agrarian settlers of the parent generation work as volunteers in order to transform orphans into independent Japanese citizens, so that they are able to live in Japan without public assistance. Furthermore, before coming to the center, the orphans spend their first four months at one of six institutions called Chûgoku Kikokusha Teichaku Sokushin Sentâ [the Center to Promote Permanent Living (in Japan) for Returnees from China]. These center names explicitly express the Japanese state's intention – that is, to make orphans return permanently to Japan, and to remake them into independent Japanese citizens.

7 In the mid-1980s, the Chinese government made an official protest to the Japanese government that the orphans who had returned to Japan were neglecting their filial obligations toward their adoptive parents. This protest interrupted the Japanese government's search for the orphans for almost a year. The interruption ended when the two governments reached the following agreements: (1) the orphans must solve their "family problems" before returning permanently to Japan; (2) the orphans, who return temporarily to Japan to see their relatives, must return to China to solve their family problems; (3) if they refuse to return to China, the Japanese government should be responsible for persuading them to do so; (4) the Japanese government should pay half the expenses required by the remaining family of a repatriated orphan in China; and (5) the volunteer organizations in Japan should make efforts to pay the other half. See Asahi Newspaper, March 17, 1984, September 5, 6, and 7, and October 27, 1986.

8 Until 1992, the adult (older than twenty years of age) or married children of orphans were not allowed to return to Japan with their parents at the government's expense. In that year, the government implemented a policy which allowed a "disabled" orphan to return with one of his or her children. Two years later, the government began to apply the same policy to any orphan older than sixty-five. In 1995, the government lowered the age threshold to sixty (Kôsei-shô 1997: 419).

9 See, for example, Yomiuri Newspaper, November 25, 1994.

10 In 2001, NHK aired a program about a woman who had refused to acknowledge her daughter – an orphan visiting Japan – because she had remarried and was entered in her second husband's house registration. Prodded repeat-

edly by an officer of the Ministry of Health and Welfare, she finally acknowledged her daughter. Yet, by then, the mother was suffering from a life-threatening illness and died shortly after.
11 I obtained these numbers from Mr. Yamamoto at the time of my interview. The current statistics are hard to obtain, presumably because some of the families of orphans fall into the category of "Chinese" immigrants in Japan.
12 Benedict Anderson argues that "post-war nomadism" is a consequence of the metropolis losing the capacity and the interest to naturalize and nationalize its millions of immigrants (1994). I agree with him only partially, and note, along with Stuart Hall (1997), that such capacity and interest has remained powerful enough to maintain colonial racism.
13 Asahi Newspaper, Evening Edition, August 15, 2001.
14 Asahi Newspaper, December 20, 2002.
15 Asahi Newspaper, August 21, 1999.

14 Negotiating work and self
Experiences of Japanese working women in Singapore

Leng Leng Thang, Miho Goda, and Elizabeth MacLachlan

The post-war movements of Japanese overseas are closely linked to the transnational economic expansion of Japanese industries since the 1960s, resulting in the dispersal of Japanese salaried men from multinational corporations to different corners of the world. Known as *chûzai-in*, these male expatriates and their families form the core of Japanese communities overseas. Often perceived by the host society as a closely knit community, they are distinct in terms of residential locale, school choice (sending their children to Japanese-language schools), consumption preferences, and membership in Japanese associations.

Chûzai-in and their families – who usually stay for an average of three years in a country – continue to dominate the image of the Japanese community in Asia. However, since the 1990s, we have witnessed the growth of non-*chûzai-in* among the Japanese transnational migrants to East and Southeast Asia. Characterized as "new Japanese expatriates" who are young, single, and female (*Straits Times*, August 24, 1994), they form a new type of immigrant from Japan. The previous flow of young women migrants out of Japan focused on moving to the West, particularly to the United States, the United Kingdom, Canada, Australia, and New Zealand. These Westbound emigrants, who started out in small numbers in the 1970s, were referred to as "spiritual migrants" rather than as "economic migrants," and were characterized by their constructed illusions about the West and Japan (Sato 1993 cited in Sakai 2000: 214).

Japanese women moving to work elsewhere in Asia since the 1990s are also well qualified as "spiritual migrants," who are driven to leave Japan because of their disillusionment with the Japanese workplace, and/or the curiosity to experience independent living overseas (rather than for economic gains) (Befu 2000: 34). Many have taken jobs as local wage earners, without the luxury of a housing and transportation allowance, and often live modestly overseas, frequently receiving less income than they would in Japan. Although they do not consider themselves to be part of the Japanese enclave, the majority have found work connected in some way to the Japanese community, particularly in (1) the headquarters, subsidiaries and factories of Japanese corporations operating in the host country, (2) travel agencies catering to Japanese tourists, and (3) a host of service-related industries – Japanese grocery stores, hair salons, medical clinics, schools – that address the needs of Japanese expatriates.

There is a general lack of statistics on such a gendered diaspora (Befu 2000: 35). Broadly speaking, the rising trend of female emigration started in the 1990s. Due partly to demand from cost-cutting Japanese firms that see hiring local Japanese women as an attractive alternative to the more expensive expatriate posting, many young Japanese women have chosen to venture abroad on their own. In addition, stories of women daring to forsake Japan to seek a new successful life overseas have been publicized in the media, no doubt contributing to its attraction.

Asia became the favored location due to increasing work opportunities, compared with more stringent visa requirements and the lack of employment in Western countries. Recruitment agencies play a major role in facilitating emigration. PaHuma Asia Co., a personnel placement company specializing in Asia, started the "Japanese women work in Asia" boom with its first career seminar on Hong Kong conducted in Tokyo and Osaka in 1993. More than 14,000 Japanese were registered with the company by early 2002, 60 percent being female. The company noted that the majority of Japanese women were registering for job placement in China and Singapore (*Japan Times*, January 14, 2003). Singapore attracts Japanese women because it is relatively easy to obtain work visas there, English is commonly used, and it has a reputation as a safe metropolitan city.

Despite the increasing numbers of Japanese women working overseas, studies on this type of emigrant are only just beginning (e.g., Ben-Ari and Yong 2000; Sakai 2000). We have explored the experiences of single working women in Singapore and elsewhere and concluded that, although they are perceived to be on the margins of both the host society and the Japanese community, they nevertheless find fulfillment in their overseas experience and feel empowered as they find opportunities for self-improvement professionally, socially, and emotionally (Thang, MacLachlan, and Goda: 2002). In this chapter, we focus on the experiences of both single and married Japanese working women in Singapore. Studies on married Japanese working women outside Japan are even more rare, as Japanese women – especially the wives of *chûzai-in* – are expected to play a supporting role as full-time homemakers. In Singapore, Japanese spouses who structure their lives around their children and husbands, live in luxury condominiums, kill time in upscale coffee houses and tea lounges, and shop in upscale department stores such as Takashimaya, have earned the affectionate title of "Taka Mamas" (*Straits Times*, October 20, 2003).

By focusing on Japanese working women in the context of transnational migration, this study juxtaposes work, motherhood, and self within the context of globalization from the perspective of Japanese emigration. How do marriage, work, and their Japanese identities intersect to influence their overseas experience? How do these roles and identities simultaneously impose constraints and personal freedom?

This chapter begins with a brief description of data collection, followed by a description of the patterns and characteristics found among Japanese working women as observed in Singapore. After a brief section on the development of the Japanese community in Singapore, we analyze women's perceptions and experiences from three perspectives. The first two are negotiating work and negotiating domestic work, and we discuss strategies for combining the two. The determination found in most women to continue working despite constraints reflects the role of work as essential to the women's life satisfaction and well-being. The third theme of our study examines Japanese women's negotiations with their own *Japaneseness* as they situate themselves as a working professional, mother, and wife outside Japan.

Data collection

Data for this study were obtained through a questionnaire survey, with a combination of open-ended questions and in-depth interviews conducted in 2000. A snowball sampling method was used through friends and acquaintances, announcements in Japanese newspapers, and distributions of questionnaires to Japanese schools and Japanese companies. We sent out a total of 410 questionnaires with self-addressed envelopes and received 194 responses (47.3 percent return rate), of which 119 (61.3 percent) were from single women and seventy-five (38.7 percent) from married working women. We further conducted in-depth interviews with twenty-four of the respondents, who provided us with further insights beyond the questionnaire replies. As far as possible, we followed up with another interview in 2003. These follow-up interviews have provided interesting trajectories for some of their life experiences.

The average ages of the single and married respondents were 31.2 years old and 35.2 years old, respectively. For single women, this is in line with the application requirement to have a few years of work experience and a tertiary degree to obtain employment visas in Singapore. While all single women were working full-time, for the married women thirty were in full-time positions while forty-five worked part-time.

Patterns and characteristics of Japanese working women

Single women

The single women in our study were representative of Japanese single women working overseas. Most obtained their jobs either through classified ads, recruitment agencies specializing in placements for Japanese, or recommendations from friends already working in Singapore. Some had signed up with recruitment agencies in Singapore and attended job interviews while vacationing, but the overwhelming majority were local hires. They held full-time positions usually as secretaries or in administrative jobs in banking, manufacturing, or securities companies. Other popular occupations included sales, marketing, and teaching positions. These jobs usually required Japanese language proficiency (Thang and MacLachlan 2002).

Married women

In general, married women found little difficulty getting a job in Singapore, especially compared to Japan.[1] Due to demands for Japanese speakers to serve the Japanese community, married women with some qualifications (such as a certificate for teaching the Japanese language, translation, or interpretation) are in high demand. In addition, their visa sometimes increases their marketability compared to single women, who must have an employment pass to be eligible. Japanese women on dependant visas or in permanent residency are preferred, especially for companies who are looking for part-timers or who would like to do away with the complications of employment visa applications. As one married respondent commented:

> I was a lecturer in Japan.... I did not expect to find a job [as a Japanese language teacher] so easily. The condition of employment was simply to have an eligible visa. I was fortunate! In Singapore, even for a Japanese housewife, age is not a concern. There are many job opportunities. In the first place, many companies would employ you if you have a visa to stay. Also, there are many jobs that require Japanese, such as a Japanese language teacher or staff in a Japanese company. I think married women have a better chance of getting a job than single women who come from Japan. This is exactly opposite from the situation in Japan.
> (D.H., part-time working wife of a Singaporean; no children)

In Singapore, wives and children of *chûzai-in* are given dependant passes based on the employment pass status of their husbands. Although they are not allowed to work as dependant pass holders, it is relatively easy for the women to obtain work permits as long as their employers are willing to apply to the Ministry of Manpower on their behalf. Women married to local Singaporeans usually have permanent residency, allowing them to work without permission from the Ministry. Due to the flexibility of being able to work part-time, married women have more work opportunities than single women.

While single women may be considered as one category (since the majority of them have similar employment experiences and work status), married working women show great differences in experience depending on whether they came as an accompanying spouse with their *chûzai-in* husbands, or as wives of Singaporeans. Hence, it is useful to categorize them into two types:

1 Working women with chûzai-in *husbands*

In our study, there are thirty-six Japanese women with Japanese *chûzai-in* husbands and six women whose husbands are non-Japanese. One-third hold full-time jobs, mostly as teachers, while the rest are part-timers. Expatriate wives such as these made up half of the *chûzai-in* migration. From a study of expatriate women from the United States, the United Kingdom, Canada, Australia, New Zealand, Japan, the People's Republic of China, Taiwan, and Hong Kong (as well as other European and Asian countries), Yeoh and Khoo (1998) conclude that as "trailing spouses," expatriate wives are generally invisible in migration.[2]

Among the Japanese, it is generally expected that overseas wives will be full-time home-makers, even if they held jobs in Japan. This is reinforced by the husbands' companies, which sometimes have clear regulations preventing accompanying spouses from working, or restricting them to working part-time. The argument is that women should support their husbands and children. Moreover, the benefits package – worth at least S$10,000 (US$6,000) a month, in addition to a luxury apartment, payment for children's education, and a transportation allowance (if not a company car) – usually mean an improvement in the family's previous living standards without the need for supplemental income (*Straits Times*, October 19, 2003). As Yeoh and Khoo (1998: 167) indicate, Japanese expatriate wives do enjoy their non-working role overseas. One of their interviewees said:

> Many Japanese ladies in Singapore do not work ... we do not need to work.... Here we can live in a large house ... we can employ a part-time maid, and everything is so cheap when compared to Japanese prices ... so we can play golf, tennis.... Why work? Why not enjoy our comfortable life?

On the other hand, more Japanese expatriate wives are also working "for fun," or "for *ikigai*" (to give life meaning), rather than for financial gain:

> I like to teach and to have international exchange with foreigners. My reason to work is to have meaning in life, and a little income. It is mostly for my own improvement.
>
> (M.R., part-time working expatriate wife; one child)

The desire to work is especially found among some expatriate wives who have no children:

> I have no children, and I feel bored. When I found that there was an administrative work opening in a Japanese company, I immediately applied. My main purpose is to have something to do; income is less important.
> (T.S., full-time working expatriate wife; no children)

However, the wives' desire to work is sometimes met with objections from the larger expatriate Japanese society (i.e., the company and the Japanese community). Some wives give in to this pressure, while others show resistance in different ways while negotiating their work.

2 Working women married to Singaporeans

Compared to the expatriate wives, Japanese women who are married to Singaporeans find little pressure in their choice to work as married women. On the contrary, they may find pressure to actively stay in the workforce. Due to the size of the country, where parents-in-law usually live near or with their children – and the affordability of employing domestic help (usually women from Indonesia or the Philippines) – being a full-time housewife has become more an exception than the rule in Singapore. It is quite common for Singaporean women to define themselves through work rather than as a mother or wife, especially when they are highly educated. This can be disturbing to women who choose to be full-time home-makers, as one forty-two-year-old Japanese expatriate wife (a former bank officer) indicated:

> Many Singaporeans I meet here ask me what I do for a living. When I say I'm a housewife, they will ask why don't I get a job. I feel a bit hurt. Does that mean I'm worth nothing without a job?
> (*Straits Times*, October 19, 2003)

In our sample, half of the working wives married to Singaporeans are working full-time, while the rest work part-time. Many of these wives of Singaporeans first came to Singapore as single working women on employment visas, which they later changed to permanent resident status upon marriage. With permanent resident status, many have began to work part-time after becoming mothers.

Compared to the wives of Japanese nationals, whose reasons for working seem to be either *ikigai* or as a hobby, the reasons expressed by wives of Singaporeans are more wide-ranging. More women in full-time employment mentioned the need to work to boost family income:

My reason to work is *ikigai*. I have always liked to teach, and this work [teaching Japanese] suits me perfectly. The pay is less important, but compared to part-time work in Japan, this job pays more; it is a double win. Since this is part-time work, I can take care of the home as well.

(G.H., part-time working wife of Singaporean; no children)

I took courses to become a Japanese language teacher while in Japan. Now I am able to use what I have learned. My reason to work is both for *ikigai* and for income.

(G.M., full-time working wife of Singaporean; two children)

I am in this job [at a travel agency] to make a living ... recently, I did think about quitting. My reason to work is for an income. I hope to allow my child to have a better education in the future. I work hard at balancing both work and family, housework and childcare.... I have thought of becoming a full-time housewife, but it would be tough to live just on my husband's income. I also wish to have more time with my child. This is difficult. [My husband] understands my feeling about work, but since he is a Singaporean, he seems to expect a dual-income family.

(S.K., full-time working wife of Singaporean; one child)

On the whole, wives of Singaporeans distinguish themselves from expatriate wives. Although some expatriate wives do work – and increasingly more are choosing to do so – the general perception of expatriate wives is still that of the Taka Mamas stereotype. The different patterns and characteristics observed among single working women, expatriate wives, and working wives of Singaporeans reflect the diversity of experiences among women depending on their connections and negotiations with the Japanese community in Singapore.

The Japanese village

Referred to as a "Japanese village" by a Japanese single working woman who belongs to a group removed from the Japanese community, this term characterizes the perception of the Japanese community as "closed" and existing in a "bubble."[3] At present, there are about 21,000 people in this Japanese community in Singapore.[4] This makes it the second largest foreign community in the country (Singapore's population of 4.1 million is 25 percent foreign). Of the three groups of women discussed in this chapter, the expatriate wives form the most integral part of the Japanese community.

The Japanese community in Singapore has developed quite differently from overseas Japanese communities in other parts of the world. In general, we can divide its development into pre-war and post-war phases.

The pre-war Japanese community dates back to the nineteenth century. In 1889, the Japanese consul recorded over two hundred Japanese living in Singapore, made up mostly of *karayuki-san* (prostitutes from Japan), some men (mostly pimps), and some others. By the early twentieth century, more elite business people came as Japan expanded its foreign trade. In 1912 and 1915 respectively, the Japanese Primary School (*Nihonjin Shôgakkô*) and the Japanese Association (*Nihonjin-kai*) were established, symbolizing the permanent social and cultural presence of the Japanese community in Singapore. In 1937, the Japanese population totaled 3,973. However, this number soon dropped once repatriation began as the Japanese invasion of China continued in the 1930s. The Japanese population swelled again between 1942 and 1945 when the island was under Japanese occupation. It dwindled again at the end of World War II, and by 1947 not a single Japanese remained (Plath 2001; Tsu 2002).

The post-war Japanese community re-emerged only in the 1970s, when Japanese businesses' overseas expansion coincided with the favorable business climate in Singapore (i.e., strong government support, cheap labor, and political stability). By some estimates, there are about 3,000 Japanese companies in Singapore, making up as much as a quarter of Singapore's gross domestic product (Ben-Ari 2002). As noted by Ben-Ari (ibid.), the post-war Japanese community is overwhelmingly made up of managers and their families, with a small minority of *tanshin funin* (Japanese office workers sent abroad by Japanese companies). Most of them are in their late thirties and early forties, with their school-age children usually enrolled in Japanese elementary or middle school. Singapore has the largest Japanese overseas education system, with two elementary schools enrolling about 1,900 students, a middle school enrolling 700, a high school enrolling about 500, and a Japanese kindergarten serving 400 children.

Because of this social makeup, Ben-Ari (2002) characterizes the Japanese community in Singapore differently from the "Little Japans" or "Little Tokyos" we find in large urban areas such as London or Los Angeles. It is more similar to the Japanese community found in Düsseldorf, with a population of all ages and diverse occupations (see Sakai 2000; Sakamoto 2000). Ben-Ari's study of Japanese managers in Singapore shows them remaining distinctively "Japanese." They speak about the uniqueness of Japanese culture, the *Nihonjin-ron* perspective, the essence of group mentality, and the need to refrain from "going native" (including maintaining a Japanese appearance, such as formal office attire despite the perennial heat in the country).

Their families also tend to stay in close proximity with other Japanese, as most congregate in certain residential areas, due partly to the influence of real estate agents in directing newcomers to certain areas, and partly for convenience (such as close proximity to Japanese schools). Some companies even confine their staff to the same residential project for ease of management. A host of services catering to the Japanese community are found ranging from supermarkets (such as Meijiya and Isetan), hair salons, travel agencies, boutiques, bookstores, cafés, video stores, clinics, radio stations, and Japanese cable channels. The Japanese Association offers social and cultural activities and programs as well. It is easy to stay within the familiar environment speaking only Japanese while away from home. Such a sheltered environment, however, could pose a dilemma for expatriate wives as they attempt to venture beyond being the expected full-time home-makers.

Negotiating work

Groupism is generally believed to be a fundamental Japanese trait forming the basis of one's identity in Japan. Many studies (e.g., Nakane 1970; Salamon 1975; Imamura 1987) have noted groupism in Japanese company housing complexes, where the hierarchical order within a company directly affects the vertical relationships among wives living in the same complex. While men conform to the group within the company structure, women negotiate with neighbors who are useful for social support but, at the same time, are also regarded as elements of social control. Through gossip, criticism, and competition, they coerce women into the group's values of traditional "good wives and mothers" still entrenched in Japanese society (Salamon 1975).

Japanese expatriate wives in the Japanese village in Singapore face many of the same problems that residents in a Tokyo housing complex (as described by Salamon (ibid.)) faced two decades earlier. Gossip and jealousy are concerns for expatriate wives who have opted to work, even if only part-time:

> I am not so bothered [by the gossip and pressures of interpersonal relationships], but to other people it must be a cause of great concern. For example, in Japanese companies where there are many Japanese employees, the wife's status is directly linked with the husband's position. In the same condominium, subtle status differences can be felt between the wives whose husbands work in big banks or big companies, and those whose husbands work in small and medium-size corporations. I also heard that in condominiums that have a large number of Japanese you can find the wives forming cliques among themselves. And to be an expatriate wife who is working in the midst of all this, you can't tell what gossip they are saying about you while you are away.
>
> (F.M., part-time working expatriate wife; no children)

Having no children has made it possible for the part-time working expatriate wife to resist the pressure to conform. For example, one expatriate wife found herself fighting a tough battle trying to juggle both her work and her hobbies. Although her husband has been very understanding – and supported her by coming home early from work to take care of their three young children when she had to go to her hobby classes or part-time job – colleagues at his workplace (and her visiting parents-in-law) were very critical. Her parents-in-law even offered to pay her a part-time income in exchange for her staying at home. "I work not for the money, but for my desire to do something meaningful. They cannot understand me at all." She was discouraged by their unsupportive attitude toward her determination to work.

However, when we re-interviewed her two years later we found that what really caused her to hang up her dancing shoes and stop her English and Chinese lessons was pressure from her neighbors. She was stressed out from being closely watched and criticized by her Japanese neighbors for straying away from the good wife and mother image (she nonetheless insisted on continuing with her part-time work on weekends). As a mother of three young children far away from her relatives, she has to depend on her neighbors for help, such as picking up her older child from the school bus after kindergarten when she needs to take the younger children to the doctor. Because of other needed favors and baby-sitting, it is necessary for her to maintain good relationships with her neighbors.

Aside from neighbors, Japanese companies also reinforce a Japanese village overseas with written or non-written rules prohibiting expatriate wives from working. Nonetheless, women who desire to work can still find various strategies such as using their maiden names to avoid identification with their husbands and their companies. Others work as volunteers (sometimes receiving only a transportation allowance, if anything, when the purpose of working is solely for self-fulfillment).

> I am professionally certified in counseling, and really wanted to work as a counselor here in Singapore, as I did in Japan. Now, I am working part-time as a counselor in a Japanese organization. Since my husband's company did not permit wives to work, I have to work as a volunteer, without any pay.
> (Y.Y., part-time working expatriate wife; no children)

Some expatriate wives are less affected by the Japanese village if their husbands' companies employ only a few Japanese, or if they deliberately avoid staying in condominiums densely inhabited by Japanese:

> Although my husband works for a Japanese company, they have very few Japanese employees, so we have little worries about company relationships. Moreover, my condominium has very few Japanese, and the wives are also not close with each other, so there are very few interpersonal relationship problems there either.
> (T.A., part-time working expatriate wife; two children)

The complexity of expatriate wives being working wives and mothers is clearly reflected in our data collection, where getting participant wives was more difficult than recruiting from the other two groups. Even among the expatriate wives who participated, they were careful in asking for details such as the source of the research funding, uses of the survey results, and the objectives of the research. They only agreed to participate in the survey after receiving permission from their husbands. In contrast, most single working women, and married women whose husbands are non-Japanese, participated freely in the surveys and interviews.

Being outsiders to the Japanese village, the single working women and working wives of non-Japanese face little difficulty at work. The problem for single working women, if any, is having no choice but to work full-time as stipulated by their employment visa. To compensate for this, single working women focus on doing what really interests them, and shift readily to other work or activities with relative ease. It is not uncommon to find that single women who have saved enough quit their jobs and return to colleges either locally or overseas. They will also job-hop, leave for jobs in another country, or return to Japan, if they are dissatisfied with their jobs in Singapore. While most expatriate wives said they expected to stay in the country for about three to five years, the single working women tended to be more vague, saying, for example, "I want to stay longer in Singapore," or "I will return to Japan some day."

Compared with single working women, working wives of Singaporeans have relatively little geographical mobility since they are mostly settled in Singapore. However, many are glad to have permanent residency status through marriage, which allows them greater job mobility:

> I have job-hopped many times in Singapore. Sometimes, I quit only because the commuting time was long. Since I speak English and have permanent residency status, I don't feel insecure about finding a new job. Anyway, it is common to job-hop in Singapore; Singapore companies are used to it, too. When you quit a company, there is no need for formalities (like in Japan). It is not troublesome at all.
>
> (T.K., full-time working wife of Singaporean; one child)

With permanent residency status, it is also easy to switch to part-time employment. One mother who was working full-time as a tour coordinator switched to part-time work as a receptionist at a Japanese medical clinic after she married a Singaporean. She compared the change in attitude about work after becoming a permanent resident:

> When I was single and working, because of visa restrictions I could have not thought about changing jobs. But after I married and received permanent residency, I became open to information on pos-

sible new positions. It is a relief to know that now I am able to leave my job any time I want.

(N.K., part-time working wife of Singaporean; two children)

As wives of Singaporeans, Japanese women are adjusting to the Singaporean expectations of a dual-income family. Although they commented that it is easier for mothers to work in Singapore, as working Japanese mothers they do feel more pressure (than Singaporean women). Nonetheless, most feel that their husbands and families are understanding and helpful about housework and childcare:

> I am able to continue working because of the help and advice I received from colleagues and friends, as well as my husband's family. I may quit if I want to, but my husband encourages me to continue working. If I had married a Japanese, I would probably have quit working either after getting married or after childbirth.
>
> (Y.N., full-time working wife of Singaporean; one child)

Among the full-time working wives of Singaporeans, one-third (five out of fifteen) consider themselves to be career women, as opposed to only one out of ten full-time expatriate wives. Among single working women, only 25 percent consider themselves to be career women. This means that as wives of Singaporeans, these full-time working Japanese women are adopting the values of Singaporean society. However, for the majority, working part-time instead of full-time, for example, becomes a way of negotiating their priorities in work and family in the host society.

Negotiating domestic work

Since the 1970s in Singapore, as women began working in greater numbers, work permits for domestic servants from neighboring countries (including Thailand, Sri Lanka, and the Philippines) were liberally granted to help these Singaporean working women (Yeoh and Huang 1998). Today, employing a live-in foreign maid has become common in Singapore, with one in seven households having live-in foreign help. In recent discussions on how to increase the birth rate in Singapore, one suggestion was to reduce the cost of the required stipend paid to the Singapore government for hiring foreign maids,[5] to make them more affordable.

Among working Japanese married women, full-time working women are more likely to employ live-in maids (as do many Singaporean families). Compared to Japan, women among our interviewees find the availability of live-in maids in Singapore useful. Alternatively, for working wives of Singaporeans, they rely on help from their mothers-in-law, or institutions such as childcare centers if there is no live-in help at home. Women also change to part-time employment as a strategy to balance work and family:

> Although I have a child, since my mother-in-law is helping me, there is no need for a maid.
> (T.K., full-time working wife of Singaporean; one child)

> My elder daughter enters school this year. As she is in the afternoon session, I have adjusted my working time from the morning to the afternoon shift so that I can stay at home in the morning to do housework and to supervise her school work. When my elder daughter goes to school, I will leave my younger daughter at a childcare center and leave for work at the same time. I return around the same time my daughter comes back from school.
> (N.K., part-time working wife of Singaporean; two children)

A majority of the respondents, though, are more in favor of employing part-time help than live-in help. One reason is because there is less need for full-time live-in help when they are only working part-time:

> When I have to work as a home tutor at night or during the weekends, I will look for a baby-sitter on a temporary basis whenever my husband is not able to stay home with our children. I prefer to do housework and childcare myself. Therefore, there is no need for a live-in maid. I will pay for part-time help on an hourly basis if I have to.
> (M.C., part-time working expatriate wife; three children)

Some respondents are wary of the employment of full-time live-in domestic maids due to negative media reports and fear of problems with maids. This is not peculiar to the Japanese women, though. Singapore families who have had unpleasant experiences with live-in maids often do not employ any either.

However, more Japanese women cited or implied "because I am Japanese" to explain why they have no intention of hiring live-in help:

> I did not hire a live-in maid. I have not heard good things from people who have one. I also feel uncomfortable being under the same roof. Most Singaporean women continue to work after giving birth, leaving their children with their own parents or in-laws, or employ maids to help. As a Japanese, I find this tough. My parents are too far away in Japan, [and] my parents-in-law have passed away; I leave my child at childcare centers when I go to work.
> (S.K., full-time working wife of Singaporean; one child)

> Well, as Japanese, we are not used to having live-in maids, so it is a difficult situation. Some years ago when I was really busy with my work

and found it difficult to take care of housework at the same time, I had employed a live-in maid. When I was trying to decide whether to quit my job completely or take up a part-time job, I easily chose to work part-time [and do away with the live-in maid].
(N.A., part-time working wife of Singaporean; no children)

It is questionable to say unequivocally that Japanese do not have maids, since many well-to-do Japanese families (such as merchant and aristocrat families) did employ live-in maids and still do (Hamabata 1990; Lebra 1993). It is, however, true that middle-class households, where the majority of Japanese identify themselves, do not engage domestic help since the domestic sphere is regarded as the women's private domain of responsibility. Moreover, as it is common for white-collar workers' wives to be full-time homemakers, coupled with the high cost of labor in Japan and the relatively small size of a typical house, the idea of employing a maid, especially a live-in maid, is non-existent to most Japanese. In situations where domestic help is not considered, we see working mothers taking part-time (instead of full-time) employment, engaging the help of relatives and neighbors, or enlisting the support of their husbands.

The burden of domestic work has often been blamed as one barrier to women's gainful employment, while also serving to deter women from having more children. Despite some respondents' views that the employment of domestic maids, especially foreign domestic maids, is too "un-Japanese," it is nevertheless a strategy some of them have chosen to employ in Singapore. Rather than considering Japanese women who employ maids as "going native," their decision should be seen as an outcome of their pragmatic negotiations to balance work and family. In Japan, as noted by Ueno (2000), the importing of foreign domestic help is already increasing.

Negotiating the Japanese self

In advising Japanese women who express interest in working overseas, one recruitment consultant constantly stresses the need for them to be proactive and independent; in other words, to have qualities not typical of Japanese women. What constitutes a typical Japanese woman? The most common terms used by our interviewees to describe the stereotypical image of Japanese women were: being polite, being supportive of men, being a professional housewife, being quiet and passive, and being self-sacrificing (putting others' interests before one's own).

While only 2 percent of both single and married working women in the survey indicated "yes" when asked whether they identify with this image, 60.6 percent answered that they somewhat agreed, and only 37.4 percent felt that they were far from typical. These results may not seem to offer strong support for the advice given to Japanese women who desire to work overseas. However, seeing oneself as a somewhat typical woman reveals much about the process of women's negotiations between the "Japanese" self and the "social" and "work" selves. Such a negotiation was evident among the Japanese women who we interviewed. In the earlier section, we noted, for example, how opinions on the employment of live-in maids are reduced to questions of culture (as well as assumptions that the domestic sphere defines the wife's and mother's responsibilities).

In interviews with single working women, we often hear them say that they are more Japanese than they thought. While the sojourning experience has changed their personality – such as becoming more confident and outgoing – they have also "returned" to become more Japanese. In the first place, many found that knowledge of Japanese culture, and their abilities to "handle" Japanese clients at work, have aided them in their process of rediscovering the *Japaneseness* in themselves.

Age plays a part in this process of rediscovery, as is seen in an interview with Miyuki Suzuki, Managing Director of Brokat Asia (a branch of a German IT company), reported in *Straits Times* (October 23, 1999). While agreeing that she is very different from the stereotypical Japanese woman, she said:

> But I don't think I'm as rebellious as before. I used to try to be unique and individualistic, and wasn't particularly bothered about what others thought about me. But now that I'm becoming 40, I guess my personality is mellowing and I appreciate things like family support and community spirit. In that sense, I'm actually becoming more Japanese than I used to be!

A conscious effort to stay in touch with matters relating to Japan is one way of maintaining the sense of *Japaneseness* for these women. This includes cooking Japanese meals, meeting with Japanese friends, and watching Japanese television programs. A majority of the women in the survey cook Japanese food at least once a week. Among the single women, more than half said they usually spend their leisure time with fellow Japanese friends.

The conflicting sense of "staying Japanese" versus "going native" is especially felt among women who are married to non-Japanese:

> I am well adapted to the local community and happy with it. I also have many local friends. As my son is attending a local school, he is really localized. I am close to my husband's family, and we go traveling together. However, at times, I still have the conscious feeling that I am Japanese. I do feel myself straying further and further away from Japanese society.
>
> (Y.N., full-time working wife of Singaporean; one child)

One full-time working wife of a Singaporean, who used to see herself as different from most Japanese, discovered after moving to Singapore that she values her *Japaneseness* after all. Although she never used to watch NHK (Japan's public broadcasting station) in Japan, after moving into her husband's house she subscribed to the station on cable television. She cooks Japanese food at least once a week and many of her friends, whom she met at her workplace, are Japanese. When we re-interviewed her two years later, she had given birth to a child and was moving to Japan. She has influenced her husband, who will move with her to Japan and spend the first year studying the Japanese language full-time before getting a job there. Meanwhile, she will work full-time to support the family, placing their child in the care of her mother. She will be different from most Japanese when she returns to Japan to work as the breadwinner of her transnational family.

Although married to Singaporeans, Japanese women make efforts to maintain ties with Japan, and where possible raise their children with immersion in both cultures. To familiarize them with their mother's culture, one part-time working wife of a Singaporean (N.K.), a member of the Japanese Association due to her company's corporate membership, went to the Japanese Association library regularly and taught her children Japanese. She intends for her children to attend local schools, and to be raised as Singaporeans who also speak Japanese and understand Japanese culture. In our follow-up interview, though, her elder daughter was already in Japan staying with her grandmother. She would live in Japan and attend elementary school there while the rest of the family remained in Singapore. According to N.K., her daughter likes the Japanese school environment and has opted to study in Japan after spending a month there during a Singapore school holiday. She thought the immersion would provide a good opportunity for her daughter to learn to become Japanese.

The above two instances of returning to Japan may be uncommon among women who are married to non-Japanese. However, they show migration as a dynamic process, where, once married, the female migrants are not necessarily permanent emigrants but may move back to their home country bringing their transnational family with them. The women – from the negative sense of perpetuating the Japanese village mentality among themselves, to preserving Japanese culture and language among their bicultural children and non-Japanese husbands – are significant players in an increasingly globalized world where women constitute part of the transnational flows.

Conclusion

This chapter has focused on the intersection of work, marriage, and being Japanese among Japanese female immigrants in contemporary Singapore.

By examining work among Japanese women, especially among Japanese expatriate wives, we challenge the stereotypical notions of Japanese expatriate wives as a non-productive, leisurely group – a shadow population to their *chûzai-in* husbands. Despite struggles with the dominant Japanese village, the determination to work among this group of expatriate wives signals the significance of work as a measure of satisfaction and meaning.

As women leave their friends, workplaces, and communities to relocate with their husbands overseas, the circumstances of being a trailing spouse often leave them in a social and emotional vacuum. Employment thus provides them with means of coping with the new environment. To Japanese expatriate wives, the workplace further provides a refuge from the competitive, suspicious, and vertical nature of relationships in the world of expatriate wives:

> I am glad that working part-time here [at the Japanese Supplementary School] allows me to meet many types of Japanese women. There are wives of *chûzai-in*, Japanese who married Singaporean, Malaysian, and Hong Kong men, as well as people who are working elsewhere on employment visas but still "moonlight" here. Among us, while they are addressed variously as Mrs. X or wife of Mr. President [of the company] outside, over here, these statuses do not matter; we are equal as *sensei* [teachers].
>
> (D.H., part-time working wife of Singaporean; no children)

Work, beyond the narrow definition of paid work, also includes community volunteering as yet another avenue to build social ties. The women's section of the Japanese Association, for example, is an active volunteer group that visits over a hundred social welfare agencies a year. These women also organize bazaars and charity events where more than S$100,000 (US$60,000) is raised yearly to support their charities (Ng 2002).

There is also a broad spectrum of community work opportunities beyond those organized by national-based associations. This includes volunteer service helplines for the Japanese, editing community magazines, or working as volunteer guides in the history museum. Women in these groups come together for a common purpose and interest, different from "neighborhood friends." They provide spaces for the cultivation of peer and social ties based more on equal exchanges and communication:

> I like history, and I would like to become a Japanese volunteer guide at the Singapore History Museum after I am settled in. It is not just to know more about Singapore; I am keen to make friends with other Japanese expatriate wives who have an interest in history. If I only have friends who are housewives from the same company, my world will become too narrow.
>
> (O.R., full-time home-maker expatriate wife; no children)

It is recognized that Japanese are dispersing across the world more rapidly, and in greater variety, than ever before (Befu 2000: 40). This is especially true among the women. As Japanese women are becoming more educated, and more globalized in outlook with their English language ability and experiences overseas (either as tourists, students, or workers), we may expect more Japanese women to step beyond Japan in search of *ikigai* through various means (including work). They are proof of the need for studies on migration in Japan to accommodate a diversity of migrant women – which include, but are not limited to, the three groups studied in this chapter: single working women, expatriate wives (who are commonly subsumed as passive followers of *chûzai-in*), and women who migrated to become wives and mothers of transnational households. A study of gendered variations in Japanese migration also contributes to the growing attention to studies of women and migration, which have so far focused mostly on migrant women as unskilled laborers in factories and domestic helpers (cf. Pedraza 1991; Huang and Yeoh 1996; Romero 1998; Kofman 2000). Thus this study is offered as a microcosm of activity that no doubt will expand greatly in the future.

Acknowledgments

This study was funded by the National University of Singapore Research Fund (R-112-000-006-112). We are grateful to the individuals who have contributed to this research.

Notes

1 In Japan, although age and gender discrimination are discouraged by law, age discrimination is still largely present, particularly among women above forty years old (Ueno 2000).
2 In Yeoh and Khoo's (1998) study of female expatriates in Singapore, 81 percent of their survey sample (N = 194) had engaged in paid work in their own countries, but only 44.8 percent continued to work in Singapore.
3 Terms coined by E. Cohen (1977) such as "environment bubble" and enclave are commonly used to characterize communities all over the world showing similar behaviors in forming shelters that have the familiarity of one's home environment, including the creation of a range of services such as restaurants or schools.
4 This is an estimate from the Japanese Embassy. It was estimated at around 27,000 in 1997, showing shrinkage due to the economic climate in the region (*Straits Times*, October 19, 2003).
5 Currently, employers have to pay a monthly stipend of S$345 (US$200) to the government on top of the salary paid to the maid.

References

Aarim-Heriot, Najia (2003) *Chinese Americans, African Americans, and Racial Anxiety in the United States, 1848–82*, Urbana: University of Illinois Press.

Abinales, Patricio N. (2000) *Making Mindanao: Cotabato and Davao in the Formation of the Philippine Nation-state*, Manila: Ateneo de Manila University Press.

Adachi, Ken (1991) *The Enemy That Never Was: A History of the Japanese Canadians*, Toronto: McClelland and Stewart. Originally published in 1976.

Adachi, Nobuko (1998) "Gender Roles, Women's Speech, and Ethnic and Community Boundaries in a Japanese-Brazilian Commune," in S. Wertheim, A. C. Bailey, and M. Corston-Oliver (eds) *Engendering Communication: Proceedings of the Fifth Berkeley Women's Language Conference*, Berkeley: Berkeley Women and Language Group, University of California, pp. 1–12.

—— (1999) "Japanese Voices in the Brazilian Forest: Cultural Maintenance and Reformed Ethnic Identity in a Transplanted Community," *World Communication*, 28(2): 68–82.

—— (2001) "Japanese Brazilians: The Japanese Language Communities in Brazil," *Studies in the Linguistic Sciences*, 31(1): 161–78.

—— (2004) "Is *Japonês* a Marker of Social Class, or a Key Term in the Discourse of Race?: Japanese 'Racial Diasporas' in Brazil," in *Latin American Perspectives*, 31(3): 48–76.

Akachi, Jesús K., Carlos, T. Kasuga, Manuel S. Hurakami, Maria E. Ota Mishima, Enrique Shibayama, and René Tanaka (2002) "Japanese Mexican Historical Overview," in A. Kikumura-Yano (ed.), pp. 204–21.

Amano, Yoshikazu (1940) *Manshû Kaitaku Nenkan: Shôwa 15 nenban* [Frontier Manchuria Yearbook 1940], Dairen: Manshûkoku tsûshinsha.

Amemiya, Kozy (1999) "The Bolivian Connection: U.S. Bases and Okinawan Emigration," in C. Johnson (ed.) *Okinawa: Cold War Island*, Cardiff, CA: Japan Policy Research Institute, pp. 53–69.

—— (2001) "The Importance of Being Japanese in Bolivia," *JPRI* Working Paper, 75 (March).

—— (2002a) "The 'Labor Pains' in Forging a Nikkei community: A Study of the Santa Cruz Region in Bolivia," in L. Hirabayashi, A. Kikumura-Yano, and J. Hirabayashi (eds), pp. 90–107.

—— (2002b) "Reinventing Population Problems in Okinawa: Emigration as a Tool of American Occupation," *JPRI* Working Paper, 90 (November).

—— (2004) "Celebrating Okinawans in Bolivia," *JPRI Critique*, XI (4: September).

Anderson, Benedict (1994) "Exodus," *Critical Inquiry*, 20(2): 314–27.

Andô, Tatsuo (1973) *Daigaku-e no Nihonshi* [University Japanese History], Tokyo: Kenbun-shoin.
Aoki, Morihisa (1995) "The Japanese Ambassador to Peru," *Revista Oficial COPANI VIII, Peru*, pp. 4–5.
Appadurai, Arjun (1996) *Modernity at Large: Cultural Dimensions of Globalization*, Minneapolis: University of Minnesota Press.
Arakaki, Makoto (2002) "The Uchinanchu Diaspora and the Boundary of 'Nikkei,'" in L. Hirabayashi, A. Kikumura-Yano, and J. Hirabayashi (eds), pp. 296–309.
Araki, Raul (2002) "An Approach to the Formation of Nikkei Identity in Peru: Issei and Nisei," in L. Hirabayashi, A. Kikumura-Yano, and J. Hirabayashi (eds), pp. 76–89.
Araragi, Shinzô (1994) *Manshû Imin no Rekishi Shakaigaku* [The Historical Sociology of the Immigrants to Manchuria], Kyoto: Kôro-sha.
Archuleta, Margaret L., Brenda J. Child, and K. Tsianina Lomawaima (eds) (2000) *Away from Home: American Indian Boarding School Experiences, 1879–2000*, Phoenix, AR: Heard Museum.
Aruego, Jose M. (1954) *Philippine Government in Action*, Manila: University Publishing Company.
Asahi Shimbun (1992) *Asahi Shimbun Japan Almanac 1993*, Tokyo: Asahi Shimbun Publishing Company.
—— (1998) *Asahi Shimbun Japan Almanac 1999*, Tokyo: Asahi Shimbun Publishing Company.
—— (2002) *Asahi Shimbun Japan Almanac 2003*, Tokyo: Asahi Shimbun Publishing Company.
Azuma, Eiichiro (2005) *Between Two Empires: Race, History, and Transnationalism in Japanese America*, New York: Oxford University Press.
Bagamaspad, Anavic and Zenaida Hamada-Pawid (1985) *A Peoples' History of Benguet Province*, Baguio: Baguio Printing & Publishing Company.
Baía, Larissa R. (1999) "Rethinking Transnationalism: Reconstructing National Identities Among Peruvian Catholics in New Jersey," *Journal of Inter-American Studies and World Affairs*, 41(4): 93–109.
Basch, Linda, Nina Glick Schiller, and Cristina Szanton Blanc (1994) *Nations Unbound: Transnational Projects, Postcolonial Predicaments, and Deterritorialized Nation-States*, Amsterdam: Gordon and Breach.
Befu, Harumi (1983) "Internationalization of Japan and Nihon Bunkaron," in H. Mannari and H. Befu (eds) *The Challenge of Japan's Internationalization: Organization and Culture*, Tokyo: Kwansei Gakuin University and Kodansha International, pp. 232–66.
—— (2000) "Globalization as Human Dispersal: From the Perspective of Japan," in J. S. Eades, T. Gill, and H. Befu (eds) *Globalization and Social Change in Contemporary Japan*, Melbourne: Trans Pacific Press, pp. 17–40.
Ben-Ari, Eyal (2002) *Going National: The Japanese Community in Contemporary Singapore*. Online. Available www.aems.uiuc.edu/HTML/UAS/BenAri.html (accessed 9 July 2005).
Ben-Ari, Eyal and Yong, Vanessa (2000) "Twin Marginalized: Single Japanese Female Expatriates in Singapore," in J. Clammer and E. Ben-Ari (eds) *Japan in Singapore: Japanese Occurrences and Cultural Flows*, London: Curzon Press, pp. 82–111.

Berrios, Rueben (2001) "Peru and Japan: Uneasy Relationship," Japan Center for Area Studies, National Museum of Ethnology, Osaka, Japan, Occasional Paper No. 10: 3–22.
Beyer, H. Otley (dir.) (1917) *Population of the Philippine Islands in 1916*, Manila: Philippine Education Co.
—— (1921) *The Non-Christian People of the Philippines*, Manila: Bureau of Printing.
Blasier, Cole (1971) "The United States and the Revolution," in J. M. Malloy and R. S. Thorn (eds) *Beyond the Revolution: Bolivia Since 1952*, Pittsburgh: University of Pittsburgh Press, pp. 53–109.
Bolivia Colonia Okinawa Nyûshoku 25 Shûnen Hensan Iinkai (1979) *Bolivia Colonia Okinawa Nyûshoku 25 Shûnenshi*, Place and Publisher unknown.
Braziel, Jana Evans and Anita Mannur (2003) *Theorizing Diaspora*, Oxford: Blackwell.
Brunhouse, Robert L. (1940) "Lascars in Pennsylvania," *Pennsylvania History*, 7: 20–30.
Calvo, Thomas (1983) "Japoneses en Guadalajara: 'Blancos de Honor' durante El Seiscientos Mexicano [Japanese in Guadalahara: 'Honorary Whites' in Sixteenth Century Mexico]," *Revista de Indias* (Madrid), 43(172): 533–47.
Campbell, Persia Crawford (1923) *Chinese Coolie Emigration within the British Empire*, London: P. S. King & Son.
Canada (1885) *Report of the Royal Commission on Chinese Immigration*, Ottawa.
—— (1902) *Report of the Royal Commission on Chinese and Japanese Immigration, 1902*, Ottawa.
—— (1947) *Report on the Re-establishment of Japanese in Canada, 1944–1946*, Ottawa: Department of Labor.
Chan, Sucheng (1986) *This Bittersweet Soil: The Chinese in California Agriculture, 1860–1910*, Berkeley: University of California Press.
Ching, Leo T. S. (2001) *Becoming Japanese: Colonial Taiwan and the Politics of Identity Formation*, Berkeley: University of California Press.
Ciccarelli, Orazio (1982) "Peru's Anti-Japanese Campaign in the 1930's: Economic Dependency and Abortive Nationalism," *Canadian Review of Studies in Nationalism*, 9(1): 115–33.
Clark, Gregory (2005) "Japan; Migration Conundrum," Online. Available at: www.japanfocus.org/217.html (accessed 25 April 2005).
Clementi, Cecil (1915) *The Chinese in British Guiana*, Georgetown, British Guiana.
Clifford, James (1994) "Diasporas," *Cultural Anthropology*, 9(3): 302–38.
Cody, Cecil E. (1959) "The Japanese Way of Life in Prewar Davao," *Philippine Studies*, 7(2): 172–86.
Cohen, E. (1977) "Expatriate Communities," *Current Sociology*, 24(3): 5–90.
Cohen, Robin (1997) *Global Diasporas: An Introduction*, Seattle: University of Washington Press.
Coman, Katharine (1978 [1903]) *The History of Contract Labor in the Hawaiian Islands*, New York: Arno.
Conroy, Hilary (1978 [1953]) *The Japanese Frontier in Hawaii, 1868–1898*, Berkeley: University of California Press.
Constantino, Renato (1975) *A History of the Philippines: From the Spanish Colonization to the Second World War*, New York and London: Monthly Review Press.
Cotia Sangyô Kumiai Chûô-kai Kankô Iin-kai (ed.) (1987) *Cotia Sangyô Kumiai Chûô-kai: 60-nen no Ayumi* [Cotia Industrial Cooperation: Its 60 Years of History], São Paulo: Tupão Press.

CWRIC (1982) *Personal Justice Denied. Report of the Commission on Wartime Relocation and Internment of Civilians*, Washington, DC: Government Printing Office.

Daniels, Roger (1962) *The Politics of Prejudice: The Anti-Japanese Movement in California and the Struggle for Japanese Exclusion*, Berkeley: University of California Press.

—— (1970) *The Politics of Prejudice: The Anti-Japanese Movement in California and the Struggle for Japanese Exclusion*, New York: Atheneum. Originally published in 1967.

—— (1988) *Asian America: Chinese and Japanese in the United States*, Seattle: University of Washington Press.

—— (2000) "The Japanese Diaspora: The New World, 1868–1990," *Pan-Japan: The International Journal of the Japanese Diaspora*, 1(1): 13–23.

—— (2004) *Guarding the Golden Door: American Immigration Policy and Immigrants since 1882*, New York: Hill & Wang.

Davids, Jules (ed.) (1973) *American Diplomatic and Public Papers: The United States and China. Vol. 17: The Coolie Trade and Chinese Emigration*, Wilmington, DL: Scholarly Resources.

Doi, Yatarô (1980) *Yamaguchi-ken Ôshima-gun Hawai Iminshi* [History of Migration to Hawaii from Ôshima County, Yamaguchi Prefecture], Tokuyama: Matsuno Shoten.

Douglass, Mike and Glenda S. Roberts (2000) "Japan in a Global Age of Migration," in M. Douglass and G. S. Roberts (eds) *Japan and Global Migration: Foreign Workers and the Advent of a Multicultural Society*, London: Routledge, pp. 3–37.

Dresner, Jonathan (2001) "Emigration and Local Development in Meiji era Yamaguchi," unpublished thesis, Harvard University.

Duus, Peter (1976) *The Rise of Modern Japan*, Boston, MA: Houghton Mifflin.

—— (1989) "Introduction: Japan's Informal Empire in China, 1895–1937. An Overview," in P. Duus, R. H. Myers, and M. R. Peattie (eds) *The Japanese Informal Empire in China, 1895–1937*, Princeton, NJ: Princeton University Press, pp. xi–xxix.

Ericson, Steven (1983) "Matsukata Fiscal Policy," *Kodansha Encyclopedia of Japan*, 4: 133–4.

Ethnic Studies Oral History Project and United Okinawan Association of Hawaii (1981) *Uchinanchu: A History of Okinawans in Hawaii*, Honolulu: Ethnic Studies Oral History Project, University of Hawaii.

FBI (Federal Bureau of Investigation) (1942) "Totalitarian Activities in Peru Today," FBI Report, May, in *Harry L. Hopkins Papers*, Franklin D. Roosevelt Presidential Library, Hyde Park, New York.

Firipin Zanryû Nipponjin Tokubetsu Chôsa Iinkai (1995) *Zanryû-sha Chôsa Hôkoku* [A Research Report on the Japanese Remaining], Unpublished papers.

Fuchs, Lawrence H. (1961) *Hawaii Pono: A Social History*, New York: Harcourt, Brace, Jovanovich.

Fujimori, Alberto (1995) "Speech of the Constitutional President of Peru," *Revista Oficial COPANI VIII*, Peru, pp. 6–7.

Fujimura, Jandira (1970) "Burajiru ni Okeru Nikkei Mura Shakai no Kôzô to sono Tenakai Katei: Nikkie Nômin o Chûshin to Shite (The Structure and Process of the Formation of Society in a Nikkei Village: Focusing on the Lives of Nikki Farmers)," *Ijû Kenkyû* [Migration Research], 7: 37–51.

Fukumoto, Mary (1997) *Hacia Un Nuevo Sol: Japonesas y Sus Descendientes en el Perú* [Toward a New Sun: The Japanese and their descendants in Peru], Lima: Asociación Peruano Japonesa del Perú.

Furnivall, J. S. (1939) *Netherlands India: A Study of Plural Economy*, London: Cambridge University Press.

Furukawa, Yoshizô (1956) *Dabao Kaitaku-ki* [The Report of Development in Davao], Tokyo: Furukawa Takushoku Corp.

Furuki, Toshihiro (2000) "Rapasu Nikkeishakai no 100-nen (A Hundred Years of Nikkei in La Paz)," in The Japanese Immigration in Bolivia Centennial Committee (ed.) *Borivia ni Ikiru: Nihonjin Ijû 100-shunenshi* [To Live in Bolivia: The Centennial of Japanese Immigration], Santa Cruz, Bolivia: Fedración Nacional de Asociaciones Bolivano-Japonesas, pp. 125–52.

Furusawa, Isojirô (1936) "Dabao no Genchi o Tazunete (Visiting Davao)," in R. Hasegawa (ed.) *Nanpô Seisaku o Genchi ni Miru* [Watching Japan's Policy in the South]. Tokyo: Nippon Gaiji Kyôkai, pp. 55–106.

Gardiner, C. Harvey (1975) *The Japanese and Peru*, Albuquerque: University of New Mexico Press.

—— (1981) *Pawns in a Triangle of Hate: The Peruvian Japanese and the United States*, Seattle: University of Washington Press.

—— (1986) "The Latin-American Japanese and World War II," in R. Daniels, S. C. Taylor, and H. H. L. Kitano (eds) *Japanese Americans: From Relocation to Redress*, Salt Lake City: University of Utah Press, pp. 142–5.

Gardner, William O. (2003) "Mongrel Modernism: Hayashi Fumiko's *Hôrôki* and Mass Culture," *Journal of Japanese Studies*, 29(1): 69–101.

Gibney, Frank (ed.) (1995) *Sensô: The Japanese Remember the Pacific War*, Armonk, New York: M. E. Sharpe.

Gloria, Heidi K. (1987) *The Bagobos: Their Ethnohistory and Acculturation*, Manila: New Days Publishers.

Gonzales, Michael J. (1985) *Plantation Agriculture and Social Control in Northern Peru, 1875–1933*, Austin: University of Texas Press.

Goodman, Grant K. (1967) *Davao: A Case Study in Japan–Philippine Relations*, Kansas City: The University of Kansas Press.

Gordon, Andrew (1988) *The Evolution of Labor Relations in Japan: Heavy Industry, 1853–1955*, Cambridge, MA: Council on East Asian Studies/Harvard University Press.

Gordon, Milton M. (1964) *Assimilation in American Life: The Role of Race, Religion, and National Origins*, New York: Oxford University Press.

Graham, Richard (1993) "1850–1870," in L. Bethell (ed.) *Brazil: Empire and Republic, 1822–1930*, Cambridge: Cambridge University Press, pp. 113–60.

Guardados, Johanna Joyce R. (2001) "The Bagobo Clata of Calinan, Davao City," in J. Guardados, A. Mercedes, M. Onggo, L. Cua, D. Lobos, A. Cruz, and M. Ompang (eds) *Mindanao Ethnic Communities: Patterns of Growth and Change*, Manila: The Center for Integrative and Development Studies, University of the Philippines, pp. 1–20.

Guerrero, Milagros C. (1967) *A Survey of Japanese Trade and Investments in the Philippines, with Special References to Philippine–American Relations 1900–1941*, Manila: University of the Philippines.

Hadfield, Peter (1995) *The Coming Tokyo Earthquake*, Boston, MA: Charles Tuttle Co.

Hagihara, Akiko and Grace Shimizu (2002) "The Japanese Latin American Wartime and Redress Experience," *Amerasia Journal*, 28(2): 203–16.

Hall, Stuart (1990) "Cultural Identity and Diaspora," in J. Rutherford (ed.), pp. 222–37.

—— (1997) "The Local and the Global: Globalization and Ethnicity," in A. McClintock, A. Mufti, and E. Shohat (eds) *Dangerous Liaisons: Gender, Nation, and Postcolonial Perspectives*, Minneapolis: University of Minnesota Press, pp. 173–87.
Hamabata, Matthew (1990) *Crested Kimono: Power and Love in the Japanese Business Family*, Ithaca, NY: Cornell University Press.
Hamada, Sinai C. (1983) "The Japanese In and Around Baguio Before the War," in Filipino Japanese Friendship Association of Northern Luzon (ed.) *Memorial: The Japanese in the Construction of Kennon Road*, unpublished pamphlet, pp. 22–5.
Handa, Tomô (1970) *Imin no Seikatsu no Rekishi: Burajiru Nikkei-jin no Ayunda Michi* [The History of Japanese Immigrants: How the Japanese Brazilians Passed This Way], São Paulo: Centrode Estudos Nipo-Brazilerios.
Hane, Mikiso (1982) *Peasants, Rebels, and Outcastes: The Underside of Modern Japan*, New York: Pantheon Books.
—— (1986) *Modern Japan: A Historical Survey*, Boulder, CO: Westview Press.
Harootunian, Harry D. (1988) *Things Seen and Unseen: Discourse and Ideology in Tokugawa Nativism*, Chicago, IL: University of Chicago Press.
Hasegawa, Ryô (ed.) (1936) *Nanpô Seisaku o Genchi ni Miru* [Watching Japan's Policy in the South], Tokyo: Nippon Gaiji Kyôkai.
Hattori, Ryûzô (1939) "Dabao ni okeru Dai-nisei Kyôiku [Education of the Nisei in Davao]," *Umi o Koete* [Over the Ocean], 2(11): 25–8.
Hayakawa, Toyohira (1940) "Bagio-shi to Zairyû-hôjin [Baguio City and Japanese Residents]," *Umi o Koete* [Over the Ocean], 3(4): 23–4.
Hayase, Shinzo (1984) *Tribes, Settlers, and Administrators on a Frontier: Economic Development and Social Change in Davao, Southeastern Mindanao, the Philippines, 1899–1941*, unpublished thesis, Murdoch University (Australia).
Hayden, Joseph Ralston (1942) *The Philippines: A Study in National Development*, New York: The Macmillan Company.
Hazama, Dorothy Ochiai and Jane Okamoto Komeiji (1986) *Okage Sama De: The Japanese in Hawaii, 1885–1985*, Honolulu: Bess Press.
Heco, Joseph (1863) *Hyoryuki* [A Castaway's Account], Edo: Publisher unknown.
—— (1895) *The Narrative of a Japanese: What He has Seen and the People He has Met in the Course of the Last Forty Years*, San Francisco, CA: American-Japanese Publishing Association.
—— (1955) *Floating on the Pacific Ocean*, Los Angeles, CA: Glen Dawson.
Helly, Denise (ed.) (1993) *The Cuba Commission Report: A Hidden History of the Chinese in Cuba: The Original English-language Text of 1876*, Baltimore, MD: Johns Hopkins University Press.
Higashide, Seiichi (1993) *Adios to Tears: The Memoirs of a Japanese-Peruvian Internee in U.S. Concentration Camps*, Honolulu: E & E Kudo.
—— (2000) *Adios to Tears: The Memoirs of a Japanese-Peruvian Internee in U.S. Concentration Camps*, Seattle: University of Washington Press.
Higman, B. W. (1972) "The Chinese in Trinidad, 1806–1838," *Caribbean Studies*, 12(3): 22.
Hinkôshô kôsho (1940) *Dai Sanji Kaitakudan Mizuho Mura Gokanenshi* [The Five-year History of Mizuho Village of the Third Immigration Group], Harbin: Hinkôshô kôsho.
Hirabayashi, Lane, Akemi Kikumura-Yano, and Jim Hirabayashi (2002) *New Worlds, New Lives: Globalization and People of Japanese Descent in the Americas and from Latin America in Japan*, Stanford, CA: Stanford University Press.

Hirano Shokuminchi Nihonjinkai (1931) *Hirano 25-nen-shi* [Twenty-five Years of the Hirano Community], São Paulo: Nippakusha.

Hirose, Naomi, Maria Teresa Senda, and Ariel Takeda (2002) "Supplementary Materials," in A. Kikumura-Yano (ed.), pp. 197–201.

Hiroshima Prefecture (1980) *Hiroshima Kenshi: Kindai Tsuushi, Jôkan* [History of Hiroshima Prefecture: Modern, Part One, First Part], Hiroshima: Toppan Printing.

—— (1991) *Hiroshima-ken Ijûshi: Shiryô-hen* [History of Hiroshima Prefecture Migration: Documents], Hiroshima: Daiichi Hôki Publishing.

—— (1993) *Hiroshima-ken Ijûshi: Tsûshi-hen* [History of Hiroshima Prefecture Migration: Narrative], Hiroshima: Daiichi Hôki Publishing.

Hitô Chôsa Iinkai (ed.) (1993) *Gokuhi Hitô Chôsa Hôkoku* [Top Secret Research Report on the Philippines], vol. 1 and vol. 2, Tokyo: Ryûkei Shosha.

Hiura, Barbara (2000) "The Japanese Cuban Experience, Part I and Part II," *Hokubei Mainichi*, September 27.

Hobsbawm, Eric (ed.) (1983) *The Invention of Tradition*, Cambridge: Cambridge University Press.

Hoffman, Katherine E. (2004) "Review of Ruba Salih, *Gender in Transnationalism: Home, Longing and Belonging Among Moroccan Migrant Women*," H-Gender-MidEast, H-Net Reviews, November. Online. Available at: www.hnet.org/reviews/showrev.cgi?path=194971100891542 (accessed 11 January 2005).

Huang, Shirlena and Brenda Yeoh (1996) "Ties That Bind: State Policy and Migrant Female Domestic Helpers in Singapore," *Geoforum*, 19(4): 479–93.

Hu-DeHart, Evelyn (1980) "Immigrants to a Developing Society: The Chinese in Northern Mexico, 1875–1932," *Journal of Arizona History*, 21(3): 275–312.

Huttenback, Robert A. (1976) *Racism and Empire: White Settlers and Colored Immigrants in the British Self-Governing Colonies, 1830–1910*, Ithaca, NY: Cornell University Press.

Ichioka, Yuji (1988) *The Issei: The World of the First Generation Japanese Immigrants, 1885–1924*, New York: The Free Press.

Ide, Magoroku (1993) *Man-mô no Ken'eki to Kaitaku-dan no Higeki* [National Interests in Manchuria and Mongolia and the Tragedy of the Agrarian Settlers], Tokyo: Iwanami.

Ikeda, Kaoru (1990) "Surôkan Idô Nikki [Slocan Relocation Diary]," in S. Tsuji (ed.), pp. 77–101.

Ikuno, Eriko (2000) "Nihon ni Okeru Nikkei Boribiajin Shakai [Nikkei Bolivian Community in Japan]," in The Japanese Immigration in Bolivia Centennial Committee (ed.) *Borivia ni Ikiru: Nihonjin Ijû 100-shunenshi* [To Live in Bolivia: The Centennial of Japanese Immigration], Santa Cruz, Bolivia: Federación Nacional de Asociaciones Boliviano-Japonesas, pp. 293–310.

Imamura, Ann (1987) *Urban Japanese Housewives*, Honolulu: Hawaii University Press.

Imin 80-Nin-Shi Hensan Iinkai (ed.) (1991) *Burajiru Nihon Imin 80-Nen-shi* [Brazil: Eighty Years of Japanese-Brazilian History], São Paulo: Tupán Press.

Inobushi, Kiyoshi (1936) "Dabao no Nipponjin [The Japanese in Davao]," in R. Hasegawa (ed.), pp. 267–314.

Irick, Robert L. (1982) *Ch'ing Policy toward the Coolie Trade, 1847–1878*, Taipei, Taiwan: Chinese Materials Center.

Irie, Hisao (1941) *Kaitakumin Mondai* [Obstacles to Immigration], Tokyo: Chûô Kôronsha.

Irie, Toraji (1938) *Hôjin Kaigai Hatten-shi* [A History of Japanese Development Abroad], vol. 1, Tokyo: Imin Mondai Kenkyû-kai.
—— (1951a) "History of Japanese Migration to Peru, Part I," trans. W. Himel, *Hispanic American Historical Review*, 31(3): 437–52.
—— (1951b) "History of Japanese Migration to Peru, Part I," trans. W. Himel, *Hispanic American Historical Review*, 31(4): 648–64.
Iriye, Akira (1972) *Pacific Estrangement: Japanese and American Expansion, 1897–1911*, Cambridge, MA: Harvard University Press.
Irwin, Yukiko and Hilary Conroy (1972) "R. W. Irwin and Systematic Immigration to Hawaii," in H. Conroy and T. S. Miyakawa (eds) *East Across the Pacific: Historical and Sociological Studies of Japanese Immigration and Assimilation*. Santa Barbara, CA: American Bibliographic Center-Clio Press, pp. 40–55.
Ishi, Angelo A. (1992) "Burajiru Nikkei Dekasegi Rôdosha to Nihon no Shinzoku (Brazilian *Nikkei Dekasegi* Workers and Japanese Relatives)," *Mare Nostrum*, 5: 69–72.
Ishihara, Fumio (1944) *Tomiya Taisa to Katô Kanji* [Colonel Tomiya and Katô Kanji], Tokyo: Chôbunkaku.
Ishikawa, Tomonori (1967) "Yamaguchi-ken ôshima-gun, Kuga-son *shôki* hawai keiyaku imin no shakai chirigakuteki kôsatsu [A Social Geographic Study of Japanese Indentured Emigrants to Hawaii from Kuga-son, ôshima-gun, Yamaguchi Prefecture]," Hiroshima Chiri Gakkai. *Chiri Kagaku* [Geographic Science], 7: 25–38.
—— (1975) "Setonai Chiiki kara no (Shutsu) Imin [Immigration from the Seto Naikai Area]," *Shigaku Kenkyo* [Research in Historical Studies], 126: 54–71.
—— (1987) "Imin to Kokusai Kôryû [Emigrants and International Exchange]," *Shin Okinawa Bungaku*, 72: 84–98.
Ito, Kazuo (1973) *Issei: A History of Japanese Immigrants in North America*, trans. S. Nakamura and J. S. Gerard, Seattle: Japan Publications, Executive Committee for the Publication of *Issei* (Japanese Community Service).
Ivy, Marilyn (1995) *Discourses of the Vanishing: Modernity, Phantasm, Japan*, Chicago, IL: University of Chicago Press.
Jacques, Leo M. Dambourges (1974) "The Chinese Massacre in Torreon (Coahuila) in 1911," *Arizona and the West*, 16: 233–46.
Jansen, Marius B. (2000) *The Making of Modern Japan*, Cambridge: The Belknap Press of Harvard University Press.
Japan Gaimushô Ryôji Ijû-bu (1971) *Wagakokumin no Kaigai Hatten: Siryô-hen* [The Development of our Nationals Abroad: Data Volume], Tokyo: Ministry of Foreign Affairs.
Japan Institute of Labor (1995) *Nikkeijin Rôdôsha no Jûkyû Shisutemu to Shûrô Keiken* [The Demand/Supply System and Employment Experiences of Nikkeiin Workers], Tokyo: Japan Institute of Labor.
Japanese American National Museum (1999) *International Nikkei Research Project First Year Report. April 1, 1997 to March 31, 1998*, Los Angeles, CA: Japanese American National Museum.
JICA (Japan International Cooperation Agency) (ed.) (1994) *Nihon o Suteta Nihonjin*, Tokyo: Soshisha.
Jomo Shinbun (ed.) (1997) *Sanba no Machi Kara: Gaikokujin to Tomoni Ikiru – Gunma, Ôizumi* [From the City of Samba: Life with Foreigners in Ôizumi, Gumma Prefecture], Gumma, Japan: Jomo Shinbun, Inc.

262 References

Jones, F. C. (1949) *Manchuria Since 1931*, London: Oxford University Press.

"Kaitakuchi no Seikatsu Shidô (A Guide to Frontier Settlement Life)"(1944) *Kaitaku* [Frontier], 8(1): 35–58.

Kajita, Takamichi (1994) *Gaikokujin Rôdôsha to Nihon* [Foreign Laborers and Japan], Tokyo: NHK Books.

Kami, Shôichirô (1973) *Manmô Kaitaku Seishônen Giyûgun* [The Patriotic Youths Corps of Manchuria-Mongolia], Tokyo: Chûô Kôronsha.

Kamohara, Hiroji (1938) *Dabao Hôjin Kaitaku-shi* [A History of Japanese Pioneering in Davao], Davao: Nippi Shimbun-sha.

Kanegae, Seitarô (1968) *Aruite Kita Michi* [The Road Where I Walked], Tokyo: Kokusei-sha.

Kasamatsu, Emi (2002) "Japanese Paraguayan Historical Overview," in A. Kikumura-Yano (ed.), pp. 230–40.

Katô, Kanji (1943) *Nô to Nihon Seishin* [Agriculture and the Japanese National Spirit], Tokyo: Chitose Shobô.

Kato, Ryuhei (1996) *Meishin* [Myth], Mexico City: Meishinkai.

Kawakami, Barbara F. (1993) *Japanese Immigrant Clothing in Hawaii, 1885–1941*, Honolulu: University of Hawaii Press.

Keizai Koho Center (ed.) (2004) *Japan 2004: An International Comparison*, Tokyo: Kezai Koho Center.

Kelsky, Karen (2001) *Women on the Verge: Japanese Women, Western Dreams*, Durham, NC: Duke University Press.

Kevles, Daniel J. (1985) *In the Name of Eugenics: Genetics and the Uses of Human Heredity*, New York: Alfred A. Knopf.

Kikumura-Yano, Akemi (ed.) (2002) *The Encyclopedia of Japanese Descendants in the Americas: An Illustrated History of the Nikkei*, Walnut Creek: AltaMira Press.

Kimura, Kai (2004) "Nihon Kindaishi kara Nuke Ochita Burajiruojûshi [The Unwritten History of Migration to Brazil in Modern Japanese History]," *Correspeondência da Aliança/Ariansa Tûshin*, 16: 4–7.

Kimura, Rei (1998) *Alberto Fujimori of Peru: The President Who Dared to Dream*, London: Eyelevel Books.

Kimura, Yukiko (1988) *Issei: Japanese Immigrants in Hawaii*, Honolulu: University of Hawaii Press.

Kin-chô-shi Hensan Iinkai (ed.) (1996) *Kin-chô-shi, Dai Ikkan, Imin: Shôgen-hen* [A History of Kinchô, vol. 1: Migrants. Volume of Interviews], Okinawa: Kin-chô Board of Education.

Kinshichi, Norio, Ikunori Sumida, Kunihiko Takahashi, and Mikio Tomino (2000) *Burajiru Kenkyu Nyû-mon: Shirarezaru Taikoku 500-nen no Kiseki*, Tokyo: Kôyô-Shobô.

Kita, Itsuo (1944) *Manshû kaitaku ron* [A Treatise on Manchurian Immigration], Tokyo: Meibundô.

Kitagawa, Toyoie (1996) "Hamamatsushi ni Okeru Nikkei Burajirujin no Seikatsu Kôzô to Ishiki: Nippaku Ryôkoku Chôsa o Fumaete [The Lives and Consciousness of the Brazilian Nikkeijin in Hamamatsu City: Based on Surveys in Both Japan and Brazil]," *Tôyô Daigaku Shakai Gakubu Kiyô* [Bulletin of the Department of Sociology at Tôyô University], 34(1): 109–96.

—— (1997) "Burajiru-taun no Keisei to Deasupora: Nikkei Burajirujin no Teijyuka ni Kansuru Nananen Keizoku Oizumi-machi Chôsa [Diaspora and the Formation of Brazil Town: A Continuing Seven-year Oizumi Town Survey about the

Settlement of Brazilian Nikkeijin]," *Tôyô Daigaku Shakai Gakubu Kiyô* [Bulletin of the Department of Sociology at Tôyô University], 34(3): 66–173.

Kiyama, Henry (Yoshitaka) (1999) *The Four Immigrants Manga*, trans. Frederik Schodt, Berkeley, CA: Stone Bridge Press.

Klein, Herbert S. (1992) *Bolivia: The Evolution of a Multi-ethnic Society*, New York, Oxford: Oxford University Press.

Kobayashi, Audrey (1989) *A Demographic Profile of Japanese Canadians and Social Implications for the Future*, Ottawa: Secretary of State.

Kodama, Masa'aki (1978) "Setonai Chiiki no Kan'yaku Imin [Government-sponsored Emigrants from the Seto Inland Sea Region]," in Y. Tetsumae (ed.) *Seto Naikai Chiiki no Shiteki Kenkyû* [Seto Inland Sea Region Historical Research], Hiroshima: Fukumin Shobô, pp. 325–60.

—— (1992) *Nihon Iminshi Kenkyû Josetsu* [Japanese Emigrant History: An Historical Introduction], Hiroshima: Keisui-sha.

Kodansha (ed.) (1993) *Japan: An Illustrated Encyclopedia*, 2 vols, Tokyo: Kodansha.

Kofman, Elizabeth (2000) "The Invisibility of Skilled Female Migrants and Gender Relations in Studies of Skilled Migration in Europe," *International Journal of Population Geography*, 6: 45–90.

Kogawa, Joy (1981) *Obasan*, Toronto: Lester and Orpen Dennys.

—— (1990) "Odoroki, Warai, Ai (Surprise, Laugh, and Love)," in S. Tsuji (ed.), pp. 48–73.

Kojima, Suguru (1996) *Nanyô Kanyo no Tajûsei to Kyôiku no Ronri* [Many Aspects of Japanese Engagement with the South Seas and Educational Logic], Pamphlet.

Komai, Hiroshi (ed.) (1998) *Shinrai: Teijû Gaikokujin Shiryôshûsei, Jôkan* [Newcomers: Data of Foreign Settlers in Japan, vol. 1], Tokyo: Akashi-Shoten.

Komiya, Kiyoshi (1990) *Manshû memori mappu* [Manchuria Memory Map], Tokyo: Chikuma Shobô.

Kondo, Dorinne K. (1986) "Dissolution and Reconstitution of Self: Implications for Anthropological Epistemology," *Cultural Anthropology*, 1(1): 74–88.

Kôsei-shô (ed.) (1997) *Engo Gojû-nen-shi* [The 50-year History of Assistance Extended to Repatriates], Tokyo: Gyôsei.

Koshiro, Yukiko (1999) *Trans-Pacific Racisms and the U.S. Occupation of Japan*, New York: Columbia University Press.

Kuga-gun yakusho (1889) "Hawaikoku dekasegi roku – Meiji 22-nen [1889 Record of Labor Migration to Hawaii]," in *Yamaguchi-ken monjokan shozô shiryô shûeihyô: Gunyakusho monjo Kuga-gun 69*, Yamaguchi-ken, Japan.

Kunimoto, Iyo (2000) "Andesu kara Amazon e: Nihonjin Borivia Shôshi [From the Andes to the Amazon: An Abridged History of Japanese Immigration in Bolivia]," in The Japanese Immigration in Bolivia Centennial Committee (ed.) *Borivia ni Ikiru: Nihonjin Ijû 100-shunenshi* [To Live in Bolivia: The Centennial of Japanese Immigration], Santa Cruz, Bolivia: Federación Nacional de Asociaciones Boliviano-Japonesas, pp. 103–24.

—— (2002) "Japanese Bolivian Historical Overview," in A. Kikumura-Yano (ed.), pp. 96–110.

Kunimoto, Iyo and Yasuo Wakatsuki (1985) *La Immigración Japonesa en Bolivia: Estudios Historicos y Socio-Economicos* [Japanese Immigration in Bolivia: History and Socio-economic Studies], Tokyo: University of Chuo.

Kuwajima, Setsurô (1992) *Manshû busô imin* [Armed Immigrants in Manchuria], Tokyo: Kyôikusha.

LaFeber, Walter (1997) *The Clash: U.S.–Japanese Relations Throughout History*, New York: Norton.
Lagos, Maria L. (1994) *Autonomy and Power: The Dynamics of Class and Culture in Rural Bolivia*, Philadelphia: University of Pennsylvania Press.
Lai, Walton Look (1993) *Indentured Labor, Caribbean Sugar: Chinese and Indian Migrants to the British West Indies, 1838–1918*, Baltimore, MD: Johns Hopkins University Press.
Laumonier, Isabel (2002) "Japanese Argentine Historical Overview," in A. Kikumura-Yano (ed.), pp. 72–88.
Lebra, Takie Sugiyama (1993) *Above the Clouds: Status Culture of the Modern Japanese Nobility*, Berkeley: University of California Press.
Lehman, Kenneth D. (1997) "Revolutions and Attributions: Making Sense of Eisenhower Administration Policies in Bolivia and Guatemala," *Diplomatic History*, 21(2): 185–213.
—— (1999) *Bolivia and the United States: A Limited Partnership*, Athens: The University of Georgia Press.
Leon-Portilla, Miguel (1981) "La Embajada de los Japoneses en Mexico, 1614. El Testimonio en Nahuatl del Cronista Chimalpahin" [The Japanese Mission to Mexico, 1614: The Testimony in Nahuatl of Cronista Chimalpahin], *Estudios de Asia y Africa*, 16: 23–36.
Lesser, Jeffrey (ed.) (1999) *Negotiating National Identity: Immigrants, Minorities, and the Struggle for Ethnicity in Brazil*, Durham, NC: Duke University Press.
—— (2003) *Searching for Home Abroad*, Durham, NC: Duke University Press.
Levitt, Peggy (1998) "Social Remittances: Migration-driven Local-level Forms of Cultural Diffusion," *International Migration Review*, 32(4): 926–48.
Li, Peter S. (1977) "Fictive Kinship, Conjugal Ties and Kinship Chain Among Chinese Immigrants in the United States," *Journal of Comparative Family Studies*, 8: 47–63.
Liberal Democratic Party (1992) *Kokusaika Jidai ni Taiô Shite: Omo to Shite Gaikokujin Mondai ni Kansuru Teigen* [In Response to the Age of Internationalization: A Proposal about the Foreign Labor Problem], Tokyo: Liberal Democratic Party.
Liddle, Joanna and Sachiko Nakajima (2000) *Rising Suns, Rising Daughters: Gender, Class, and Power in Japan*, London and New York: Zen Books.
Lie, John (2001) *Multiethnic Japan*, Cambridge, MA: Harvard University Press.
Lind, Andrew W. (1968 [1938]) *An Island Community: Ecological Succession in Hawaii*, Westport, CT: Greenwood.
Lone, Stewart (2001) *The Japanese Community in Brazil, 1908–1940: Between Samurai and Carnival*, New York: Palgrave.
Luna, Juan Luis Z. Jr. (1990) *Philippine Almanac: Book of Facts 1990*, Manila: Aurora Publications.
Maeda, Hiroshi (ed.) (1986) *San Juan Ijuchi 30-nenshi* [La Historia de 30 Años de la Imigración Japonesa en San Juan de Yapacaní, Santa Cruz, Bolivia 1955–1985], Santa Cruz, Bolivia: Colonia Japonesa San Juan.
Maeda, Yunosuke (1941) "Dabao ni Okeru Manira-asa Saibai to Hôjin [Cultivation of Manila Hemp and the Japanese in Davao]," *Umi o Koete* [Over the Ocean], 4(2): 74–7.
Maeyama, Tadashi (1979) "Ethnicity, Secret Societies, and Associations: The Japanese in Brazil," *Comparative Studies in Society and History*, 21(4): 589–610.
—— (1981) *Hisôzoku-sha no Seishin-shi: Aru Nikkei Burajiru-jin no Henreki* [History of

the Psychology of Non-successors: A Case Study of a Japanese Brazilian], Tokyo: Ochanomizu Shobô.
—— (1996) *Esunishiti to Burajiru Nikkeijin* [Ethnicity and Nikkei Brazilians], Tokyo: Ochanomizu Shobô.
—— (1997) *Ihô ni 'Nihon' o Masuru: Burajiru Nikkeijin no Shûkyô to Esunisiti* [Worshipping Japan in a Foreign Country: Japanese Brazilian Religions and Ethnicity], Tokyo: Ochanomizu Shobô.
Makabe, Tomoko (1995) *Picture Brides: Japanese Women in Canada*, Toronto, ON: Multicultural History Society of Ontario.
Manshû Kaitaku-shi Kankô-kai (ed.) (1984) *Nagano-ken Manshû Kaitaku-shi: Sôron* [The History of the Colonization of Manchuria by the Agrarian Immigrants from Nagano Prefecture: An Overview], Nagano: Nagano-ken Kaitaku Jikô-kai.
Manshû Takushoku Iinkai Jimukyoku (1938) *Manshu imin teiyo* [Manchuria Immigration Handbook], Hoten: Manchukuo.
Manuel L. Quezon Papers (1919) Series IV, Box 165, Manila: National Library of the Philippines.
Masterson, Daniel M. (1991) *Militarism and Politics in Latin America: Peru from Sanchez Cerro to Sendero Luminoso*, Westport, CT: Greenwood Press.
Masterson, Daniel M. and Sayaka Funada-Classen (2004) *The Japanese in Latin America*, Urbana, IL: University of Illinois Press.
Meagher, Arnold J. (1978) *The Introduction of Chinese Laborers to Latin America: The 'Coolie Trade,' 1847–1874*, San Francisco, CA: Chinese Materials Center.
Medina, Laurie Kroshus (1997) "Defining Difference, Forging Unity: The Co-construction of Race, Ethnicity, and Nation in Belize," *Ethnic and Racial Studies*, 20(4): 757–80.
Miller, Stuart C. (1969) *The Unwelcome Immigrant: The American Image of the Chinese, 1785–1882*, Berkeley: University of California Press.
Ministry of Justice (1994) *Shutsunyukoku Kanri Gyôsei no Genjyô to Tômen no Kadai* [Administration of Immigration Control and Current Topics], ed. Immigration Control Policy Committee, Tokyo: Ministry of Justice.
Ministry of Labor (1991) *Gaikokujin Rôdôsha ga Rôdômento ni Oyobosu Eikyôto ni Kansuru Kenkyûkai* [Research Group Study on the Impact of Foreign Laborers], Tokyo: Ministry of Labor.
—— (1992) *Gaikokujin Rôdôsha ga Rôdômentô ni Oyobosu Eikyôtô ni Kansuru Kenkyûkai Senmonbukai* [Expert Research Group Study on the Impact of Foreign Laborers], Tokyo: Ministry of Labor.
Mintz, Sidney (1985) *Sweetness and Power: The Place of Sugar in Modern History*, New York: Viking Penguin.
Miyao, Susumu (1991) "Imin Kûhaku Jidai to Dôbô-shakai no Konran (The Time of No Immigration and the Chaos of Japanese Society in Brazil)," in Imin 80-Nin-Shi Hensan Iinkai (ed.) São Paulo: Tupãn Press, pp. 140–229.
Miyoshi, Masao (1979) *As We Saw Them: The First Japanese Embassy to the United States*, Berkeley: University of California Press.
Mizuki, John, Masato Ninomiya and Hironobu Kai (2002) "Japanese Brazilian Demographic Information," in A. Kikumura-Yano (ed.), pp. 143–7.
Mori, Hiromi (1994) "Nikkei Shûdanchi ni totte no 'Dekasegi' no Motsu Imi: San Nikei Shûdanchi no Dekasegi Keitai to Eikyô no Taihi o Tôshite (The Meaning of 'Dekasegi' for Areas of Nikkeijin Concentration: A Comparison of the

Composition and Influence of Dekasegi in Three Nikkei Communities)," *Ijyû Kenkyû* [Migration Research], 31: 40–57.
Mori, Koichi (2003) "Identity Transformations among Okinawans and their Descendants in Brazil," in J. Lesser (ed.), pp. 47–65.
Morimoto, Amelia (ed.) (1991) *Población de Origin Japones en el Perú: Perfil Actual* [Origins of the Japanese Population in Peru: A Contemporary Profile], Lima: Comisión Conmemorativa del 90 Aniversario de la Inmigración Japonesa al Perú.
—— (2002) "Japanese Immigrants and Their Descendants in Peru, 1899–1998," in A. Kikumura-Yano (ed.), pp. 248–58.
Moriyama, Alan Takeo (1985) *Imingaisha: Japanese Emigration Companies and Hawaii*, Honolulu: University of Hawaii Press.
Murphy-Shigematsu, Stephen (2000) "Identities of Multiethnic People in Japan," in M. Douglass and G. S. Roberts (eds) *Japan and Global Migration: Foreign Workers and the Advent of a Multicultural Society*, London: Routledge, pp. 196–216.
Myerhoff, Barbara (1980) *Number Our Days*, Carmichael, CA: Touchstone Books.
Myers, Ramon H. and Saburo Yamada (1984) "Agricultural Development in the Empire," in Ramon H. Myers and Mark R. Peattie (eds) *The Japanese Colonial Empire, 1895–1945*, Princeton, NJ: Princeton University Press, pp. 420–54.
Nakagawa, Martha (2000) "*Camaraderia* Miyasaka – Japanese Cuban Nisei," *Pacific Citizen*, 29 (September): 1–8.
Nakahara, Zentoku (ed.) (1943) *Bagobo-zoku Oboegaki* [A Memoir of the Bagobos], Tokyo: Kaizô-sha.
Nakamura, Gongoro (1981) "Selection of Overseas Emigrants," in *Uchinanchu: A History of Okinawans in Hawaii*, Honolulu: University of Hawaii, Ethnic Studies Oral History Project, Ethnic Studies Program.
Nakamura, Takeo (1939) "Dabao Zairyû Hôjin no Genjô [The Current Conditions of Japanese Residents in Davao]," *Umi o Koete* [Over the Ocean], 2(11): 6–8.
Nakane, Chie (1970) *Japanese Society*, Berkeley: University of California Press.
National Archives (1952) "Memorandum to Coolidge" from Tigner, November 15, 1952, Subject: Completion of SIRI *Study of Ryukyuan Emigration Problem and Latin American Opportunities*, National Archives: RG/319. DA-CA. E: #60. Correspondence of the Public Affairs Division, 1950–1964, Box 30. File: Ryukyuan Emigration to Bolivia.
—— (1954) "Japanese Government Warns GRI to Use Prudence in Selection of Bolivian Emigrants," *Daily Okinawan Press Summary-Okinawa Shimbun*, National Archives: RG/319, DA-CA. E: #60, Box 30. File: Ryukyuan Emigration to Bolivia, December 1950 to December 1964.
—— (1956) Office Memorandum of Dept of State from Mr. Sullivan (FE) to Mr. Robertson (FE) on "Pentagon Proposal to Bring Ryukyuan Farm Workers to the U.S.," dated August 24, 1956, National Archives: RG/59, Dept of State. General Records, 1955–1959; Central Decimal File; Box 5115; File: 894C.06/12-2055.
Ng, Wai Min (2002) "The Japanese Association and the Kowloon Club: A Study of the Japanese Community from a Comparative Perspective," in H. Hiromachi (ed.) *The Culture of Association and Associations in Contemporary Japanese Society*, Senri Ethnological Studies no. 62. National Museum of Ethnology, Osaka, Japan, pp. 75–92.
Nichiman Nôsei Kenkyû-kai (1942) *Manshû Kaitaku Kondankai Sokkiroku* [Record of a Conference on Immigration to Manchuria], July 1, Tokyo: unpublished confidential report.

Nihonjin Borivia Ijûshi Hensan Iinkai (ed.) (1970) *Nihonjin Borivia Ijûshi* [History of Japanese Immigration in Bolivia], Tokyo: The Ministry of Foreign Affairs.

Nihonjin Ijû 100 Shûnen Hensan Iinkai (2000) *Nihonjin Ijû 100 Shûnenshi: Boribia ni Ikiru* [The 100-Year Anniversary of Japanese Immigration: To Live in Bolivia], Santa Cruz: Federación Nacional de Asociaciones Boliviano-Japonesas.

Niiya, Brian (ed.) (2001) "Nikkei," in B. Niiya (ed.) *Encyclopedia of Japanese American History* (2nd edn), New York: Checkmark Books, p. 303.

Ninomiya, Masato (2002) "Japanese Brazilian Historical Overview," in A. Kikumura-Yano (ed.), pp. 116–26.

Ninomiya, Masato and Naomi Hoki Moniz (2002) "Bibliographic Essay of Japanese Immigrants and Their Descendants," in A. Kikumura-Yano (ed.), pp. 127–9.

Nojima, Toshihiko (1989) "Susumetai Nikkeijin no Tokubetsu Ukeire [Proposal for the Special Admission of the *Nikkeijin*]," *Gekkan Jiyû Minshû* [Free Citizens Monthly], November: 92–9.

Nolte, Sharon and Sally Ann Hastings (1991) "The Meiji State's Policy Towards Women, 1890–1910," in G. Bernstein (ed.) *Recreating Japanese Women, 1600–1945*, Berkeley and Los Angeles: University of California Press, pp. 151–74.

Normano, J. F. and Antonello Gerbi (1943) *Japanese in South America: An Introductory Survey with Special Reference to Peru*, New York: Institute of Pacific Relations.

Nuttall, Z. (1906) "Earliest Historical Relations between Mexico and Japan," *American Archaeology and Ethnology*, 4: 1–47.

Office of Strategic Services (OSS) (1943) "Memorandum, Number, 12294, December 20, 1943, Record Group, 226, U.S. National Archives, College Park, Maryland.

Ogasawara, Yuko (1998) *Office Ladies and Salaried Men: Power, Gender, and Work in Japanese Companies*, Berkeley: University of California Press.

Ogawa, Tsuneko (1995) *Sokoku-yo: 'Chûgoku Anryû Fujin' no Han-seiki* [My Fatherland: The Half-century Life of Women Who Have Been Left in China], Tokyo: Iwanami.

Ôgimi, Chôtoku (1935) *Hirippin Guntô An'nai* [Guidance for the Philippine Islands], Tokyo: Kaigai Kenkyûsho.

Oguma, Eiji (1995) *Tan'itsu Minzoku Shinwa no Kigen* [The Myth of the Homogeneous Nation], Tokyo: Shin'yô-sha.

—— (2002) *A Genealogy of "Japanese" Self-images*, trans. David Askew, Melbourne: Trans Pacific Press.

Ohno, Shun (1991) *Hapon: Firipin Nikkeijin no Nagai Sengo* [Japanese: The Long Agony of the Philippine Nikkei After World War II], Tokyo: Daisan Shokan.

—— (2000) *Kankô Kôsu denai Firipin* [Another Philippines], Tokyo: Kôbunken.

Ohnuki-Tierney, Emiko (1990) "The Ambivalent Self of the Contemporary Japanese," *Cultural Anthropology*, 5(2): 197–216.

—— (1993) *Rice as Self: Japanese Identities through Time*, Princeton, NJ: Princeton University Press.

Oiwa, Keibo (ed.) (1991) *Stone Voices: Wartime Writings of Japanese Canadian Issei*, Montreal: Véhicule Press.

Okabe, Makio (1990) *Manshû Imin Kankei Shiryô Shûsei: Kaisetsu* [Collected Materials on Manchurian Immigration: An Interpretation], Tokyo: Fuji Shuppan.

Okihiro, Gary Y. (1991) *Cane Fires: The Anti-Japanese Movement in Hawaii, 1865–1945*, Philadelphia, PA: Temple University Press.

Ong, Aihwa (2002) "The Pacific Shuttle: Family, Citizenship, and Capital Circuits,"

268 References

in J. X. Inda and R. Rosaldo (eds) *The Anthropology of Globalization: A Reader*, Oxford: Blackwell, pp. 172–97.

Orient Year Book [Restricted] (1942) Tokyo: The Asia Statistics Co.

Pak, Katherine (2000) "Foreigners are Local Citizens Too: Local Governments Respond to International Migration in Japan," in M. Douglass and G. S. Roberts (eds) *Japan and Global Migration: Foreign Workers and the Advent of a Multicultural Society*, London: Routledge, pp. 244–74.

Panikkar, K. M. (1959) *Asia and Western Dominance*, London: Allen & Unwin.

Pastrana, Juan Jiménez (1983) *Los Chinos en la Historia de Cuba, 1847–1930* [The Chinese in the History of Cuba, 1847–1930], La Habana: Editorial de Ciencas Sociales.

Pedraza, Silvia (1991) "Women and Migration: The Social Consequences of Gender," *Annual Review of Sociology*, 17: 303–25.

Perez, Louis (1998) *The History of Japan*, Westport, CT: Greenwood Press.

—— (2002) *Daily Life in Early Modern Japan*, Westport, CT: Greenwood Press.

Philippines Commission of the Census (1941) *Census of the Philippines: 1939*, vol. 2, Manila: Bureau of Printing.

Plath, David (2001) *Under Another Sun: Japanese in Singapore*. Video documentary, 56 minutes, University of Illinois at Urbana-Champaign and National University of Singapore.

Prime Minister's Office (2000) *Seron Chosa Nenkan: Zenkoku Seron Chosa no Genjyo* [Annual Public Opinion Surveys].

Radin, Robert (1984) "Rice Riots of 1918," *Kodansha Encyclopedia of Japan*, vol. 6, Tokyo: Kodansha, pp. 310–11.

Reischauer, Edwin and Albert Craig (1978) *Japan: Tradition and Transformation*, Boston, MA: Houghton Mifflin.

Richardson, Peter (1982) *Chinese Mine Labour in the Transvaal*, London: Macmillan.

Rocca Torres, Luis (1997) *Japonesas bajo el sol de Lambayeque* [The Japanese under the Sun of Lambayeque], Lambayeque, Peru: Universidad Nacional Pedro Ruiz Gallo.

Romero, Mary (1998) "Maid in the USA," in J. J. Macionis and N. V. Benokratis (eds) *Seeing Ourselves: Classic, Contemporary, and Cross Cultural Readings in Sociology*, Upper Saddle River, NJ: Prentice Hall, pp. 277–83.

Ropp, Steven Masami (2002) "The Nikkei Negotiations of Minority/Majority Dynamics in Peru and the United States," in L. Hirabayashi, A. Kikumura-Yano, and J. Hirabayashi (eds), pp. 279–95.

Ropp, Steven Masami and Romy Chavaz de Ropp (2002) "An Interview with Francisco Miyasaka, President of the Japanese Cuban Association," *Amerasia Journal*, 28(2): 129–46.

Rosaldo, Renato (1989) *Culture and Truth: The Remaking of Social Analysis*, Boston, MA: Beacon Press.

Rosenberger, Nancy (2001) *Gambling with Virtue: Japanese Women and the Search for Self in a Changing Nation*, Honolulu: University of Hawaii press.

Ross, Mark Howard (1997) "Culture and Identity in Comparative Political Analysis," in M. Irving Lichback and A. S. Zuckerman (eds) *Comparative Politics: Rationality, Culture, and Structure*, Cambridge: Cambridge University Press, pp. 42–80.

Roth, Joshua (2002) *Brokered Homeland: Japanese Brazilian Migrants in Japan*, Ithaca, NY: Cornell University Press.

Roy, Patricia E. (1989) *A White Man's Province: British Columbian Politicians and Chinese and Japanese Immigrants, 1858–1915*, Vancouver: University of British Columbia Press.
Rubinger, Richard (1986) "Education: From One Room to One System," in M. Jansen and G. Rozman (eds) *Japan in Transition: From Tokugawa to Meiji*, Princeton, NJ: Princeton University Press, pp. 195–230.
Rutherford, Jonathan (1990) "A Place Called Home," in J. Rutherford (ed.) *Identity: Community, Culture, Difference*, London: Lawrence & Wishart, pp. 9–27.
Ryukyu Shimpo (1995) November 15.
Saber, Mamitua (1975) "Majority–minority Situation in the Philippines," *Mindanao Journal*, 2(1): 22–3.
Safran, William (1991) "Diasporas in Modern Societies: Myths of Homeland and Return," *Diaspora*, 1(1): 83–99.
Saiki, Kikuko (1996) "For Mario: Life Has Unexpected Turns After All," in R. Kato (ed.), pp. 106–24.
Saiki, Masaru (1996) "Building 50 Model Five-Story Towers: A Recollection of a 90-Year-Old Man Who Has Lived in Mexico for 67 Years," in R. Kato (ed.), pp. 93–105.
Saito, Hiroshi (1976) *Burajiru no Seiji: Barugasu kara Gaizeru e no Gekidô Seiji-shi* [Brazilian Politics: The History of Political Upheaval – from Vargas to Geisel], Tokyo: The Simul Press.
—— (1983) *Atarashii Burajiru: Rekishi to Shakia to Nihonjin* [The New Brazil: History, Society, and Nikkiejin], Tokyo: The Simul Press.
Sakai, Junko (2000) *Japanese Bankers in the City of London: Language, Culture and Identity in The Japanese Diaspora*, London: Routledge.
Sakamoto, Rei (2000) "The Japanese Community in Düsseldorf," *Pan-Japan: The International Journal of the Japanese Diaspora*, 1(2): 15–35.
Sakuda, Alejandro (1999) *El futuro era Perú: Cien años o más de inmigración japones a* [The Future was Peru: One Hundred Years or More of Japanese Immigration], Lima: ESICOS.
Salamon, Sonya (1975) "The Varied Groups of Japanese and German Housewives," *The Japan Interpreter*, 10(2): 151–70.
Sandmeyer, Elmer C. (1973) *The Anti-Chinese Movement in California*, Urbana: University of Illinois Press.
Saniel, Josefa M. (1966) "The Japanese Minority in the Philippines Before Pearl Harbor: Social Organization in Davao," *Asian Studies*, 4(1): 103–26.
Sawada, Mitziko (1991) "Culprits and Gentlemen: Meiji Japan's Restrictions of Emigrants to the United States, 1891–1909," *Pacific Historical Review*, 6(3): 339–59.
Saxton, Alexander (1971) *The Indispensable Enemy: Labor and the Anti-Chinese Movement in California*, Berkeley: University of California Press.
SCAP, GHQ (1996) *Nihon Senryôshi: Population* [History of the Non-military Activities of The Occupation of Japan 1945–1951], vol. 4, trans. T. Kuroda and M. Obayashi, Tokyo: Nihon Tosho Center.
Schattschneider, Ellen (2001) "Buy Me a Bride: Death and Exchange in Northern Japanese Bride-doll Marriage," *American Ethnologist*, 28(4): 854–80.
Scheper-Hughes, Nancy and Carolyn Sargent (1998) *Small Wars: The Cultural Politics of Childhood*, Berkeley: University of California Press.
Schiller, Nina Glick, Linda Basch, and Cristina Szanton Blanc (1995) "From

Immigrant to Transmigrant: Theorizing Transnational Migration," *Anthropological Quarterly*, 68(1): 48–60.
Schumpeter, Joseph (1951) *Imperialism and Social Classes*, Philadelphia, PA: Orion.
Schurz, William L. (1959) *The Manila Galleon*, New York: Dutton.
Schwartz, Larissa N. (1998) "The Inconveniences Resulting from Race Mixture: The Torreon Massacre of 1911," in L. N. Schwartz (ed.) *Chinese America: History and Perspectives 1998*, San Francisco, CA: Chinese Historical Society of America.
Sellek, Yoko (2001) *Migrant Labour in Japan*, New York: Palgrave.
Sheffer, Gabriel (1986) "A New Field of Study: Modern Diasporas in International Politics," in G. Sheffer (ed.) *Modern Diasporas in International Politics*, London and Sydney: Croom Helm, pp. 1–15.
Shibata, Ken'ichi (1941) "Hôjin no Hitô Shinshutu-shi (A History of Japanese Advancement in the Philippines)," *Firipin Jôhô*, 45: 15–21.
—— (1942a) *Dabao Kaitaku-ki* [A Description of Pioneering in Davao], Tokyo: Kôa Nippon-sha.
—— (1942b) *Nanyô no Rekishi to Genjitsu* [A History and Reality of the South Seas], Tokyo: Teikoku Sangyô Hôki-sha.
Shimaki, Kensaku (1940) *Manshû kikô* [Manchuria Travelogue], Tokyo: Sôgensha.
Shinpo, Mituru (1986) *Kanada Nihonjin Imin Monogatari* [Japanese Immigration Story in Canada], Tokyo: Tsukiji-shokan.
Shirota, Yoshiroku (1985) *Dabao Imin-shi o Aruku* [Tracing the History of Japanese Emigrants in Davao], Fukuoka: Ashi Shobô.
Smith, Thomas Carlyle (1988) "Peasant Time and Factory Time in Japan," in T.C. Smith (ed.) *Native Sources of Japanese Industrialization, 1750–1920*, Berkeley: University of California Press.
Sôga, Yasutarô (Keihô) (1953) *Gojû-nenkan no Hawai Kaiko* [My Fifty Years Memoirs in Hawaii], Osaka: Osaka Kosoku Printing.
Spickard, Paul R. (1989) *Mixed Blood: Intermarriage and Ethnic Identity in Twentieth-century America*, Madison: University of Wisconsin Press.
Stearman, Allyn MacLean (1985) *Camba and Kolla: Migration and Development in Santa Cruz, Bolivia*, Orlando: University of Central Florida Press.
Stephens, Sharon (1995) "Introduction: Children and the Politics of Culture in 'Late Capitalism'," in S. Stephens (ed.) *Children and the Politics of Culture*, Princeton, NJ: Princeton University Press, pp. 3–48.
Stewart, Watt (1951) *Chinese Bondage in Peru: A History of the Chinese Coolie in Peru, 1849–1874*, Durham, NC: Duke University Press.
Sugano, Masao (1939) *Tsuchi to tatakau* [Soil and Struggle], Tokyo: Manshû ijû kyôkai.
Sugimoto, Howard H. (1978) *Japanese Immigration, the Vancouver Riots and Canadian Diplomacy*, New York: Arno Press.
Suzuki, Jôji (1992) *Nihonjin Dekasegi Imin* [Japanese Dekasegi Immigration], Tokyo: Heibonsha.
Tajiri, Tetsuya (1991) "Nihon Imin no Hajimaru made [Until the Beginning of Japanese Emigration to Brazil]," in Imin 80-Nin-Shi Hensan Iinkai (ed.), pp. 11–34.
Takaguchi, Yasuaki (1944) "Manshû no Ishokujû: Kaitakuchi no Aiiku [Necessities of Life in Manchuria: Raising Children in Frontier Settlements]," *Kaitaku* [Frontier], October, 8(5): 48–54.

Takaki, Ronald (1983) *Pau Hana: Plantation Life and Labor in Hawaii, 1835–1920*, Honolulu: University of Hawaii Press.
—— (1989) *Strangers from a Distant Shore: A History of Asian Americans*, New York: Penguin.
—— (1998) *A Larger Memory: A History of Our Diversity with Voices*, Boston, MA: Little, Brown.
Takeda, Ariel (2002) "Japanese Immigrants and Nikkei Chileans," in A. Kikumura-Yano, (ed.), pp. 178–91.
Tamura, Yoshio (ed.) (1953) *Hiroku: Daitôa senshi: Manshû-hen: Ge* [The Unknown History of the Greater East Asian War Manchuria: Final Part], Tokyo: Fuji Shoen.
Tanaka, Stefan (1993) *Japan's Orient: Rendering Pasts into History*, Berkeley: University of California Press.
Tegtmeyer Pak, Katherine (2000) "Foreigners are Local Citizens Too: Local Governments Respond to International Migration in Japan," in M. Douglass and G. S. Roberts (eds) *Japan and Global Migration: Foreign Workers and the Advent of a Multicultural Society*, London: Routledge, pp. 244–74.
Thang, Leng Leng and Elizabeth MacLachlan (2002) *The Second Wave: Japanese Working Women in Singapore*, Video documentary, 23 minutes, National University of Singapore and University of Illinois at Urbana-Champaign.
Thang, Leng Leng, Elizabeth MacLachlan, and Miho Goda (2002) "Expatriates on the Margins: A Study of Japanese Women Working in Singapore," *Geoforum*, 33: 539–51.
Tigner, James Lawrence (1956) "The Okinawans in Latin America," unpublished thesis, Stanford University.
—— (1963) "The Ryukyuans in Bolivia," *Hispanic American Historical Review*, 43(2): 206–29.
Tinker, Hugh (1974) *A New System of Slavery: The Export of Indian Labour Overseas, 1830–1920*, London: Oxford University Press.
Titiev, Mischa (1951) "The Japanese Colony in Peru," *Far Eastern Quarterly*, 10(3) (May): 227–47.
Tôa Keizai Chôsa-kyoku (1933) *Chamusu Imin no Jikkyô* [Report on Immigration Conditions in the Jiamusi Area], Tokyo: Tôa Keizai Chôsa-kyoku.
—— (1936) *Saikin no Firipin* [The Philippines Nowadays], Tokyo: Tôa Keizai Chôsa-kyoku.
—— (1939) *Nanyô Sôsho: Dai-gokan: Firipin-hen* [Series on the South Seas, vol. 5: The Philippines], Tokyo: Tôa Keizai Chôsa-kyoku.
Tomiyama, Ichirô (1990) *Kindai Nippon Shakai to 'Okinawajin'* [Modern Japanese Society and the Okinawans], Tokyo: Nippon Keizai Hyôron-sha.
Totman, Conrad (1993) *Early Modern Japan*, Berkeley: University of California Press.
Tsu, Timothy (2002) "Japanese in Singapore and Japan's Southward Expansionism, 1860–1945: Historical Notes for 'Under Another Sun,'" Online. Available: <http://www.aems.uiuc.edu/HTML/UAS/Tsu.html> (accessed July 10, 2003).
Tsuda, Takeyuki (1999a) "The Motivation to Migrate: The Ethnic and Sociocultural Constitution of the Japanese-Brazilian Return Migration System," *Economic Development and Cultural Change*, 48(1): 1–31.
—— (1999b) "The Permanence of 'Temporary' Migration: The 'Structural Embeddedness' of Japanese-Brazilian Migrant Workers in Japan," *Journal of Asian Studies*, 58(3): 687–722.

—— (2003a) "Homeland-less Abroad: Transnational Liminality, Social Alienation, and Personal Malaise," in J. Lesser (ed.), pp. 121–61.

—— (2003b) *Strangers in the Ethnic Homeland: Japanese Brazilian Return Migration in Transnational Perspective*, New York: Columbia University Press.

Tsuda, Takeyuki and Wayne A. Cornelius (2004) "Japan: Government Policy, Immigrant Reality," in W. A. Cornelius, P. L. Martin, and J. F. Hollifield (eds) *Controlling Immigration: A Global Perspective*, Stanford, CA: Stanford University Press, pp. 439–77.

Tsuji, Shin'ichi (1990) *Nikkei Kanadajin* [The Japanese Canadians], Tokyo: Shôbunsha.

Uemura, Naoki (1992) "Beikoku no Reisengaiko to Latin America no Kakumei: Boribia-kakumei to Guatemara-kakumei no Hikaku [U.S. Cold War Policy and Latin American Revolutions: The Bolivian and Guatemalan Cases]," *The American Review*, 26: 89–107.

Ueno, Chizuko (2000) *Kindai Kazoku no Seiritsu no Shuen* [The Rise and Fall of the Modern Family], Tokyo: Iwaba Shoten.

Umehara, Hiromitsu (1976) "Firipin ni Okeru Tochi Shoyûken Kakutei Jigyô ni Kansuru Ichi Kôsatsu [Land Title Policy in the Philippines during the American Period]," *Ajia Keizai*, 17(1–2): 57–71.

United States Governor of Guam (1901–41) *Annual Report of the Governor of Guam*. Original typed reports to the Secretary of the Navy, Washington, DC: NA Microfilm, 3 Rolls, No. 10-37-5, and copies in collection of the Micronesian Area Research Center of University of Guam, United States, Seattle: University of Washington Press.

Valentine, James (1990) "On the Borderlines: The Significance of Marginality in Japanese Society," in E. Ben-Ari, B. Moeran, and J. Valentine (eds) *Unwrapping Japan: Society and Culture in Anthropological Perspective*, Honolulu: University of Hawaii Press, pp. 36–57.

Van Sant, John (2000) *Pacific Pioneers: Japanese Journeys to America and Hawaii, 1850–80*, Urbana: University of Illinois Press.

Wakatsuki, Yasuo (1979) "Japanese Emigration to the United States, 1866–1924: A Monograph," *Perspectives in American History*, 12: 387–516.

—— (1987) *Hatten Tojôkoku e no Ijû no Kenkyû: Borivia ni okeru Nihon Imin* [Study of Emigration to a Developing Country: Japanese Immigration in Bolivia], Tokyo: Tamagawa Daigaku Shuppanbu.

—— (1995 [1991]) *Shinpan: Sengo hikiage no kiroku* [New Version: The Records of Postwar Repatriation], Tokyo: Jiji Tsûshin-sha.

Watanabe, Masako, Masanori Ishikawa, Ryoko Anada, Harumi Yuge, Hironori Watanabe and Angelo Ishi (1992) "Nikkei Dekasegi no Kyûzô ni Tomonau Nihon Shakai no Taiô to Mosaku [The Rapid Increase in Japanese-descent Migrant Workers and the Resulting Response and Uncertainty of Japanese Society]," *Meiji Gakuin Daigaku Shakaigakubu Fuzoku Kenkyûjo Nenpô* [Meiji Gakuin University Sociology Division Affiliated Research Institute Annual Report], 22: 55–85.

Watson, James (2004) "Presidential Address: Virtual Kinship, Real Estate, and Diaspora Formation: The Man Lineage Revisited," *Journal of Asian Studies*, 63(4): 893–910.

Weglyn, Michi (1976) *Years of Infamy: The Untold Story of America's Concentration Camps*, New York: William Morrow.

Weiner, Myron (1986) "Labor Migrations as Incipient Diasporas," in G. Sheffer

(ed.) *Modern Diasporas in International Politics*, London and Sydney: Croom Helm, pp. 47–74.
Westney, D. Eleanor (1983) "Emigration," *Kodansha in Encyclopedia of Japan*, vol. 2, Tokyo: Kodansha, p. 201.
Winkler, Karen (1999) "Historians Explore Questions of How People and Cultures Disperse Across the Globe," *Chronicle of Higher Education*, January 22: A11.
Yabiku, Mosei (ed.) (1987) *Burajiru Okinawa Imin-shi* [History of Okinawan Immigrants in Brazil], São Paolo: The Okinawan Association in Brazil.
Yamada, Gôichi (1962) "Manshû ni Okeru Hanman Kônichi Undô to Nôgyô Imin: Chû [The Anti-Japanese Movement in Manchuria and Agricultural Immigration: Middle Part]," *Rekishi Hyôron* [Critical History], 143 (July): 62–77.
Yamagami, Kenichi and Eijun Suketake (1994) *Japan's Constitution and Civil Law*, Tokyo: Foreign Press Center.
Yamaguchi Prefecture (1963) *Yamaguchi-ken Bunkashi: Tsûshi-hen* [Cultural History of Yamaguchi Prefecture: Narrative] (revised edn), Yamaguchi Prefecture, Hofu City: Ômura Insatsu.
Yamamuro, Shin'ichi (1993) *Kimera* [Chimera], Tokyo: Chûô Kôronsha.
Yamanaka, Keiko (1996) "Return Migration of Japanese-Brazilians to Japan: The *Nikkeijin* as Ethnic Minority and Political Construct," *Diaspora*, 5(1): 65–97.
Yanami, Ren'ichi (1936) "Nankô Henken [The Voyage in the South Seas Here and There]," in R. Hasegawa (ed.), pp. 163–93.
Yeoh, Brenda S. A. and Shirlena Huang (1998) "Negotiating Public Space: Strategies and Styles of Migrant Female Domestic Workers in Singapore," *Urban Studies*, 35(3): 583–602.
Yeoh, Brenda S. A. and Louisa-May Khoo (1998) "Home, Work And Community: Skilled International Migration and Expatriate Women in Singapore," *International Migration*, 36(2): 159–86.
Yoneyama, Lisa (1999) *Hiroshima Traces: Time, Space, and the Dialectics of Memory*, Berkeley: University of California Press.
Yoshida, Kensei (2001) *Democracy Betrayed: Okinawa Under U.S. Occupation*, Bellingham, Washington, DC: Western Washington University.
Yoshida, Yosaburo (1909) "Sources and Causes of Japanese Emigration," *Annals of the American Academy of Political and Social Science*, 34: 377–87.
Yoshida, Yoshiaki (1993) "Abaka wa Moeru [*Abaca* is Fired]," in Dabao Kai (ed.) *Senka ni Kieta Dabao Kaitaku-imin to Minara-asa* [Settlers in Davao, Who Disappeared in the War, and Manila hemp], Tokyo: Dabao-kai, pp. 388–460.
Yoshino, Kosaku (1992) *Cultural Nationalism in Contemporary Japan: A Sociological Enquiry*, London: Routledge.
Yoshiya, Nobuko (1940) "Manshû Tairiku no Tsuchi ni Ikiru Hitobito [The Agricultural Immigrants of Continental Manchuria]," *Shufu no Tomo* [The Housewife's Companion], November: 83–90.
Young, Arthur M. (1938) *Imperial Japan, 1926–1938*, New York: William Morrow.
Young, Louise (1998) *Japan's Total Empire: Manchuria and the Culture of Wartime Imperialism*, Berkeley: University of California Press.
Zaide, Gregorio F. (1957) *Philippine Political and Cultural History: The Philippines Since the British Invasion*, vol. 2 (revised edn), Manila: Philippine Education Company.
Zo, Kil Young (1978) *Chinese Emigration to the United States, 1850–1880*, New York: Arno.

Index

abaca 86, 87, 99n6; cultivation 87, 94; industry 96; lands 88; plantation *see* plantation(s); planters *see* planter(s); prices 87; production 91
African(s) 1–3, 25–6, 29, 104, 198, 200
African: communities 9; Peru's 201; slaves 117, 142
African American(s) 29, 194
Afro-Brazilian Culture 15
Afro-Caribbean slavery 26
agricultural: area 164; assimilation 91; colonist(s) 71, 73–5, 78–9, 82–3, 84n6; colonists' expectations 82; colonization 79, 83; colonization program 77; colony 31; community/communities 77, 79–80, 122; companies 87; conditions in Japan 37; differences 93; economic output 37; heart 149; improvement programs 58; land (Japan) 37; philosophy 112; practices 80; produce 81; product 92; production 81, 188; public lands 87; sector 143; settlements 76–8, 80–1; similarities 90; society 27; specialists 81; tasks 72; villages 54; workers 199
Agricultural Development Cooperative 184
agriculture 29, 32–3, 43, 45, 62, 78–9, 146, 198; Californian 32; Hawaiian 62; *see also* Peruvian agriculture
Aizu-Wakamatsu: group 53; samurai 53
Algeria 194
Aliança (Brazil) 111–13, 120
Amazon: area 115, 120n9; Basin 197; region 175–7, 181, 188, 189n5; river 198
American Popular Revolutionary Alliance *see* Popular Revolucionaria Americana

Andô, Tarô 54
anthropologists 1, 127
anti-Asian: constitution 64; movement 166; sentiment 33
anti-Japanese 98; activity 32, 73, 146; card 148–9; demonstration 167; elements 72; feelings 143, 148, 151, 183; forces 72; guerrillas 96; hostility 196; leaflets 200; legislation 32; measures 33, 163; movement 150, 166; platform 112; prejudice 151; protests 116; racism 123; racists 123; rhetoric 64; riots 144, 165; sentiment(s) 122, 144, 148, 160, 162–5, 167, 189n6, 200; treatment 178
APRA *see* Popular Revolucionaria Americana
Argentina 22n7, *48–50*, 149, 151–2, 156, 159–60, 162, 166, 170n9, 190n13
Asia 9, 11, *18*, 20, 25, 35, *48*, 53, 98, 236–7, 250
Asian(s) 2, 25, 28–9, 33, 104, 109, 122, 157, 165, 195, 198; ancestry 33; Canadian-born 33; clientele 122; communities 2, 142, 240; countries 240; customs 117; families 108; history 30; immigration 25; mainland 35, 219; migrant(s) 2, 33; migration 25; minority 203; predecessors 25
Asian American(s) 2, 195
Associación Nikkei de Callao 157
Australia 28, 30, 47, *48–9*, 53, 236, 240

Bagobo 88, 90, 93, 99n7, 99n8, 100n14, 100n15, 100n16, 100n19, 100n22, 101n26; appearance 88; chieftain 88; community/communities 88, 90; families 90; friends 90; Japanese–Bagobo 91; language *see* language;

Index 275

parentage 90, 100n16; parents 91; relatives 90–1; tradition 91
Bagobo-ized 88
Bastos (Brazil) 111–13, 115–16
Bayaba Plantation Company 88
bicultural children 251
birth rate 13, 122, 183, 247
blood 195–6, 211, 214; life-blood 191; mixed-blood 95, relatives 227; sweat and 129; tax 39, 210
bloodiest incident 27
bloodshed 116
bloodstream 158
bloody night 27
Bolivia 10, 17, *48, 50,* 119n1, 120n9, 148, 152, 156, 159–60, 162–3, 169n1, 170n10, 175–9, 181–5, 187–8, 189n2, 189n3, 189n5, 190n12, 190n15, 196–7, 201; acceptance of immigration 179; bread-basket 179; development 179; eastern regions 201; economic and social activity 177; economy 178; leading producers of soybeans, wheat, rice 188; Okinawan 201; president 179; Santa Cruz 198; tin 179
Bolivian(s) 162, 175–7, 183, 187–9, 189n12, 197, 201; Amazon region 177; *see also* Amazon; community/communities 175, 177–8, 188; economy 177–8; government(s) 176, 178, 185, 187, 189n12; nationality 187; officials' acceptance 183; population 162; situation 178; society 175, 177–8, 188–9; wives 201
Boliviano Japonesas 169, 189
Bowring, Sir John 28
BRATAC association (Brazil) 112, 114, 116, 120n11, 120n12
Brazil 9–10, 14–15, 21, 22n2, 22n7, 31, 46–7, *48–51,* 102–7, 109–11, 113–19, 119n1, 120n4, 120n5, 120n9, 120n12, 120n15; national income 104; president *see* Getúlio Vargas
Brazil Colonial Association *see* BRATAC
Brazilian(s) 14–15, 21, 106–9, 112–13, 116, 118–19; army 116; cities 119; citizenship 107, 110, 120n6; culture 15, 110; education 110; elite attitudes 104; government 104, 115, 117; identity 110; landlords 106; middle and upper classes 119; neighbors 116; newspapers 116; Nikkei *see* Nikkei; Nikkei returnees *see* returnees; rainy season 108; region 102; society 103, 106, 109–10, 117, 119; school 116; teachers 116
Brazilian-ness 21
bride(s) 89, 91; continental 76, 78; family 91; picture 32–3, 63, 121; residence 91
bridegroom 91; marriage 91
British Columbia (Canada) 30, 33, 121–4, 128–30, 136
British Columbia Security Commission 129
Buddhist(s) 110, 122, 130; altars 113; ceremony 110; congregation 109; deities 231; karma 63; monks 11, 110, 120n8; mortuary memorial tablets *see ihai*; practices 113; temple(s) 92, 109
Burajiru Takushoku Kumiai see BRATAC

California 8, 28–32, 47, 53, 128, 170n8, 178, 194
California Gold Rush *see* gold rush
Callao (Peru) 146–7, 153, 157, 199; Lima-Callao *see* Lima
Canada 8, 10, 21, 22n2, 22n3, 25, 30–3, 47, *48–50,* 114, 121–4, 127–8, 136, 138, 140, 236, 240; Japanese 33; other ethnic minorities 125; shortage of manpower 136; true nature 140
Canada–United States border 33, 122
Canadian(s) 33, 127–8, 138–40; born Asians *see* Asians; citizens 122–4, 128, 131, 141; community/communities 121, 124; count 30; culture 127; factions 140; fishermen 33; *see also* Japanese Canadian fishermen; fishing vessels 123; government 8, 30, 33, 124, 138, 140–1; history 122; mosaic 124; naturalized 138–9; passenger ships 121; population *see* Japanese Canadian population; *see also* Chinese Canadian population; racism *see* racism; society 124, 126; west 26, 29, 33
Canadian–American border *see* Canada–United States border
Caribbean 25–8; area 27; islands 26; slavery 26
caucasian: leadership 66; non-caucasian foreigners 214
caudillo 154
Centro Cultural Peruano-Japonés 152

276 Index

Centro Nikkei Estudios de Superiores 157
Chiapas (Mexico) 142; immigrants 142
chieftain(s) *see datu*
Chile 10, *50*, 148, 159–60, 163, 166
Chilean(s) 163–4, 167; authorities 167; businessmen 163; experiences 163; society 163; views 166
Chilean Japanese 166
China 15–6, 21, 25–8, 30, 35, 45, *49*, 51, 53, 66, 98, 176–7, 217, 237, 240, 243; Indochina 96
China Friendship Commission 223–33, 234n3, 234n6, 234n7
Chinatown 33
Chinese 1–3, 15–16, 22, 25–33, 34n3, 34n6, 34n7, 41, 58, 73, 74, 75, 79–80, 82–3, 90, 121–2, 151, 192–3, 198, 200–1, 201n5, 215, 217–18, 220–1, 224–6, 228–9, 231–3, 245; adoptive parents 220, 227, 231–2; anger 74; citizens 15, 221, 225, 228; communicative competence 16; communist parties 234n3; community/communities 73, 79; coolie(s) 199; coolie trade 25; diaspora(s) *see* diaspora(s); emperor *see* Pu-yi; family/families 73, 220, 223, 228–9; farmer(s) 74, 80, 223; foster-parents 16; government 26, 30, 224, 234n7; identity/identities 218; immigrant(s) 26, 28–30, 218, 235n11; laborer(s) 26–9, 52, 142; leader(s) 74, 219; merchant(s) 199; migrants 3; morality 26; name(s) 220; nationality 220, 230; neighbor(s) 74; parents 15–16, 221, 227, 232; ports 26; relatives 227; residents 73; seamen 25; sentiment(s) 164; society 16, 227; state 224; volunteer(s) 225; workers 26
Chinese America(n) 29–30
Chinese Canadian population 30
Chinese Exclusion Act 29
Chinese Japanese 229, 233; war orphan(s) 233
Chinese Peruvians 200
cholera 143, 148
chûzai-in 236–7, 239–40, 252–3
citizen(s) 5, 8, 10, 12–13, 29, 32–3, 35, 52–3, 58, 170, 227; American 101n27, 161; Brazilian 107, 110; Canadian 122–3, 140; Chinese 15, 131, 218, 221, 225, 228; Davao 85; Filipino 94; Japanese 14, 16, 93, 98, 193, 217, 230, 232, 234n6; Japanese Brazilian 163 native 187; naturalized 29, 33, 129; non-citizens 165; Peruvian 8, 161, 165, 170n6, 170n7; rights 167; U.S. *see* citizens, American
citizenship(s) 7–9, 22n1, 33, 87, 94, 156, 167, 195–6, 218, 221, 229–33; American 161; 101n27, 181; Canadian 124, 128, 141; cultural *see* cultural; rights 7; Filipino 94, 96, 98, 101n27; Japanese 86, 98, 129, 171n14, 186, 229–31; local 216n9; Peruvian 149, 151; Philippine *see* citizenship, Filipino; U.S. *see* citizenship, American
class(es) 4, 11, 16, 39, 45, 63, 65, 79, 83, 169, 194, 196, 198, 200–1, 205, 245; different 127; distinctions 36; first 133, lower 11, 103; lower-middle 148; middle 202, 249; obligations 36; organized; second 16, 93 127; social 102; society 28; stereotype 65; 135; subordinate 198; upper 119
classic diaspora *see* diaspora
classical age 228, 235
classification(s) 3–4, 209
classified 3, 6, 8, 99n7; ads 238–9
Clifford, James 4
Clinton, Bill 12
climate 25, 41, 86, 89, 123, 160, 243, 253n4
coffee 104, 111, 112; beans 104; crisis 104; house 237; plantation(s) 102, 104–5, 111–13, 117; trees 106, 111
Cohen, Robin 3
Cold War 179, 188
Colonia Okinawa 186, 188
Conquesta City (Brazil) 106
continental bride *see* bride(s)
Conroy, Hilary 28
Cuba 10, 22n3, 26, *50*, 159, 162, 164–5, 170n8, 194
Cuba Commission 26, 28
Cuban: descent 170n8; government 164; issei *see* issei; Japanese *see* Japanese Cubans
Cuban Revolution 164, 169
cultural 2, 35; abilities 207; activities 111, 145, 152, 203, 205, 244; affinities 22n1; apart 148; aspects 211; assimilation 12; attributes 210; authentication 208; barriers 216n7; battles 233; behavior 206–7; center 152; *see also* Japanese Peruvian

Index   277

Cultural Center; citizenship 3; communities 100n9; complexion 7; confrontations 21; construction 5; context 1; cosmopolitanism 157; differences 207; discontinuity 126; discrimination 158; distance 127; diversity 203; encounters 211; events 15; evidence 158; expectations 20; group 2; heart 149; heritage 203; homogeneity 213; identity/identities 2, 4–5, 7, 15, 22, 232–3; ideologies 3, 20; impact 10, 147; inferior 105; insecurity 7; insularity 149; integrity 1; knowledge 208; minority/ minorities 99n7, 100n9, 100n19; nationalism 211, 213; patterns 145, 148, 158; positions 1; presence 243; pressure 1; problems 16; process 1; proficiency 204; qualities 211; rituals 146; schema 208; similar 209; situation 7; solidarity 143, 153; symbols 15; tensions 104; ties 157; traditions 155; traits 147, 211; values 15, 156; *see also* bicultural
Cultural Revolution (China) 225
culturally 188, 204; alien 206, 211; apart 148; assimilated 214; attributes 203; Brazilian 203–4, 209–10, 212; Brazilian Nikkeijin 203; comprehended 213; different 203–4, 209–11, foreign 204, 213; incongruous 212; isolated 110; Japanese 203, 209, 220; similar 213; structured 208
culture(s) 2–5, 19, 21–2, 50n1, 62, 64, 92–3, 95, 127, 157, 194–6, 201, 209–10, 213, 216n10, 221, 225, 229, 232, 250–1; dominant 212; hybrid 6; popular 202; subcultures 21; *see also* Afro-Brazilian culture; Brazilian culture; Canadian culture; ethnic culture; Japanese culture

da Gama, Vasco 30
datu 88, 90–1, 100n14, 100n15
Davao 85–97, 99n2, 99n4, 100n17, 100n18, 100n22, 100n25, 100n26, 100n28; citizens 85; city 85, 92, 99n4, 99n7, 100n12, 100n16, 100n22, 100n23, 100n25, 100n28, 100n33; der Sur 99n7; events 99n4; Filipino residents 93; issei *see* issei; Japanese Association 93; Japanese community 88, 93; Japanese Elementary School 89, 95; Japanese migrants 90; Okinawan community 93; province 92, 94
"Davaokuo" 92
dekasegi 177; Brazilian 14; diaspora *see dekasegi* diaspora; migrant(s) 6, 21; movement 119; worker(s)/migrant labor(s) 13–14, 22n7, 62, 119
diaspora(s) 1–9, 14, 20–2, 33, 34, 48, 195, 237; African 1–3, 9; Chinese 25; classic 69; community/communities 4, 5, 15; *dekasegi* 15; displaced 7, 9; ethnic 3; gendered 237; incipient 7–9, 16, 20; Japanese 1, 5, 7, 9, 13, 16–17, 21, 25, 30–1, 35, 46, 50, 142, 171n12; Jewish 4; labor 3; long-term and permanent-resident 7, 17–18, 20–1; minority *see* model or positive minority; model or positive minority 7, 11–12; modern 21; Nikkei 7, 13, 15, 20; Okinawa 16–17, 21; Permanent-resident *see* long-term and permanent-resident; prototypical 3; trade 3; variations 253; victim 3
diasporee(s) 2–4, 6, 8, 13, 17, 20–1; displaced 13; incipient 14; Japanese 11; minority, model or positive 13; Nikkei 13
discrimination 8, 10, 16, 29, 32–3, 84n11, 93, 97, 117, 121, 124–6, 158, 163, 207, 212–14, 225, 229; cultural *see* culture; ethnic 12, 207, 212; gender 253n1; racial 20, 109; social 7
Doi, Yatarô 67n3

East Asia 25, 66, 176, 181, 217, 221, 229, 233
East Asian(s) 25, 66, 176, 181; contract workers 31
economic: achievement 112; activity/activities 146, 152, 165, 177; advancement 13; assistance 98, 154; bases 177; benefits 45, 63; bonds 7; bubble 14; calamity 104; capital 22; change 42; climate 41, 253n4; competition 167; complexion 7; conditions 80, 98, 146, 156; confrontations 21; context 1; contribution(s) 85, 102; crisis 202; depression 107; developer(s) 71; development 92, 98, 150, 179; difficulties 81; discrepancy 221;

economic: achievement – *contd.*
  distress 53; doldrums 20; failure 81; future 5; gain(s) 52, 236; goals 230; growth 45, 79, 83; hardships 6, 20, 46, 104, 148, 229; importance 154; inefficiencies 80; influence 8; insecurity 7–8, 19; institutions 122; interest 179; issue 111; Japan's 14, 71, 98; losses 98; marginality/marginalization 4, 8; migrants 236; motivation 150; networks 153; news 153; niche 33; opportunity/opportunities 3, 17, 145, 155; output *37*; positions 1; power 45, 113; pressure 1; problem(s) 16; process 1; purposes 102; realities 81; reason(s) 44, 169; reform(s) 38–9; refugees 110; relationship 9; restriction(s) 8; rigors 149; role(s) 26; security 106, 144, 158; shortfall(s) 79; situation 7, 22, 80, 92, 186; stability 144; status 89, 93, 203; straits 83; structure(s) 102–3, 156; success 6, 12, 20–1, 27, 32; undertones 221; upheaval(s) 36; viability 81; well-being 81; woes 148
economically: assimilated 6; marginalized 2; segregated 215; successful 27; vibrant region of Bolivia 188
economics 2, 79
economy: Bolivian *see* Bolivian economy; world *see* world economy
education 9, 11–13, 16, 19, 22n2, 22n4, 36, 52, 55, 60, 65, 68, 94–5, 97, 103, 110, 112, 114, 116–19, 140, 146, 153, 187, 193, 240, 242–3; education program 65
educational: achievement 55; institutions 122; organizations 165; principle 95, 101n29; status 203
Ehime (Japan) 43
Eighty Percent Law, 1932 (Peru) 8
El Nacional 143
embranquecimento 109
Emigration Promotion Ltd. 186
Emigrant Association *see imin-gaisha*
emigrants 7, 20, 43, 45–7, 48, 52–66, 67n1, 67n4, 68n14, 68n15, 71, 75, 92, 111, 180, 183, 190n12, 237, 251; behavior 52; couple 75; earnings 66; experience 82; failure rate 65; home 58; *see also* Japanese emigrants; image 16; Japanese 30; laborers 52; life 8; Nikkei *see* Nikkei; outcomes 58; resources 63; services 56
emigration 11, 17, 27–8, 30–1, 35–6, 37, 41–3, 44, 45–8, 51n5, 52–4, 56–8, 60–4, 66, 67n2, 67n4, 68n11, 68n13, 71, 92, 97, 102, 156, 175, 178, 180–5, 189, 189n7, 237–8; agency/agencies, association(s), companies *see imin gaisha*; history 186; period 58; plan 182; pro-emigration propaganda 71, 78, 82–3; project(s) 111, 180–3; records 119n1; system 52; *see also kan'yaku imin*
Engels, Friedrich 33
Estado Novo 9
ethnic: affinity 203, 205, 213; anomalies 209; assumptions 209; attitudes 92, 209; avoidance 206; boundaries 3, 202–3, 211, 213; community 163; consciousness 114, 203; conflict 6, 14, 88, 212; cultures 110; cultural events 15; diaspora *see* diaspora; differences 211; discrimination 12, 207; display 207; diversity 212; enclave(s) 33, 122; foreigners 92; group 3, 13, 22, 22n1, 31, 47, 60, 64, 88, 91, 99n5, 99n9, 100n9, 101n30, 119, 177, 188; homogeneity 202, 209, 212–13; identity/identities; *see* identity/identities; incongruity 209; interaction 205; Japanese 202–3, 212; minority/minorities 124–5, 204, 233; neighborhood communities 106; performance(s) 208, 214–15; prejudice 93; reactions 211; rejection 206; relevance 203; resistance 207–8; segregation 98; situation 7; society 215; solidarity 15; stereotype 125; strife 111; symbols 15
Ethnic Studies 193
ethnically 203, 207, 210–11, 213, 215, 216n11; different 212; homogenous 92; segregated 212
ethnicity 4, 21, 22n1, 82, 103, 119, 169, 196, 199, 201, 216n11, 218, 229, 232–3; mono-ethnicity 211
Euro-American countries 202, 215, 216n1
European immigrants 109, 183
Exclusion Act 29, 32, 34n6, 47, 193, 201; *see also* Immigration Exclusion Act, 1924 (U.S.)

farmers 8, 11, 36, *37*, 38–41, 43–5, 50n1, 73–4, 79–81, 90, 94, 106–7, 112, 118, 142, 152, 162, 164, 178–9, 181, 218, 223
Filipino/a 85–92, 94–8, 99n7, 99n8, 100n9, 100n14, 100n15, 101n27, 194, ambassadors 85; citizens *see* citizens; community 88, 96, 98; guerrillas 97–8, 101n31; language *see* language; parentage 94, 101n31; wives 85, 94, 97; *see also* Philippines school; society
Fujimori, Alberto 142–5, 151, 154–8
Fukuoka (Japan) 88

gaichi 217–18
gambari-ya 123; *see also* kachi-gumi
Gannen-mono 53
Gardiner, Harvey C. 1, 159–62, 165–6, 168, 170n3, 170n4, 170n5, 170n6, 170n7, 171n12, 171n15
gender(s) 157, 194, 196, 201, 216n11, 221; diaspora *see* diaspora; discrimination *see* discrimination; imbalance 149; ratio 29, 31; role 76
Gentlemen's Agreement 31–3, 47
geta 147
globalization 228, 233, 238; guarantees 50; studies 1
gold *see* gold rush
Gold Hill (California) 31
Gold Mountain 28
Gold Mountain, New 28
gold rush 128; California 28; Klondike Gold Rush 128
golden: age 194; bust 109; door 29; period 177
"good wives and wise mothers" 76
government-sponsored emigration *see kan'yaku imin*
Guam 36, *48*, 53, 100n17
gunzoku 85
Great Tokyo Earthquake (1923) 40–1

Hall, Stuart 4–5
Handa, Tomô 104
hantavirus 189n8
hapa 193, 195
Hapon see Otro Hapon
Hara, Yasutarô 55, 58–61, 64, 67n3
Hawaii 21, 25–32, 34, 34n6, 36, 46–7, *48*, 53–6, 58–60, 61–4, 66, 100n21, 192–4, 196, 199; bound group 61; dependence 60; Republic of 60, 66
Hawaiian(s) 192; agriculture 62; Board of Immigration 56; Bureau of Immigration 68n14; Collections 66; government 53; immigrants 65; islands 65; Japanese 60; Japanese population 31; pidgin English 194; plantation 31
Heco, Joseph 34n10
Hirano: community 108–11; district 107; issei *see* issei; residents 110; Shokumin-chi *see* Hirano community; survivors 109; tragedy 111
Hiroshima (Japan) 17, 43–4, 54, 56, 60–1, 63–4, 67n1, 67n3, 67n5, 68n11, 68n12, 90, 148,
Hirano, Umpei 107–11, 117
Hiroshima Governor *see* Miki Nabeshima, Jôgyô Senda
historians 1, 30, 34n2, 43, 55, 111, 191
Hong Kong 28, *48–9*, 237, 240, 252

Ichioka, Yuji 1
Ide, Magoroku 217
identity 5, 16, 110, 118–19, 188, 195, 220–1, 223, 229, 232, 244; card 180; collective group/collective 4, 209; collective national 224; *see also* national identity; community's 110; construct 3; dual 110–11; *see also* singular identity; ethnic 1–4, 12, 20–1, 114, 119, 209, 211; ethno-national 204, 206, 208–9, 211; national 63, 203, 211–12; personal 102–3, 110; politics 98, 232; self-identity 86; singular 195; *see also* Brazilian identity; Chinese identity; cultural identity; ethnic identity; Japanese Brazilian identity; Japanese Brazilian group identity; Nikkei identity; social identity
Igarapava (Brazil) 106
Igorot 88–90, 100n11, 101n30; Japanese-Igorot 91
ihai 107
Ikeda, Arichika 127
Ikeda, Kaoru 121, 127–8, 132, 135, 140, 141n1
imin see immigrant(s)
imin-gaisha 9, 66, 104, 111, 147, 183, 187, 190n14, 200
immigrant communities 176
immigrants 3, 7–9, 15, 17, 28–9, 31–2, 35, 43, 45, 62, 79, 103, 105–7, 110–11, 114, 117–19, 121–2, 143–4, 147–8, 157, 166–7, 171n14, 175–6, 178,

immigrants – *contd.*
181–2, 184–9, 190–1, 197, 199, 202–3, 212–3, 215, 216n9, 216n13, 235n12; *see also* Chinese immigrants; Hawaiian immigrants; Indian immigrants; Japanese immigrants; Okinawan immigrants
immigration 2, 17, 25, 27–33, 35, 47–8, 50, 56, 68n14, 89, 96, 102, 104, 114, 120n5, 143, 145, 151–3, 157, 159, 171, 175–6, 178–9, 181, 184–5, 188, 189n12, 190n13, 193, 202, 205, 211–31, 215; Japanese immigration; *see also* Okinawan immigration
Immigration Exclusion Act,1924 (U.S.) 31, 47, 65, 67
Immigration Law, 1936 (Peru) 8
Immigration Law, 1889 (Brazil) 104
Indian immigrants 27
Indochina *see* China
Indonesia *48–9,* 92, 241
institutions *see* economic institutions; educational institutions; and political institutions
intermarriage(s) 6, 86–92, 101n26, 152, 166, 205, 216n7; rate 93, 145; *see also* marriage
intermarriers 88, 91, 94–6, 99n5
internationalization 202–3
internees 5, 12
Irish 1; labor 52
issei 85–98, 99n7, 100n20, 101n26, 121–2, 124–7, 144–6, 148–9, 152–3, 162, 164–7; aging 144; collaboration 98; Cuban 165; Davao 101n26; Filipino wives 97; generation 145; hard labor 86; Hirano 110; immigrants 167; intermarriage *see* intermarriage; intermarriers *see* intermarriers; living standard 93; narrative 93; North American 125; Okinawan 100n20; oral history 126; Peru's 145, 149; pioneers 148; population 124; residents 89; rural 89

Japan–Bolivia Immigration Pact 187
Japan National Farmer Union *see Nihon Nômin Kumiai*
Japanese: ancestry 5, 9, 15, 22n1, 35, 47, 86, 97, 142–3, 160–1, 163, 166, 177; citizen(s) *see* citizens; citizenship *see* Citizenship; civilians 11; colonists 15, 79, 82, 228; culture 50n1, 107, 157–8, 177, 207, 209–10, 243, 250–1; descent 1, 5, 14, 22n1, 35, 102, 122–3, 155, 160, 162–5, 170n6, 170n11, 203–4, 208, 213–14; diaspora *see* diaspora; education 9, 22n2, 114, 116; *see also* Japanese school; emigrant(s) 7–8, 46–7, *48,* 64–5, 183; ethnic identity 12; *see also* ethnic identity; families 15, 106, 108, 185, 249; farm dialects 14; *see also* Japanese language; fishermen 8; government 10, 13, 15–17, 35, 39, 52–4, 58, 64–6, 71, 74, 81, 86, 97–8, 100n17, 105, 109, 111–14, 116, 118, 120n9, 138, 170n10, 176–7, 182–8, 189n7, 193, 212–13, 217–18, 221, 224, 226, 228–31, 233, 234n3, 234n6, 234n7; immigrant(s) 8–9, 16, 31–2, 85–7, 91, 93, 99n2, 104–7, 109, 117, 121–4, 142–3, 149, 152, 160, 164, 171n14, 175–80, 184–6, 188, 189n5, 251; intermarriages *see* intermarriages; internees *see* internees; Japanese-Igorot *see* Igorot; language *see* language; migrants 8, 11, 85, 105, 108, 114–6, 120n13, 143; national(s) 10–11, 17, 21, 35, 48, *49,* 98, 123, 138–9, 152, 212, 241; nationality 94–8, 101n27, 187–8, 221, 223, 225, 227–31; newcomers 9, 80; North American internees *see* internees; overseas settlements 9; performers 9; populations *see* populations; property 8, 87; *see also* property; school 9, 11, 95–6, 107, 112, 149, 238, 243, 251; urban 11; vegetable 89; workers 8
Japanese American Citizens League (JACL) 5
Japanese Americans 1, 10, 12, 32–3, 123, 161, 181, 201; community 5; *see also* Japanese overseas community; filmmaker *see* Emiko Omori
Japanese–Bagobo *see* Bagobo
Japanese Bolivians 162, 175–7, 188; community 175, 177–8, 188; groups 177; population 162; *see also* population
Japanese Brazilians 103, 109, 112–16, 118–19, 163, 165, 167, 202–14, 216n2, 216n3, 216n4; activities 111; community/communities 102, 105, 111, 116, 216n2; concentration 102; *dekasegi see* dekasegi; elites 103; group identity 103; identity 102–3;

immigrants 209; non-Japanese Brazilians 113, 116, 163; sense of self 103; society *see* society
Japanese Canadian(s) 12, 33, 121–9, 138–9; community/communities 121, 124; culture 127; fishermen 129; history 122, 124–6, 134; poet *see* Joy Kogawa; population 121–4; *see also* population
Japanese–Canadian Redress Settlement 124
Japanese–Chinese relations 223
Japanese communities 2, 9–11, 15, 20, 57, 80, 102, 105, 111, 113–14, 118–19, 148, 236, 242; overseas 1, 17, *18*, 64, 236, 243
Japanese Cuban(s) 169, 170n10, 170n11; experience 170n8
Japanese Exclusion Act 32
Japanese Filipino Association 101n33
Japanese Immigration Cooperation Agency (JICA) 156
Japanese Latin Americans 14, 156, 158–61, 167–9, 170n2; experiences 159, 171; redress movement 168
Japanese Mexicans 165
Japanese Orphans Organization 101n33
Japanese Overseas Associations 186
Japanese Peruvian(s) 10, 142–4, 146–7, 149–52, 156–8, 160–1, 165–9, 170n4, 170n6, 170n7, 170n10, 171n15, 178, 200; community 144–5, 147, 149, 151, 154; Cultural Center *see* Centro Cultural Peruano-Japonés; migration 155; ; Peruvian-born Japanese 8; population145; *see also* population
Japanese Peruvian Oral History Project 171n15
Japanese–Philippine relations 98
Japaneseness 9, 15
Japantown 8
Jewish 1, 9; diaspora *see* diaspora; expatriate communities 1; identity 1; migration 3
Jiamusi (Manchuria) 71–3; Chinese residents 73
Jizô 231–2; *Manshû* 232
judo club 122

kachi-gumi 114–18, 163, 169
Kagawa (Japan) 43
Kamohara, Kôji 88
Kantô Dai-shinsai see Great Tokyo Earthquake

Kantôgun see Kwantung Army
kan'yaku imin 52, 67n2
Katô, Kanji 72, 78, 84n1
Kato, Yûzaburô 40
Kawasaki, Eiji 187
King, William L. M. 33
Kita, Itsuo 81
Kogawa, Joy 125
koji see orphans
Kokusaika see Internationalization
konketsu 214
Korea 35, 45, *48–9, 51,* 65, 71, 214
Korean(s) 41, 71, 198, 214–15; emigration 71; Japanese 213–14; minority 41
Kumamoto (Japan) 54
Kwantung Army 71–5, 77, 79, 82–3

La Paz (Bolivia) 177, 181, 185–6
language 3–4, 9, 14, 61, 63, 65, 85, 93, 95, 116–17, 126, 153, 161, 196, 201, 206–7, 210, 221, 227, 251; ability 107; *see also* linguistic ability; Bagobo 88; barrier 127, 224; English 67n1, 253; Filipino 95; foreign 114; Japanese language school 162, 165, 205; Japanese newspaper 145, 153; Japanese proficiency 158, 239; Japanese skill 153; Japanese: 9, 14–15, 67n1, 95, 116, 119, 122, 160, 201, 204, 210, 229, 236, 251; language 3–4, 9, 14, 61, 63, 65, 85, 93, 95, 116–17, 126, 153, 161, 196, 201, 206–7, 210, 221, 227, 251; Portuguese 108; Portuguese proficiency 158; native 91, 96, 100, 117; religious 63; teacher 239, 242
Latin America 1, 6, 10, 12–3, 22n7, 27, 34n2, 36, 47, 142–3, 148, 151–2, 154, 156–60, 168–9, 178–9, 181–3, 196; Japanese language newspaper 145; issei 152; *see also* issei; latin American nations
Latin American(s) 14–15, 156, 165, 208; cities 14; countries 159–60, 163, 166–7, 171n14; government 166; guest workers in Japan 158; heritage 15; history 181; Japanese communities 10; *see also* Nikkei Latin American communities; Japanese internees 12; *see also* internees; Japanese *see* Japanese Latin Americans; nations 10, 22n3, 150, 198; *see also* Latin American countries;

Latin American(s) – *contd.*
  Nikkei communities 12; *see also* Latin American Japanese communities; Nikkei/Nikkeijin 15, 144, 155, 158, 202; *see also* Nikkei; political leaders 154; residents 159
Lima (Peru) 144, 146, 149, 150, 152, 155, 157, 161, 165, 200; Lima-Callao 143, 145, 149, 152; newspaper 26
linguistic 127, 216n7; abilities 207; barrier 126; gap 126; problem(s) 16; proficiency 204
linguistically isolated 57
Little Tokyo 122
Luzon 86, 88–9, 100n11, 101n33

McClatchy, V.S. 193
make-gumi 114–18, 163, 169; *see also* kachi-gumi
malaria 108–9, 111, 120n5, 181
Manchukuo 45–6, 71–2, 75, 78, 82–3, 92
Manchuria 11, 15–16, 21, 45–7, *48*, 71–9, 81–3, 84n3, 84n4, 92, 149, 217–20, 222–3, 225–6, 228–9, 230–2, 233n1; economic growth 83; expatriate community 83; resources 81; security 82
Manchurian: diet 79; frontier 76; soil 80
Manchurian Incident (1931) 71, 96
manila hemp *see abaca*
Maria Luz incident (in 1872) 198–9
marriage(s) 13, 20, 27, 32, *51*, 59, 90–4, 145, 147, 157, 196, 216n7, 226, 238, 241, 246, 251; arrangements 63; gifts 91, 100n16; mixed 67n7; out-marriage 90, 201; tribal marriage 94; *see also* intermarriage(s)
Marx, Karl 33
masungit 93
matapong 93
Matsukata, Masayoshi 38, 53, 58
Meiji 31, 35–6, 38, 40, 42, 44, 53, 65, 90, 154, 195, 200; Emperor 193; government 38–9; Restoration 40, 50n1
Meiji Colonization Company 197
Meijiya 244
mestizaje 145
mestizos/mestizas 95–6, 99n5, 101n32, 166, 197–8
Mexicali (Mexico) 164

Mexican(s) 26–7, 142, 145, 164–5, 168, 196, 201; cookbook 196; foods 196
Mexico 25, *48*, *50*, 148, 159–60, 164–5, 168, 196, 199; *see also* new Mexico
migration 1–3, 6, 17, 21, 25–6, 28–9, 31, 35–6, 50, 52–3, 56, 65–6, 67n1, 68n14, 143–4, 147, 155, 157, 170n10, 176, 179–80, 196, 198, 202–3, 206–7, 212–13, 216, 218, 237, 240, 251, 253; migration system 52; *see also* emigration, immigration
migrant(s) 1, 3, 6, 8, 10, 14, 16, 18, 20–1, 43, 52, 54–5, 56, 58, 64–5, 67, 85–6, 88–9, 90, 99n1, 102, 104–5, 107, 109, 112–17, 119n1, 120n13, 143–5, 148–9, 156–7, 176–7, 194, 199–20, 202–3, 206, 208, 211–12, 236, 251, 253; *see also* Asian migrants, Japanese migrants agrarian *see* migrant farmers; camaradas *see* migrant farmers; community/communities 2, 93; economic 236; farmers 8; 102, 113; labor 1, 14, 52, 67 spiritual 236; workers 8–9, 13–14, 21, 52, 54, 60, 62–3, 67, 111, 121, 158, 194, 199
military 11, 17, 36, 39, 72–3, 79, 82–3, 85, 96, 98, 101n31, 126, 150, 160, 177, 180–1, 183, 219, 220, 233; *see also* gunzoku
mimoto see identity
Minas Gerais 106
mine/mining 128, 130–1, 179, 190n15, 199
miner(s) 178–9
Minister: of Agriculture, Bolivia 187; of Agriculture, Japan 179, 184, 187; of Agriculture and Forestry, Japan 45; of Colonial Affairs, Japan 72; of Foreign Affairs, Japan 101n32, 182–4, 186, 189, 189n7, 217; of Health and Welfare, Japan 220, 235n10; of Labor, Japan 212
Ministry of Justice, Japan 212
miso paste 81, 131, 139, 196
Mizobe, Osao 88
mochi 146–7
modernization 41–2
Morioka Emigration Company 197, 199, 200
Movimiento Nacionalista Revolucionario (MNR) 178
multicultural setting 233
multiculturalism 124
Mutô, Nobuyoshi, Marshall 72

Index 283

Nabeshima, Miki 61, 63
Nagata, Shigeshi 112
Nagano (Japan) 46, 112, 218–19, 222–3, 229, 233n1
Nagasaki 39, 45
naichi 217–18
naichi-jin 148
National Association of Japanese Canadians (NAJC) 124
nationality *51*, 216n11, 218; *see also* Bolivian nationality, Chinese nationality, Japanese nationality
nattô 196
New Mexico 159, 171n15
New Zealand 30, *48*, 236, 240
Nihon Nômin Kumiai 41
Niigata (Japan) 46, 127, 148
Nikkei 1, 6–7, 10–12, 14–15, 17, 20–1, 22n1, 48, *50*, 97–8, 99n5, 110, 113, 118–19, 122–4, 142–7, 149, 152–3, 155–8, 162–3, 168–9, 170n8, 170n9, 173, 205–6, 214–15, 216n12, 216n12; activists 12; *chichi* 157; community/communities 6, 21, 99n3, 155, 157; *dekasegi see dekasegi*; dialects 14; emigrants 156; history 125; identity 114; immigrants 204–5, 208, 212–14; labor 140; Latin Americans 12, 15, 22n7, 144, 155, 158; Latin American community 32; migrants 156; non-Nikkei foreigners 203, 213; population *see* population; returnee *see* returnee(s); workers: 1, 205
Nikkeijin 85–6, 96–8, 99n3, 99n4, 202–15, 216n5, 216n7; Latin American 202; Nikkeijin-kai 97, 101n28, 101n33; Pan-American *see* Pan American; Philippine 85; population *see* population
nisei 9, 22n2, 85–6, 94–8, 99n5, 100n16, 100n23, 101n26, 101n28, 101n30, 101n32, 101n33, 102, 122, 124, 126, 129, 138–41, 143–5, 151–3, 157, 162, 164–5, 187, 203, 210; *mestizo* 86, 90, 94–8, 101n28, 101n31, 101n33; Okinawa 99n5, 100n24, 100n25
North America 1, 10–12, 17, *18*, 20, 27, 31–2, 36, 109, 115, 127, 162
North American(s) 1, 5, 12, 47, 125, 186; minority 12
Notestein, F.W. 189n10

Ohita (Japan) 45
Ohta Development company *see* plantation
Okayama 43, 90, 100n12
Okinawa 16–17, 54, 92–3, 100n20, 101n26, 148, 156, 173, 175–6, 178–83, 186–8, 189n2, 190n15, 195–8, 201, 201n4,
Okinawan(s) 7, 16–17, 21, 85, 92–4, 99n5, 100n18, 100n19, 100n20, 100n24, 100–1n25, 101n26, 146–8, 152, 157, 175–6, 180–8, 193, 195, 197, 201, 201n4; colonists 198; community/communities 93, 181; emigrants 92; *see also* emigrants; emigration 92, 180–1, 184, 189n7; government 180, 186; identity 188; immigrants 93, 100n21, 148, 181–2, 186–7, 189n7; *see also* immigrants; immigration 180–2, 185, 187–8; *see also* immigration; migrants 16, 50n5; *see also* immigrants; migration 196; *see also* migration; workers 197
Okinawan Association of Hawaii 193
Okinawan Mutual Aid Society 152–3
Omikoshi 85
Omori, Emiko 5
Opium War 30
orphans 13, 15–16, 97–8, 101n32, 101n33, 218, 220–33, 234n3, 234n6, 234n7, 235n11
Osaka (Japan) 158, 196, 237
Otro Hapon 93
Overseas Immigration Agency *see imin-gaisha*

Pacific War 122
PaHuma Asia Co. 237
Pan-African community 2
Pan-Africanists 4
Pan American 155, 157; Nikkei 155
Pan-Nikkei community 6
Paraguay *48*, *50*, 119n1, 152, 156, 159, 164–5, 190
Parker, Daniel 34n7
Pearl Harbor 122–3, 128, 141, 149–50, 162–4
personalismo 154
Peru 8–10, 26–8, 30–1, 47, *48*, *50*, 93, 119, 142–61, 165–7, 170n4, 170n6, 176–7, 183, 189n6, 197–201; Japanese community 144–5, 149–50; president *see* Alberto Fujimori

284 Index

Peruvian 8, 143–5, 147–8, 149–55, 157–9, 161, 165–6, 168, 170n6, 170n7, 171n13, 171n15, 199; agriculture 198; community 144, 147, 149, 151; culture 143, 152, 154, 158; government 150–2, 160, 165, 198; universities 153
Philippine(s) 48, 51, 85–7, 89, 91–5, 97–8, 99n3, 99n5, 99n6, 99n7, 100n9, 100n10, 100n17, 100n19, 101n27, 101n28, 101n29, 101n30, 101n32, 101n33, 241, 247; citizenship land law 90; citizenship law 94; government 87, 94, 96, 99n7; national *see* national(s); Nikkeijin *see* Nikkeijin Philippine society *see* society; *see also* Filipino/a
Philippine–Japan Centennial Celebration 85
Philippine Nikkeijin association 97, 101n33; *see also* Nikkeijin-kai
Philippines' Public Land Act 87
picture brides *see* bride(s)
pidgin English *see* Hawaiian
plantation(s) 16, 25, 27–8, 56, 62, 87, 104, 106, 109, 117, 143, 148, 199; *abaca* 88, 90, 93; *abaca* company 87; abaca corporations 87–8; coffee *see* coffee; corporations 87; cotton 26; farm-hands 105; *see also* plantation workers; Furukawa Plantation Company 87; Guatapará Plantation 107; Hawaiian Plantation(s) *see* Hawaiian; labor 2–3, 103, 104, 117; managers 117; migrant 111; non-plantation society 57, 199; Ohta Development Company 87; owners 16, 28, 56, 88, 104, 109, 148, 199; store 109; sugar 26, 62, 193; workers 57, 62, 105, 193, 199
planter(s): *abaca* 86, 96; society 31; sugar 147
political 1–2, 4, 6–8, 12–14, 16–17, 21–2, 35, 45, 65, 92, 103, 111, 117, 142–5, 153, 156, 168, 180–2, 189n3; capital 22; confrontation(s) 21; economy 45; empowerment 167; exiles 28, 31; instability 175; institutions 122; leaders 154; marginalization 103; movements 20; power 36, 111, 113, 149, 189n3; problem(s) 16; refuges 53; relationships 9, 122; rights 13–14; stability 243; strategy 45

politically marginalized 2, 117
politics 2, 98, 143, 148, 201, 232
Popular Revolucionaria Americana (APRA) 148–9
populations 2, 22n1, 50, 102, 162; Japanese 1, 6, 10, 13; Nikkei/Nikkeijin 170n8, 205
prejudice 16, 32–3, 64, 122, 126, 146, 150–1, 160, 163–4, 206, 214; *see also* ethnic prejudice; racial prejudice
pressure *see* cultural, economic, political, social
problem(s) *see* economic, cultural, linguistic, political, social
propaganda: pro-emigration *see* emigration
property 8, 10, 33, 61, 82, 86, 90, 129, 136, 141, 167, 197
Pu-yi (of the Quing Dynasty) 45

race 21, 50, 64, 103, 145, 151, 167, 169, 192–4, 200–1, 209, 213, 216n10, 216n11, 218, 221, 229, 232–3
racial 1, 6, 12, 22n1, 64, 97, 167, 198, 211, 214, 216n7; bias 93; discrimination 20, 109, 121; marginalization 20; minority/minorities 121, 124; prejudice 100n19, 126; superiority 171n14; supremacy 229
racialist 64
racialization 201
racialized 194, 200–1; hierarchy 215
racially 203, 209–11, 213–14
racism 1, 6, 30, 123, 229, 232, 235n12
Reagan, Ronald 12
redress 12, 39, 98, 124–6, 168, 225; awards 12; settlement 126; *see also* Japanese–Canadian Redress Settlement
returnee(s) 27, 35, 66, 100n20, 101n26, 218, 228, 231, 234n6; *dekasegi* 6; returnees 1, 14, 21
rice 37, 38, 41–3, 46, 71, 78, 82, 106, 108, 111–12, 130, 146–7, 188, 232
Roosevelt, Theodore 32, 144, 150, 153
Roth, Joshua 1
Royal Hawaiian Agricultural Society 27
Russo–Japanese War 218
ryôsai kembo see "good wives and wise mothers"

Sacramento Bee 193
Safran, William 3–4

Index 285

Sago Palm Hell *see* Sotetsu Jigoku
sake 38, 60, 79, 81, 147
Sakura-maru 147, 199
samba 208, 214
San Francisco Peace Treaty (1951) 180
Sankaku Minasu 105–8
sansei(s) 97, 144–5, 147, 152–3, 157, 203, 207, 210
school 9, 20, 22n9, 32–3, 36, 55, 64–5, 89–90, 92, 95, 105, 119, 120n15, 128, 133–4, 136–7, 139, 145–7, 153, 157, 192, 194, 198, 201n1, 225–6, 230, 236–7, 243, 245, 248, 250–2, 253n3; children 158, 243; Filipino 95; Japanese 9, 11, 95–6, 101n29, 107, 112–13, 149, 238, 243; Japanese language 122, 161, 165, 236; schooling 11, 55, 119, 158; teachers: 65, 160; temple 11; segregation 29
Senda, Jôgyô 60–1
settlement(s) 9, 12, 68n15, 71, 73–83, 84n1, 84n8, 88, 102–3, 105, 108–13, 121, 124, 126, 146, 149, 164, 175–6, 181–8, 189n1, 203, 219, 223
settler(s) 10–1, 29, 71–2, 75, 86–90, 92–4, 100n14, 103, 106, 108–9, 110, 112–13, 116, 120n14, 123–4, 126, 131, 200–1, 219–20, 222, 234n6
sex ratios 30, 89
sexuality 194, 196, 201
Shiimi-sai 147
Sino–Japanese War (1894) 39, 58, 233
Shinto 63, 92, 105
Singapore 21, *48–9*, 236–53, 253n2
Singapore School Holiday 251
Singaporean 247
social 1, 3, 5–8, 10, 13–14, 16, 19, 21–2, 36, 41–2, 44–6, 55, 71, 82–3, 92, 102–6, 109, 111, 113, 117, 119, 126–7, 144–5, 150, 152, 157–8, 177–9, 180, 182–3, 186–7, 200–1, 204–6, 208, 212, 215, 232, 243–4, 250, 252; alienation 205; assimilation 12; bases 177; bounds/boundary 7, 14; capital 22; classes 102; club 113; condition(s) 98, 114, 146; confrontation(s) 20; discrimination 7; exclusion 204, 206; formation 200–1; identity 10, 119, 126; imperialism 44–5; instability 181; isolation 6; justice 45; losses 98, 227; marginalization 4, 8, 203, 206; mobility 11, 118; networks 47, 153; pressure 1, 52, 59, 65; segregation 216n4; separation 206; solidarity 156; stability 179
socialism 41
socialists 41, 169
socially 3, 45, 82, 93, 117, 203–6, 213, 215, 237; assimilated 6; bond(s) 7; inferior 105; marginalized 8; separated 206
society 1–2, 4–5, 8, 12–14, 19, 21, 27, 30–1, 57, 64–5, 92, 103, 109, 110, 114, 117–19, 121–4, 126, 154, 156, 163, 169, 195, 203, 209, 233, 236–7, 247; class 28; Filipino 95, 99n7; global/globalizing 21; Japanese Brazilian 103, 111, 115, 118; multi-ethnic 215; Philippine *see* Filipino; *see also* Bolivian society; Brazilian society; Chinese society; Japanese society
sociocultural 160
socioeconomic 9, 203; marginalization 215
socio-economically segregated 215
sociologists 1, 99n7
socio-psychological 125
Sôga, Yasutarô 55, 58, 67n3, 68n14
sojourner(s) 29, 31, 48, 91, 145, 153, 155–6, 191, 206
Sotetsu Jigoku 92
South America 6, 12, *18*, 120n12, 150, 168–9, 182, 184, 202
Southeast Asia 25, 98, 194, 220, 236
soy sauce 81, 139, 196, 201
soybean(s) 78–9, 81–2, 188, 196, 201
Steveston (British Columbia, Canada) 122
sugar 34, 92, 123, 133–4, 136, 142, 149, 184–5, 199

Taeuber, Irene B. 189n9
Taft, William H. 32
Taiwan 45, *48–9*, 65, 240,
Takaki, Ronald 1
Takamori, Yasutarô 90, 100n13
tea lounges 237
Terauchi, Masatake 42
Texas 159, 161, 171n15, 178
Thompson, Warren S. 189n9
Tijuana (Mexico) 164
Tokugawa shoguns 35–6, 39–40,
Tokugawa, Yoshinobu 36
Tokyo 32, 39–40, 85, 140, 152, 154, 157, 182, 187, 218, 225, 230–1, 237, 243–4
Tômiya, Kaneo 72, 78
tonkonbyô 78

286 *Index*

tradition 15, 22n9, 28, 46, 48, 57, 62–5, 80, 85, 91, 118, 126–7, 140, 146–7, 149, 155, 180, 195, 209, 232, 244; Japanese 147, 203
transcultural blending 216n11
transnational 1, 212, 251, 253; economic 236; labor 202; migrant(s) 3, 18, 21, 121, 212–13, 236–7; ties 212
transnationalism 2–3, 212
tuberculosis 76, 84n3

United Kingdom *49*, *51*, 236, 240
United States 2, 8, 10, 12–13, 17, 21, 22n2, 22n3, 25, 27–33, 34n9, 46–7, *48–51*, 67n2, 86, 91, 97, 99n6, 100n17, 114, 122–3, 127, 144, 150–1, 153, 156, 159–69, 170n2, 170n5, 170n6, 175–82, 184, 186–7, 193–4, 199, 220, 236, 240; U.S.–Japan relations 96
U.S.–Bolivia Immigration Pact 185, 187, 190n13
U.S. Civil Administration of the Ryûkyû Islands (USCAR) 180–4

Vancouver (Canada) 33, 122–3, 128–9, 132–3, 135–6
Vargas, Getúlio 114–15
Viet Nam 194
Villa, Francisco 27

wages 14, 30, 60, 80, 104, 132, 134, 143, 147, 156, 200, 215
Wakamatsu *see* Aizu Wakamatsu
war 2, 5, 10–12, 15–16, 35, 40–1, 43, 45, 71, 81–3, 84n8, 85–6, 91, 93, 96–8, 101n30, 101n33, 101n32, 102–3, 107, 114–15, 118, 120, 122–3, 126, 128, 135–6, 141, 144, 149–53, 160–4, 165, 170n9, 171n15, 176–7, 194, 198, 201, 221, 223, 226, 230;civil war 179, 220; post-war 5, 11, 77, 107, 115, 119, 122, 124–5, 151–2, 169, 171n14, 175–6, 178, 180–1, 183, 185, 187–9, 220, 231, 235n12, 236, 243; pre-war 7–8, 10, 85, 88, 91–4, 101n26, 101n28, 101n29, 102, 122–3, 125, 164–8, 175–6, 178, 180–3, 188, 190n12, 242–3; war orphans 97; *see also* Cold War; Opium War; Pacific War; Sino–Japanese War; Russo–Japanese War; World War I; World War II
wartime 71, 79, 81, 83, 121–2, 124–6, 140, 141n4, 151–2, 214
Webster, Daniel 34n7
Whelpton, Pascal K. 189n9
Wilson, Woodrow 32
world economy 52
World War I 41, 87, 170n5, 219,
World War II 1, 5, 9–12, 16–17, 35, 43, 45, 47, *48*, 67n2, 83, 85, 92, 97–8, 99n6, 100n16, 102–3, 107, 111–12, 114–16, 118, 121–2, 124, 128, 143, 145–6, 148–53, 159–60, 163, 166, 170, 175, 178, 180, 189n6, 197, 219, 221, 231–2, 243; *see also* Pacific War

Yamaguchi (Japan) 43, 54–64, 67n3, 68n13, 148
Yamamoto, Gonbei 40
yobiyose 65, 67n2, 143, 149
yonsei 97, 144–5, 147, 152, 157
Yon-Ijûchi 111
Yoshida, Enzô 88

zanryû fujin 221
zanryû koji 220–1, 227, 234n4,
zôri 147

CPSIA information can be obtained
at www.ICGtesting.com
Printed in the USA
BVOW06s2040221216
471683BV00002B/11/P